INDIGENOUS
MISSOURIANS

INDIGENOUS MISSOURIANS

Ancient Societies to the Present

Greg Olson

UNIVERSITY OF MISSOURI PRESS

COLUMBIA

Library of Congress Cataloging-in-Publication Data

Names: Olson, Greg, 1959- author.
Title: Indigenous Missourians : ancient societies to the present / Greg
    Olson.
Description: Columbia : University of Missouri Press, [2023] | Includes
    bibliographical references and index.
Identifiers: LCCN 2022048796 (print) | LCCN 2022048797 (ebook) | ISBN
    9780826222824 (hardcover) | ISBN 9780826223203 (paperback)
    ISBN 9780826274878 (ebook)
Subjects: LCSH: Indians of North America--Missouri--History.
Classification: LCC E78.M8 O47 2023 (print) | LCC E78.M8 (ebook) | DDC
    977.8004/97--dc23/eng/20221108
LC record available at https://lccn.loc.gov/2022048796
LC ebook record available at https://lccn.loc.gov/2022048797

∞™ This paper meets the requirements of the
American National Standard for Permanence of Paper
for Printed Library Materials, Z39.48, 1984.

Typeface: Minion Pro

Front cover photo: Cody Goff is an enrolled member of the Ho-Chunk Nation of
Wisconsin and a member of the bear clan. He is a men's northern traditional pow-
wow dancer, a union laborer from Local 662, and a patched member of New Breed
Motorcycle Club, Fulton, Missouri Charter. Cody lives in Jamestown, Missouri.
Photograph Courtesy of Shane Webster, Oneida Nation of Wisconsin.

Background cover photo: Detail of the For the People Pow Wow Staff, which is carried
into the dance circle during grand entry. Photo by Greg Olson.

Back cover: Map of Extent of Settlement in Mississippi Valley by William Clark, 1816.
National Archives and Records Administration, Washington, D.C.

This book was made possible with the generous support of
The State Historical Society of Missouri

To my brother, friend, and mentor
Larry Sellers (1949-2021)

Contents

Contents

Illustrations

Illustrations

Maps

Acknowledgments

Our accomplishments rarely are the product of simple hard work and effort. When we succeed, it is because others took the time to help us, educate us, or to offer us important teachings. I have been able to complete this project only through the help of many people who endeavored to lend me a hand.

I would like to thank the State Historical Society of Missouri for its generous support of my work over the years. I conducted much of the research for this book while I was a fellow at the Center for Missouri Studies in 2020. I am especially grateful to Beth Pike and Kevin Walsh for providing me with opportunities to publicly share my research and findings.

A portion of this work appeared previously in the society's *Missouri Historical Review*. I would like to thank John Brenner and Kimberly Harper of the journal's editorial staff for their hard work in preparing that article for publication.

I also appreciate the work of Andrew Davidson, Robin Rennison, and everyone at the University of Missouri Press for their support during the more than two years it has taken to see this project through.

The sheer scope of this book forced me far out of my academic comfort zone as I engaged with scholarship about topics that were new to me. For this reason, it has been important for me to seek input and advice from colleagues in related fields. I would especially like to express my sincere appreciation to Dr. Candace Sall, Director of the University of Missouri's Museum of Anthropology, and Dr. William Foley, Professor Emeritus at the University of Central Missouri, for their help. They provided important feedback and pointed me toward sources and considerations I would have otherwise overlooked. Dr. Tai Edwards, Director of Johnson County Community College's Kansas Studies Institute, went far above and beyond the call of duty by providing significant editorial guidance.

The Iowa Tribe of Kansas and Nebraska's Preservation Officer and Council Vice President Lance Foster has been an important resource and supporter of my work for over two decades. I would also like to thank Chris Morey, a member of the Iowa Tribe, who generously provided me with information he has collected about the Tribe of Mic-O-Say, of which Chris was a member. Thank you to all my Báxoje friends who have encouraged me over the years. Nancy McCracken Blue also eagerly provided me with material for this book, which included personal photographs of her late husband Bob Blue and her family.

My former colleagues at the Missouri State Archives, Shelly Croteau, Christina Miller, and Erika Woehlk helpfully provided me with images and documents that appear in this book.

Thank you to Sara Wilson, current Executive Director, and Jackie Lewin, former Executive Director of St. Joseph Museums, Inc. for supporting and encouraging my work for several years. Former members of the museum's staff, Sarah Elder and Trevor Tutt, have been instrumental in steering me toward important resources in the museum's collection.

I have also been the beneficiary of many years of support and teachings from the late Larry Sellers and other elders and members of our sundance tiospaye. This family has broadened my horizons and helped me see beyond the limitations of my own experiences. Thank you as well to all of the people who have shared traditional knowledge, teachings, ceremonies, and oral histories with me over the years. Wa-do. We wa nah. Wopila. Warígroxi ke. To the best of my ability, I have tried to use this knowledge to inform the way in which I approached this project.

Finally, thank you to my family, especially my wife Chris, who has been a strong supporter of my work for more than thirty-five years.

Preface

In May 1962, forty-six-year-old Elinor Fields was heavily involved in many aspects of her community. A member of the Pawnee Nation, Fields had been a sergeant in the US Army during the Second World War. After returning home to Pawnee, Oklahoma, she had become a member of the Indian Women's Pocahontas Club, an all-Indigenous women's organization formed in 1899, for the purpose of caring for "our culture, our heritage, and our communities." By 1950, Fields was contributing to the club's weekly "Indian News" column in the *Pawnee Chief*. A decade later, the column would appear under her byline. "Indian News" was the kind of small-town newspaper feature rarely seen today. It covered the social events and the comings and goings of Pawnee community members. In putting each week's column together, Fields made it her business to know about local weddings, funerals, graduations, birthdays, anniversaries, and who had visited whom. As an active member in her tribal community, it is little wonder that "El," as she was known, was one of about a dozen Pawnees called upon to make the three-hour car trip to Neosho, Missouri, on Saturday, May 12, to represent the nation in an "Indian program."[1]

When the Pawnee delegation reached Neosho, they found the streets of the town of seventy-five hundred people filled with a crowd of eight thousand. The crowd had gathered that day to pay homage to seventy-three-year-old Thomas Hart Benton who had returned to Neosho to bask in a "homecoming" celebration held in his honor. Benton, who had left his hometown in 1912 to eventually become a world-renowned artist, was celebrated in Neosho by the likes of former President Harry Truman and the artist Charles Banks Wilson. The activities included the unveiling of a new portrait Wilson had completed of Benton, performances by folksingers, a press conference, and a gala dinner for five hundred guests.

The Pawnees had been asked to participate in the festivities as a way of commemorating the many trips that young Tom Benton had made into the Indian Territory, the eastern border of which was just fourteen miles away, to hunt and fish. Their performance might also have reminded Benton of his childhood when Indigenous people were a common sight in the streets of Neosho. As their exhibition ended, El Fields invited Benton to join them. What followed was described as an impromptu "Pawnee two-step" with Benton and Fields leading a line of dancers around a circle in the Newton County Courthouse square.[2]

IMAGE 1: Pawnee dancer Elinor "El" Fields does a "Pawnee two-step" with artist Thomas Hart Benton near the Newton County Courthouse in Neosho, Missouri. Fields and other Pawnee dancers were participating in a home-coming celebration for Benton in on May 12, 1962. *Photo courtesy of the Missouri State Archives*

It is telling to see the beaming Benton navigate his way across the square as he held hands with El Fields. The Pawnee two-step, which differs from the Texas two-step, is a staple of powwows across the country. It is one of the few powwow dances in which couples step together while holding hands. It also provides women with a rare opportunity to extend invitations to the dance partner of their choice. In fact, men who refuse a dance invitation run the risk of having to give the asker a small gift. In some ways, the role of women in the two-step is in line with traditional Pawnee culture in which women held much of the power and made many of the important decisions. Though it was Fields who had extended the dance invitation, asking Benton to participate in an exhibition of her culture, Benton appears to have quickly assumed control. The artist, who during his long career had rendered dozens of Indigenous people—not always flatteringly—in his regionalist paintings and murals, turned the women's two-step into a spectacle that he controlled. The dancers were there, after all, to commemorate his life. So, it seemed natural for Benton, the guest of honor, center of attention, and a white male, to lead the way.

The spectacle of Benton leading Fields and the Pawnees in the two-step, photos of which were printed in newspapers around the country, can be seen as exemplary of Missouri's general attitude toward Indigenous people. Originally planned by Thomas Jefferson as a place in which displaced Natives from east of the Mississippi River could be resettled—at least temporarily—to live without white interference, the state had removed all Indigenous nations from its borders by 1837. Two years later, Missouri law required any Native person who entered the state to have written permission from a government Indian agent in order to do so.[3]

From that time on, the people of Missouri considered themselves to live in a state in which Indians, at least the "real" buffalo robe-wearing, face-painting, arrow-shooting Indians of their imagination, no longer existed. This perceived absence of Indigenous people is particularly noticeable in the state's history. Natives have only appeared in the annals of Missouri's past when they presented a significant challenge or obstacle to settler colonialists' hunger for land and natural resources. Once many were successfully deported to Kansas, Nebraska, and the Indian Territory in the 1830s, and no longer signified a threat to the state's white settlement, Natives completely disappeared from Missouri's story. This erasure of Indigenous people from the state's boundaries and the story of its past has had long-lasting consequences. The presence, experiences, and rights of the Indigenous people who remained in Missouri over the past one hundred seventy years has been ignored and forgotten. For the most part, non-Natives now have no concept of, or connection to, their Indigenous neighbors, nor do they comprehend the long process of colonialism that has defined the history of Indigenous people. As a direct result, we live in a state where a large percentage of the general population is genuinely mystified as to why Native people object when fans of the Kansas City Chiefs enact the "Tomahawk Chop" in Arrowhead Stadium. As the Cree-Métis archaeologist Paulette F. C. Steeves recently has observed, "The cleaving of links between contemporary Indigenous populations and ancient homelands and links between ancient and contemporary people denies Indigenous identities and rights and fuels discrimination and social and political disparities."[4] No, Missouri has never danced well with Indigenous people, and on those rare occasions when we do, non-Natives insist on taking the lead.

In part, this book grew out of my concerns over the way in which Missouri's bicentennial was commemorated in 2021. I had hoped that planners of the festivities both in the state and in my hometown of Columbia would have used the anniversary to revisit the role that slavery and settler colonialism had in creating the Missouri we know today. Perhaps I was naïve in my expectation that a commemoration of the past would encompass *all* of the past. While a few organizations engaged in such discussions, they were generally ancillary to the greater celebration. This book is my small effort to correct what I see as a missed opportunity.

I have also been motivated by a question I was first asked over twenty years ago and have been asked many times since, "Which Indian tribes lived here?" In these queries, "here" often meant Missouri in general, but sometimes referred to specific counties or areas of the state. My initial response to these questions has been: "It depends on the time period." The Indigenous nations that lived here at the very beginning of European colonization were not the same as those who lived here at the time of the Louisiana Purchase, nor were they the same people who lived here at the time of the last Ice Age. People have always been mobile, looking for new opportunities and better lives. Yet, despite mobility and change, the Indigenous presence in what is now Missouri has remained constant.

I have also been asked on more than one occasion by non-Natives whether writing a history of Missouri's Indigenous people has been an overly depressing endeavor. I think this concern comes from the assumption that all "real Indians" have now vanished. However, in researching and writing this book, I have learned that again and again, and over the past twelve millennia, whenever Native Missourians have faced challenges to their survival, they have found ways to persevere. If anything, this continued resilience and adaptability in the face of overwhelming adversity has left me feeling optimistic about the state's Indigenous future.

Over the past few years, I have given a number of presentations about Missouri's Indigenous past and have found that people generally know very little about the topic yet are often eager to learn more. This persuaded me that there was a need for a history of the state's Indigenous people. In writing this book, I had two main goals. First, I set out to tell Missouri's Indigenous history as the continuous story of a presence that has lasted at least twelve thousand years, and perhaps much longer. Second, I wanted to show the enduring adaptability and resilience that has enable Natives to have remained here for such a long time.

I want Missourians to have at their disposal a book that does not segregate the state's Natives into those who lived here during the so-called era of "prehistory," and those who occupied the state during what has been labeled as the "historical" period. I wanted to write a book that presented Native history in the state as one long arc and to focus on the presence of a people who have lived here for many millennia, and whose connections to this place are longer, deeper, and fundamentally unlike that of non-Natives.

Missouri has been the beneficiary of excellent monographs about ancient Missourians written by such non-Native scholars as W. Raymond Wood, Michael J. O'Brien, Carl H. Chapman, Eleanor F. Chapman, Carol Diaz-Granados, James R. Duncan, Timothy R. Pauketat, and Gayle J. Fritz. Similarly, the history of Missouri's Indigenous people in the decades between European contact and 1840 has been equally well covered by such historians as William E. Foley, Carl J. Eckberg, Tanis C. Thorne, Michael Dickey, J. Frederick Fausz, Jacob F. Lee, Patricia Cleary, Kathleen DuVal, Peter J. Kastor, Mark William Kelley, Tai S. Edwards, and others. I have also been informed by the work of, and conversations with, Indigenous scholars from various nations. These historians include Vine Deloria, Jr. (Lakota), John Joseph Mathews (Osage), Louis F. Burns (Osage), Lance Foster (Ioway), and Kent Blansett (Cherokee, Creek, Choctaw, Shawnee, and Potawatomi descent), George "Tink" Tinker (Osage), Robert Warrior (Osage), Paulette F. C. Steeves (Cree/Metis), Roxanne Dunbar-Ortiz, Jimmy Beason (Osage), Thomas "Ed" Smith (Osage descent), Larry Sellers (Osage), and many others.

By synthesizing much of the existing scholarship on Indigenous Missourians and adding a fair amount of my own original research, I have fashioned a long view of Missouri history that examines more than twelve thousand years during which Native people lived in this state. I am certainly not the first to present a long view of Indigenous presence. In the 2000s, Colin G. Calloway and Stephen Aron both offered far-reaching frontier histories of the Midwest and West. In his 2006 *American Confluence: The Missouri Frontier from Borderland to Border State*, Aron laments that, "Too often, frontier historians dismiss the precolonial past as mere prehistory." He goes on to point out that by taking a longer view of history, we can see commonalities shared by Indigenous people and colonial nations. "Like Europeans from various kingdoms, these Indians of diverse backgrounds brought distinct histories that later molded their responses to colonial intruders."[5] It is Calloway, however, who takes his long view of the American West back to the continent's first inhabitants, whom he calls "pioneers," in his 2003 book, *One Vast Winter Count: The Native American West before Lewis and Clark*. A proper book about the American West, writes Calloway, must "stretch back thousands of years before Europeans arrived."[6]

More recently, historians have begun to publish books that take a much-needed long view of specific places. One very recent example is *We Are the Land: A History of Native California* by Damon B. Akins and William J. Bauer Jr. Though the book, published in 2021, is too recent to have served as a model for this one, it was written in the same spirit and covers the history of California in much the same way as I have endeavored to cover that of Missouri. Akins and Bauer write about the efforts of contemporary California Natives to reassert their sovereignty over traditional lands and the degree to which the issue of Indigenous rights has caught by surprise the general public, most of whom had assumed the state's Indians had long ago vanished. "Histories that ignore how California's Indigenous People lived within the state's boundaries for centuries, maintained relationships with the land, and shaped the state's history undermine the sovereignty of contemporary California Indian communities," by perpetuating ignorance and erasure of the people and their issues.[7]

Given that this book is supposed to be a history of Indigenous Missourians, some readers may be surprised at the amount of time I devote to discussions of government policies and erroneous and racist theories regarding Ice Age migration, Mound Builders, Ozark Cliff

Dwellers, and the like. I dwell on these topics at some length because these are all elements of settler colonialism. Indigenous people not only suffered from physical removal and colonization, but they were also the victims of intellectual and cultural erasure. The challenges Indigenous Missourians face today are the direct result of centuries of settler colonial thought and action. To me, it is difficult to trace Indigenous survival and resilience without identifying and discussing the nature of the obstacles that settler colonialism has placed before them.

As we now recognize the importance of encouraging Indigenous people to tell their own stories, I must make clear that I am not Native. I have written extensively about Indigenous history in Iowa, Missouri, and Kansas and worked with Native people and communities for the past twenty-five years. Nonetheless, I cannot claim to speak from the perspective of anyone other than a white male who is now in his sixties. In order to augment my own perspective, I have included interludes in which Indigenous voices can be heard, telling the story of their presence, perseverance, and survival. Even so, I apologize in advance for anything I may write in these pages that inadvertently misrepresents Indigenous people and communities. Like Colin G. Calloway, a historian who is also not Indigenous, I can only say that "I don't write Indian history, I write American history that includes Indians."[8]

Finally, a word about terms. In this text, I have used the terms *Indigenous* and *Native* interchangeably. The word *Indian* tends to be archaic, and many in the Native community today use *Native* or *Indigenous* as a way of moving away from that word. Whenever possible, I have tried to refer to individuals or groups of people by their tribal affiliation. I have used the word *Indian* when referring to organizations, such as the American Indian Movement, National Congress of American Indians, and the Kansas City Indian Center. I have also employed the word *Indian* in describing laws and policy decisions that use the word in their titles.

INDIGENOUS
MISSOURIANS

Voices

At the beginning of time . . .

. . . when the Sac and Fox people came from the East they saw only the Sun shining on a barren land. There were no mountains, no water, no trees, no rocks, no animals, no birds, no humans, nothing. Nothing but the flat ground. The people wondered how they were to survive in such a place without food, water, or shelter.

In one of the families were twelve brothers. The Twelve Boys set out to find food and water and to discover what might be found out in the land. They walked for many miles and days but found nothing.

Then one day they encountered an elderly man and woman sitting beside their path. The old couple asked each of the boys what he sought and what he desired.

Each boy said he wanted to serve his people.

The first boy said, "I want to bring my people the gift of water, that they may continue to survive."

"You can serve your people as you want," said the old couple. "You can sacrifice your physical life here, and in return you will receive life everlasting as the Water Spirit. Water is life. All living beings are dependent on water to sustain life. All natural waterways serve as the lifeline of this Grandmother Earth."

The first boy accepted. "It will be an honor to serve my people as the Water Spirit."

The Water Spirit represents life and is the Lead Spirit in ceremonies. Sac and Fox people offer prayers of gratitude to the Water Spirit in recognition of the boy's sacrifice and the life it brought to the people.

The second boy said, "I want to bring my people the gift of communication with the Creator."

The old couple told the second boy, "The Creator likes to smoke tobacco but will keep none of it for himself. Instead, the Creator gives it all to the care of the Sac and Fox. You can serve your people as the Sacred Tobacco, the Creator's gift to the Sac and Fox.

"The responsibility of planting and reaping must be taken care of by a special man in the tribe, and all men must follow the rules that govern the usage of this special tobacco. When Sac and Fox people wish to speak to the Creator, they first offer him a smoke. Through the Sacred Tobacco is the door opened to offer prayers in ceremonies, for help, for family, home, safe travel, and daily aid."

The third boy said, "I want to bring my people the gift of shelter, warmth, medicine, and fruit."

"You will begin the Tree nation," said the old couple. "Each tree species is related and has a male and female of each tree who can start a family. Through the Tree Spirit, all trees continue their specific responsibilities though each individual tree completes a life cycle and depends on its children to carry on. Older trees are the grandmothers and grandfathers to the people."

Even today, before a Sac and Fox cuts down a tree, he makes an offering of the Sacred Tobacco to thank the third boy for his sacrifice and explains his need for the wood.

The fourth boy said, "I want my people to have the gift of knowledge and prayer."

The old couple said, "Rock carries all the knowledge of Grandmother Earth and humanity. Your first job is to create the hills and mountains. The cycle of the Rock family can be seen in the various rocks and their layers, and rocks house substances such as gold and coal. Rocks support the crust of Grandmother Earth. Because of his knowledge, Rocks are used in Sac and Fox ceremonies. Flint rock is the Chief of the Rock Nation, and his spark lights the sacred fires."

The fifth boy said, "I want to bring my people the gift of cleansing and purification to keep their spirits strong and healthy."

The old couple told him, "An unwanted spirit can be from the accumulation of daily stress, adversity, ill will, bad luck, or hard times. The Cedar Spirit will know if a heart is sincere and can remove a bad spirit and protect the people by cleansing. Cedar will lift the spirit of one who is sad or grieving. You will remain green all the year round to remind the people that Cedar is an everlasting, living spirit and always there when needed."

The Sac and Fox still use Cedar to purify ourselves and our homes as well as to aid healing in times of sorrow.

The sixth, seventh, and eighth boys said, "We want to bring our people the gift of food and nourishment, that they may never hunger."

"Corn, Bean, and Pumpkin are the favorite foods of the Creator," said the old couple. "Through your sacrifice, He gives these three foods to humanity. You and your families have a kinship with all foods and will forever feed your people. Through the Corn, Bean, and Pumpkin Spirits Sac and Fox people can receive blessings."

Corn, Beans, and Pumpkins are the lead foods in ceremonies, and the Sac and Fox offer prayers of thanks and appreciation to the sixth, seventh, and eighth boys.

The ninth boy said, "I want to bring my people the gift of a healthy environment through life in the water."

The old couple said, "The Fish Spirit represents all those who live in the waters. Many families live in various parts of the land and oceans. You contribute to the health of the land and sea through your interaction with plants and animals. The Fish world is a huge world of its own and is vitally necessary to all of humanity, so much so that the people will form a kinship with the Fish and become a clan, a family, so named."

The Sac and Fox still depend on all who live in the waters for physical and spiritual health and have many uses for the reeds that grow along the waters.

The tenth boy said, "I want my people to have the gift of many brothers and sisters who will help them in their lives through provision and protection."

"The Spirit of All Wild Animals is in all four-leggeds," said the old couple. "Through this spirit the animals have offered themselves to provide food, shelter, and clothing. The sacrifice of All Wild Animals is so important to humanity that the people will also form clans as a relationship and kinship to an animal spirit and honor their contributions."

Today the Sac and Fox are born into clans named for the water and animal life and receive their Indian names from them.

The eleventh boy said, "I want to bring my people gifts from the sky."

"There is life and purpose for All Things That Fly," said the old couple. "There are birds who fly the highest and nearest to our Creator and carry our prayers to Him. There are birds who carry medicine, who provide food, who are guardians, and who can give warnings. All the birds, insects, and flying things keep our Grandmother Earth fruitful and healthy and bring messages from the Creator to those who can understand them."

Today the Sac and Fox still keep aware of the messages from and hold sacred the feathers of the winged people.

The twelfth boy said, "I want to help keep Grandmother Earth healthy as a gift to my people."

The old couple said, "The Spirit of All Things That Crawl has the responsibility to aid in the environmental cycles that keep Grandmother Earth healthy. All Things That Crawl not only walk upon the surface of this grandmother but also live within her body and tend to the foods and medicines that come from her."

The crawling people often lead the Sac and Fox to healing herbs and plants.

"Remember that the Creator is behind each gift given," said the old couple now. "He gave humanity a pristine world to inhabit. Abuse of those with whom you share the world is an abuse unto yourself. In all living things are living spirits. Remember the Twelve Boys who sacrificed themselves that all may live."[1]

—A Sac and Fox oral tradition

The Little Ones came from the stars. In those days they were all *Tzi-Sho*, or Sky People, pure, clean, and noble. However, as they descended to the earth, dislodging acorns from red oak trees with their outstretched arms as they drifted down, they found that this unfamiliar world was divided into land and water and that it was a chaotic place that could unleash thunderstorms, cyclones, snow, and ice on them. They discovered after their descent, that they too had become disorganized. To overcome this, the Little Ones organized themselves into three groups, the Water People, the Land People, and the Sky People.

Though the Little Ones were unsure why *Wah'Kon-Tah* had sent them to this new place, they believed that their purpose was to become caretakers of earth, or the Sacred One. With the Water People in the lead, and the Land and Sky people following in that order, they began to wander the land, familiarizing themselves with their new surroundings. Along the way, they met the buffalo, who gave the Little Ones squash and four colors of maize. The buffalo instructed them how to use the various parts of its body to make shelter, clothing, and tools. The Little ones later met the crayfish, who brought them the four sacred colors of earth: black, red, yellow, and blue. Along the way, they met plants, trees like the cedar, and other animals. All the nations who lived on the land instructed the Little Ones how to use the gifts they had to offer. As a result, the Little Ones prospered.

The Water People took the name *Wah-Sha-She*, or Name Givers. The Land People became *Hun Ka*, or Sacred Ones, and the Sky People retained their name *Tzi-Sho*, or Sky Lodge. Yet they came to understand that as a people they were not whole. They would not become a complete nation until they became united with the *U-Tah-No'n-Dsi*, or Isolated Earth People. After wandering some time, the Little Ones found the village of the Isolated Earth People. They were wary of the village, however, because it was a place of death and chaos. Only the Water People were brave enough to sit with the leader of the Isolated Earth People and smoke the sacred pipe. In doing so, the two groups became relatives and the Isolated Earth People prepared to leave their chaotic village and follow the Water People. Along the way, they joined the Land People and the Sky people. All of them sat down to smoke and establish kinship ties. From then on, they were one people divided into two groups, the Sky People, *Tzi-Sho*, and the Land People, *Hun Ka*. The *Hun Ka* were further divided into two subgroups Land and Water People. Together, they all became known as *Ni'-u-kon-çka*, Children of the Middle Waters. Much later, the White People would call them Osages.[2]

—Osage oral tradition

When they emerged on land, the Bear clan thought they were the first people. For a long time, the earth had been only water, but with the emergence of land, the Bear clan came out of the water. Once on the land, they were surprised to discover the tracks of many animals. They followed the tracks to see who the other creatures on the land might be. Soon, they came across the Beaver clan. In those days, all the creatures on the earth, even the plants and trees, spoke the same language and could communicate with one another. "Let us be brothers and travel together," the Beavers told the Bears. "We shall prove useful to each other some time." As the two clans traveled on, they met the Elk clan. The Elks said: "Let us be brothers and go on together . . . because we may need one another."

As the three clans traveled together, *Ma^un*, Creator, showed the Elks how to make fire and taught all the clans how to cook their food. The clans wanted to learn more from *Ma^un* but were not sure how to express themselves to him. The Creator showed the Bears how to make a pipe bowl out of stone. He taught the Beavers how to make a wooden stem for the pipe. When put together, the two parts became the sacred pipe, or *ráhnuwe*. *Ma^un* instructed them to smoke native tobacco in the pipe. When the smoke rose into the sky, *Ma^un* would know they wished to speak to him.

Meanwhile, the Eagle clan had become tired of living in their home in the sky. They found an opening in the sky that allowed them to make their way down to earth. When they landed, they too thought they were the first people until they saw tracks on the ground. They followed the tracks and met the Bear, Elk, and Beaver clans. The Eagles were soon joined by other clans from the sky, the Buffalo, Owl, Pigeon, and Snake. These Sky People also had a pipe, which they smoked with the Bears, Elks, and Beavers, who were all Earth People. They decided to join together to become one nation, the Chiwere. The Earth clans and the Sky clans decided that they would share leadership responsibilities for the people. The Earth People, led by the Bear clan, would lead in the autumn and winter, while the Sky People, led by the Buffalo clan, would lead in the spring and summer. Over time, the Chiwere would organize themselves into four groups, the Ioways, Missourias, Otoes, and Winnebagos (Ho-Chunks).

And that's when I came home.[3]

—Ioway oral tradition

Chapter One

Fire and Ice

THE OSAGES SPEAK OF A time when only the highest blufftops emerged above the water. In those days, "large and monstrous animals" traveled up the Mississippi and Missouri Rivers from the east. Upon their arrival, these large invading mammals clashed with the animals that already lived here. These battles between the animals were so violent that Osage hunters were afraid to leave their camps. As a result, their people became very hungry. One of the largest clashes took place near what is now known as Rocky Ridge. The combat was fierce and many of the animals were slaughtered. Afterward, the Osages offered the carcasses to *Wah'Kon-Tah*, who buried them in the Pomme de Terre River. From that time on, the Osages referred to the river as the Big Bone River, and they made an annual sacrifice at that spot, which they considered to be sacred.[1]

As the last Ice Age drew to a close, both mammoths and mastodons lived in what is now Missouri. Mammoths tended to prefer grazing in open areas, while mastodons sought out wooded regions. Other large mammals that inhabited the region included bison, bears, camels, deer, horses, and musk oxen. While successfully hunting any one of these species required skill and strength, killing an animal that was the weight and height of a school bus was undoubtedly treacherous. An adult mammoth, a relative of the modern-day elephant, could weigh ten tons or more and stand at least twice as tall as a human at the shoulder. Mastodons, which were more common in Missouri, were slightly smaller and had shorter legs.

Such a hunt was a group effort, as teams of humans, sometimes aided by domesticated dogs, would try to zero in on an individual mastodon rather than attacking an entire herd. Juveniles or females were the preferred targets, as they were sometimes smaller and less dangerous to kill. Hunters may have used a variety of strategies in pursuing their prey.

Tracking megafauna with such large feet and significant weight was not difficult. When the opportunity arose, hunters would have thrown spears at the animals. Because it was hard to pierce the Mastodon's hide with a spear, the hunt could go on for miles as the wounded animal tried to flee. Sometimes, hunters would use fire to help trap and frighten targeted animals. Hunting mastodons was less difficult, however, if the megafauna could be trapped at a watering hole or a slough. There, the animal's size could be a liability and it could become mired in mud. It appears that this is what happened at a site now known as the Kimmswick Bone Bed in eastern Missouri. Twelve thousand years ago, hunters killed multiple mastodons and other animals at a site that was near water. Because of the number of species and individual animals found at the site, it seems likely that hunters used it as a kill site for a time.[2]

Twelve thousand years later, a German immigrant from Saxony, Albert Carl Koch, had settled in St. Louis, where from 1836 until 1841 he exhibited such curiosities as life-size wax figures, a live alligator, and a six-legged lamb in his successful "museum." While the unusual and bizarre were his bread and butter, Koch's true passion was collecting fossil vertebrates, an ambition that led him to conduct excavations at three sites in Missouri. The best-known of the three is Kimmswick, which is located about twenty miles south of St. Louis. Koch also explored sites in the Pomme de Terre River valley in Hickory County and on the Bourbeuse River in Gasconade County. At the Bourbeuse River site in October 1838, Koch found man-made stone artifacts lying among the bones of a very large mammal. He also noticed that some of the bones of the animal appeared to have been charred by fire. Though he was an archaeologic neophyte, Koch believed he had found convincing evidence that ancient people had hunted mastodons and mammoths in Missouri. Skeptical scientists, confident that humans and megafauna could not possibly have coexisted, vehemently attacked Koch's discovery as a hoax. Disappointed, he apparently sold the stone artifacts to the Royal Museum at the University of Berlin, Germany.[3]

Undeterred by his detractors, Koch assembled another set of bones he had found during his Missouri excavations. Believing he had found a new giant species of extinct mammal, which he proclaimed to be the *Leviathan Missouriensis* and later, the *Missourium Theristocaulodon*, he displayed the bones in his museum. "Citizens of Missouri," the promoter barked, "come and see the gigantic race that once inhabited the space you now occupy, drank of the same waters which now quench your thirst, ate the fruits of the same soil that now yields so abundantly to your labor." The public's reception of Koch's new "monster" was so positive that he closed his museum and traveled throughout Europe to exhibit the skeleton. After scientists discovered that Koch's leviathan was an incorrectly assembled mastodon, the Museum of Natural History in London purchased it. It remains there to this day.[4]

Koch had no way of knowing that one day he would be vindicated and that the stone artifacts he had found among the bones near the Bourbeuse River likely were signs of human-megafauna cohabitation. More than a century later, archaeologists excavating the Kimmswick site would also find bones and stone points lying together. Kimmswick, now known as Mastodon State Historic Site, became one of the earliest sites in North America to prove that ancient Indigenous Missourians had hunted and butchered mastodons.[5]

Ideas and attitudes informed by settler colonialism have clouded research into the early history of Indigenous people in North America. In some cases, incorrect narratives have been put forth because of cultural bias from scholars in the field of archaeology which, even in the twenty-first century, has predominantly been the domain of white men. In other instances, especially in the nineteenth and early twenties centuries, unscrupulous or poorly trained examiners or undisciplined methods led to a variety of mistakes in the field. Over time, however, field methods and training for archaeologists have improved, science and technology have advanced, biases have been pointed out, and the western scientific story of Missouri's ancient inhabitants has begun to emerge in some detail.

All of this is not to say that the emerging narrative is settled or that it has generated unanimous agreement. Even today, the quest to determine precisely who the first Missourians were, where they came from, and how they got here is bound to raise more questions than answers. Among those non-Native academics who are attempting to unravel the complex story of the first Missourians' beginnings and migration, there seems to be one generally agreed-upon narrative.[6] Though it is constantly being challenged and updated, the general scientific timeline of the arrival of North America's first people unfolds something like this: *Homo sapiens*, from whom modern humans are descended, first separated from Neanderthals between 500,000 and 400,000 years ago in Africa. At some point, between 100,000 and 50,000 years ago, *homo sapiens* left the African continent and began to spread out across the globe. By about 35,000 years ago, a few had made their way to modern-day Siberia, and 10,000 years after that, some were living near what is now the Bering Strait. By that time, one of the Siberian groups had separated from the others and, over the next ten millennia, developed DNA traits that made them genetically distinct from Eurasian people. Scientists believe that these were the ancestors to today's Native Americans.[7]

By about 30,000 years ago, the earth's climate had cooled in what is commonly known as the Pleistocene Ice Age. Great ice sheets had developed in present-day Canada and other points in the far northern hemisphere. During the height of this period, sometimes called the Last Glacial Maximum (LGM), the glaciers were so massive and contained so much of the world's water that ocean levels may have been as much as two hundred eighty feet lower than they are today. This, in turn, exposed land over the Bering Strait that connected the continents of Asia and North America. Now known as Beringia, the exposed land was far more than a narrow passageway. It was a large subcontinent that at one time was a much as six hundred twenty miles wide. Based on a study of sea-level change and the fact that similar stone tools have been found on both sides of the Bering Strait, many scientists have hypothesized that the first Americans crossed Beringia anywhere between 26,500 to 12,000 years ago and from there eventually made their way into North and South America. Archaeologists first thought that these hearty paleolithic people, whom they call Paleoindians, were big-game hunters who followed the trail of mastodons, mammoths, musk oxen, or giant bison. This was based largely on the fact that these large mammals did indeed share the landscape with the ancient people, and that the most plentiful artifacts those people left behind for archaeologists to find were stone tools and hunting points. Once on the North American continent, the hunters were believed to have traveled southward along an ice-free corridor, which was situated east of the Canadian Rocky Mountains between the Cordilleran and Laurentide ice sheets.[8]

Indigenous Americans have their own traditions regarding their arrival in North America that often contradict those of the academy. The Lakota scholar and writer Vine Deloria Jr., who was a strong proponent of the knowledge and traditions about this continent that Native people have learned and kept for millennia, famously attacked the Bering "Land Bridge" Migration theory from a Native perspective in his 1995 book *Red Earth, White Lies: Native Americans and the Myth of Scientific Fact.* Deloria pointed out that, not only had the theory not been conclusively

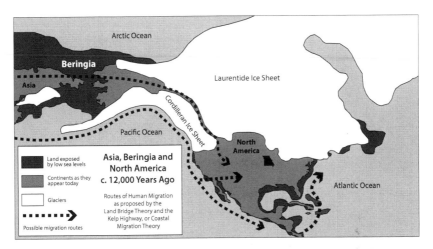

MAP 1: According to the Land Bridge Migration Theory, melting glaciers at the end of the last Ice Age provided a route for humans to travel from Asia to North America around 12,000 years ago. The Kelp Highway, or Coastal Migration Theory, suggests that humans sailed along the coast of Beringia. *Map by the author*

verified by archaeological research, but that it did not mesh with the oral traditions of the Lakotas and many other Indigenous peoples. "American Indians, as a general rule, have aggressively opposed the Bering Strait migration doctrine because it does not reflect any of the memories or traditions passed down by the ancestors over many generations," writes Deloria. "Some speak of transoceanic migration in boats . . . while others speak of the experience of a creation." After a lengthy, point-by-point rebuttal of the theory in *Red Earth, White Lies*, Deloria argued that either Native Americans originated on this continent, or that they arrived from another continent far earlier than archaeologists previously believed.[9]

In recent years, scientific evidence has slowly begun to move in a direction that supports many facets of Deloria's argument. By some accounts, the subcontinent of Beringia was not a particularly hospitable place for human or animal life during the Ice Age. Ecologist Paul Colinvaux proposed that the region could not have supported people or large mammals until the massive glaciers had begun to retreat in earnest around 14,000 years ago. Prior to that time, much of Beringia would have been tundra. As temperatures warmed and humidity rose, parts of the subcontinent would have become a steppe, or a grass-dominated landscape punctuated by wetlands with marshes, shallow ponds, and occasional forests of alder and dwarf birch. Because the archaeological record does show the existence of several species of megafauna on each side of the land bridge, some who have pointed to a "productivity paradox," questioning how even this landscape could support animals as well as humans.[10]

Deloria also attacked the theory of an Ice-Free Corridor (IFC) that supposedly allowed humans to make their way south through present-day Canada and into the United States. Some scholars have pointed out that such an IFC would only have been open as the Ice Age came to an end and the Cordilleran and Laurentide ice sheets began to recede between 12,000 and 11,000 years ago. These dates have become increasingly problematic as radiocarbon dating and other advances in archaeological methodology indicate that several sites in the United States had been occupied before the Ice-Free Corridor would have become a viable migrations route.[11]

Cree-Métis archaeologist Paulette F. C. Steeves has persuasively argued that the archaeological record does not support the theory that the first people in the Americas came from a single migration of Asians through the IFC after the Last Glacial Maximum (LMG). Prior to about 25,000 years ago, or the beginning of the LGM, Beringia was a viable migration route. She points to fossil evidence that shows mammals have migrated between Asia and North American for "millions of years." Citing the work of Duane Froese and colleagues, who have identified at least two major migrations of bison between the two continents, one at 195,000 to 135,000 years ago and another at 45,000 to 21,000 years ago, Steeves makes the case for the possibility that numerous human migrations to North America occurred long before the LGM. She believes the evidence shows that "people have been in the Western Hemisphere for over 60,000 years and likely over 100,000."[12]

Anthropological geneticist Jennifer Raff has recently written about an "Out of Beringia" migration model. She points out that south central Beringia was a lowland coastline during the LGM, between 50,000 and 11,000 years ago, and it could have supported both humans and animals. She hypothesizes that an isolated group of humans lived there for a long period of time during the LGM. Raff writes that, if true, "Beringia wasn't a crossing point, but a homeland, a place where people lived for many generations, sheltering from an inhospitable climate and slowly evolving the genetic variation unique to their Native American descendants." Evidence has led her to believe that people may have lived in

Beringia as long as 32,000 years ago and that people were living in the Americas 16,000 to 17,000 years ago and possibly as long as 25,000 years ago.[13]

Other scholars have considered migration routes that bypassed central Beringia. In 1979, Knut Fladmark, a Norwegian archaeologist working in British Columbia, proposed the possibility that ancient people had not only bypassed the Ice-Free Corridor, but also the inhospitable Beringian inland by migrating from Asia to North America along the Pacific coast. Fladmark and his supporters point to evidence that suggests the coast would have thawed far earlier than the inland—some claim as early as 17,000 to 16,000 years ago—and that a "kelp highway" would have provided enough resources to support both humans and animals.[14] They also argue that Asians were experienced in sea travel and had been using watercraft for substantial journeys anywhere from 40,000 to 25,000 years ago. Fladmark's Coastal Migration Theory helped explain the appearance of humans on the continent before the glaciers had completely retreated.[15]

Thanks to these theories, the stereotypical image of the migratory Ice Age big-game hunter following megafauna across Beringia has been diminished in favor of images of maritime migrants living in more temperate coastal shorelines. As anthropologist Thomas D. Dillehay has observed, humans were here earlier than scientists previously believed, and they were both big-game hunters *and* "plant-food gathers." As we shall see, hunters of mastodons, mammoths, and giant bison certainly played their part in the earliest human history of Missouri.[16]

An alternate land bridge theory, now known as the "North Atlantic Ice-Edge Corridor Hypothesis" or, more commonly, the "Solutrean Theory," was first proposed in 1872 by Charles Conrad Abbott, a former Civil War surgeon from New Jersey. After discovering the presence of ancient humans in the Delaware River valley, he observed that the stone tools he had found there were similar to those made by Paleolithic people from Europe. "Man in a rude state, with habits similar to those of the River-drift hunter of Europe," wrote Abbott, "lived upon the banks of the ancient Delaware . . . at the close of the glacial epoch." This led him to theorize that Paleolithic Europeans had colonized North America. The theory was refined in the 1940s by archaeologist Frank Hibben, who apparently altered evidence to make it appear that artifacts he unearthed in a New Mexico cave were 20,000 years old, the same age as the Solutrean culture of France.[17]

However, with the refinement of radiocarbon dating in the mid-twentieth century, Abbott's artifacts turned out to be several thousand years newer than he had believed them to be and Hibben's altered evidence was discounted. As a result, the theory was largely discredited and lost favor with archaeologists until the 1990s, when Bruce Bradley and Dennis Stanford published their book *Clovis and Beyond*. Bradley and Stanford argued that Solutrean people from southern France used watercraft to migrate to North America during the Ice Age. In a model reminiscent of Fladmark's Coastal Migration Theory, they proposed that the Solutreans had followed the margins of the ice bridge that connected the two continents, subsisting on marine animals along the way. The theory is largely predicated on the similarities found in the tools of the Solutreans and the Clovis people of North America.

As the presence of several pre-Clovis sites, which are older than 11,250 years, have been recently verified in North America, Bradley and Stanford have revised their hypothesis to address a major flaw in their theoretical connection between Solutreans and Clovis people. Solutrean people lived about 23,000 to 18,000 years ago while Clovis people lived about 11,500 to 10,500 years ago. Had Solutrean people been the direct ancestors of Clovis people, one would have suspected them not to have been separated by a gap of 10,000 to 5,000 years. The appearance of pre-Clovis people, who may have lived in North American well before 11,500 years ago, helped Bradley and Stanford close that time gap.[18]

While several archaeologists, such as David Meltzer and Lawrence Straus, have been critical of the Solutrean Theory, one of the most recent critics has been former University of Missouri Professor of Anthropology Michael J. O'Brien. After Bradley and Stanford published their revised thesis in 2012, O'Brien and several of his colleagues challenged the two archaeologists on a few points. In brief, O'Brien and his colleagues charged that they were unconvinced by Bradley and Stanford's evidence of similarities in the tools made by the Clovis and Solutrean people. They pointed to the lack of any evidence to show that either of the groups used watercraft or had ever subsisted on marine life. They also cited radiocarbon dates that did not support the idea that Clovis culture in North America had emanated from the east coast and spread westward, as well as the lack of DNA evidence to show the presence of ancient Europeans. Finally, O'Brien and his colleagues noted that, even with the discovery of pre-Clovis sites in North America, there was still a sizable time gap between the appearance of the two groups. Much of their critique of the

Timeline of Indigenous Presence in Missouri

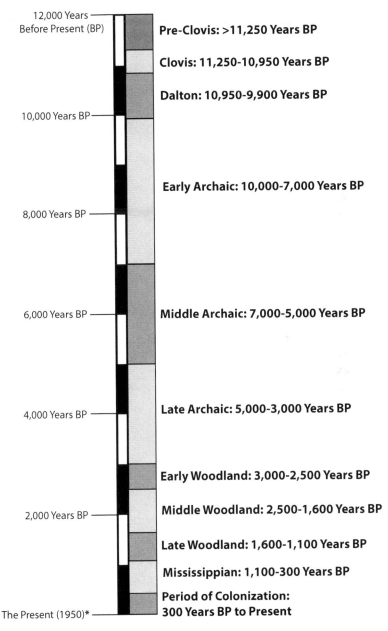

12,000 Years Before Present (BP)

Pre-Clovis: >11,250 Years BP

Clovis: 11,250-10,950 Years BP

Dalton: 10,950-9,900 Years BP

10,000 Years BP

Early Archaic: 10,000-7,000 Years BP

8,000 Years BP

Middle Archaic: 7,000-5,000 Years BP

6,000 Years BP

Late Archaic: 5,000-3,000 Years BP

4,000 Years BP

Early Woodland: 3,000-2,500 Years BP

Middle Woodland: 2,500-1,600 Years BP

2,000 Years BP

Late Woodland: 1,600-1,100 Years BP

Mississippian: 1,100-300 Years BP

**Period of Colonization:
300 Years BP to Present**

The Present (1950)*

*Archaeologists have chosen the year 1950 as a reference point for 'the present.'
That date was chosen because radiocarbon dating was invented in the late 1940s.

Solutrean Thesis centered on a stone point and a portion of a mammoth skull that Bradley and Stanford used as supporting evidence. The items had been unintentionally dredged up from near Chesapeake Bay in 1970. Because of the way they had been obtained, there was no archaeological context to hint at the age of the artifacts. However, radiocarbon testing has since dated them to be 10,000 years older than Clovis culture. So certain was O'Brien in his belief that this discovery was not credible evidence, that he was quoted in a widely distributed article generated by the University of Missouri as saying, "Until the inaccuracies are cleared up, there is really no reason to accept the find as evidence of anything connected with the early peopling of North America."[19]

Like the Land Bridge Theory, this explanation for the peopling of North America raised several important cultural issues for Indigenous people. It has also become highly politicized. Long a propaganda talking point used by white supremacists, the idea that Native people were not the first or only ancient inhabitants in North American had been used in attempts to deny them of their Indigenous rights. Since the time of Charles Abbott, European Americans have implemented the Solutrean Theory to stake an ancient claim to the continent and discount the cultural achievements of Indigenous cultures. This in turn has been used to justify the process of settler colonialism. It also has led some in the scientific community to decry those who promote what they believe is a fringe theory as "extremely irresponsible." In response, Bradley has said that "We can't stop doing science because somebody might misappropriate something."[20]

The Clovis Era (and Before)

Humans have lived in Missouri for at least twelve thousand years—quite possibly longer. Missouri's first inhabitants were likely drawn to the region by its abundance of resources. Because of its geographical location near the confluence of three of the continent's most important waterways, the Missouri, Ohio, and Mississippi Rivers, Missouri is ideally situated to attract people and wildlife. Since river valleys were also important transportation routes, early denizens of the region had easy access to travel in and out of the area in any direction. These rivers also supported a great variety of plant, mammal, and aquatic life capable of sustaining humans.[21]

Missouri is also unique in that it is located at the point where the western prairies meet the southeastern forests. During the last centuries of the Pleistocene era, North America was nearing the end of the Ice Age and the Mississippi River Valley was shifting with the warming climate, from mixed evergreen and deciduous forests to more predominantly deciduous forests of oak and hickory. Meanwhile, the northern and western portions of the state were covered with a mixture of tallgrass prairie punctuated by stands of deciduous trees that generally followed the river valleys.[22]

In 1975, Missouri Archaeologist Carl H. Chapman allowed that it was possible that people, whom he called "Early Man," may have lived in Missouri earlier than 14,000 years ago. A decade later, Michael O'Brien and Ray Wood placed the date of Missouri's first humans around 11,250 years ago, though they too were open to the possibility that settlement may well have occurred earlier. Pressure to verify earlier settlements has led the archaeological community to develop better techniques and strategies for examining new and existing sites in Missouri, and some sites do hold promise. Late twentieth-century investigations at the Kimmswick site in Jefferson County have dated some aspects of it at 12,800 to 13,300 years ago. Researchers at the Big Eddy site in Cedar County have found evidence of human habitation that they date to nearly 13,000 years ago.[23]

The ancient people who occupied Missouri around 11,000 years ago were part of what archaeologists now call the Clovis culture. Though Clovis era people likely belonged to different social groups, they seem to have adopted some of the same cultural traits as defined by the distinctive stone hunting "tool kits" they left behind. The trademark tool in the kit is a stone point, which is characterized by a fluted face, gently outwardly curving edges—archaeologist call them lanceolate shaped—and a concave base. Stone points are important in our understanding of the people who made them, as they reveal much about the level of technology their makers possessed and help us determine what species of animals these groups hunted.

Because the defining feature of Clovis culture is a tool and not a specific group of people, some archaeologists, such as Dillehay and Steeves, believe that defining them as a distinct culture obscures a more nuanced view of the migration of people across the continent. Referring to the Clovis point as "The first great American invention," Dillehay writes that it has become the "icon" of North American migration during the late Pleistocene era, albeit a deceptive one. He argues that by lumping together similar points from across the continent under the category of

Clovis, archaeologists have created false continuities that "misrepresent and underestimate [the] cultural diversity" of Ice Age groups. "It takes more than a single tool type to define a cultural group," writes Paulette Steeves. Focusing on Clovis points, writes Dillehay, makes it easy to overlook assorted adaptations across various environments. Though Clovis technology was widespread throughout North America, we can't assume that this correlated with the omnipresence of a "Clovis people."[24]

Clovis culture is particularly enigmatic for several reasons. The points, which are named for Clovis, New Mexico, the town near the site where they were first discovered, are found throughout the United States. Though nearly ubiquitous, however, Clovis points were made for less than a millennium. Dates for Clovis activity vary around the country. Some archaeologists have claimed it began as early as 13,000 years ago. Gary Haynes has dated the general timeframe for Clovis from 11,500 to 10,500 years ago. In the Great Plains and Southwest, O'Brien and Wood have determined that Clovis was only active for three hundred years, from 11,200 to 10,900 years ago. Clovis tools are also distinctive because, in most places where they have been found, they remain the oldest artifacts that can be verifiably dated. For decades, this has led many to believe that Clovis were the first people in North America and Missouri.[25]

The Clovis era people are also shrouded in mystery because they abruptly stopped making their distinctive points at about the same time as the continent's megafauna vanished. Before 11,000 years ago, Missouri's environment supported several species of large mammals, including musk oxen, ground sloths, bison, horses, mammoths, and mastodons. By 11,000 years ago, they had all become extinct, not just in Missouri, but across the continent. The timing of these extinctions has led to a long-running disagreement over whether these mega mammals were killed off by Clovis hunters, or whether the warming late-Pleistocene climate drove them to extinction.[26]

The so-called "Overkill Theory" grew out of the discovery of Clovis points among the bones of mastodons in a small number of archaeological sites like Kimmswick. The hypothesis seemed to be further supported by the fact that stone hunting tools were the defining artifacts of Clovis culture. This appeared to indicate that a rapidly growing population of people using Clovis tools had become specialized super predators who systematically over-hunted mammoths, mastodons, horses, camels, and a few other species over the course of a thousand years. Some have theorized that the hunters' task may have been made less difficult by the fact that some animals, like ground sloths, were slow-moving, while others may have lacked sufficient fear of potential predators to flee from them.[27]

However, Ice Age megafauna were more likely to have been the victims of climate change. Around 11,000 years ago, the Late Wisconsin glacier period was coming to an end. As the climate in North America became warmer, glaciers retreated northward, followed by the decline of the coniferous forest environment that supported many species of grazing mega mammals. Deciduous forests and grasslands overtook various places in Missouri, and there is evidence that around 10,900 years ago a significant drought occurred, which may have affected the availability of water. The drier climate and loss of food sources would have put stress on populations of large animals, which would in turn have made them easier prey for hunters.[28]

Additionally, new evidence suggests that Clovis era people were not specialized big-game hunters at all. Instead, it is more likely that they were "opportunistic scavengers." These bands of hunter-gatherers were adept at recognizing opportunities for exploiting their environment to feed themselves. This exploitation might include such technological undertakings as building fish weirs to enhance their ability to harvest aquatic life or understanding how to use fire and stones to process nuts for consumption. While the evidence shows that Clovis era people did kill mammoths, mastodons, and other large mammals, the activity does not seem to have constituted their primary means of sustenance. Rather, these large mammals were simply another resource to be exploited when the opportunity arose. While seeds and nuts were labor intensive to prepare, a large mammal provided what archaeologist Nicole Waguespack has termed "greater post encounter return" once it is successfully hunted. In other words, one mammoth kill produced a greater amount of food for less expended labor than did other, more labor-intensive sources. For this reason, Clovis era people may have preferred to hunt mega mammals when they were available but were adept at other means of procuring food when they were not.[29]

Bands of Clovis era people were likely small and moved often in search of food. The entire group was heavily involved in food gathering, hunting, and food preparation. Applying current assumptions about gender roles and the work performed by different genders in Clovis societies is problematic. "Gender and sex may be aligned," writes Jennifer

Raff, "or they may not. . . . We can't assume we know what a person's gender was simply because we can determine their biological sex." Because Indigenous societies have diverse conceptions of gender, we must consider the likelihood that ancient gender roles did not conform to those later imposed by Christian colonizers.[30]

Waguespack, E. James Dixon, and others have pointed out that our masculine-centered perception of Clovis era people as being primarily big-game hunters comes from the fact that stone hunting tools are among the few artifacts they seem to have left behind. Waguespack writes that many of the organic artifacts made by women, "pass under researchers' trowels" because they have decomposed over the millennia. While Clovis era women performed tasks crucial to hunting, such as locating and driving game, their work in gathering and preparing edible plants and nuts was critical to group survival, especially when plant-based foods were needed to supplement their diet due to a lack of game. Women also served as leather workers, house builders, and burden carriers and likely helped produce some of the stone tools for which the Clovis period is known. More recently, archaeologist Randy Haas and others have challenged the perception that only men hunted prey. After finding a 9,000-year-old female skeleton buried with a hunter's toolkit in Peru, Haas and his colleagues did a statistical analysis of other burials. They studied 429 burials that contained hunter toolkits in both North and South America. All the burials were between 14,000 to 8,000 years old. Of the twenty-six burials in which the gender of the hunter's remains could be determined, eleven were found to be female. Based on this, they hypothesize that as many as 30 to 50 percent of all big-game hunters could have been women.[31]

Early Archaic Period

Even though Clovis points stopped being produced in Missouri 10,900 years ago, humans did not disappear from the landscape. Around 11,000 to 10,000 years ago, as the Pleistocene era was ending, the Holocene era was beginning, and ancient people were utilizing every area of the state.[32] There was a slow transition away from early hunter traditions to the Early Archaic tradition of hunter-foragers. This period was characterized by changing climate, flora, and fauna. Smaller mammals, such as deer and rabbits, replaced the large megafauna in the diets of Early Archaic people. The hunter's stone toolkit changed, too, likely to adapt to the new environment. Clovis points were rapidly replaced by so-called Dalton points. The latter fluted only near the base and tended to have a more streamline lanceolate shape, serrated edges, and often bases that resemble fish tails. Dalton points are ubiquitous in Missouri, having been found in all 114 of the state's counties.[33]

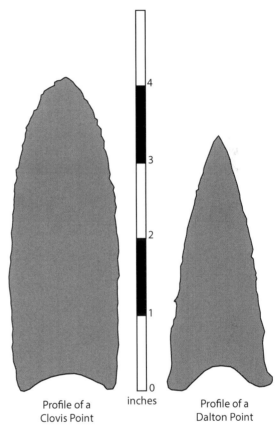

IMAGE 2: Both Clovis point and Dalton points are found in Missouri. Clovis technology dates from about 11,500 to 10,500 years ago. As the Pleistocene era ended and the climate became generally warmer, Indigenous people adapted to the new conditions by creating smaller Dalton points, which were better suited to hunting deer and rabbits. *Drawing by the author*

Profile of a Clovis Point

inches

Profile of a Dalton Point

Missouri archaeologists O'Brien and Wood have lamented the fact that, despite the large number of Dalton points found in the state, very little is known about the people who made them. Archaeologists believe that they chose to live near small streams adjacent to locations where prairies and forests met. While these people hunted and ate small mammals, birds such as turkeys, and turtles, snakes, and fish, they also ate hickory nuts and black walnuts. They used their distinctive points to hunt by launching them from atlatls, which were levers that, when swung in the direction of prey, launched the points with enough velocity to kill. Stone pestle and mortars show evidence that seeds and nuts were also important dietary staples. They also produced stone tools called Dalton adzes for wood working. Adzes could be used to both plane and chop wood to make atlatls, handles for knives, digging sticks, and snares. The presence of bone and stone awls at archaeological sites indicates that the people who lived in them were sewing together hides for clothing. Chapman cites the discovery of a buried partial human skeleton near what may be a ceremonial structure at Graham Cave in Montgomery County, to suggest that Early Archaic people also may have participated in spiritual rituals.[34]

Even as Indigenous people covered the state, the environment continued to undergo significant change as the Ice Age ended. Perhaps most dramatic among these alterations was the shifting of the Mississippi River. Melting glaciers in Canada had produced a huge reservoir of water. Known as Lake Agassiz, it was larger than all five of the present-day Great Lakes combined and covered much of what is now Manitoba. Around 8,200 years ago, the lake released a catastrophic amount of water, which gushed down what is now the Minnesota River into the Mississippi River. The extreme force of the release caused the Mississippi to jump from the west side of Crowley's Ridge to the east side and created some of the lowland swamps of the bootheel region.[35]

Middle Archaic Period

Nine thousand years ago marked the beginning of what archaeologists call the Middle Archaic Period, which would last for roughly six thousand years. It was also at about that time that a climatic event called the Hypsithermal began. During this time, the predominance of dry winds from the west created generally warmer, drier weather patterns in Missouri. This created an environment in which prairie grasses spread farther south and east while the hardwood forests retreated to wetter, low-lying areas. The animal population shifted in favor of those species that were better suited to live in prairie and grassland environments, such as jackrabbits, deer, and prairie chickens. Plant life also changed, and there is some evidence that by the peak of the Hypsithermal, around 7,000 years ago, the lack of moisture caused grains, seeds, and nuts to become smaller and some larger mammals to became scarce.[36]

In the face of environmental challenge early Archaic people adapted to their changing surroundings through innovation. One advance was the use fire to control the landscape. Intentional burning, or pyroregeneration, of both grassland and wooded areas enhanced hunting by creating better browsing vegetation for animals like deer, while keeping the landscape free of debris in which prey might hide. Burning could also improve growing conditions for many of the berries and nuts that people ate. Early Archaic stone toolkits are another innovation that illustrates the ways in which people were exploiting their environment, as the variety of tools became more diverse and more specialized for both hunting and foraging. At this time, people were engaged in what O'Brien and Wood call a "mobile foraging economy." In the warm seasons, people lived in camps in the river bottoms. As the weather cooled, they would move upland to hunt and collect seeds and nuts.[37]

By about 7,000 years ago, Archaic technology started to become more complex. Stone tools continued to diversify, as did the technology used to make them. This period also marked the appearance of stone axes and celts. These tools were made by grinding stones into smooth shapes rather than chipping them. Twined fiber technology was also becoming more common in the Middle Archaic Period. Archaeological investigations at Arnold Research Cave, in Callaway County, produced some rare examples of woven sandals, shoes, foraging bags, and fabrics made from the leaves of rattlesnake master, a plant that resembles yucca. One sandal found in the cave was made about 8,000 years ago, during the Early Archaic Period, and currently holds the distinction of being the oldest open-toed sandal known in the world.[38]

Though Archaic people continued to live in or near river valleys, they began moving onto river bottom terraces, river bluff bases, and even on bluff tops. Because they adapted to the changing climate, Archaic people began to move less often and establish connections to specific places. This produced a body of environmental knowledge about local resources that was passed down through generations. Along with this more sedentary lifestyle came signs of social hierarchy and the appearance of non-utilitarian objects of social value. It was also at this time that people began to bury the dead in specific cemetery spaces.[39]

Late Archaic Period

Around 5,000 years ago, the Hypsithermal came to an end. The climate in Missouri became generally cooler and wetter, allowing forests to reclaim grassland in some places. According to Chapman, the state's most populated regions at that time were likely the prairie north and northeast, while the western prairies likely had the sparsest population. When viewing this period of history, is important to keep in mind that food sources and stone tools varied in different regions of the state according to localized environmental conditions. However, in general, a growing population forced late Archaic people to become adept at exploiting a wide variety of birds, animals, and plants for consumption. For the first time, evidence suggests that people were beginning to domesticate plants, such as squash, gourds, sunflowers, and goosefoot, a plant that has edible leaves and seeds. O'Brien and Wood refer to this early form of agriculture as "incidental domestication," while Chapman hypothesizes that humans may have observed how seeds buried in trash piles grew and experimented with planting them in select locations. These early experiments would have involved the simple clearing of small plots of land on which to cultivate wild plants.[40]

Along with small garden-like plots, specific sites related to food production began to appear at this time. While earlier Archaic people often moved their entire camps when it was time to collect and process seeds and nuts, later people developed sites away from towns exclusively to produce black walnuts, pecans, hazelnuts, hickory nuts, and acorns. In the Late Archaic Period, a wider variety of artifacts associated with specific kinds of food production appeared as well. The so-called "Sedalia digger," for example, was an adz used primarily for digging up plant roots. Manos, pestles, and hammerstones were tools used in food-processing sites, specifically to grind seeds roots and plants.[41]

Anthropologist Gayle Fritz of Washington University in St. Louis has written that the first plant to be domesticated in the ancient Midwest was the bottle gourd. Seeds from the plant dating back 5,000 to 4,500 years have been found at Phillips Spring in Benton County, Missouri. Also found at the site were pepo squash seeds from roughly the same period. These "container crops" were useful as both food and vessels for seed storage, among other things. By about 4,000 years ago, "oily-seeded crops" such as sunflowers and marshelder, or sumpweed, also were domesticated and, due to their high fat content, contributed significantly to the Late Archaic diet. Soon, these crops were augmented by "starchy-seeded crops" such as little barley, maygrass, erect knotweed, and chenopod, a relative of quinoa.[42]

Cultural and spiritual practices became more elaborate in the late Archaic Period as camps evolved into towns, and people became more sedentary. At the same time, some sites appear to have been chosen for purely cultural or ceremonial reasons. For the first time, burial mounds appeared, usually on blufftops. One of the earliest late Archaic burial mounds in Missouri is Hatton Mound in Monroe County, but mounds from the era can be found in other parts of the state as well. Many people were buried in the Hatton Mounds. Some bodies were laid under stone slabs and rocks. Some of those interred there were buried with tools such as grooved axe heads, flint knives, and shell ornaments. In the western Ozarks, two late Archaic mounds, one in Hickory County and one in Polk County, each contained a single human. Both figures were buried with projectile points. The presence of these tools and cultural objects in the mounds seems to indicate that those conducting the burial saw themselves as sending the deceased off on some sort of journey.[43]

The Woodland Period

As the Archaic Period came to an end, humans entered the Woodland Period. The characteristics that define Woodland people are the cultivation of plants, the construction of earthen burial mounds, and the widespread making and use of pottery. As we have seen, cultivation and burial mounds first appeared during the Archaic Period in Missouri, though they appeared at other times in other areas. However, the use and making of pottery is a more reliable marker of the Woodland Period, which in Missouri began 2,600 years ago and ended 1,100 years ago. Chapman refers to Woodland Period people as "prairie-forest potters," because of their intense use of foraging and making of pottery. The making of ceramics had first appeared in Missouri between 4,000 and 3,000 years ago, but it was a very rare phenomenon until 2,600 years ago. The earliest Woodland pots, called Marion Thick, were heavy and made of paste-like clay tempered with large chunks of material that protruded through the vessel's finished surface. Pots were made by stacking coils of clay and smoothing the coils together by hand. Then, placing one hand inside the pot, and holding a wooden paddle wrapped in cord in the other hand on the outside, artisans would shape the pot. These rustic containers are cylindrical in shape, have flat bottoms, and often carry surface marks made by the cording or course woven material. It appears that once the pottery dried, it was fired above ground, perhaps covered in flammable material that was then ignited.[44]

The appearance of Black Sand pottery, roughly 2,400 years ago, illustrated technological improvements over Marion Thick. Black Sand pots were made of a harder clay tempered with smaller bits of sand and other materials formed into more refined vessel shapes with thinner walls. Black Sand pottery is also often decorated with incised lines and simple geometric shapes. This type of pottery appears in central and northeastern Missouri, as well as in eastern Iowa, Western Illinois, Wisconsin, and southern Minnesota. At roughly the same time, pottery in southeastern Missouri showed influences from the lower Mississippi River Valley. Named Tchula, this pottery is tempered with limestone and impressed on the exterior with fabric or wrapped cords like pottery fragments found in the lower Ohio and Mississippi River Valleys.[45]

Beginning about 2,200 years ago, a dizzying array of pottery subtypes began to appear throughout Missouri. These variants of Havana pottery, named for a location in Illinois where it was first excavated, were defined by the various design motifs stamped and incised on the surface of pots. Temper material became finer, which made it possible for artisans to make small clay effigy figurines and pipes depicting animals and humans. Though Havana pottery appears to have originated in Illinois, it influenced pottery made as far west as Oklahoma. This widespread influence has caused archaeologists to ask whether this is due to the migration of people into Missouri from the east, or whether the Havana style spread through the area because of trade and the exchange of ideas and knowledge.[46]

Chapman's term "prairie-forest potter" also refers to Woodland Period people's ability to get the most possible food from the environment in which they lived. This is known as "primary forest efficiency." People of this era tended to situate their towns in locations where they had easy access to forests, streams or rivers, and the prairie glades. While people cultivated plants, their main sources of food came from the wild plants, wildlife, and marine life found in these prairie-forest regions. Archaeologists believe that Woodland Period people ate a larger percentage of seeds than did their predecessors. They especially favored starchy seeds from plants like goosefoot, knotweed, maygrass, and little barley. However, an excavation in Lincoln County, Missouri, turned up nearly two dozen different types of edible nuts and seeds. It is not known whether this heavy reliance on nuts and seeds was necessary to compensate for the lack of other food sources like wildlife, or if Woodland people's efficiency at foraging simply led them to rely on what was readily found nearby.[47]

Heavy foraging allowed for a more sedentary lifestyle in which people were increasingly likely to stay in a particular place for longer periods of time. The extensive knowledge that foragers and hunters had gained about utilizing the resources in their immediate environment allowed them to feed more people with less exertion. This made it possible for villages to become larger and remain in one location longer. This trend accelerated when, about 2,250 years ago, people began to move away from the incidental domestication of plants toward specialized domestication of gourds and sunflowers. Early agriculture not only allowed villages to support greater numbers of people, but it also made year-round habitation of some places possible and, in places where food plots needed tending, necessary. Large, semi-permanent settlements also attracted people from locations where foragers, hunters, and farmers were less successful. By this time, notes archaeologist Mark F. Seeman, Woodland people "lived in worlds of their own creation. They not only interpreted the landscape in ways that were meaningful to them but added to it a variety of buildings, monuments, pathways, fields, and public spaces."[48]

A sedentary lifestyle allowed for the development of more elaborate burial practices. Around 1,800 to 1,900 years ago, mounds of the Woodland Period began to exhibit what archaeologists refer to as Hopewell influences. While the name comes from a large complex of earthen mounds found in southern Ohio, Hopewell traits traveled through Indiana, Illinois, and into Missouri. Archaeologist Robert Hall has referred to Hopewell as a "phenomenon" because of the difficulty of defining exactly what it was. He points to Joseph Caldwell's useful statement that Hopewell was not a "culture per se," but "material evidence of an episode of interaction between several regional traditions."[49]

Some portions of Missouri, especially along the Missouri and Mississippi River Valleys, were included in the Havana Hopewell sphere of influence between 2,070 and 1,700 years ago. Centered along the Illinois River, this sphere spread widely to parts of Wisconsin, Iowa, Michigan, and Indiana. In Missouri, two variances of the influence have been identified. The Kansas City Hopewell, near the confluence of the Kansas and Missouri Rivers, and Big Bend Hopewell, which is located farther down the Missouri River near the Grand and Chariton Rivers. Archaeologists have identified three types of Havana Hopewell settlements, including permanently occupied villages or "base camps," ceremonial camps related to blufftop burial mounds, and regional transaction sites located in floodplains. Havana Hopewell people subsisted on hunting and the gathering and cultivation of domestic plants, of which maize constituted a small portion.[50]

Even with the widespread Hopewell influence, the details of mounds around Missouri vary. In them, the human remains were usually interred in a crypt-like structure made of logs or stone. The crypts were then covered with dirt in the form of a low cone or mound. It was not unusual for other bodies, perhaps added later, to be buried in the periphery of mound structures. One of the hallmarks of Hopewell burial mounds is the presence of nonutilitarian artifacts made of exotic materials in graves. Objects made from materials such as obsidian, copper, and catlinite appear in mounds located far from the places where such materials are found. This points to the fact that Woodland people participated in a sophisticated and far-reaching network of trade and exchange.[51]

Because of trade in exotic minerals used in mounds, Chapman has suggested that a "Hopewell Interaction Sphere" existed for a wide variety of materials and purposes but was most active in the distribution of ceremonial and cultural innovations, such as burial customs and beliefs related to death. Practical skills, such as tool and pottery making, tended to be more influenced by local adaptations. The most activity in trade networks seems to have occurred in regional transaction centers, such as the Havana center along the Mississippi River, north of the Missouri River, and Lower Illinois River. Other regional sites occurred along the Missouri River between Kansas City and the Iowa border, along the Big Bend of the Missouri River in Saline and Lafayette Counties, and the Cooper Center in extreme southwest Missouri.[52]

Trade made an impact on other parts of Hopewell culture beside burial customs. Exchange networks created a support system by which local settlements struggling with food insecurity might turn to other groups nearby for assistance. This served as an important protection against the unpredictability of the environment. Trade activity also may have led to social hierarchy, creating a class of local elites who had access to highly valuable trade goods. A system of hierarchy may also have formed around those who either had hereditary status or enjoyed prominence because of some sort of personal achievement. In any event, it seems to have been the bodies of these elites who were interred in ceremonial mounds.[53]

O'Brien and Wood point to evidence suggesting that during the middle part of the Woodland Period, people began to affiliate into what we now call "tribes" or "nations." Such affiliations gave participants several advantages, including the distribution of risks and benefits in an uncertain world. Tribal groups helped disseminate information and allowed for the delegation of the responsibilities for decision making. Finally, tribal affiliations helped individuals define their allegiances during times when diverse groups met together to participate in ceremonies, trading, or warfare.[54]

For several decades in the early and mid-twentieth century, some archaeologists posited that portions of extreme southeast Missouri had been left out of the Hopewell Interaction Sphere. This "hillbilly hypothesis of Ozark nondevelopment" was based on the work of Mark R. Harrington, who excavated several rock shelters and caves in the White River valley of northwest Arkansas and the Cowskin River valley in southwest Missouri in 1922 and 1923, and Samuel Dellinger, who excavated sites in the region between 1928 and 1934. Because the caves were dry, Harrington and Dellinger found numerous organic artifacts like baskets, clothing, and wooden objects. They found very little pottery, and no bows and arrows—which were a late Woodland innovation—and only slight evidence of agriculture. Because they were working in the days before radiocarbon dating and were sifting through layers of artifact stratification that were extremely difficult to sort out, Harrington and Dellinger thought they were looking at the refuse of a single Woodland Period of cultural occupation that had lasted for "a very long time." Harrington dubbed the cave occupants the "Ozark Bluff Dwellers." To explain the presence of artifacts that were clearly more recent and different from those made by the Bluff Dwellers, Harrington hypothesized that the shelters had been briefly occupied by a culture from outside the region, which he called the "Top-Layer" people.[55]

Based on what they found and did not find in the shelters, Harrington, Dellinger, and a small number of other archaeologists created a narrative about the Bluff Dwellers based on several incorrect assumptions. They hypothesized that the Bluff Dwellers lived in the western Ozarks during the Woodland Period but, because of the rough terrain in the region, were largely isolated from and lived a far more primitive existence than did people who lived just a few hundred miles east of them in the Mississippi River Valley. Bluff Dwellers lived year-round in rock shelters and caves and made complex baskets and fabrics. They raised corn and squash, but relied mainly on hunting deer, bear, elk, and other mammals, which they did with outdated atlatls technology, for sustenance. Dellinger and one of his co-authors, a physician named Elmer Wakefield, claimed that the Bluff Dwellers were a unique race of people whose origins and subsequent disappearance were shrouded in mystery. Despite the complete lack of evidence, they claimed Bluff

Dwellers were unusually short in stature and had sloping heads and a very tenuous genetic connection to the Indigenous people of today.[56]

The story of the vanished race of Ozark Bluff Dwellers caught on with the popular press by the end of the 1930s and persisted for decades, eventually making its way into popular histories of Missouri and Arkansas and school textbooks. The Federal Writer's Project's *Arkansas: A Guide to the State* (1941) informed its readers of the mysterious people who "fell far short of the cultural levels attained by the prehistoric inhabitants of the rest of the state and then vanished." As late as 1970, the popular Taney County, Missouri, historian Elmo Ingenthron wrote that if the Ozark Bluff Dwellers had, in fact, coexisted with Hopewell culture, they, "were immune to the cultural developments of those other people living at no great distance from them." Historian Brooks Blevins points out that such passages created a myth of the backward Bluff Dwellers that, going even that far back in history, portrayed the Ozarks both as a place of "cultural refuge," and as a haven for hillbillies.[57]

By the mid-twentieth century, however, archaeologists began to push back against the myth of the Ozark Bluff Dwellers and to correct Harrington and Dellinger's numerous false assumptions. The duo's most glaring misconception of the shelters and caves had been that they were evidence of a single cultural occupation when, in fact, the sites showed nine millennia of human presence that spanned the Archaic, Woodland, and Mississippian periods. The absence of pottery and other artifacts in the caves was because the rock shelters were never used as year-round homes. While people in the Archaic Period may have spent considerable time there, by the late Woodland Period, the caves were often used as food processing centers.

Most important, archaeologists now recognize that Woodland era people living in the Ozarks "do not appear to lag behind adjacent regions in any meaningful way." Nonetheless the myth of the Ozark Bluff Dwellers still survives in the popular imagination, largely, write archaeologists Linda Rees and Jamie Brandon, because the romantic story of a vanished race is easier to grasp than the complicated, multi-layered story unearthed by modern research techniques. The myth also remains potent because of the way it neatly dovetails with the harmful stereotype of Ozarks people as somehow "premodern and ignorant." By the end of the twentieth century, archaeologists were able to lay the myth to rest, especially after James Allison Brown systematically spelled out the case against it in his 1984 book, *Prehistoric Southern Ozark Marginality: A Myth Exposed.*[58]

About 1,600 years ago, the Hopewell Interaction Sphere appears to have suddenly evaporated. The nature of this seeming reduction in trade and intergroup contact remains the topic of much debate. Some archaeologists have suggested that the reduction in exchange might have been due to an interregional economic collapse. Archaeologists James Theler and Robert Boszhardt point out that exotic minerals such as copper, flint, and shells stopped being traded, and that the elaborate Hopewell stone effigy pipes were replaced by simple elbow pipes made of stone or clay. They are unable, however, to come up with an explanation for the cause of such a collapse. Nonetheless, the variety and quality of artifacts in Late Woodland sites seem lackluster. According to archaeologist Richard Yerkes, "Late Woodland artifact assemblages are known more for what they lack than for what they are." Pottery was largely without decoration and lithic points and tools did not appear to be as carefully worked as had earlier examples.[59]

Chapman termed this change a "retrogression," citing the ebb of ceremonial life and communication. He reported that during the Late Woodland Period, a new emphasis on "locally oriented cultures" was underway. Mortuary ceremonies and mounds became less elaborate. Chapman believed that small scale agriculture and the "specialized exploitation of resources" gave way to more generalized hunting and gathering. Populations became more dispersed, moving inland from the river valleys, and, other than the bow and arrow, advances in arts, crafts, and technology seem to have waned considerably. Chapman hypothesized that while the Hopewellian Interaction Sphere deteriorated in general, it seemed to remain open to information from the south. This made it possible for influences from Mesoamerica to make their way to the Midwest via present day Arizona, New Mexico, and Texas. While these influences first became established in the Late Woodland Period, they would play a greater part in shaping the Mississippian Culture that was yet to come.[60]

Other archaeologists, however, take exception to this grim scenario. Countering Chapman's argument, O'Brien and Wood maintain that using the presence of Hopewell influence and exchange as a metric by which to judge the success of Missouri cultures was somewhat beside the point. They suggest that the bonds that tied local groups, or tribes, together were becoming more vibrant at this time. Trade, they argue, did continue during the Late Woodland Period but that Hopewell items were only a small part of that exchange.[61]

Archaeologists Dale McElrath, Thomas Emerson, and Andrew Fortier have argued that the Late Woodland Period is best understood as a time when people in Missouri and the Midwest went through three major transformations. The first was the initial formation of tribal societies about 1,600 or 1,700 years ago. "Late Woodland Native societies," they write, "are recognizable because they were welded together from the diffuse social networks established in . . . earlier times." The second transformation was marked by the widespread adoption of the use of the bow and arrow about 1,400 years ago. This was accompanied by population increase and a shift toward increasingly complex societies. The final transformation was the reliance on maize and other grains as major food sources about 1,100 or 1,200 years ago. This helped to create the foundations of the agricultural-centered societies upon which Mississippian culture would thrive. "Despite the absence of dramatic spectacles and fancy paraphernalia," writes Fritz, "Late Woodland populations were clearly successful at feeding themselves and reproducing across the landscape. . . . Many of them were good enough at food production to deserve the label 'farmers.'"[62]

Though some archaeologists still view the Late Woodland as a period of "good gray cultures," known for the drabness of the material culture that has survived, O'Brien and Wood see it as a period that "set the stage for several significant changes in how the inhabitants of parts of Missouri arranged themselves across the landscape and how they interacted with each other after 900 A.D."[63]

Voices

In the sun lives the Lord of Life. In the moon lives Old-Woman-Who-Never-Dies. She has six children, three sons and three daughters. These live in the sky. The eldest son is the Day; another is the Sun; another is Night. The eldest daughter is the Morning Star, called "The Woman Who Wears a Plume;" another is a star which circles around the polar star, and she is called "The Striped Gourd;" the third is Evening Star.

Every spring Old-Woman-Who-Never-Dies sends the wild geese, the swans, and the ducks. When she sends the wild geese, the Indians plant their corn, and Old-Woman-Who-Never-Dies makes it grow. When eleven wild geese are found together, the Indians know the corn crop will be very large. The swans mean that the Indians must plant gourds; the ducks, that they must plant beans.

Indians always save dried meat for these wild birds, so when they come in the spring they may have a corn feast. They build scaffolds of many poles, three or four rows, and one above the others. On this they hang the meat. Then the old women in the village, each one with a stick, meet around the scaffold. In one end of the stick is an ear of corn. Sitting in a circle, they plant their sticks in the ground in front of them. Then they dance around the scaffolds while the old men beat the drums and rattle the gourds.

Afterward the old women in the village are allowed to eat the dried meat. In the fall they hold another corn feast, after the corn is ripe. This is so that Old-Woman-Who-Never-Dies may send the buffalo herds to them. Each woman carries the entire cornstalk, with the ears attached, just as it was pulled up by the roots. Then they call on Old-Woman-Who-Never-Dies and say, "Mother, pity us. Do not send the cold too soon, or we may not have enough meat. Mother, do not let the game depart, so that we may have enough for winter."

In the fall, when the birds go south to Old-Woman, they take back the dried meat hung on the scaffolds because Old-Woman is very fond of it.

Old-Woman-Who-Never-Dies has large patches of corn, kept for her by the great stag and by the white-tailed stag. Blackbirds also help her guard her corn patches. The corn patches are large; therefore, the Old Woman has the help also of the mice and the moles. In the spring the birds go north, back to Old-Woman-Who-Never-Dies.

In the olden time, Old-Woman-Who-Never-Dies lived near the Little Missouri. Sometimes the Indians visited her. One day twelve came, and she offered them only a small kettle of corn. They were very hungry, and the kettle was very small. But as soon as it was empty, it at once became filled again, so all the Indians had enough to eat.[1]

—Mandan oral tradition

There were once ten brothers, six of whom were good hunters, three poor hunters, while the last was the hero of this tale. The eldest boys all killed big game, and the other three killed only turkeys, raccoons, and skunks respectively. One day it was announced that there was to be a great race around the world, and the tenth boy told the three poor hunters to get boughs and make a sweat lodge. The boys did this, while the six who were good hunters jeered and laughed at them and made their own lodge. However, after they had sweated, the youngest brother pulled at their hair till it was very long, then he too sweated and became handsome. He put on his best clothes, placed his human head earbobs in his ears, and came out. When the elder brothers saw how fine the younger ones looked, they became very jealous. On the day of the race all the brothers appeared at the appointed spot. The contest was to be against a party of giants who had mucus hanging from their noses and who always won. The whole tribe was to try against them on this occasion in hopes of wiping them out, for the people had lost many of their number through these giants, who always bet a life against a life. Human-head-earrings won the race and slew the giants, in which he was assisted by two friends that he had made, Turtle and Blackhawk.[2]

—Robert Small and Julia Small (Otoe)

She planted as many hills as she desired, taking the grains from a woven sack flung on her back, woven of nettle or buckbrush runners. She formerly, and at least ceremonially, painted her forehead with one red and one blue line across the breadth and one red and one blue short line running vertically on each cheek.

Her song as she planted, beating the rhythm with her feet and the planting stick, was one of the most beautiful of all the many songs of the Little Ones [Osages].

I have made a footprint, a sacred one.

I have made a footprint, through it the blades must push upwards.

I have made a footprint, through it the blades radiate.

I have made a footprint, over it the blades float in the wind.

I have made a footprint, over it the ears lean toward each other.

I have made a footprint, over it I pluck the ears.

I have made a footprint, over it I bend the stalks to pluck the ears.

I have made a footprint, over it the tassels lie gray.

I have made a footprint, smoke rises from my lodge.

I have made a footprint, there is a cheer in my lodge.

I have made a footprint, I live in the light of day.[3]

—*John Joseph Matthews (Osage)*

Chapter Two

The Morning Star and the Evening Star

CORN, OR MAIZE, ORIGINATED IN the western hemisphere and is thought to have first been grown in present-day Mexico. Maize is a somewhat unique crop in that it cannot grow wild and is solely dependent on humans for its survival. Scientist now believe that it was first domesticated about nine thousand years ago from a wild grass called teosinte, which grows in central Mexico's Balsas River valley. Because the inch-long cobs on the teosinte plant produce no more than a dozen hard seeds (modern corn cobs can each produce up to one thousand kernels), archaeologists Douglas J. Kennett and Keith M. Prufer speculate that the plant was first harvested for the sweet juice inside its stem, which may even have been fermented to create alcohol for consumption. Over time, humans bred the crop to produce a greater number of larger kernels. By about 4,500 to 4,000 years ago, maize had become a dietary staple in Mesoamerica.[1]

Eventually, Indigenous farmers, who were primarily women, hybridized and adopted its cultivation across the continent. It made its way to the Mississippi River Valley either through the Southwest or through the Caribbean. Woodland farmers first began to grow the crop in the Midwest about 2,200 years ago. Woodland people were not dependent on the crop for sustenance, but they may have used it in ceremonies. During the period of the Hopewell interaction, very little maize seems to have been planted in the Midwest. It was not until about 1,250 years ago that some groups of people in the region began to plant it for sustenance. By that time, hybridization had produced ears of corn that contained up to twelve rows of kernels. The rise in maize cultivation coincided with a changing climate that brought warm and moist air into Missouri for three centuries, starting from about 1,300 to 1,000 years ago. According to archaeologists Michael J. O'Brien and W. Raymond Wood, early corn production in Missouri first took place in the Bootheel region among the meander belts of the Mississippi River floodplain. Maize was also planted extensively on the east side of the Mississippi River, between the Illinois River and the Kaskaskia River, in an area known today as the American Bottom. Because corn was less tolerant of heat, drought, and insects than native edible plants, it seems likely that Indigenous farmers had to experiment considerably to determine how best to grow it in that location. Nonetheless, by about 1,100 years ago, corn was an important part of the ancient Midwestern diet.[2]

Due to a combination of natural reproduction and the immigration of people mostly from the Illinois River valley, the population of the Mississippi River Valley had been growing for several hundred years. Because maize eventually became a reliable crop that helped sustain that growth, people slowly devoted an increasing amount of time, energy, and land to its cultivation. While this diverted time and resources from hunting and growing other crops, the dividend was apparently worthwhile. According to archaeologist Amber VanDerwarker, through experimentation with land quality and seed selection, the people of the Mississippi River Valley became "maize experts." Because Indigenous people learned how to successfully store maize, the plant evolved from being a garden crop eaten immediately after harvest to an important commodity that was stockpiled in communal caches for future use. While the intense farming of maize coincided with population growth in the Mississippi River Valley, archaeologist Jeffrey S. Alvey cautions us that evidence does not support the assumption that maize alone created the increased population levels. As we have already seen, Woodland people had successfully grown gourds, squash, oily-seeded crops, and starchy-seeded crops, and Mississippian farmers had continued to cultivate all of them.[3]

Early Mississippian Period

Between about 1,200 and 1,000 years ago, some settlements in southeast Missouri and the American Bottom became permanent agrarian communities. Archaeologist Carl H. Chapman labeled the period between 1,100 to 800 years ago the "Village Farmer Tradition" because people throughout the region were becoming more reliant on permanent fields in river valleys and the "efficient, organized exploitation of most natural resources." More recently, other archaeologists have called this era the

Early or Emergent Mississippian Period. Though village farmer settlements ranged in size, most of them had become more socially organized. Towns and villages began to be arranged around an open central plaza, at the center of which was often placed a tall, painted wooden pole, which signified village identity or a common ancestor. Dwellings exhibited a new "trench wall" technology in which house walls were built as modular units, sometimes in offsite locations, and set upright in trenches that outlined a square or rectangular floorplan. Other items of material culture changed as well. Pottery, previously tempered with various types of crushed stone or sand, now was tempered with burned and crushed mussel shells. Like their Woodland predecessors, Early Mississippians built burial mounds. Mounds constructed after 1,200 years ago were, however, often truncated at the top to accommodate flat ceremonial platforms.[4]

Archaeologists have traced some of the cultural ideas that shaped Early Mississippians to the Coles Creek people who lived in the lower Mississippi River Valley in present-day Louisiana. They were heirs to a tradition of mound building that predates the mounds found in the large Mississippian settlement of Cahokia, which was located across the Mississippi River from present-day St. Louis. It is widely believed that, like maize, many of the cultural influences that shaped the Mississippians made their way into the Mississippi River Valley from Mesoamerica. Archaeologist have found evidence of trade between the people of present-day Mexico and modern New Mexico and Arizona. From there, it is possible that trade goods and cultural ideas spread to the Caddoan people of Texas and Oklahoma and on to Cahokia.[5]

As Mississippian culture developed in the American Bottom and in southeast Missouri, the transformation of groups from the Late Woodland to the Mississippian Period proceeded somewhat differently than did those living elsewhere in the state. For much of present-day Missouri, Late Woodland cultural traits continued throughout much of the Mississippian Period, even though many Woodland groups had regular contact with Mississippian people. Burial mound excavations in central and north central Missouri appear to show that the people who made them tended to exhibit Woodland traditions, though O'Brien and Wood point to the fact that many of these mounds were first excavated in the early twentieth century and accurately dating them has been challenging. So-called Boone Phase burial mounds, dating from 1,550 to 800 years ago, tended to be placed on bluffs overlooking major rivers, especially the Missouri River and its lower tributaries. Many types of burials, including cremated remains, disembodied skulls, and entire skeletons can be found, sometimes together in a single mound. Grave offerings are few and limited to pottery, clay or stone pipes, and shells or shell beads. While their home village sites in the center of the state have not been well documented, it seems that they subsisted on native plants raised on low bottomland terraces, freshwater aquatic resources, and game.[6]

Though many of the mounds and cairns in the Ozark Highlands were built during the early Mississippian period, between 1,000 and 700 years ago, they exhibit the characteristics of Late Woodland burials. These were generally made of rock and earth on bluff tops overlooking streams. Often, the mounds held rock chambers or platforms. While people in this region continued the Archaic Period practice of living in river valleys and camping in caves and rockshelters, they also built larger, open village sites on elevated terraces in larger stream and river valleys. Late Woodland people in the Ozark Highlands subsisted on a wide variety of mammals, but most often ate deer, turkeys, and raccoons. They also consumed many freshwater mussels and cultivated some maize and native plants such as goosefoot.[7]

Chapman cited some evidence for at least one Mississippian-style platform mound in the White River valley in far southwestern Missouri. Other mounds in southwest Missouri have been found to contain Caddoan-influenced grave goods and, occasionally, maize. This area was located adjacent to Caddoan people who lived in the Arkansas River valley. In places like Spiro Mounds in northeast Oklahoma, the Caddoans exhibited Mississippian influences, and they conducted trade with settlements like Cahokia in the American Bottom. It is difficult to say, however, whether the people who lived in southwest Missouri were Caddoans or closely allied with them.[8]

In northeast Missouri, Late Woodland village sites have been found in a wide variety of geographical locations. Early in the period, around 1,300 years ago, the population in this corner of the state increased significantly. Not only are settlements found in river valleys on high bottomland terraces, but they are also on bluffs near streams. Even though the region is near the American Bottom, Early Mississippian culture traveled south along the Mississippi River rather than north, and the Woodland traditions in northeast Missouri continued with only some

Mississippian influences. However, the number of village sites appears to have dropped dramatically during the Early Mississippian period. Archaeologists theorize that as the climate warmed about 950 years ago, prairies overtook some forest regions in northeast Missouri and some of the village sites built during the previous population boom had become unsustainable.[9]

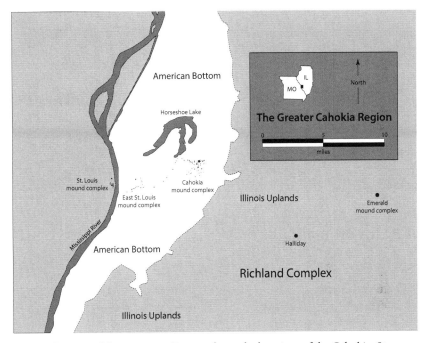

MAP 2: This map of the American Bottom shows the locations of the Cahokia, St. Louis, and East St. Louis mound complexes and the adjacent farming region during the years 1050 to 1150. *Map by the author*

One of the areas of Missouri that shows a significant Mississippian influence is near the confluence of the Kansas and Missouri Rivers. Pottery, stone tools, maize farming, and mound burials from the Steed-Kisker phase show a mixture of Cahokian and eastern Great Plains influences. Archaeologist believed at one time that this location had been settled by Mississippian immigrants from the American Bottom. It is more likely, however, that the region was heavily influenced by Mississippian traits brought up the Missouri River through trade and exchange.[10]

Prior to about 1,000 years ago, Early Mississippian influences seem to have been strongest in eastern Missouri, from the Missouri River south to the lowlands between the St. Francis and Mississippi Rivers. Mississippian communities developed there and were evident inside a triangle formed at the three corners by Cape Girardeau, Memphis, Tennessee, and the St. Francis River valley on the western edge of the Missouri Bootheel.[11]

However, the center of the Mississippian tradition was located across the Mississippi River in the American Bottom. Archaeologists have cited several characteristics that marked the transition from Woodland to Mississippian culture. One of the most visible of these is a dramatic change in material culture. This included shell-tempered pottery, bow and arrow use, trench wall houses, and stone elbow and effigy pipes. Characteristics also included increased maize agriculture, trade and exchange between regions, large permanent communities, public structures, and social stratification.[12]

Mississippian Period

After 1,000 years ago, a handful of large communities, each centered around ceremonial mounds, began to develop in the Mississippi River Valley. The largest of these was Cahokia, located just seven miles east of the present site of St. Louis. We do not know what the people who lived in Cahokia 1,000 years ago called their city. Its present name comes from the Cahokia people of the Illinois Confederacy, who lived near the site at the time of European contact in the seventeenth century. Situated in the rich farmland of the American Bottom, which archaeologist Timothy R. Pauketat has referred to as "ancient America's Corn Belt," Cahokia was a ceremonial center and the seat of local government. Prior to about 1,000 years ago, the town had already been home to more than a thousand people, many of whom may have migrated from smaller towns in the region. Even so, the Cahokia of the first half of the eleventh century was likely an ethnically homogenous place where people spoke the same language and shared similar cultural traditions.[13]

Suddenly, in the mid-eleventh century, a dramatic incident, or series of events, occurred that would alter Cahokia quickly and significantly. No one knows just what occurred, but something triggered a massive acceleration of the Mississippian culture that had been steadily developing up to that time. It also brought a new wave of migration into the American Bottom. Some have suggested that the change may have been caused by a military event. Others believe it might have had something to do with a major natural or spiritual event. Pauketat, who has spent most of his professional career studying Cahokia and the surrounding area, has theorized that the spark that inspired the town's sudden transformation was an exploding supernova that lit the northern hemisphere's day and nighttime sky for two days beginning on July 4, 1054. Given that the Mississippians closely observed the sun, moon, and stars, such an occurrence would have been of great significance to them. Whatever the specific cause may have been, it inspired the town of Cahokia to undergo an immediate and drastic makeover during the next fifty to one hundred years.[14]

Sometime during the decade of the 1050s, "old" Cahokia was razed and a new, magnificently planned ceremonial city was built in its place. The civic and ceremonial center of "new" Cahokia was a huge Grand Plaza, which covered nearly fifty acres, or about the land mass of thirty-five modern American football fields. The plaza was artificially leveled with earth and gravel and became the site of huge feasts, religious ceremonies, and games of chunkey. The plaza was surrounded by neighborhoods of trench-wall houses, each with a steep pitched hipped roof covered in thatch. Each neighborhood of houses was connected to its own smaller plaza and mound groups.[15]

Immediately north of the Grand Plaza stands Monk's Mound. At one hundred feet in height, the mound, which is named for Trappist monks who lived on top of it in the nineteenth century, is the largest pre-Columbian structure built in North America. Containing 730,000 cubic meters of earth, clay, and limestone, the completed Monks Mound featured four main terraces. On the highest terrace stood a council house, possibly the place where decisions regarding the community were made by priests or councilors. At 4,300 square feet, it is thought to be the largest Mississippian building ever constructed. On the second highest terrace was a small conical mound that acted as the axis upon which all the city was laid out.[16]

For decades, archaeologists believed that it may have taken up to two centuries to construct the enormous mound. Recently, however, archaeologist Timothy Schilling has estimated that Monks Mound was built quickly, in at least three separate stages beginning in the late eleventh century. Each stage of construction likely took between five and fifteen years to complete, with intervals between the construction stages perhaps lasting several years. There is evidence that during these intervals, the mound developed serious erosion problems that had to be rectified. Schilling hypothesizes that part of the instability was caused by

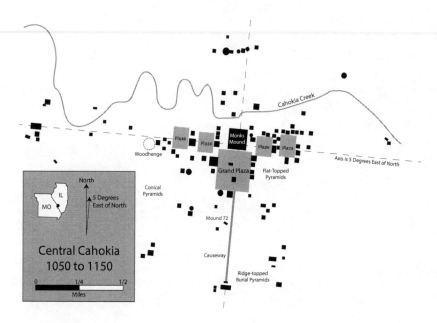

MAP 3: Central Cahokia as it looked between 1050 and 1150. Note that the axis upon which the city is organized is centered on Monks Mound. Also notice that the axis does not align with the four cardinal directions but is offset by five degrees. *Map by the author based on a map by Timothy R. Pauketat*

the hasty pace of construction. "Sediments were placed so rapidly," he writes, "that weathering or soil formation did not have time to occur." In fact, archaeologists and engineers working to stabilize the mound in 2007 were able to differentiate individual basket-loads of dirt from loose fill and sod blocks that surrounded them. Layers of limestone pavers mark previous mound platforms and indicate the points at which one stage of construction ended and another began. The 2007 excavation also revealed large cypress posts set vertically in what would have been the top of earlier stages of the mound. The collapse of these posts after placement seems to have exacerbated the instability of some mound sections.[17]

South of the plaza, an elevated causeway extended a half mile through a swamp. The causeway connected the plaza with two offertory platforms, several ridge-top burial mounds, and terminated at a large earthwork known as Rattlesnake Mound. Just west of the causeway, about halfway to Rattlesnake Mound, archaeologists have uncovered the remains of dozens of men and women in a ridge-top earthwork

IMAGE 3: A view of Cahokia's central precinct as seen from the south as it would have looked around the year 1150. The Grand Plaza is in the foreground and Monk's Mound is in the background. *From a Painting by Lloyd K. Townsend, 1982, Courtesy of Cahokia Mounds State Historic Site*

known as Mound 72. Some in the mound had been interred ceremonially after death, while others appear to have been ritually executed at the site.[18]

North and east of the Grand Plaza was another smaller plaza, as well as more mound groups and residential neighborhoods. An ancient road, which was still visible in the nineteenth century, led east across the American Bottom and up the river bluffs to the Emerald Mound group, which is believed to have served largely as a ceremonial site. Between Cahokia proper and the Emerald site stretched the Richland Farming Complex, which sat on the uplands away from the river bottom. At its height, around the year 1150, Cahokia may have had a population of between ten thousand and fifteen thousand people. As the urban center grew, it needed a dependable source of food for its large population. While Cahokia was being rebuilt, the landscape around it was also reordered. Woodland villages were mostly abandoned and replaced by planned individual farmsteads and nodal farming communities. Each of the complex's communities was spiritually linked to Cahokia by ceremonial structures, and larger towns also served as administrative centers. The Richland complex may have once been home to between five thousand and seven thousand farmers who formed a network that supplied Cahokia with the food that it needed. Richland farmers, the vast majority of whom were women, not only grew maize but also grew sunflowers, which made up a large part of Cahokians' diet, as well as squash, sumpweed, little barley, erect knotweed, and chenopod.[19]

As many as one in three of these farmers were born outside of the American Bottom, with many of them coming from the middle and lower Mississippi River Valley and the lower Ohio River valley. To get a sense of the diversity of people that emigrated to the Cahokian world, consider one small village of about two hundred to three hundred people located about ten miles southeast of Cahokia in the Richmond complex. Archaeologists working on what is now known as the Halliday Site were confused to find that the style of much of the material culture found in the village was out of step with that which had been found in other Cahokia-related sites. Pauketat described the findings as "either old fashioned or foreign to the region." Archaeologists were further surprised to find that, while Cahokian sites tend to be tidy, the Halliday site was strewn with ancient trash. Apparently, life was hard for the farmers living in this and other nearby towns. Their diet was poor, containing far too much corn and not enough protein. Pauketat judges that they lived "the closest thing to a peasant lifestyle that had ever existed in pre-Columbian North America." By focusing on the unique style of pottery the people of the Halliday Site made, archaeologists have determined that they had either immigrated from southeast Missouri or were the descendants of Missourians from that region. Like immigrants today, these people had banded together to form a community in their new homeland and brought their culture, which in this case included Varney Style pottery, with them. But, also like immigrants of today, they had adopted some parts of the local culture. In the case of the Halliday Site people, they adopted the Mississippian game of chunkey.[20]

Chunkey, a game that originated around 1,400 years ago in western Illinois and Eastern Missouri, was a cultural unifier for the people of Cahokia and its outlying districts, and important matches attracted large crowds of spectators. In the game, players tried to knock over a rolling chunkey stone, which was about the size of a hockey puck, by hurling long spear-like poles to stop it as it rolled along the ground. Specific rules for the game varied from place to place. The game was more than a cultural pastime, it was sometimes played to settle disputes that otherwise might have led to violence. The fact that competitors traveled long distances to play chunkey at Cahokia is evident by the wide distribution of the city's distinctive stones throughout the Midwest.[21]

West of Monks Mound, the Grand Plaza, and Cahokia's urban complex of one hundred twenty mounds, more earthworks and residences extended to the Mississippi River and beyond. One-half mile west of the plaza was a series of structures archaeologists have called the American Woodhenge. The site consists of at least five circles of varying sizes, the largest having a diameter of four hundred twenty feet. Each circle was outlined by regularly spaced cypress posts planted vertically in the ground in multiples of twelve, likely to coincide with the annual cycle of the sun. Archaeologist believe these circles allowed the people of Cahokia to observe and trace the movements of the sun.[22]

Beyond Woodhenge, a string of mounds ran southwest along what was then the south bank of Cahokia Creek. The largest of these was Powell Mound located about two miles west of the Grand Plaza. At three hundred ten feet long, one hundred seventy feet wide, and thirty-five feet tall, it was the second largest mound in the Cahokia district. From Powell Mound, which was destroyed to make the land farmable in 1930, more mounds formed a line, three or four more miles long, leading the way to present-day East St. Louis, Illinois.[23]

With forty-five mounds, East St. Louis was the second largest mound complex in the Cahokia region. Evidence gleaned from recent archaeological excavations indicates that this area was planned and constructed at the same time during which Cahokia was rebuilt. In the 1960s, archaeologists assumed that none of the East St. Louis complex remained, and an interstate highway was built through the heart of the site. Excavations since then have shown that the mound group and many residences seem to have generally followed the path of what is now Interstates 55 and 64, beginning about one mile east of the Mississippi River and running farther east to the point at which Interstate 64 veers to the south. From that spot, more mounds extend for a mile in a generally northern direction. Recent excavations on the north and south sides of the highway have uncovered "nearly 1,500 structures, more than 70 large monumental post features, about 3,600 cache, or storage, pits, and several burial areas, as well as the base of a heretofore unknown rectangular mound," all built between the years 900 and 1200. Archaeologist have also uncovered evidence of a "widespread" fire that ravaged much of the St. Louis complex sometime in the late twelfth century. Whether this devastation was the result of an accident, conflict, or ritual is unknown. Because of its proximity to the Mississippi River, East St. Louis, and its sister mound complex across the river in St. Louis, Missouri, were, archaeologists believe, major market centers for the Cahokia complex. Cahokia Creek would have provided a direct link to move goods and people between the river and central Cahokia.[24]

On the Missouri side of the Mississippi River, a third mound complex occupied the site of present-day downtown St. Louis. Though the main group contained only twenty-six mounds and was less than a mile long, the St. Louis group was nonetheless impressive. A three-tiered structure now known as Falling Gardens Mound created a sort of stepped transition from the levee, up the gentle bluff in the vicinity of what is now Biddle Street and North 1st Street. On the bluff top was a plaza. Much smaller than Cahokia's Grand Plaza, the St. Louis plaza was anchored by large mounds at both its north and south ends and surrounded by homes. Each of the large mounds at the ends of the plaza had structures that may have served as temples on top of them. Approximately one-half mile north of the plaza, located near present-day Interstate 70 between North Broadway and North 1st Street, was Big Mound. The site of the mound is currently marked with a plaque mounted to a large granite boulder.

Nearly five miles south of the main mound group is a single earthwork now known as Sugar Loaf Mound. This is the sole remaining mound in the city of St. Louis. In 2007, the Osage Nation purchased the property to preserve the structure. Archaeologists have varying interpretations of the earthwork. Andrea Hunter, the Osage Nation's Tribal Preservation Officer, believes Sugar Loaf Mound, which sits on the edge of a river bluff, may have been a three-tiered structure like Falling Gardens Mound. However, because only a single tier of the structure remains, other archaeologists have hypothesized that it was originally a simpler conical mound. Other Mississippian mounds were once located west of the St. Louis waterfront: approximately sixteen of them were situated in Forest Park; nine near what is now the Grand Basin; and seven on top of Art Hill, just east of the St. Louis Art Museum. Nearly a dozen miles west of Forest Park, more mounds have been discovered along Creve Coeur Creek, near the towns of Chesterfield and Creve Coeur. Archaeologist Mark Leach, who has studied the area in detail, believes that Mississippian people lived in the area and added to these mounds, which were likely originally built in the Woodland period. Farther south along the Missouri side of the Mississippi River, in an outlying region that was still within one- or two-days' traveling distance of Cahokia,

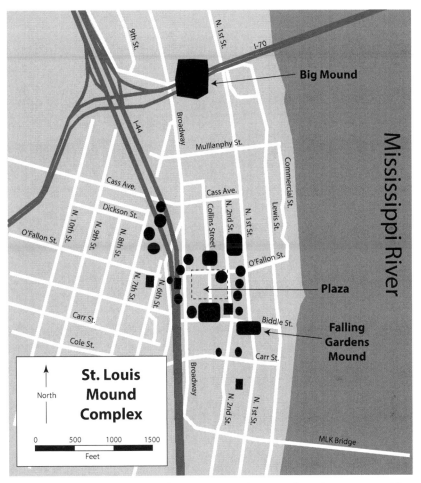

MAP 4: The St. Louis mound complex superimposed on a modern city street map. *Map by the author based on maps by Mark Leach and Titian Ramsay Peale*

another farming district provided much-needed food to fuel the central city and its suburbs.[25]

North America had never before produced a phenomenon like Cahokia. Estimates of between ten thousand and fifteen thousand people living in Cahokia proper and as many as forty thousand people living in what might be called Greater Cahokia (which would include St. Louis, East St. Louis, the Richland Farming Complex and other related areas), made it one of the largest metropolitan areas on the planet at the turn of the twelfth century. At its height, Cahokia exerted authority over nearly everyone who lived within a fifty-miles radius of Monks Mound, and it had an indirect cultural impact on people living as far away as present-day Wisconsin, Ohio, Kansas, and Oklahoma. Figurines sculpted in Cahokia from flint clay dug in eastern Missouri have been found hundreds of miles away at Spiro Mounds in eastern Oklahoma, and carved long-nosed God maskettes made in Cahokia have been discovered along the Little Sioux River valley in northwest Iowa, the Gahagan site in Louisiana, and Florida's Grant Mound.[26]

Archaeologist have struggled to explain how this large and powerful zone of influence was created and maintained. Experts believe that Cahokia was a home-grown phenomenon that emerged from the Woodland people who had lived in the American Bottom for centuries. As we already have seen, most Woodland groups created ceremonial mound burials, planted maize and other field crops, and lived within some level of social hierarchy. As Mississippian culture developed, the people of the American Bottom absorbed influences from the migrants who settled among them, even while continuing to develop their own cultural ideas. The sprawling sphere of influence seems to have been made possible by the convergence of changes in agricultural production, civic authority, and spiritual beliefs and expression. Social anthropologist Melissa R. Baltus has speculated that Cahokia experienced "a deliberate push for change using a social or religious agenda," in which "People reinterpreted traditional practices and reinvented cosmologies, using new materials and negotiating new social relationships."[27]

The role food production played in helping to bring about an increase in population in the American Bottom was critical. Some archaeologists believe that the connection between food crops and the growing population seems to have developed into a cycle of dependency. While more crops allowed for a greater number of people to inhabit the American Bottom, increased population growth also necessitated the planting of an ever-increasing number of acres. Since Cahokian society was based on hierarchy and relied on division of labor, that would only exacerbate the need for farmers to produce more food. To collect the required surplus, civic leaders not only carefully plotted the use of farmland in their districts, but they likely required farmers to turn over a portion of their crop each year as "tribute." This surplus was then used to feed artisans, earth movers, builders, priests, civic elites, and other persons who did not produce their own food.[28]

All the planning, building, and delegating necessary to build this influence must have come from a very strong and centralized authority that, at least for now, we still know little about. Clearly, power radiated outward from Cahokia, where elites directed the region's spiritual activities, public works, and economy, while lesser elites held power over outlying provinces. At this point, we cannot say with any certainty whether those who directed public activities were civic, military, or spiritual leaders. Possibly, they were a combination of all three. It is also not known whether Cahokia's elites inherited their status from ancestors, or if their power was ascribed to them based on military prowess or because of some special spiritual or metaphorical strength.

How Cahokian leaders succeeded in harnessing such an extraordinary amount of centralized power over tens of thousands of people also remains a mystery. VanDerwarker believes the answer to this enigma lies in food production. She has written that a "constellation" of environmental factors, economic decisions, and religious beliefs "allowed medieval Cahokian leaders to harness the potential of maize and other grains toward enlarging and enriching their dominion." She goes on to hypothesize that by controlling grain surplus through the act of exacting tribute from provincial farmers, leaders were able to fund massive public works projects and spectacular rituals that were expressions of the magnitude of their power.[29]

Religious leaders—who could be women or men—were able to access power by using the Earth Mother deity to exploit the people's reliance on grain. Thomas Emerson has written that Cahokians established what he calls a cult of Earth Mother. As keepers of esoteric knowledge and rituals related to Earth Mother, this small elite group projected a special metaphysical relationship with the deity upon which the public relied so heavily. Cahokians needed the priests and priestesses to appeal to Earth Mother and keep her placated so that she might favor them with bountiful harvests. One of the ways Cahokian leaders achieved this was by making the cosmology related to Earth Mother and other natural forces manifest in the physical layout of the ceremonial complex. Archaeologists William F. Romain and Timothy R. Pauketat have proposed that all of Cahokia was platted with the movement of the moon and Mississippian cosmology in mind. "If Cahokia's designers sought to incorporate symbolism invoking plentiful harvests and prolific fertility," writes Romain, "then what better way to do so than to consecrate the entire city to the Earth Mother-Moon Goddess by connecting the city's primary axis and major mounds to her night-time sky manifestations."[30] Romain has also demonstrated that two of Cahokia's nearby satellite complexes, the Sponemann and BBB Motor sites, physically relate to Monks Mound in a way that align with specific lunar positions. At both sites, archaeologists have discovered carved figurines of Earth Mother. Made from red flint clay, which was mined west of present-day St. Louis, these figurines reinforce Cahokia's connection between this force and the moon and kept her image ingrained in the memories of those who saw them.[31]

Another of the ways Cahokian spiritual leaders addressed the force was through elaborate theatrical ceremonies. Cahokia is well-known as a place where human sacrifices occurred. Many of those who were sacrificed were once thought to have been servants and assistants who were made to travel to the Beneath World with important religious and civic leaders who had died. However, based partly on the fact that many of the dead were buried in possible alignment with the moon, Romain suggests that the two hundred sixty persons found interred under a ridge-topped earthwork known as Mound 72 had been sacrificed as tribute to Earth Mother. Sacrifices were one way in which Cahokians upheld their part in the reciprocal relationship they had with this essential force of the natural world. By offering Earth Mother the human life forces of those who were sacrificed, Cahokians hoped that she would bestow on them the gift of life necessary to maintain the relationships between fertility and plentiful harvests. Pauketat has suggested that the sacrifices at Mound 72 and other ridge-topped mounds may have been part of staged theatrical ceremonies intended to be seen by many people. Key to these ceremonies were the themes of death and reincarnation, which also fell under the purview of Earth Mother. Pauketat writes that these ceremonies were "designed as a means of making a statement [to the public] regarding the consolidation of ancestral and celestial power at Cahokia."[32]

Gayle Fritz is a paleoethnobotanist who has studied ancient humans' interactions with the plants around them. She has argued that much of the power in Cahokia came from "the most highly respected and spiritually powerful" female farmers in the American Bottom and Richland Farming Complex, who "performed the duties and rites necessary to ensure reproduction of crops, families, and the larger social order." She favors a hypothesis in which women of child-bearing age belonged to sodalities or societies whose patron was an Earth Mother deity. She sees Cahokia not as a society in which there was "elite control and collusion between priests and chiefs intent on securing domination over rural populations," but rather as one in which rural women performed important rituals invoking this Earth Mother force. "It's likely that women's critical knowledge of domesticated crops and wild food plants would have earned them positions of power and respect at every level of the society."[33]

Archaeologists know from excavations at Cahokia and its affiliated communities that an Earth Mother figure played a central role in the spiritual life of Mississippian people, though there has been some disagreement as to the exact identity of this figure. While some have identified her as Corn Mother, or Corn Maiden, the bringer of maize, Fritz suggests that she is Old-Woman-Who-Never-Dies, the guardian of all the vegetation that people use or eat in their daily lives. To support her argument, Fritz points out that a careful inspection of some well-known red flint clay carvings of Earth Mother show that they do not depict women with corn plants, as has been previously suggested. She argues that two of these figures are growing gourds and holding sunflower seed heads. While the difference between the deities of Corn Mother and Old-Woman-Who-Never-Dies may seem subtle, it points to a critique put forward by some archaeologists who claim the importance of maize in creating and sustaining Cahokia has been exaggerated. They contend that this emphasis on maize has given us a biased and inaccurate view of Mississippian culture that privileges male elites, chiefs, and priests over female farmers and seed keepers.[34]

To grasp the prominence of the Earth Mother in Mississippian culture, it is important to better understand the people's cosmology, which was divided into the Above World, the Middle World, and the Beneath World. Connecting these three worlds was a central vertical axis that served as a portal between them. This axis was often manifest by the vertical poles erected in the center of Mississippian village plazas or on the tops of ceremonial mounds or by a sacred tree. Another important aspect of this cosmology, "as fundamental as gravity is to our world vision," writes F. Kent Reilly III, an expert on Mississippian art and culture, is the idea of dualistic oppositions. The Mississippian world was full of tension between the forces of good and evil, natural and supernatural, feminine and masculine.[35]

The Above World was the home of mostly benevolent deities. The daytime sky was where the Sun, or creation force, lived with the

Thunderbirds and other birds—often falcons—who represented the wind and lightning. The night sky was the home of the Path of Souls, or Milky Way. This was the road the dead traveled on their journey to the underworld. The night sky was also the home of another of the most important deities in Mississippian life, Red Horn, or He-Who-Wears-Human-Heads-As-Earrings, who lived in the Orion constellation. The Middle World, where humans and four-legged creatures live, was often perceived to be the back of a turtle that was floating at sea. For this reason, our continent is sometimes referred to, even today, as Turtle Island. The Beneath World was the domain of the Underwater Panther, who was part panther and part snake. It is sometimes also known as a Piasa, a name given to the creature by Father Jacques Marquette, who along with Louis Joliet observed a large painted carving of the creature on a bluff near present-day Alton, Illinois, in 1673. This deity had the ability to stir up the lakes and rivers with its tail, causing whirlpools and dangerous waves capable of swallowing humans. The Beneath World was also the realm of Earth Mother, and could be reached via the Path of Souls, or through caves, lakes, and rivers.[36]

If the Mississippian world was based on the relationships that existed between dualistic oppositions, the counterpart of Earth Mother may well have been the figure of Red Horn, or He-Who-Wears-Human-Heads-As-Earrings. We know about Red Horn because his exploits were preserved in the oral traditions of the Ioways and the Winnebagos, or Ho-Chunks, and recorded at the beginning of the twentieth century. According to archaeologist David H. Dye, "He-Who-Wears-Human-Heads-As-Earrings' highly crafted iconography was foundational to Mississippian conceptions of the afterlife and the rebirth, reincarnation, and requickening of human life."[37] His regalia is marked by long red braided hair, a feathered cape, earrings in the shape of human heads, and bilobed arrows, which are symbols that appear to be a hybrid of a pipe, a bow and arrow, and an atlatl. On his forehead He-Who-Wears-Human-Heads-As-Earrings wears an ogee palette, which is a symbolic portal through the constellation Orion to the Path of Souls.[38]

He-Who-Wears-Human-Heads-As-Earrings was a Mississippian cultural hero who was associated with war and is alternately known by some as Morning Star. The competitions in which he participated in the sagas were not games but rather contests between life and death. In the words of Dye, the hero fights, "in order that humans might overcome death through rebirth and achieve immortality through reincarnation."

"He-Who-Wears-Human-Heads-As-Earrings provides a mechanism for Mississippian warriors to extend their lives through reincarnation."[39] Dye has proposed that, like the saga of Earth Mother, the myth of He-Who-Wears-Human-Heads-As-Earrings was exploited by Cahokian leaders to help them acquire and maintain power over the public.

Like Earth Mother, or Old-Woman-Who-Never-Dies, He-Who-Wears-Human-Heads-As-Earrings was depicted in flint clay figurines. However, while Earth Mother figurines were nearly always found near Cahokia, male warrior figures and likenesses of He-Who-Wears-Human-Heads-As-Earrings tended only to be found in Mississippian communities outside of the American Bottom, such as the Spiro Mounds site in eastern Oklahoma and the Shiloh site in southwest Tennessee. In addition to figurines, likenesses of He-Who-Wears-Human-Heads-As-Earrings have been discovered in cave pictographs, most prominently in Picture Cave in Warren County, Missouri, and Gottschall rock shelter site in Wisconsin. Picture Cave features about four hundred painted images dating between 1,100 and about 950 years ago. An image of Morning Star, or He-Who-Wears-Human-Heads-As-Earrings, in the cave depicts him as a warrior in battle. He has vertical black lines painted on his face and torso and he wears an arrow headdress. He is identified by the small human head he wears in his ear. In his left hand, he holds a bow and in his right hand, a severed head.[40]

Other likenesses linked to He-Who-Wears-Human-Heads-As-Earrings that were widely distributed are the so called Long-nosed maskettes. These were made of copper or carved from marine shells. Meant to represent the human heads worn in the deity's ears, these maskettes bear a striking resemblance to the one depicted in the Picture Cave painting and tend to conform to a very specific design. The faces are usually shield-shaped with a small slit mouth and what have been described as "google eyes," which are simple small dots for pupils surrounded by simple circles. From the center of the shield-shaped face projects the long nose for which the maskettes are named. Often these noses are curved or bent. This is thought to signify reincarnation through adoption. People of many Indigenous cultures adopted war captives or friendly allies to take the place of dead relatives. As part of the kinship ceremony, the adoptee's nose was often cut or notched.[41]

Long-nosed God maskettes have been found near Cahokia, in St. Louis's Big Mound, as well as in Iowa, Wisconsin, Florida, and Louisiana. The late Robert L. Hall, an anthropologist who specialized in

IMAGE 4: This drawing of Red Horn, also known as He-Who-Wears-Human-Heads-As-Earrings or Morning Star, is based on a one-thousand-year-old painting found in Picture Cave in Warren County, Missouri. This image depicts him as a warrior in battle. He has vertical black lines painted on his face and torso and he wears an arrow headdress. He is identified by the small human head he wears in his ear. In his left hand, the figure holds a bow and in his right hand, a severed head. *Drawing by the author*

Mississippian spirituality, speculated that, much like the peace medals European colonial powers gave to Indigenous leaders during the eighteenth and nineteenth centuries, the wide distribution of figurines and Long-nosed Gods was an act of diplomacy. "The maskettes could have functioned within a ritual," Hall wrote, "to create fictions of kinship between the powerful leader of a large polity and his political clients in outlying areas."[42] The maskettes, which were limited in number, not only signified a bond between the one who possessed it and Cahokian leaders, but they also elevated that person's level of prestige within his own community.

Alternately, the Long-nosed God maskettes may have elevated one's authority through something resembling cosplay. Citing the fact that archaeological excavations usually uncover Long-nosed Gods near human skulls, James R. Duncan and Carol Diaz-Granados, who specialize in Indigenous rock art, have suggested that Mississippians wore the ornaments, both in life and in death, to embody their cultural hero. It is possible that those who wore maskettes did so as a means of metaphysically harnessing the power of the force by emulating it.[43] Archaeologist Michael Fuller believes this is the case as well with the likeness of Morning Star, or He-Who-Wears-Human-Heads-As-Earrings, found in Picture Cave. Fuller suggests that the "figure represents an actual person—a warrior who has taken the head of an elite individual."[44] Citing Osage oral tradition, Fuller believes the warrior is in the act of presenting the severed head to a sacred bird to claim his war honors. If this interpretation is correct, we might assume that the unnamed warrior wore Long-nosed god maskettes in his ears to summon the power of the cultural hero to assist him in his campaign. Perhaps the maskettes were awarded to the warrior based on acts of bravery or military prowess and symbolized his own elite status.

Ultimately, the nature of the power Cahokian elites held over the public seems to have been based on a covenant. The public relied on leaders to leverage their special relationships with the deities to keep the dualistic oppositions that always characterized the world in balance. If the leaders fulfilled that responsibility, the public would support them by performing specialized tasks, paying tribute, or doing whatever might be necessary to help maintain order. If the crops were plentiful, the people were fertile, and both human and metaphysical enemies remained at bay, the covenant held fast, and Cahokia prospered. However, an empire built on the massive production of food is also an empire highly vulnerable to drought, crop disease, and other conditions that can lead to crop failure.

In the American Bottom, that covenant seems to have begun to show signs of strain about nine centuries ago. There are a variety of theories, which include both climatic and social causes, regarding the reason for this breakdown. The most popular theories about the factors contributing to Cahokia's decline are those which posit the likelihood that the city had lost the ability to support itself. Cahokia was a complex sphere of influence that seems to have been founded on the principle of extravagant excess. Its massive public spaces and ceremonial earthworks were matched in scale by the huge ceremonies and feasts Cahokians hosted. The large number of sacrificed humans who were buried in ridge-topped mounds attest to the excessive nature of the priests' theatrical ceremonies. Feasts were no less extravagant. Archaeologists have uncovered a 195-foot-long borrow pit that had been dug for fill when the Grand Plaza was constructed and was later repurposed as a garbage pit. Based on an analysis of the pit's contents, investigators believe some of the feasts that took place in the plaza could have served thousands of guests. Pauketat has written that a single feast, served over a period of just a few days, could have required as many as 3,900 deer, 7,900 ceramic vessels, and "enough smoking tobacco to produce more than a million charred tobacco seeds." The amount of labor expended in gathering, storing, and preparing that surplus food and in preparing the vessels and other materials for such feasts was surely a heavy tax on human and environmental resources.[45]

Cahokia's extravagant use of natural resources seems to have coincided with a change in the climate. A global event called the "Medieval Warm Period" had taken place during the height of Cahokia's inhabitation, from about the years 950 to 1225. After about 1225, however, global temperatures began to cool, and North America entered what has been called the "little Ice Age," which lasted until about 1850. Two recent studies present theories that after the year 1100, climate change led Cahokia to suffer either a lingering drought or persistent flooding. Using data collected from tree rings, Pauketat and his colleagues Larry V. Benson and Edward R. Cook have proposed the theory that the years of abundant rain and warm air that had characterized the rise of Cahokia ended around the year 1100. Beginning at that time, the American Bottom entered a period of intense and persistent drought that would last for about 150 years. As fields dried up, the farmers of the Richland Farming Complex moved away, leaving the region nearly abandoned within a century. Not only did the drought periods cause crop failure, but also they reduced the amount of wildlife and freshwater marine life available for food.[46]

Conversely, a team led by archaeologist Samuel Munoz has proposed that Cahokia experienced its rapid rise during a period of aridity that kept the American Bottom largely flood free during the Medieval Warming Period. Using sediment cores from the floodplain, the team plotted the occurrence of flood events near Cahokia and claim that around the year 1200 the city experienced its first significant flood event in more than five hundred years. They write that the event "was of a magnitude sufficient to inundate croplands, food caches, and settlements across the floodplain, and would have forced residents to temporarily relocate." After the year 1200, flooding seems to have become a more common event in the American Bottom. This naturally caused a significant disruption in farming. Aside from immediate crop loss, clearing fields and restoring food production likely would have taken the community more than one entire growing season.[47]

This conclusion seems to have been confirmed by the work of archaeologists Neal Lopinot and William Woods, who theorized that deforestation in the Cahokia region a thousand years ago led to soil erosion that would have caused "frequent, severe, and unpredictable local floods."[48] However, recent research at Cahokia conducted by a team led by geoarchaeologist Caitlin Rankin concludes that there is no evidence of increased flooding in Cahokia near the end of its occupation. "We do see some negative consequences of land clearance early on [in the city's history]," Rankin told *The New York Times*, "but people deal with it somehow and keep investing their time and energy into the space." In fact, evidence uncovered by Rankin shows that Cahokian farmers learned to carefully manage their environment. It was only after European Americans clear-cut nearby bluffs for coalmines in the nineteenth century that significant flooding events occurred.[49]

While no one can say with any certainty what led to the abandonment of Cahokia, environmental and political forces were both likely involved. Whatever the cause, the city center population dropped from fifteen thousand at its height to between fifty-two hundred and seventy-two hundred during the twelfth century. One century after that, only about three thousand to four thousand five hundred people remained in the community. VanDerwarker believes some of that population moved from Cahokia into outlying agricultural regions where competition for food was less intense. Similarly, archaeologist Alvey notes an apparent population shift from lowland areas, like Cahokia, to upland regions around the year 1200. Evidence also suggests that some Cahokians moved across the Mississippi River into the Cairo Lowlands of southeast Missouri's Bootheel. The strain of a changing climate, population movements, and alterations in status and the division of labor is likely to have led to social unrest. As Munoz writes, "Cahokia's leaders appear to have been unable to maintain the impression of security and stability following the economic upheaval created by the return of large floods" or persistent drought.[50]

The fact that population centers like East St. Louis and Cahokia became fortified during the second half of the twelfth century leads us to believe that social unrest turned violent, though it is difficult to know just who threatened these communities. Some archaeologists have speculated that violence occurred when much of the East St. Louis complex was destroyed by fire. Evidence of other walled compounds that also burned down in the eleventh and twelfth centuries can be found in southern Wisconsin and in the Illinois River valley.[51]

At Cahokia, a twenty-foot-high stockade, nearly two miles in length, was built to encircle Monks Mound and the Grand Plaza. Between 1200 and 1275, manpower was largely diverted away from building or enlarging ceremonial mounds and directed toward the upkeep of the wall. With fewer farmers producing food in the outlying areas, the complex's population continued to dwindle rapidly. After 1275, Cahokians began to build homes inside the fortified area on what were once ceremonial and public spaces. The city was no longer the center of cultural and religious influence it once had been. By 1350 the city of Cahokia was abandoned. The life span of this once powerful community encompassed just three hundred years.[52]

Journalist Annalee Newitz cautions us against using the term *collapse* when discussing Cahokia's abandonment. Instead, she urges us to see it as a mark of deliberate social change. Archaeologists have revealed that Cahokia is an urban palimpsest that shows signs of having been rearranged and rebuilt numerous times as the needs of the people who lived there changed. Cities, she writes, are "ecosystems whose components are always transforming, and whose boundaries expand and contract naturally." Evidence suggests that environmental factors did alter the way the people of the American Bottom interacted with the land and with their spirituality. At some point, as Cahokia became more fragmented, the various immigrant groups who had come together to build the complex began to return to their old traditions. "Woodland people followed the call of a great revival," writes Newitz, "and settled in Cahokia to build an urban farming society before eventually moving on again." Abandonment "doesn't mean that something terrible happened [in Cahokia]," commented Caitlin Rankin. "It could be that people found other opportunities elsewhere, or decided that some other way of life was better."[53]

The city and its surrounding complex left a lasting legacy in the region. According to Pauketat and Susan Alt, Cahokians would "alter the geopolitical landscape of North America, spread and intensify the cultivation of maize and 'Mississippianize' people" throughout most of the central continent. Yet, even in places where Mississippian influences were strong, like the Steed-Kisker complex near present-day Kansas City, archaeologist Dale Henning has observed that "this influence was altered immediately by [a] receptive indigenous population."[54] In other words, those who received Mississippian ideas through trade and exchange seemed to filter them through their own traditions and those of others with whom they had contact. Cahokian influence never really seems to have taken hold in faraway places, even though its power over other Mississippian communities in the south and east was strong. In the end, for all its size, Cahokia's direct power over populaces never spread much beyond the boundaries of the American Bottom.

Today, we are hard pressed to explain who the people of Cahokia were and what happened to them. At its height around the year 1100, the ceremonial center and its outlying areas were made up of a mixture of immigrants from all over the region, as well as people whose roots in the American Bottom dated back for centuries. It is likely that as Cahokia's population declined, people spread out in a good many directions. Some may have returned to places where their ancestors had lived before coming to the complex. Among those groups who may have made up the population of Cahokia at one time or another are Algonquin, Muskhogean, Caddoan, and Siouan-speaking people. Hall wrote that the Algonquins, which include the Illinois, Kaskaskias, and Peorias, all of whom would live in the American Bottom later, arrived at the Mississippi River from points east too late to be a part of Cahokian culture. While Muskhogean-speaking people like the Chickasaws, Choctaws, and Creeks descended from Mississippians, they lived far to the south and east of Cahokia. Caddoan-speaking people surely had contact with Cahokians and served as a conduit of influences between Mesoamerica and the American Bottom. However, Hall believes that they were not residents of the Cahokia complex.[55]

Most often linked to Cahokia by archaeologists are the Chiwere Siouan and Dhegihan Siouan-speaking people. The Chiwere group's descendants are the Missourias, Ioways, Otoes, and Ho-Chunks. Some historians maintain that the Chiwere Siouan people originally inhabited the Ohio and Tennessee river bottoms with their Dhegihan Siouan-speaking kinsmen throughout the Woodland period and migrated westward to the Mississippi River Valley with them.[56] However, the Chiwere place their origins near Green Bay, Wisconsin, a place they call Red Earth or *Máyan Shúje*. From about the twelfth century up to the time of European contact, the Chiwere were core members of a culture archaeologists call the Oneotas. According to oral tradition, a portion of the group moved south along the Mississippi River, leaving their Ho-Chunk relatives in Green Bay. When the Chiwere reached the mouth of the Rock River in northern Illinois, another group, which would become *Báxoje*, or Ioways, elected to settle there. By 1300, the remaining Chiwere people had made their way to the Missouri River and were living near the mouth of the Grand River. From there they split one final time. The people who would become Otoes moved up the Missouri River into a region that included present-day Missouri and Nebraska. Those who remained called themselves *Nyut^achi*, or the People of the River's Mouth. We know them today as the Missourias. As we will see, the Oneotas were contemporaries of the Cahokians. They lived near them, had contact with them, and adopted some of their influences. However, they are not generally thought to have been a part of the Cahokian complex.[57]

The Dhegihan Siouan-speakers are ancestors of today's Quapaws, Kanzas, Poncas, Omahas, and Osages. According to Hunter, the Dhegihans left their homes on the upper Ohio River and began traveling toward the Mississippi River Valley with their Chiwere Siouan-speaking relatives during the Middle Woodland period, reaching the Mississippi River sometime in the Late Woodland period, around the years 400 to 500. Other archaeologists have placed their arrival sometime between the sixth and tenth centuries, or even later. Once the group reached the Missouri River, the Quapaws decided to travel south toward the mouth of the Arkansas River, while the rest of the Dhegihan group moved to the north, toward the Missouri River. By the time Cahokia was developing, the Dhegihans had splintered again, with the Omahas and the Poncas moving up the Missouri River, to be followed later by the Kanzas. These divisions are generally thought to have also been a part of the Oneota group. Meanwhile, most archaeologists agree that the Osages were in the vicinity of Cahokia while it was at its peak. However, there remains some debate regarding their place in that culture.[58]

University of Missouri archaeologist Carl Chapman struggled for much of his career to determine where the Osages fit into the cultural milieu of Missouri during Mississippian period. At first, he placed them among the Oneotas in the Van Meter State Park area. He later thought they may have been among the people who lived near the Caddos in the Oklahoma, Kansas, Arkansas, Missouri border area. Still later, he suggested they may have been Mississippians who lived in southeast Missouri's Cairo Lowlands. In their review of Chapman's assessment, O'Brien and Wood state the Osages were probably related to Oneota culture but not likely to have spent much time in southwest Missouri until after European contact. They write that the Osages did share cultural similarities with "Mississippi River Valley Dhegihans" and Algonquins, likely because they lived in that region until around 1300.[59]

Citing Chapman, among others, and oral traditions, Osage historian Louis F. Burns indicates his ancestors retained many of their Woodland traditions into the Mississippian period. Burns points out the similarities between Woodland design and Osage symbols. He also recalls the Osage tradition of morning devotions at sunrise, which he said has Mayan influence and dates from the Mississippian phase. Finally, he claims that as the Osages always loved the freedom of the hunting lifestyle, they likely would not have become sedentary farmers. While they would have adopted some advantages of Woodland agriculture, "they apparently always, right up to historic times, lived on the fringes of Woodland culture." Burns reminded his readers that the Osages were originally six bands who came together to form a single nation. He believed that the three bands of the Those Who Were Last to Come people, who would later be known to Europeans as the Little Osages, were most certainly Mississippian people. However, he did not place them at Cahokia, but rather farther south, at the Arkansas River, or perhaps in the Missouri Bootheel.[60]

Recently, historians and archaeologists have been exploring the possibility that the Osages were not only Mississippians, but that they were also an integral part of the Cahokia complex. Hunter has not only placed the Osages in the Cahokia vicinity during the complex's highpoint, but she has also tied them to the construction of mounds such as Sugarloaf Mound in St. Louis along the Mississippi River.[61]

The anthropologist and archaeologist Alice Beck Kehoe has turned to the fieldwork conducted by Francis La Flesche, an Omaha anthropologist who worked at the turn of the twentieth century, to directly place Osages in the heart of Cahokia. La Flesche was particularly interested in Osage traditions of spirituality, and he recorded songs and rituals. According to anthropologist Garrick Bailey, La Flesche's work differs from that of many other anthropologists because he "was not interested merely in describing Osage ritual; his primary objective was to explain Osage ideals, beliefs, and concepts."[62] Working on the hypothesis that the traditions of the Osage priests recorded by La Flesche go back seven hundred years or more, Kehoe compares them to archaeological data from Cahokia's figurines, mounds, and woodhenges to draw a number of connections. On her analysis, Kehoe concludes that the "congruence of so many [archaeological] features with the holy [Osage] texts enhances credibility," that Cahokians were Osages, or at least Dhegihan.[63]

None of these theories have been proven, however, and as Pauketat has observed, "It appears likely that many, probably most ancient midwestern, southern, and Plains Indians were in one way or another entangled in a history that began at Cahokia."[64]

Meanwhile, in southeast Missouri, Mississippian culture, which had developed there around the same time as it had at Cahokia, continued even after the abandonment of the larger community. Sometime after the year 900, several large, fortified villages appeared between Crowley's Ridge and the Mississippi River in the Cairo Lowlands. Each of these larger population centers was the heart of a Mississippian "chiefdom," which likely would have had smaller satellite villages, burial mounds, and farmsteads all managed by hierarchical leaders, like those found in Cahokia. While these towns likely had contact with Cahokians, they do not seem to have lived under their direct control. Instead, they developed their own, independent, form of Mississippian culture. One of the largest civic and ceremonial sites in the Cairo Lowlands is now known as Towosahgy, an Osage word meaning "old village." At the urging of Chapman, the site was purchased by the State of Missouri in 1967 and is now part of Towosahgy State Historic Site. This and other villages seemed to have reached their peak in the first half of the fourteenth century, as Cahokia was being abandoned, so it is possible that some people from the American Bottom moved to the Cairo Lowlands.[65]

While these large communities flourished, several smaller, less well-organized settlements, which also had burial mounds but lacked fortifications, developed south and west of the Cairo Lowlands, in the Bootheel between the Mississippi River and the St. Francis River. Many of these were located near the Missouri-Arkansas border in the Pemiscot Bayou in Pemiscot County, Missouri. These villages stood among the meander belts of the Mississippi River backwater. As the course of the river stabilized, it left behind a "levee and point bar" landscape that consisted of heavy forested natural levees surrounded by wetlands of cypress and cottonwood trees. O'Brien has observed that during the late Mississippi Period, this was an extremely productive environment that attracted people who had the technology to adapt to it.[66]

Late Mississippian Period

Though the settlements of Pemiscot Bayou were less well organized than those in the Cairo Lowlands, they managed to persevere, and even to thrive, as the Cairo Lowlands was largely abandoned at the beginning of the Late Mississippian Period, sometime around the year 1400. Archaeologists are at a loss to explain why the Central Mississippi River Valley became what archaeologist Stephen Williams has labeled a "Vacant Quarter" in the late fourteenth and early fifteenth century. According to Williams, the region of abandonment is centered around the convergence of the Ohio and Mississippi Rivers, which included eastern Missouri as far south as New Madrid. Some hypothesize that the chiefdoms became more centralized, and population of the large communities grew as people moved in from outlying areas. This put strain on food production, which led to many of the large population centers being abandoned, though some outlying areas may have continued to be sparsely populated. There is also evidence that suggests there were catastrophic earthquakes along the New Madrid Seismic Zone around the year 1450, tremors of the same magnitude as those that took place in 1811 and 1812. It appears that after the seismic events in the fifteenth century, much of the population that left the Cairo Lowlands moved south into northeast Arkansas, western Tennessee, and south of New Madrid into the Pemiscot Bayou.[67]

The bayou settlements are known for their exquisite pottery, often made in the shape of human heads, squat human figures, or cat monster effigy bowls. Such pottery is frequently found in mounds with burials and has led amateur collectors to scavenge burial mounds since the mid-nineteenth century. Because of the nature of this unscientific digging, it has been difficult to determine much else about the people or

IMAGE 5: Human Head Effigy Jar, from the Late Mississippian Culture, 1350–1550. This pot came from the Chickasawba Site, located just south of the Missouri Bootheel in Mississippi County, Arkansas. Similar effigy jars have been found in the Pemiscot Bayou region of Missouri. *From the collection of the Nelson-Atkins Museum of Art. Photograph by Daderot, reproduced under the Creative Commons CC0 1.0 Universal Public Domain Dedication*

their lifeways. Archaeological investigations of the burials reveal that the people of the bayou region were generally healthy, though they were likely over-reliant on a diet of maize. Life expectancy for newborns was nearly thirty years, though adults showed signs of skeletal stress that likely came from their sedentary agricultural lifestyle. Excavation of Pemiscot Bayou sites also generally produce Spanish artifacts, showing that the settlements survived well into the mid-sixteenth century and the time of Hernando de Soto's visit to northern Arkansas.[68]

In many ways, the Mississippians' neighbors and contemporaries, the Oneota people, had succeeded in developing and maintaining a more sustainable cultural model, one that survived up to the time of European contact. Mississippi River Valley archaeologists James Theler and Robert Boszhardt have written that "the Oneota Culture was born of the marriage between Late Woodland people and Middle Mississippian ideas."[69] While archaeologist David Benn has described Oneota as a "unique transformation of culture," Lynn Alex has written that it is unlikely to have been made up of a single cultural group. Aside from the Chiwere and Dhegihan Siouan-speaking people mentioned earlier, Dakota Sioux, and even some Algonquin people may have shared what Hall called "Oneota Interaction." Hall uses the term to identify the group as a "network of relationships that resulted in the spread of a pattern of economic adaptions and styles of artifacts throughout the Upper Mississippi Valley during the late Mississippi period."[70]

The origin of the Oneota Culture remains an enigma. Because of the cultural traits those people share with the Mississippians, some scholars have speculated that perhaps Oneota people were immigrants who left Cahokia. Others have theorized they were Woodland people who adopted Mississippian traits, or perhaps were a group who migrated to the area from another region. The earliest manifestation of the tradition occurred in eleventh-century Wisconsin, prior to Cahokia's peak. By 1150, evidence of Oneota Culture with Mississippian influences reached the Mississippi River near present-day St. Paul, Minnesota. One theory, put forward by Theler and Boszhardt, is that the Oneota tradition was an adaptation that Woodland people turned to when confronted with population increase in the Mississippi River Valley around the year 950. As interior river valleys became more crowded, mobility became increasingly limited. For the first time, some river valley village sites were occupied year-round. This, in turn, altered the annual subsistence cycles, as competition for game increased and whitetail deer populations thinned out and grew scarce. Out of necessity, people restricted in their movement turned to a more intense farming of maize and harvesting of freshwater mussels. Because they learned to diversify their sources of foods, Oneotas were better able to withstand the persistent droughts of the late twelfth and early thirteenth centuries than the Mississippians seem to have been.[71]

The Oneotas were successful in adapting to life in mixed grasslands, forests, and wetlands. By the year 1200, they occupied southern
Wisconsin and northern Illinois and began to make their way up the
Missouri River. By 1300, Oneota people had reached their maximum
expansion into parts of eleven present-day states, including most of
southern Minnesota, Wisconsin, Iowa, northern Illinois, and northern
Missouri. One century later, they retreated from some of their recently
occupied land, consolidated their culture into larger communities, such
as Utz and Leary, and enjoyed a century of relative stasis, which archaeologist R. Eric Hollinger has referred to as "Pax Oneota."[72]

Archaeologist Thomas Edward Berres, who has written extensively
about Oneota culture, has observed that Oneotas and Mississippians
had regular contact with each other and were "continually transformed
and re-created" through this interaction.[73] Indeed, the two cultures
shared some material culture, most notably shell-tempered pottery,
Long-nosed god maskettes, and the cultivation of maize. They also had
similar spiritual beliefs and shared the same basic cosmology. Though
Oneotas and Mississippians both produced shell tempered pottery, they
are stylistically distinct from one another. In fact, Oneota culture is often referred to as a pottery culture. Their squat, round, olla-shaped vessels with constricted necks and flared rims are a unique marker used by
archaeologists to identify their presence at excavation sites. Oneota sites
are also marked by the presence of red catlinite disc pipes, inscribed
catlinite tablets, hoes made of bison or elk scapulas, freshwater clam
shells, and both ground and chipped stone tools.[74]

The culturally diverse groups who participated in the Oneota
Interaction were bonded together by ritual and ceremony. Often these
ceremonies took the form of adoptions, called *Hunga* by the Chiwere
and Dhegihans, which were meant to bring new members into a family,
perhaps to replace ones who had died. Other times, ritual adoptions
were more broadly performed as a diplomatic tool that served to unite
individuals, families, or clans, in a kinship of trade or military alliances.
Such adoptions carried mutual responsibilities and helped individual
groups mitigate the many risks they faced in their daily lives. At the
heart of adoption ceremonies was the sacred pipe, which the Europeans
called the calumet and the Chiwere called the *ráhnunwe*. The ceremonial use of pipes, which are traditionally made from soft red catlinite stone
found in southwestern Minnesota, originated on the plains and arrived
in Missouri in the thirteenth century.[75]

The sacred pipe and the ceremonies that went along with it helped form the basis of a political and social structure that was far more egalitarian than that found in Cahokia. Oneota seems to have been an aggregate group of cultures brought together by mutual need and consensus. Rather than submitting to the control of a centralized power structure like the one we believe ruled Cahokia, Oneota people had many kinds of leaders who manifested their power through "general will." Power was not ascribed to Oneota leaders; it was gained through various personal qualities. Paramount among these qualities was generosity. Leaders gave away what wealth they possessed in a way that would do the most common good. They sponsored ceremonies, hosted feasts, and organized civil activities and projects. Leaders participated in important discussions, but decisions were reached by group consensus.[76]

Despite this apparent collegiality between groups, the Oneota were heavily involved in warfare. Evidence indicates that as early as the eleventh century, they were in violent conflict with non-Oneota groups. Hollinger suggests that Oneota groups may even have become a threat to Cahokia in the late twelfth century. In areas into which Oneotas expanded, archaeologists have discovered signs of violence as well as evidence that Oneota people occupied the villages of some of those whom they had vanquished. One cause of violence may have been related to the very kind of reciprocity agreements that Oneota people practiced. Without a strong centralized power, most groups were nearly equal in strength, so raids, most probably over resources or unfulfilled obligations, were more common.[77]

Berres has written that, while the division of labor and knowledge among Oneota people was segregated by sex, gender roles could be described as "separate but equal." Men were involved in chores such as hunting, fishing, butchering, and warfare. They also cleared land for agriculture, quarried stone, worked with copper and lead, and built lodges and boats. Women were involved in farming, cooking, food preservation, and hide working. They also were responsible for childcare and burying the dead. While men were most often the community leaders, there is evidence to suggest that women could also fill the leadership role among some groups. In other cases, women tended to exercise power through the ownership and management of households. Berres points out that there are also certain "swing roles" that could be held by either men or women. These generally included positions as healers, medicine people, or dream interpreters.[78]

Missouri's best-known Oneota site is Utz, located in what is now Annie and Abel Van Meter State Park in Saline County. Set on the bluffs overlooking the Missouri River, Utz has been occupied at least since the Woodland Period and is best known as the one-time home of the Missouria people. Chapman was part of a team that investigated the site in 1939 and 1940. The team found burials, European trade goods, pottery, cache pits, sandstone arrow shaft abraders, bone tools, and inscribed catlinite tablets. Later excavations discovered footprints of both rectangular and oval-shaped lodges made of wooden posts. It is likely that one of the reasons the Missourias chose the village site was because of its location near the confluence of the Missouri, Chariton, and Grand Rivers. Not only did this help provide the mixed forest, but the wetland prairie landscape the Oneotas preferred also offered them easy access to trade routes. The discovery of other sites in the immediate region, such as Gumbo Point, Guthrey, Plattner, and Utlaut, indicates that there was a significant Oneota occupation in central Missouri.[79]

On a blufftop near Utz sits the only Oneota earthwork in the state. Known as the Old Fort, the earthwork covers more than six acres of what was once prairie. The site gets its name from the fact that it is an enclosure made by twin parallel ditches which resemble ramparts. Inside the fortified area were four burial mounds that were opened by grave robbers in the nineteenth century. Though it is tempting to interpret the earthwork as a fort built for protection, the lack of artifacts found within it seems to indicate that it was a ceremonial site.[80]

Another cluster of known Oneota sites can be found on both sides of the Missouri River between St. Joseph, Missouri, and the Kansas-Nebraska border. These sites indicate that the Oneota people living on the eastern edge of the Great Plains had contact with western cultures and had made different cultural adaptations than those living farther north and east. King Hill, located in St. Joseph's south side, provides a high overlook toward the west and the river bottom and seems to have been both a burial site and a village site. Henning, who led an excavation of the site in 1966, believed the site was related to Dhegihan members of the Oneota who had moved west, probably those who would become Kanzas. The excavation seems to indicate that King Hill was occupied by the Oneota for a long period of time, thus giving archaeologists an opportunity to examine their long-term habits.[81]

On the Missouri River's western bluffs, other Oneota sites are located near the Kansas towns of Doniphan and Fanning. Perhaps the

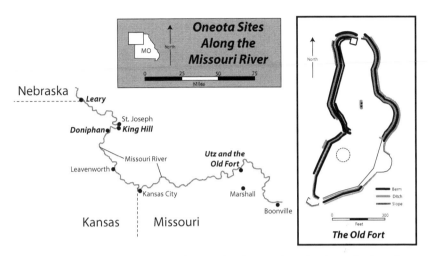

MAP 5: The location of Oneota sites discussed in the text. (Map by the author). A plan of the Old Fort in what is now Annie and Abel Van Meter State Park in Saline County Missouri. *Map by the author. Plan by the author based on a drawing by W. Raymond Wood*

best-known site in the area is Leary, located on the reservation of the Iowa Tribe of Kansas and Nebraska, on the Kansas-Nebraska border. At the time of its Oneota occupation, Leary would have been located on the south bank of the Big Nemaha River, which connected it to the Great Plains, and was less than two miles from the Missouri River. This location provided those who lived there with easy access to Oneota villages upstream in Iowa and Minnesota, and downstream to central Missouri and the Mississippi River Valley. Archaeologists believe that its location on the western edge of the Oneota occupied territory made it an important center for exchange and trade. Leary was ideally situated to transport catlinite from Minnesota to Illinois and Wisconsin. It was also a supply point for communal bison hunts undertaken in northcentral Kansas by Oneota groups from as far north as the Dixon Site on the Little Sioux River in northwest Iowa, as early as the fourteenth century.[82]

Finally, there is evidence of Oneota occupation on the Osage River near the Missouri-Kansas border. Like the sites in northwest Missouri and northeast Kansas, this region was inhabited by Dhegihan people. Citing the fact that the Dhegihan record in western Missouri is less well understood than that of the Chiwere, O'Brien and Wood write that it is difficult to know whether these were Oneota Villages, or those of the Osages and Kanzas.[83]

Because Oneota culture survived into the period after European contact, it is difficult to know when groups ceased to be Oneotas and began assuming the tribal identities we know today. In the early seventeenth century, the arrival of Europeans had begun to uproot populations in the eastern part of the continent. At about the same time as French traders and missionaries began to arrive in the Mississippi River Valley after 1763, Algonquins carrying firearms arrived and pushed the Oneotas west of the Missouri River. By that time, both Chiwere and Dhegihan Siouan-speaking groups had assumed separate tribal identities and were known by distinct names.

Voices

Now this is what the old men have said and handed down to us.

Once something appeared in the middle of the lake (Green Bay). They were the French; they were the first to come to the Winnebago. The ship came nearer, and the Winnebago went to the edge of the lake with offerings of tobacco and white deerskins. There they stood. When the French were about to come ashore they fired their guns off in the air as a salute to the Indians. The Indians said, "They are thunderbirds." They had never heard the report of a gun before that time and that is why they thought they were thunderbirds.

Then the French landed their boats and came ashore and extended their hands to the Winnebago, and the Indians put tobacco in their hands. The French, of course, wanted to shake hands with the Indians. They did not know what tobacco was, and therefore did not know what to do with it. Some of the Winnebago poured tobacco on their heads, asking them for victory in war. The French tried to speak to them, but they could not, of course, make themselves understood. After a while they discovered that they were without tools, so they taught the Indians how to use an ax and chop a tree down. The Indians, however, were afraid of it, because they thought that the ax was holy. Then the French taught the Indians how to use guns, but they held aloof for a long time through fear, thinking that all these things were holy.

Suddenly a Frenchman saw an old man smoking and poured water on him. They knew nothing about smoking or tobacco. After a while they got more accustomed to one another. The Indians learned how to shoot the guns and began trading objects for axes. They would give furs and things of that nature for the guns, knives, and axes of the whites. They still considered them holy, however. Finally they learned how to handle guns quite well and they liked them very much. They would even build fires at night so that they might try their guns, for they could not wait for the day, they were so impatient. When they were out of ammunition they would go to the traders and tell their people that they would soon return. By this time they had learned to make themselves understood by various signs.[1]

—Winnebago, or Ho-Chunk, oral tradition

In the latter part of the seventeenth century, the European came to them.

On this certain day, the history thereof garbled in tribal memory, two pale men came up the river with two of the *Ni-Sho-Dse* [Smokey Water People] warriors. They had hair on the backs of their hands and on their faces, and their hair glistened in the sun as it showed itself from the V of their Algonkian buckskin shirts. Their eyes and their mouths were almost hidden by hair. Their mouths were like the den of an old, male, bank beaver overhung by rootlets.

. . . Not knowing what to call these strangers, they would refer to them as *I'n-Shta-Heh*, Heavy Eyebrows.[2]

—John Joseph Mathews (Osage)

It is probable that both Coronado and de Soto met separate bands of Osages in the early-1540s. The surviving descriptions of Osage legends certainly indicate they did. One of Coronado's descriptions fits the Osages better than any other Indians, and this description was given in sight of the mountains (hills with blue haze) to the east (the Osage Hills or Flint Hills?). De Soto apparently met some Osages and mistook them for the Kansas. Long before Radisson mentioned them in 1659 and Marquette eleven years later, the Osage knew of the Euro-American presence. It would have been entirely in keeping with the Osage character if they had remained unseen while observing the white men.[3]

—Louis Burns (Osage)

Chapter Three

Bison Robes and Metal Utensils

FOR AT LEAST TWELVE MILLENNIA, the Indigenous people who lived on the land that is now Missouri were free to exercise complete autonomy over their lives. Their existence had been guided by cultural values and spiritual beliefs grounded in the land on which they lived and hunted. While Native nations sometimes fought one another over land, hunting rights, or economic opportunities, the rules of warfare were well understood by both sides.

Beginning in the seventeenth century, however, Native people in Missouri found themselves subject to laws and policies based on religious and cultural concepts developed half a world away. These foreign ideas, first carried to the continent by European colonizers, sought to legitimize the desire of Christians to take control of Native land without regard for the sovereignty of Indigenous nations. Native people were engaged in a conflict in which they did not immediately understand the rules by which their opponents fought. As Shawnee/Lenape lawyer Steven T. Newcomb has observed, "Indian people were not the ones who mentally developed the ideas that constitute and structure" the laws by which they found themselves governed.[1]

Europeans had developed these concepts and laws over centuries during which they exploited people and resources for profit, even on their own continent. As Indigenous historian Roxanne Dunbar-Ortiz has pointed out, "entire [European] nations, such as Scotland, Wales, Ireland, Bohemia, the Basque Country and Catalonia, were colonized and forced under the rule of various monarchs." Local resources fell under the control of royalty while the peasantry, who had been forced off their land, were compelled to sell their labor, which the monarchs used to extract these same resources for their own profit. The maintenance of this system of exploitation required monarchies to have well-trained standing armies with effective weaponry. Thus, from the eleventh through the thirteenth centuries, when Europeans exported these tactics to the Middle East during the Crusades, they were already well-practiced in the methods of colonization.[2]

The Doctrine of Discovery

Those who perpetuated the mistreatment of land and people justified doing so by a legal principle known as the Doctrine of Discovery. Generally, the doctrine held that when a European Christian nation "discovered" a non-Christian region, the former automatically gained the Right of Ownership, or sovereign and property rights, over the land and any people who might be living on and using it. While indigenous inhabitants retained what was called the Right of Occupancy, or Aboriginal Title, to the land, the discovering or conquering nation held the exclusive right to purchase the land from them, should they choose to sell. Under the Doctrine of Discovery, conquering European nations also gained the sole right to engage in international, political, and commercial activity with the indigenous nations.[3]

The terms *conquer* and *discover* are used synonymously here because a European nation generally needed only to be the first Christian power to step foot on a non-Christian nation's land to "conquer" it. The result of the doctrine was that, unbeknownst to them, Native people's exclusive rights to the land on which they lived and their sovereign right to determine their own political and commercial activities, were in danger simply because a foreign power had come upon them.[4]

Some scholars have argued the Doctrine of Discovery was originally derived from God's biblical command to Abraham in Genesis 1:28 to "subdue the earth, and exercise domain over all living things."[5] Pope Innocent IV decreed in 1240 that this command applied to Christians who invaded the lands of so-called infidels in the Muslim world. If pagans were violating God's natural laws, he reasoned, Christians were justified in invading their lands and usurping their rights. Not coincidentally, expeditions of mercenary armies into the Middle East and North Africa became extremely lucrative as soldiers returned home with troves of looted goods.[6]

European sovereigns began to see it as their divine duty to dispatch colonizers to new shores in order to fulfill God's will and, not incidentally, fill their own treasuries. Thus, when Spain's King Ferdinand and Queen Isabella agreed to underwrite Christopher Columbus's western voyage, they were as interested in any new lands he might "discover" as they were in the possibility that he would find gold and new opportunities to expand commerce. Upon Columbus's return, the royal couple quickly petitioned Pope Alexander VI to validate their rights to the islands upon which their Italian emissary had landed and claimed in their name.[7]

In response, the Pontiff issued a Papal Bull in May 1493 that clarified the rights of European explorers. In the document, he gave Spain and Portugal the exclusive right to explore and colonize lands "not previously possessed by any Christian owner." He held that, because it was the duty of Christians to convert their earthly flock, the Church had the authority to grant title of infidel lands to European nations that conquered them.[8]

Outside the sphere of the Catholic Church, England, too, was eager to participate in the rush to colonize new land. Even though she had been excommunicated from the Church in 1570, Queen Elizabeth chose to comply with the Pope's rules of conquest because she wanted Europe to recognize England's claims to new land. Thus began a competition between Spain, Portugal, France, and England to lay claim to the so-called New World. As other European powers joined the Age of Discovery, disagreements often arose over land claims. In part, these quarrels were based on varying ideas of what constituted discovery. Were nations, for example, required to settle on land in order to validate their claim to it? Or were simple rituals of discovery, such as flag and cross plantings, enough to authenticate legal possession?[9]

Spanish Exploration

Indigenous people in the middle of North America first came face to face with aspects of this new world order in the mid-sixteenth century. In 1541, two Spanish expeditions very nearly made their way to present-day Missouri. Approaching the heart of the continent from opposite directions, Francisco Vázquez de Coronado, a thirty-year-old provincial governor in New Spain, in present-day Mexico, and Hernando de Soto, the governor of the Spanish colony of Cuba and a veteran of the war to conquer the Incas, explored the region around Missouri in their search for gold and riches.

In February 1540, Coronado left northwestern Mexico at the head of a large *entrada* or expedition of two hundred men on horseback, seventy soldiers on foot, a thousand Indigenous servants and enslaved people,

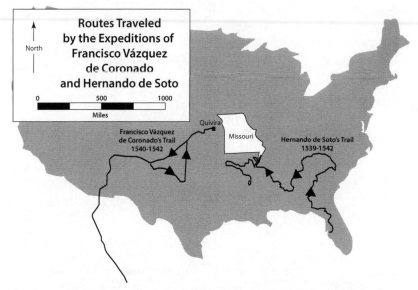

MAP 6: The journeys of explorers Francisco Vázquez de Coronado and Hernando de Soto brought them very close to Missouri in the mid-sixteenth century. Some have speculated that de Soto's forays along the Mississippi and St. Francis Rivers may have taken either him or one of his detachments north of the 36th parallel into what would later become the Missouri Bootheel. After spending the winter of 1541–1542 near Little Rock, Arkansas, de Soto died of illness, leaving the remainder of his force to make its way to the safety of Mexico City. *Map by the author*

and hundreds of head of horses, mules, cattle, and other livestock. The object of the expedition was to find the fabled Seven Cities of gold, called "Cibola." Cibola was a word for bison that the Spanish had heard the Indians use, which they then applied as a placename, probably in reference to the Pueblo tribes whose adobe complexes glinted with the mica schist found in their rock walls. The Spaniards' explorations took them north into present-day Arizona, where they visited several Native towns, but found no gold. While wintering on the Rio Grande River in present-day New Mexico, an Indigenous prisoner, known to us only as "the Turk," regaled Coronado with tales of his wealthy homeland, the kingdom of Quivira, located to the north and east of them. Determined to find the kingdom and its riches, Coronado set out with a small party in June 1541.

In July, the explorers reached a Quivira, or Wichita, village north of the Arkansas River. Though there was no sign of gold, the people of the village were welcoming, leading Coronado to remain in the area for the next three weeks, exploring around present-day Salina, Kansas. Despite their disappointment at the dearth of precious metals, the Spaniards were impressed with the commercial potential of the region's fertile soil. Still one hundred fifty miles west of the Missouri River, Coronado was discouraged from traveling farther east. The Wichitas told him that he would have no luck finding gold because the people who lived in that direction did not have great cities. Instead, the Wichitas replenished the Spaniards' exhausted food supply and provided them with guides to lead them back to the Arkansas River. It is quite likely the Wichitas were eager to see the Spaniards, whom they the judged to be poor, ignorant, and completely lacking any respect for kinship and reciprocity, go back in the direction from which they had come. As historian Kathleen DuVal has written, the Spaniards had "overstayed their welcome, and gave nothing in return." It may have been these same bad-mannered characteristics that led Coronado to central Kansas in the first place. Some scholars have speculated that the Turk had taken advantage of Coronado's lust for gold to purposely lead him away from the people of New Mexico and send him on what the Turk well knew would be a costly and time-consuming fool's errand.[10]

De Soto, too, was on a search for gold that brought him to the middle of the North American continent. In the words of the journalist Charles Mann, "For four years his force wandered . . . searching for gold and wrecking almost everything it touched."[11] Their journey had begun at Tampa Bay in 1539, and took them through parts of present-day Florida, Georgia, South Carolina, Tennessee, Alabama, and Mississippi before bringing them to the Mississippi River two years later. Along the way, they came into contact with several small late Mississippian chiefdoms but failed to locate the riches they desired. De Soto's men used force rather than friendship to sustain themselves as they traveled, often killing and stealing from Indigenous people to meet their own needs and desires. As they passed through chiefdoms, the Spaniards often ensured their safe passage by capturing the leader, called a mico, of the chiefdom, holding him hostage until they departed.[12]

By the time de Soto arrived at the confluence of the Arkansas and Mississippi Rivers, his expedition had lost many of its men and most of its horses. In 1541, he explored much of northeast Arkansas, making forays along the Mississippi and St. Francis Rivers that may have taken either him or one of his detachments north of the 36th parallel into what would later become the Missouri Bootheel. After spending the winter of 1541–1542 near Little Rock, Arkansas, de Soto died of illness, leaving the remains of his beleaguered force to make its way to the safety of Mexico City, the capital of New Spain.[13] While the expeditions of Coronado and De Soto failed to make Spain rich, they both left lasting legacies in the middle of North America. Indigenous people, who had been subjected to great cruelty, especially at the hands of De Soto's men, were left with an understandable wariness of Europeans. The Spaniards' marauding and warring had also upset the balance of power that may have led to the collapse of some late Mississippian chiefdoms.[14]

French Colonialism

Due largely to the disappointing lack of gold or silver in the heart of the continent, European expeditions did not return to the region for one hundred twenty years. The first Europeans known to have visited Indigenous Missourians on their own land were not Spanish, but French. Jesuit Father (or Père) Jacques Marquette and trader Louis Joliet stopped at the Illinois town of Peouarea at the confluence of the Mississippi and Des Moines Rivers on June 25, 1673. In the decades since the explorations of de Soto and Coronado, both France and England had established settlements on North America. French explorers first probed the St. Lawrence seaway, founding the village of Quebec in 1608. By the 1670s, French settlements dotted the Great Lakes region.[15]

Over the years, Native trading partners had told the French about a large river, which the Sioux called the Mesippi, that ran through the center of the continent. Hoping that the river would provide passage to the Pacific Ocean, the French colonial government hired Joliet to explore the river and follow it to its mouth. Leaving Mackinac in mid-May 1673, Marquette and Joliet led a seven-man expedition into Green Bay. From there, they made their way to the Wisconsin River, entering the Mississippi at the present-day site of Prairie du Chien, Wisconsin, on June 17.[16]

Once on the river, Marquette and Joliet introduced themselves to members of at least two of the Native nations inhabiting present-day Missouri. Having traveled two weeks without having seen any other humans, the French travelers were intrigued when they noticed a path leading inland on the Mississippi's west bank just below the Des Moines River. Following the trail for six miles, they were surprised to find three large Illinois towns located on the south bank of the Des Moines River. The town of Peouarea alone had nearly three hundred longhouses, and, all told, as many as eight thousand people may have called the area home. The Peorias were part of the much larger Algonquin Illinois, or Illiniwek, nation. Though the Illinois are often referred to as a "confederacy" of as many as seventeen small nations, some historians have speculated that these groups were actually distinct bands of a single nation. By the 1670s, the powerful Illinois were spread along both sides of the Mississippi River from below the Ohio River to well above the Des Moines River.[17]

The Illinois were fairly recent arrivals to the region, having emigrated there between 1600 and 1630. They had ventured west from their homeland south of Lake Erie in search of connections to the burgeoning bison trade in the Midwest. In the process, they vanquished the Ho-Chunks, who controlled much of the trade in northern Illinois and southern Wisconsin. By the 1630s, the Illinois had reached the Mississippi River and encountered another set of foes, the Ho-Chunks' Chiwere relatives, the Ioways. After forcing the Ioways to retreat northwest to the headwaters of the Des Moines, the Illinois built the town of Peouarea on the site their defeated enemies had vacated. From there they controlled commerce from southern Lake Michigan to the Missouri River, trading European goods supplied by the Iroquois, to the Osages, Missourias, and Quapaws, all of whom brought them bison robes and enslaved Natives from the west.[18]

Four Peoria elders welcomed the French travelers into their town and offered to smoke two sacred pipes with them. They then invited Marquette and Joliet to visit one of the nation's leaders in a neighboring village. The Illinois in that village honored their guests with gifts (a young, enslaved male and a pipe), an elaborate pipe ceremony, and a feast. The popularity of the pipe and its related rituals seems to have been especially strong among Indigenous people in Missouri just prior to European contact. Its appeal likely had to do with its connection to the spiritual world and the sense that, in times of uncertainty, pipe rituals helped restore a sense of balance. As had been the case with the Oneotas and Mississippians, the Illinois pipe ceremony, which included singing, a choreographed mock battle, and oratory, was a ritual form of adoption. By sharing their sacred pipes and honoring the Frenchmen with the ceremony, the Illinois let it be known they wished to accept them as family. According to archaeologist Robert Hall, Indigenous people used the pipe ceremony as "the de facto mechanism for intergroup trade," noting that the ceremony was "more than just suited to the circumstances of the times. It helped create the circumstances" by which strangers, including Europeans, created personal and economic bonds. As family, Marquette and Joliet were likely expected to reciprocate the bonds of kinship by become trading partners.[19]

There is symbolism in the fact that the first two white men known to visit Indigenous Missourians in their own towns were a trader and a priest. As historian Carl Ekberg has written, "Religious faith and commercial interests were the twin interests that drove much of early French exploration in North America."[20] By the time of Marquette and Joliet's arrival in Peouarea, the Peorias were familiar with French traders and black-robed missionaries. Indeed, the presence of European-made trade goods in the towns suggested that some of these same Illinois were likely to have visited missions and trading posts on the western Great Lakes. Still, the arrival of the two Frenchmen offered the Peorias the promise of a direct connection to French goods. By adopting a trader into their nation, the Illinois hoped they would be able to bypass the Iroquois, with whom they had to deal for French goods, and trade directly with the French.[21]

Staying only briefly among the Peorias, Marquette and Joliet soon resumed their voyage down the Mississippi. Just above the Arkansas River, they visited members of another Indigenous nation, one with hunting lands that stretched into what would become Missouri, the Quapaws. The Quapaws had first settled on the east side of the Mississippi, where they had encountered de Soto's men in 1541. Now weakened by diseases and encountering pressure from other nations, such as the Illinois and Chickasaws, the Quapaws moved west, across the river, in the mid-seventeenth century. There, they ran into violent resistance from the region's more established residents, the Caddoan-speaking people to the west and the Yazoos, Tunicas and Koroas to the south. At the time of Marquette and Joliet's visit in 1673, the Quapaws were living near the St. Francis and White Rivers, in what is now northeastern Arkansas and southeastern Missouri.[22]

Like the Peorias, the Quapaws, in their town above the Arkansas River, heartily welcomed the visitors. Quapaw welcoming ceremonies were elaborate, sometimes lasted for days, and included singing, dancing, and eating. Marquette and Joliet were taken to the Quapaw town of Kappa, where the Natives fed them, smoked with them, and made it clear that they too wanted to become trading partners with them. Though the Quapaws did have access to European trade goods, their location amid unfriendly nations forced them to acquire trade goods indirectly through intermediaries. Like the Illinois, they were eager to establish direct trade links to items such as cloth, metal tools, ammunition, utensils, and firearms that might give them an advantage over their adversaries.[23]

Though early French explorers and traders found the Quapaws to be polite, mild, and generous, they also proved to be shrewd in their business dealings. The Quapaws feared that, should Marquette and Joliet continue on their southern journey, their enemies, too, would have the opportunity to make trade alliances with the French travelers. To prevent this, the headmen of the Quapaws discouraged the expedition from proceeding downriver, warning Marquette and Joliet that the people who lived in that direction had guns and were likely to attack them. Convinced by that time that the Mississippi River did not empty into the Pacific Ocean and satisfied with the Quapaws' description of the course of the river below the Arkansas, the members of the expedition paddled upriver on their way back to the Great Lakes, where they would report their findings to the colonial governor of New France.[24]

During their brief inspection of the Mississippi River, Marquette and Joliet likely gained very little knowledge about the complex network of the Indigenous people who lived on the land to their west. While they had encountered the Illinois and the Quapaws, present-day Missouri was also home to the Missourias, Osages, and Otoes and was used for hunting by the Choctaws when the French explorers visited in 1673.

Hunting partially within the boundaries of extreme southeastern Missouri were the Quapaws' neighbors, the Chickasaws. The Chickasaws were the descendants of the Chicazas, a Late Mississippian people who had lived along the Tombigbee River in Alabama. The Chickasaws are the close Muskhogean-speaking relatives of the Choctaws, with whom they likely once lived. As the centralized power of the Mississippian chiefdoms diminished, the Chickasaws migrated to the region around Tupelo, Mississippi, between 1550 and 1650. With only about four thousand members, they were a small but formidable nation with territory extending onto the west side of the Mississippi River at the time of European contact.[25]

In the north and northwest portion of what would become Missouri were the Chiwere Siouan-speaking Otoes and Missourias. From their village at Utz in Saline County, the Missourias were a dominant force in lower Missouri River valley trade. Along with the Missourias, the

MAP 7: Jesuit Father Jacques Marquette and trader Louis Joliet are considered to be the first Europeans to have visited what would become the state of Missouri when they stopped at the Illinois town of Peouarea, near the confluence of the Des Moines and Mississippi Rivers, in 1673. This map shows the general location of Indigenous nations living in present-day Missouri at that time. *Map by the author*

regions' other dominant people were the Osages, who called themselves *Ni'-u-kon-çka*. By the time of European contact, the Osages controlled most of present-day Missouri south of the Missouri River. A miscommunication with one group of Osages who called themselves *U-Dse-Ta*, or the Down Under People, led early European visitors to refer to them as the Little Osages. Settlers then began to think of the remainder of the nation as the Big, or Great Osages. The Little Osages, allies of the Missourias, lived near them along the Missouri River, where they too are associated with the village at Utz. The Great Osages lived farther south and west, in villages largely clustered around the Osage River in present-day Vernon County, Missouri. This general configuration of Indigenous nations was far from static. Historian Stephen Aron has referred to Missouri as the "American Confluence," because it was a place where both major waterways and various groups of people converged and mingled. The movement of Indigenous nations in this region was ever-fluid, even prior to European colonization.[26]

As Indigenous people in the area would soon discover, subsequent French expeditions were not only larger than the first, but they also harbored the far more ambitious and long-lasting objectives of colonization. René-Robert Cavelier, the Sieur de La Salle, had petitioned the powerful French King Louis XIV to allow him to establish trading posts and conduct trade on the Mississippi River and its tributaries. The crown approved the request on the condition that La Salle travel to the mouth of the Mississippi River within five years to scout for possible sites on which to build a North American French port. Among the trading posts La Salle and his lieutenant, Henri de Tonti, established on the Illinois River were Fort Crevecoeur, near Pimiteoui, a Peoria town of seven thousand to eight thousand people located near present-day Peoria, Illinois, and Fort St. Louis, near a town of the Kaskaskias at Starved Rock (in Illinois) in 1680. In the region there were also settlements of Miamis, Mascoutens, Meskwakis, Kickapoos and Ioways.[27]

The Illinois had mixed feelings about two new trading posts being located so near to their towns. Though La Salle had promised them that the French would sell them weapons and ammunition—items the Illinois certainly desired—they knew that a French presence would disrupt their own lucrative business moving goods between French traders in the Great Lakes and other Native groups to the south and west. Since their arrival in the region, the Illinois had been strong and numerous enough to exert control over the middle portion of the Mississippi River. Much of the trade in furs, enslaved Indigenous captives, and European goods flowed between the Great Plains and the Great Lakes.

Acting as trade intermediaries, the Illinois were exploiting the increasing Indigenous demand for French trade goods, especially firearms and other items made of metal, for their own purposes. While trade goods made life easier for Native people, their reliance on manufactured items gradually separated them from some of their cultural traditions. As they replaced bone awls, ceramic kettles, and stone axes they once made by hand with more durable manufactured metal trade goods, crafts people gradually stopped making these items for themselves. The rituals of fashioning utensils from the bones of animal relatives, from the grandfather rocks, or from the clay that was part of grandmother earth—rituals that were deeply tied to Indigenous concepts of their place in the natural world—gradually diminished, signaling a significant change in the relationship between Indigenous people and the natural world.[28]

The introduction of European trade goods into the Mississippi River Valley also drastically altered the economics of Indigenous communities. Millennia-old economic traditions built on subsistence were changing, as Native people began to participate in the colonial model of the market economy. Writing about the Osages, historian Willard Rollings observed that they "acquired the new weapons, animals, and tools, and in so doing they partially adopted European approaches to resource management and use." In this new economy, Indigenous hunters were not only forced to harvest animals for food, but also they were killing them for trade. Increased hunting stressed animal populations and demanded that Natives allocate more human resources to the act of hunting, which in turn took available labor away from other important tasks necessary for sustenance.[29]

European trade was also the source of some intertribal mistrustfulness. When the Iroquois, who had been expanding westward from their home south of Lake Ontario, discovered the French trading posts located next to Illinois towns, they attempted to prevent a French-Illinois alliance by attacking the Illinois. What ensued were a deadly series of battles that lasted for years. Though the Illinois were eventually able to turn back the Iroquois invasion, other nations, such as the Sacs, Foxes, Chickasaws, and even the French, were pulled into the fight. All these conflicts created animosities that would cause problems for the Illinois in the future.[30]

La Salle fulfilled his promise to Louis XIV in 1682 when he descended the Mississippi River, leaving Lake Michigan on the still-frozen Illinois River on January 4. Carrying a catlinite pipe with him as a symbol of peace, La Salle was eager to meet and befriend Indigenous people along the way for the purpose of establishing trade connections. An unidentified group of Natives met the expedition at the mouth of the Missouri River on February 13. They explained to La Salle that on the river were "a great number of large villages, of many different nations; that there are arable and prairie lands, and an abundance of cattle [bison] and beaver."[31] The following day, the Frenchmen stopped on the Mississippi's east bank at a village of the Tamaroas, members of the Illinois confederacy, but found that the inhabitants of the village were away hunting.

On February 24, five Chickasaw hunters encountered members of the La Salle expedition who were searching for one of their men near the mouth of the Ohio River. The Chickasaws offered to take La Salle to their village to meet with their headmen. After walking for more than a day and realizing the village was much farther away than they had been led to believe, La Salle turned back, sending the Chickasaws on with presents. Before resuming their river descent however, La Salle ordered his men to construct a small fortification, which they called Fort Prudhomme, after the member of the expedition they had been searching for, and whom they had located a few days before moving on.[32]

On March 3, Quapaws sighted the flotilla of Frenchmen near Kappa, the same town where they had welcomed Marquette and Joliet. After determining the French had come in peace, the Quapaws embraced these newcomers much as they had their predecessors. "All of the village . . . came to the river to receive us." wrote Father Zenobius Membré, the chronicler of the expedition. "They built us cabins, brought us wood to burn, and provisions in abundance. For three days, they feasted us constantly. . . . We, in return, made them other little presents, which they greatly admired." No doubt, the Quapaws were hoping that they might enhance their power in the region by establishing close kinship ties with the French and thus gaining increased direct access to French trade goods.[33]

Ten days later, La Salle made good on another objective of the French crown when he conducted a ritual of discovery and laid claim to the surrounding land. He solemnly planted a cross and plaque bearing King Louis XIV's coat of arms near Kappa, naming the land around him Louisiana, in the king's honor. He then declared that he was taking "possession in the name of His Majesty, and of his heirs and successors to the crown, of the country of Louisiana and of all its lands, provinces, countries, peoples nations, mines, minerals, ports, harbors, seas, its straits and roads." Father Membré recounted that the Quapaws expressed "great joy" over these symbolic objects, even rubbing their hands over their bodies after having caressed the cross. No doubt impressed by the solemn nature of La Salle's ceremony, the Quapaws understood these objects to have great importance for their guests and likely believed that by planting them on Quapaw land, the French had formed a deep connection with them. To ensure the safety of these valuable objects, the Quapaws erected a palisade around them after La Salle's departure.[34]

What the Quapaws had no way of knowing was that under the Doctrine of Discovery's principle of land contiguity, European international law would now recognize the entire Mississippi River watershed as a French colony. In essence, the Quapaws, and all the hundreds of thousands of other indigenous people who lived in that watershed, now had a European landlord. In order to preclude any possible questions of legitimacy to France's claim, La Salle seems to have repeated this ritual of discovery at least two more times during his trek, once among the Natchez people in late March and again when he reached the Gulf of Mexico around April 9, claiming all of the new Territory of Louisiana, which consisted of most of the Mississippi River basin, for France.

In the short term, La Salle's mission to open trade in the lower Mississippi River Valley was not as successful as France had hoped. A subsequent expedition to establish a French colony on the gulf coast went so badly that La Salle was murdered by his own men in 1687. In the long term, however, the expedition had claimed an enormous amount of land for France and helped to create opportunities for trade with and the colonization of Indigenous people in the Mississippi River Valley.[35]

Because Indigenous people who lived on the west bank of the Missouri greatly outnumbered the newcomers, they held the upper hand in their relations with them and believed a French presence would benefit their lives both commercially and militarily. According to historian Kathleen DuVal, the Quapaws initially "neither surrendered to nor resisted colonialism. Neither would have made sense to them, given the weakness of the French." Instead, the Quapaws were able to draw Europeans into their own "patterns of land and resource allocation, subsistence, goods exchange, gender relations, diplomacy and warfare."[36]

This became apparent when Henri de Tonti returned to the mouth of the Arkansas River in the spring of 1686 to establish a trading post. La Salle had granted Tonti land and had given him permission to trade in that location during their visit four years earlier. Upon Tonti's return, the Quapaws assumed the role of landlord, giving him permission to "borrow" land near their towns in exchange for trading with them. Arkansas Post would be the first French enterprise on the west side of the Mississippi, and even though it would be shuttered by 1700, the French had become convinced there was money to be made by extracting resources from the mid-continent and proceeded to build other, more permanent, establishments.[37]

By the beginning of the eighteenth century, the French had become familiar visitors in the Mississippi River Valley, Travelers to the area included not only government sanctioned traders and missionaries, but also independent—some might call them rogue—traders and trappers known as *coureur de bois*. France's first permanent settlements in the Illinois Country, a designation that was then used to describe territory on both sides of the Mississippi River, were the villages of Cahokia and Kaskaskia. Cahokia, founded in 1699, began as a mission created by the Seminarians of Quebec and was named after the Cahokia people of the Illinois Confederacy. The mission and village were located near the confluence of the Missouri and Mississippi Rivers, near the remains of the great early Mississippian city of Cahokia, which the Europeans also named after the Illinois tribe. The missionaries believed the spot would be an ideal place from which to convert the nearby Cahokias, Tamaroas, and Peorias, of the Illinois Confederacy, to Catholicism. However, because of its location, the village became more successful as a trading post, not only for the Illinois, but also for nations west of the river like the Osages and Missourias.[38]

Fifty miles to the south, the town of Kaskaskia, which Ekberg has described as the "undisputed metropole of the Illinois Country during the French regime in Louisiana," was founded in 1703. This settlement also began as a mission, albeit one established by a different order of Catholic missionaries, the Jesuits. First located at Starved Rock, on the Illinois River, the mission was relocated at least twice before finally being moved to a site near the confluence of the Mississippi and Kaskaskia Rivers. Just four years after its founding, the village boasted a multiethnic population of twenty-two hundred. Many of the town's residents were members of the Kaskaskia nation, who lived at the periphery of the village. Like Cahokia, Kaskaskia also became an important trade hub, eventually shipping pelts and other commercial goods to New Orleans, after that important port was founded in 1718.[39]

French *habitants*, or settlers, and Indigenous people generally lived together peacefully in the Illinois Country. Not only did the multiethnic population of the Illinois Country work and socialize together, but they also often intermarried. In the early years of New France, officials had believed that the marriage of Frenchmen and Native women would be an efficient method of converting the Indigenous population to Christianity. Once they became Christians, they expected the Native women would spread religion to their families. In addition, French traders favored the concept of intermarriage because it created kinships and commercial ties to Native families that were good for business, something they had learned from Indigenous people.[40]

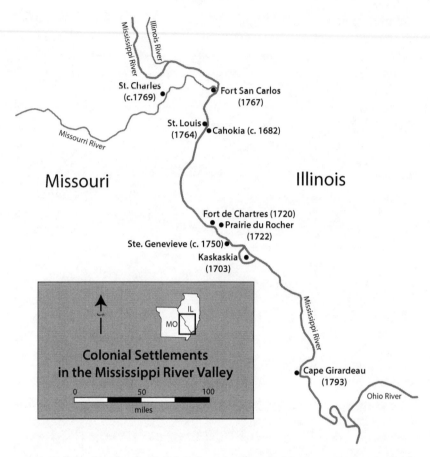

Map 8: Eighteenth-century colonial settlements along the Mississippi River. *Map by the author*

In practice, however, the goals of missionaries and the traders collided. Traders found it beneficial to adapt to the customs of the Indigenous population and to marry and adopt Native people in accordance with Indigenous traditions. This, however, conflicted directly with the missionaries' efforts to convert Natives to Christianity and indoctrinate them in European culture. The crown became especially concerned when it was apparent that the influence of Indigenous women was leading many Frenchmen to "become savage." Historian Tanis Thorne has observed that the French worried coureur de bois who lived "in between" cultures would "turn the Indian nations against the vulnerable French settlements either deliberately, by lies and other provocations, or inadvertently, by their offensive behavior." Fears about the lack of morality among the coureur de bois in the Illinois Country led one observer to declare that the French trappers and traders were "weak and slack enough to marry Illinois women, which often creates disorders among both nations that are very difficult to avoid." Paramount among these "disorders" were worries over the dilution of the French gene pool and that *Métis*, or French-Indigenous offspring, were naturally "libertine, slothful and knavish" and "worse than the Indians themselves." As Thorne has pointed out, the French believed that "their political loyalties were not firm and their morality was substandard."[41]

However, historian Robert Morrissey contends that marriages between French men and Indigenous women became the "bedrock of the community, allowing the colonists and local Indians to form a strong bond through kinship." The couples had come together to "create successful agrarian households. These relationships created a social order that, in the end, allowed the French to achieve their colonial goals of assimilating the Indigenous population, albeit, not in the manner in which the colonial government had envisioned. Intermarriage put them in tension with the empire, but it was a hallmark of the local culture.[42]

Missionaries were not completely unsuccessful in their attempts to recruit members of the Illinois Confederacy into their churches. While the Cahokias, Peorias, and Tamaroas living in the area around the French town of Cahokia distrusted the missionaries, in part because of the illnesses they brought with them, the Kaskaskias were more tolerant of French culture and religion, and even adapted to the European agricultural methods of the French habitants. Conversely, the Jesuits of Kaskaskia, unlike the more Francophile Seminarians, were often inclined to adapt to Native ways of living. By 1690, Kaskaskias, especially women, joined the Catholic Church in significant numbers. In 1696 alone, Father Jacques Gravier claimed to have converted more than two thousand Indigenous Kaskaskias at the mission. Of course, conversion to Christianity does not mean the Illinois groups abandoned their own spiritual traditions. Rollings observed that Osages were often attracted to the "vivid ceremony, dramatic expressions, and ritual" of Catholic services, even though the ceremonies were conducted in Latin, and the theology of Christianity had little to offer them. Their connection to the religion, writes Rollings, was almost always "external" which left the Osages room to hold on to much of their own spirituality.[43]

Additionally, those Natives whom Gravier counted as converts may also have viewed Church membership as a means to achieve economic or political status that was unrelated to spirituality. A case in point can be seen in the extraordinary life of a Kaskaskia woman, Aramepinchieue. Born in 1677, she was the daughter of a Kaskaskia headman named François-Xavier Rouensa. In the early 1690s, Aramepinchieue joined the Catholic Church and took the Christian name Marie Rouensa while her people still lived on the Illinois River. When Marie was seventeen, her father offered her as the bride of the nearly fifty-year-old Frenchman Michel Accault. Accault, who had been a part of La Salle's original expedition, had since become a successful trader. The headman Rouensa believed that the marriage would enhance his status among the Kaskaskias by giving him direct access to French trade goods. Marie, however, was reluctant to marry Accault, in part because he was a lapsed Catholic and well-known for his decadence. By some accounts, Marie's father was so enraged by her unwillingness to marry the trader that he tore off some of her clothing and sent her out of his cabin only partially clothed and humiliated. After fleeing to the chapel and consulting with Father Gravier, Marie agreed to the marriage. She may have decided that marriage to a prominent European like Accault might give her a place of prominence in her community that would allow her to persuade more of her Kaskaskia people to become Christians. Among her first converts were said to be her parents and her notoriously wayward husband.[44]

Sometime around 1700, the Kaskaskias left their village on the Illinois River and, attracted by closer proximity to French traders and prime farmland, migrated south to the Mississippi River. They settled on the west bank of the Mississippi near the mouth of the River Des Peres, across from the town of Cahokia. Father Gravier reestablished the Jesuit mission at the new site, and a number of French and Tamaroas also joined the settlement. In 1702, Accault died or, as some have claimed, simply disappeared. During that winter, Marie gave birth to the couple's second son, whom she named Michel, Jr. The following year, the Kaskaskias left the River Des Peres village and continued their journey south. Later that year, Marie Rouensa became one of the founding citizens of the village of Kaskaskia. There, she married a second Frenchman, Michel Philippe. The couple lived as prominent citizens of Kaskaskia, owning both real estate and enslaved Natives.[45]

By the end of first decade of the eighteenth century, French missionaries and traders were well established in the Illinois Country. However, military and government representatives of the French crown did not arrive until early 1719. In May of that year, a Canadian, Pierre Dugué Sieur de Boisbriant, landed at Kaskaskia with a flotilla of government officials, lead miners, and soldiers from New Orleans. De Boisbriant was working under the auspices of the Company of the Indies, or Company of the West, which held a royal patent on all the land La Salle had claimed for France. De Boisbriant had been directed by the crown to investigate the potential for lead mining, build a base of military operations, and establish some semblance of a colonial government in Upper Louisiana, which would include most of present-day Missouri, Illinois, and Indiana. For a base of operations, he chose a site seventeen miles north of Kaskaskia on a flat prairie near the Mississippi River and began to construct Fort de Chartres on 1719. The original wooden fort would be reconstructed twice before the French built a solid stone structure in the 1750s. That fort lasted long enough for the British to take possession of it from 1765 until 1772. A reconstructed Fort de Chartres still stands today on the site of the original near Prairie du Rocher, Illinois.[46]

The introduction of a French colonial government in the Illinois Country immediately created tensions with Native people in the region. In an attempt to end intermarriage between Frenchmen and Illinois women, de Boisbriant forced Indigenous people to be segregated into their own towns. Those more traditional members of the Illinois confederacy, the Cahokias, Peorias, and Michigameas, were wary of the missionaries and tended to support this segregation on the grounds that it allowed them to minimize contact with French influence over their people. Eventually, many of them left their towns near French Cahokia to return to the Illinois River. For more assimilated Indigenous Illinois women living in French Kaskaskia, such as Marie Rouensa, the move toward segregation created problems. In order to maintain their status and connection to the Church, they had to separate themselves from their Indigenous relatives and remain with their French husbands, thus becoming even more integrated into French colonial society.[47]

Of course, the Illinois and Quapaws were not the only Native Missourians trading with French colonists during the early eighteenth century. The disruption caused by French traders in the mid-continent was far-reaching and in one way or another affected every nation living there. France's ever-expanding trade networks created competition and conflict among some Indigenous people, even as other Native nations welcomed the French and worked diligently to become trade partners with them. In the Upper Mississippi Valley, the Foxes clashed with the French at the turn of the eighteenth century. The Foxes controlled rivers in Wisconsin through which French traders needed to pass to transport goods from the Great Lakes to the Mississippi River. To retain control of these rivers, the Foxes launched a series of attacks on traders. Because they were so few, the French were forced to rely on their Native trading partners, the Missourias, Illinois, and Osages, to help them fight the Foxes.

The conflict led to a prolonged war that began with a siege on Fort Pontchartrain, the French fort at Detroit, by the Foxes and their allies the Sacs, Mascoutens, and Kickapoos in 1712. As the call went out for Native supporters to help the French defend the fort, Osage, Illinois, and Missouria warriors traveled more than five hundred miles from their homes in Missouri and Illinois to help. While these three nations were, no doubt, interested in maintaining their beneficial alliances with the French, they were also likely equally eager to help vanquish the Foxes, whom the Osages called *Ca-Ge-Wa* or Hard to Kill People, and who had begun to encroach on Missouria and Osage hunting lands. With the help of the Missourias and their allies, the Foxes and Mascoutens were defeated at Fort Pontchartrain.[48]

French Trade in the Heart of Missouria Country

It was during their mission to assist the French at Fort Pontchartrain that the Osages and Missourias encountered a French coureur de bois by the name of Étienne Veniard Sieur de Bourgmont, who had apparently been among those who traveled to the fort to help defend it. Then in his early thirties, Bourgmont had fled his native France as a teenager to escape indebtedness. Once in New France, he joined the military and became the commander of Fort Pontchartrain in 1706. His reputation became tarnished, however, when bungled peace talks with a group of Ottawas led to an attack on the fort in which two Frenchmen and thirty Ottawas died. While it appears that Bourgmont was never punished for his inept handling of the incident, he soon deserted the military and began operating as an independent trader. Perhaps sensing that the Osage and Missouria nations represented untapped trade opportunities, he decided to return with them to their home on the Missouri River in 1712. Legend has it that Bourgmont was smitten with a Missouria woman and followed her to the Missouria village. However, Osage historians

Louis F. Burns and John Joseph Mathews both claim that Bourgmont first stayed with the Osages, and that he lived with a woman from the Elk Clan and, according to Burns, had "several" Osage children.[49]

At the time of Bourgmont's arrival, many Missourias lived on the south side of the Missouri River in a single town located in present-day Saline County. The so-called Little Osages lived nearby. The Missouria town was surrounded by prairies and conveniently located near the river, just a few miles from the point at which the Grand and Chariton Rivers empty into it from the north. This allowed them to monitor and control both Indigenous and French traders as they passed through the region. The main Missouria town was located on or very near to a site that their Oneota ancestors had occupied as early as 1350. The village was large, probably thirty to forty acres in size, and contained dozens of dome-shaped lodges covered in woven cattail mats. The Missourias farmed, hunted, fished, and gathered wild plants and roots. Deer, elk, wild turkeys, and fish were plentiful. Hunters would also travel west from their home for annual buffalo hunts.[50]

It is likely that Bourgmont saw French trade goods such as beads, knives, kettles, rings, and bracelets in the Missouria town when he arrived there in 1712. While Missourias had been doing business with French traders in the Illinois Country and northern Mississippi River since at least the 1690s, Bourgmont is the first French trader known to have lived in their village with them. Like the Quapaws and Illinois, the Missourias performed elaborate welcoming rituals of kinship for village guests. These ceremonies were likely quite like those recorded by Frenchman Nicolas Perrot when he visited the Missourias' close Chiwere relatives, the Ioways. Perrot described being carried on a buffalo hide into the lodge of the village headman. There, the leader ritually wept over Perrot, presented him with a pipe, and fed him pieces of buffalo tongue. Bourgmont reciprocated the Missourias' overtures of kinship by marrying a Missouria woman and fathering a son, who was born in 1714.[51]

As a newly made relative of the Missourias, Bourgmont was expected to use his trade connections to benefit the nation. To this end, Bourgmont set out with his wife and a few other Missourias to trade in the Illinois Country in 1713. Word that he was living with the Missourias angered members of the French colonial government, as did charges that he was creating unrest among the Illinois and Miamis by bringing British traders to the Illinois Country from the East Coast. Louisiana Governor Antoine Lamothe, sieur de Cadillac ordered that Bourgmont be arrested, but by early 1714, he was once again living in the Missouria town.[52]

Despite the fact that Bourgmont was officially a fugitive, Cadillac hired him to work as an explorer and ambassador to the Indigenous nations of the Missouri River on behalf of the French colonial government. In 1719 Bourgmont received a commission to be a captain in the colonial military and was named Commandant of the Missouri River. By this time, French officials had become concerned about the interest the Spanish, who controlled most of what is now the Southwestern United States, were showing in the Loup River region of present-day Nebraska. France sent Bourgmont up the Missouri River to make a trade agreement with Spain, or, failing that, to build a military installation on the river. Attempts to negotiate with Spanish colonial officials must not have succeeded because, during the winter of 1723–1724, Bourgmont oversaw the construction of Fort Orleans on a site across the river from the Missouria town.[53]

The new fort became an important center of commerce for the Great and Little Osages as well as the Missourias. Members of these nations visited it often to trade with their friend Bourgmont, whom they called the Wanderer. The fort also attracted members of other Native nations, who came to trade with the French and were especially interested in securing weapons and ammunition. While at the fort, visitors likely interacted with the missionary Father Jean Baptiste Mercier, who tried, apparently without much success, to convert them to Christianity. The installation was garrisoned by a military detachment of forty men, which included a young cadet named Louis St. Ange de Bellerive. St. Ange would later become the commandant at Fort de Chartres and go on to represent both the French and Spanish governments in St. Louis.[54]

With the new fort in place, the French now had a western base from which to influence the trade, warfare, and alliances of Natives living on the Missouri River and beyond. Bourgmont viewed the people and land of the Missouri River Valley as resources to be exploited and was intent on creating and maintaining Indigenous alliances that were beneficial to the French. At the same time, he militarily opposed alliances seen as detrimental to French colonial goals. For example, Bourgmont utilized "forceful methods" to prevent France's allies, the Otoes and Ioways, from making pacts with Sacs and Sioux, who were enemies of the French.[55]

Bourgmont was also focused on the West and planned to continue efforts to make a trade agreement with the Spanish colonial government and to travel to the villages of the Plains Apaches, also known to the French as Padoucas, to make a trade alliance with them. Such a pact would have been beneficial, because the Padoucas were actively trading with the Spanish, most notably for horses. The French wanted to make inroads with the Padoucas, whom they hoped would help them gain access to Spanish mines and Pacific Oceans ports. The Osages worried about this expansion of trade and influence in the West, fearing that it would compete with their own power there. At the same time, they realized that any attempt to stop Bourgmont or the French would jeopardize their valuable trade alliance with them.[56]

For their part, French officials in New Orleans worried that peace with the Padoucas would bring an end to the lucrative trade they were conducting in enslaved Padoucas. Slavery had existed in Native culture long before European contact. Enslaved Indigenous people were usually prisoners of war or captives taken specifically as a form of trade currency during raids on enemy villages. Because men often were killed in battles in which captives were taken, women and children tended to be more commonly enslaved. Often, these captives, who could be traded to other nations, would eventually be adopted by families wanting to replace deceased loved ones. However, enslaved people could also be treated severely by their captors. Historians Carl J. Ekberg and Sharon K. Person have written that the Illinois used the same word, *nitaia*, for both dogs and enslaved persons. After the arrival of the French, however, the nature of Indigenous enslavement changed. Because the French population in Louisiana was so small, they desperately needed laborers to operate mines, farms, and other lucrative resource extraction operations. Aware of the situation and eager to keep the balance of trade strong on their side, the Kanzas, Osages, Missourias, and Illinois actively traded Indigenous slaves, whom they had captured from western nations, like the Padoucas or Comanches, to the French. Enslaved African and Indigenous people were common and would eventually make up a sizable portion of the population of French colonial towns such as Kaskaskia, Chartres, Cahokia, and later, Ste. Genevieve and St. Louis. At the time he lived at Fort Orleans, Bourgmont enslaved several people. One of them, a woman named Marie-Angélique, would travel to France with him when he returned in 1725.[57]

On July 3, 1724, Bourgmont left Fort Orleans on an expedition to make trade inroads with the Padoucas in what is now central Kansas. With him was an escort of one hundred Missourias and sixty-four Osages, along with two enslaved Padoucas, which Bourgmont planned to return as a sign of good will. Along the way, the entourage stopped at a large Kanza village. Archaeologists today believe the village stood on the west bank of the river, halfway between the present-day towns of Atchison, Kansas, and St. Joseph, Missouri, at what is now known as the Doniphan archaeological site. Because of their position along the Missouri and Kansas Rivers, the French needed the Kanza, sometimes called the Kaws, as allies to keep trade moving smoothly on those water routes. Once they reached the Kanza village, however, many members of the expedition, including Bourgmont, were stricken with fever. This caused all but twenty Osages and Missourias in the entourage to return home to avoid contracting the illness. To complete the mission, Bourgmont was able to use the threat of trade sanctions to cajole one thousand one hundred Kanza men, women, and children to accompany him to the village of the Padoucas, even though the Kanzas considered the Padoucas their enemies. Along the way, Bourgmont became so ill that he had to be carried back to the Kanza village. Proceeding under the command of one of his lieutenants, the column covered much of the same country around Salina, Kansas, that Coronado's men had traveled a century and a half earlier before finally reaching a Padouca village. There, after an exchange of gifts and the ritual of smoking pipes, the French established ties with the Padoucas while encouraging a pact of peace between the Kanzas and the Padoucas.[58]

Upon his return to Fort Orleans in October 1824, Bourgmont, by then recovered from fever, undertook one last mission. He was assigned to bring Missouria, Osage, and Otoe representatives to France to meet with French officials, first in New Orleans, and later in Paris. The trip signified the importance France placed in these three nations for the success of their North American commercial ventures. Likewise, the Indigenous diplomats hoped this would be an opportunity to secure their place in France's trade network. As one Missouria headman admitted, "it would be shameful for our tribe not to obey the request made by great chief," King Louis XV, for them to visit.[59]

In New Orleans, colonial officials added an Illinois representative to the delegation and decided to limit the Missourias, Osages, and Otoes to one delegate each. In addition, the Missouria were allowed to include the headman's daughter, known to history only as Ignon Ouaconisen, or the Missouria Princess. After an eventful journey during which their first ship sank near Mobile Bay, the delegation arrived safely in Paris on September 20, 1785. For two months, they toured France and met with dignitaries, including the fifteen-year-old King Louis XV. Ignon Ouaconisen married one of Bourgmont's soldiers, a Sergeant Dubois, and was baptized at the Cathedral of Notre Dame. Though they were dazzled by the sights of Paris, the Indigenous delegates professed to be somewhat confused about the purpose of their trip. "We have been told the King and the Company [of the Indies] requested the presence of representatives from each of our tribes," the Missouria headman said at one of their public events. "Here we are before you without knowing what you wish of us." Laden with gifts, the entourage left Paris in late November without ever really knowing the answer to the question.[60]

Bourgmont stayed behind, never to return to North America. He lived out the rest of his life in France, where his efforts in North America had earned him the noble title of squire. After returning to his home country, Bourgmont set free an enslaved Padouca, Marie-Angélique. In 1732, she married and had a son in the town of Fresnes, just outside Paris. Ignon Ouaconisen returned to the Illinois Country with her husband and the rest of Bourgmont's Indigenous delegation in early 1726. After Sergeant Dubois was killed in a skirmish, she settled in Kaskaskia, where she married a militia captain.[61]

Though the French colonial government ordered Fort Orleans to be closed in 1728, it continued to operate in a diminished capacity. Until 1736, the post served as a garrison, guarded by just eight soldiers under the command of Louis St. Ange de Bellerive. The fort's missionary, Father Jean-Paul Mercier, attempted to continue his work there for some years. But in the end, he too abandoned his efforts among the Osages and Missourias. He reported that as long as the French had proven useful to their trade and provided access to weapons and ammunition, these Indigenous Missourians tolerated his efforts to convert them. However, once Fort Orleans had been downsized and French trade ceased, the Father was no longer welcome.[62]

Bourgmont had helped the French make important inroads into Louisiana. His travels had greatly expanded France's geographical and cultural knowledge of the area. He had also brought French trade goods directly into the villages of Ioways, Otoes, Osages, Missourias, and Kanzas, among others. Bourgmont also influenced the balance of power among Indigenous nations by providing French allies with trade goods and weaponry. With France's abandonment of the fort and the retirement of their friend Bourgmont, the Osages and the Missourias suddenly faced new challenges as they worked to secure their own trade networks.[63]

Indigenous Nations End French Plans for Empire

Because both the Osages and Missourias considered Bourgmont to be their relative, and because he had been their active trading partner, he had benefited from their assistance in his explorations of the Missouri River and points west. Other French traders, however, were not so fortunate. As the Missourias and Little Osages controlled trade traffic on the Missouri River above the Grand River, and the Great Osages did much the same on the Osage and Arkansas Rivers, French traders who followed in Bourgmont's wake without Osage and Missouria approval had to navigate blockades to trade with the Padoucas, Pawnees, Kanzas, or Omahas.

In the spring of 1719, Missourias and Little Osages stopped trader Charles Claude du Tisné as he passed their villages on the Missouri River. Though he threatened to end French trade with them, they refused to allow him to proceed. A few months later, Tisné tried to get past the Great Osages while traveling overland to trade with the Padoucas and Wichitas. The Osages greeted him in a friendly manner, but again refused to allow him to continue. This time, however, his threats to end French trade with them had the desired effect. They allowed Tisné to proceed, but only after they relieved him of all but three of the muskets he planned to trade in the West. To sabotage Tisné's trade mission, the Osages sent a messenger ahead to the Wichitas to warn them that he was a slave trader who planned to capture them. When he arrived at the Wichita village, it took Tisné quite some time to persuade its residents that his mission was one of trade.[64]

That same year, the trader Jean-Baptiste Bénard de la Harpe and his Caddoan guides met an Osage war party while trying to slip past the Osages via the Red River on their way to trade with the Wichitas. The Osages stopped him and threatened to kill la Harpe's guides. It was only after he gave the Osages presents that he and his men were allowed to leave, presumably in the direction from which they had come. As these incidents became more common, Missourias and particularly Osages became more vigilant in guarding their territory, protecting their own trade networks, and preventing the French from trading with their adversaries in the west. Mathews has written that Osages "confiscated goods being carried to their enemies, and they killed Frenchmen when they could do so with impunity." However, when they did kill, Osages were careful to select low-level members of the trade expedition as their victims. They knew the French Governor of Louisiana in New Orleans, Jean-Baptiste Le Moyne de Bienville, was far less likely to order retaliation against them for the murder of a *voyageur*, a French-Canadian trapper and trader, than for the murder of an expedition leader.[65]

In the meantime, the French, too, were experiencing trade-related problems. The Company of the Indies, which held a royal patent on all trade in Louisiana, had suffered economic setbacks that forced it to retreat from its expansion into the heart of the Missouri River. Financial troubles had been a major contributing factor in their decision to close Fort Orleans. By 1732, the company's fortunes were so desperate that they petitioned the King to assume control of trade once again in the colony. In the absence of company oversight, however, the crown was unable to control trade on the Missouri River. Company-licensed traders were replaced with coureurs de bois, who were focused only on personal profit and were wholly unconcerned about the welfare of France and the French colonial government's relations with Indigenous people. Natives began to complain to French authorities that these rogue traders were cheating them, acting violently toward them, and shipping large amounts of brandy into their villages. This volatile mixture of unchecked greed, violence, and use of alcohol led to the murder of several Natives and whites. As the number of illicit traders increased, so did the incidents of violence. While the French had long relied on the work of coureurs de bois to prop up their fledgling trade empire, it had become clear that they would have to be reined in.[66]

Finally, the colonial government was forced to act. In 1744, Louisiana Governor Bienville ordered the nearest French authority, Chevalier de Bertet, the commandant at Fort de Chartres, to send a small detachment of soldiers to the Missouria village to detain some particularly troublesome French traders. Then, in an attempt to stop the violence and regulate trade, Bertet granted a five-year monopoly of the entire Missouri River to a Canadian trader, Joseph Deruisseau. This allowed Deruisseau to forbid anyone else from trading on the river as well as to confiscate the goods of any trader caught defying the rules. As part of his operation, Deruisseau had a small stockade, called Fort Cavagnal, built nearly a hundred miles above the Missouria and Osage villages, near the confluence of the Missouri and Kansas Rivers.[67]

By the middle of the eighteenth century, the Indigenous people who had welcomed French traders and soldiers into the Mississippi and Missouri River valleys almost a century earlier, had begun to wonder about the viability of the relationships they had forged with their European business partners. The French colonial government was floundering, and many Native nations in Louisiana were becoming wary of its motives and actions. Over the years, relationships between government officials and Natives had shifted, and alliances were becoming nebulous. France had become distracted from its colony when it became entangled in a series of wars with the British. One, King George's War, had led to a naval blockade of New France in 1744. For more than a year, the French were unable to ship new trade goods to the Mississippi River Valley. As a result, traders and government officials lacked the gifts they needed to forge and renew long-standing kinship ties with Native allies.[68]

In short, the French had simply never succeeded in building a viable empire in the heart of the North American continent. While Natives in Louisiana had been able to integrate them into their existing trade ventures, the French had never had the strength to pursue their own agenda for the region without relying heavily on Native assistance. This dependence on Indigenous allies had led them to be drawn into several conflicts between Native groups that had been costly and had damaged their reputation among potential allies. One example was the French war with the Chickasaws. At the beginning of the eighteenth century, the Chickasaws, along with their allies, the Choctaws and the Quapaws, controlled trade traffic on the lower Mississippi River. Meanwhile, the Illinois and their allies the Miamis controlled the upper Mississippi and Wabash Rivers. When these two powerful nations went to war with one another, the French, in an effort to protect their own trade interests, were forced to enter the fray on the side of the Illinois.[69]

The Chickasaws represented two significant threats to French trade. First was their control over traffic on the lower Mississippi, where they often attacked French traders. Second, and perhaps more worrisome, was the Chickasaws alliance with Great Britain. Chickasaws had been long-time trading partners with the British, who brought goods overland from Charleston, in the Province of Carolina, which they traded to the Chickasaws for hides, beeswax, honey, salt, and Indigenous slaves. The British had established the settlement of Charleston in about 1670 and since that time it had become an important seaport. Their alliance with the Chickasaws, as well as with other nations in present-day Alabama and Mississippi, provided the British with a trade route to the Mississippi River, where they threatened French trade.[70]

French mismanagement of many of their battles against the Chickasaws, and the embarrassing defeats that followed, led even their allies to question the wisdom of continuing to support them militarily. Subsequent rumors, perhaps instigated by the British, of a widespread Indigenous conspiracy to kill French citizens living in the Illinois Country seemed to be confirmed by a Miami-led attack on villages in December 1751. In retaliation, the commandant of Fort de Chartres, Jean-Jacques Macarty Mactigue, urged a force of four hundred to five hundred Foxes, Sacs, Menominees, and Sioux to retaliate by raiding Cahokia and Michigamea towns, killing and injuring as many as seventy people on June 1, 1754. Despite the Miami leader Le Loup's adamant denials that his people had plotted to kill them, French troops and allied Indigenous fighters burned the Miami town of Picillany to the ground later that month. Historian M. J. Morgan has proposed that this attack, which caused the death of at least one British trader who was in the Miami town, marked the proper beginning of a conflict that would forever change things in the region.[71]

And yet, historian Robert Morrissey challenges us to look beyond France's apparent failures. "Far more interesting than the question of success or failure," writes Morrissey, "is understanding the nature of colonialism itself as a complicated system mutually created by diverse, entangled peoples." While the French Crown may never have gained a firm foothold in their colony, colonialism was nonetheless taking place. While Indigenous and even enslaved people were able to resist falling under the direct control of the French government, they created what Morrissey calls an "idiosyncratic colonial order." Though it may not have adhered to the plans set forth by the French government, it nonetheless upset traditional Indigenous orders of society, economics, and kinship.[72]

Voices

My father, we Osage and Missouri think as do our elder brothers, the Illinois. We shall do all they wish, and it is well that the English do not come here, for we shall always aid our brothers in preserving their lands; besides we know only the Frenchman for our father. Never have we heard our ancestors speak of another nation. They have always told us that it was the French who gave us life and supplied our needs. They advised us never to lose their hand. We still hold it my father, and it shall never escape from us.

Why do you, Englishman, not remain on your lands, while the red nations remain on theirs[?] These belong to us. We inherit them from our ancestors. They found them by dint of wandering. They established themselves there and they [the lands] are ours; no one can contest them. Leave, depart, depart, depart, and tell your chief that all the red men do not want any English here. Pay good attention to what we tell you. Do not insist on remaining here longer. Leave and do not come back anymore. We only want to have the French among us. Adieu, leave.[1]

—Anonymous Osage and Missouri headmen

Chouteau is a trader, let us suppose by his talent. He has the sole right of going to the Osages to carry them their needs, and without doubt to sustain them in their rogueries. We, if one of us steals a horse, or any other thing, are treated as thieves and as bad savages. In the same manner if anyone of us becomes intoxicated, and tries to commit any extravagance, one hears immediately: "They are dogs; they must be killed. Results have proved it." They spare us in nothing and treat us with harshness. It is quite the contrary for the Osages when they steal, pillage, and kill. They get nothing but caresses, and are supplied with everything. This is the way you whites are regarded by us.[2]

—Picanne (Miami)

The Osage had a set of policies which they followed with great consis tency, such as their fixed policy of opposition to intruders. Their distinction among three types of intruders was clearly defined. A traveler or party who crossed Osage territory uninvited but who used only what was necessary in their passage was one type of intruder. Uninvited individuals or groups who plundered the resources were a second type of intruder. The third type of intruder was those people who settled on Osage lands without invitation.[3]

—Louis F. Burns (Osage)

Chapter Four

Relatives and Enemies

IN THE SUMMER OF 1764, nearly six hundred Missouria men, women, and children arrived at a new French trading post that was taking shape just south of the confluence of the Mississippi and Missouri Rivers. Having been uprooted by a conflict with the Great Osages, the Missourias intended to settle in the area, in hopes that they could find a place of refuge from their enemies. A month earlier, on July 17, they had presented themselves to Captain Louis St. Ange de Bellerive, the commandant of the mostly deserted Fort de Chartres, asking for protection from the Great Osages. Lacking the manpower to protect the Missourias and the funds necessary to keep them at Fort de Chartres, St. Ange eventually persuaded them to leave, with the understanding that they would return to their village on the Missouri River.

Instead, the Missourias crossed the Mississippi River to a new post being constructed by a French trading firm owned by Gilbert Antoine Maxent and Pierre Laclède. The post would be called St. Louis. As more than two dozen earth mounds just north of the new settlement attested, the location had long been an important place for Indigenous people, and it was land on which the Missourias still had a legal right to settle. When Laclède, who was nervous at the appearance of hundreds of Indigenous people near his trading house, arrived on the scene, Missouria leaders explained their intentions. According to Laclède's nephew, Auguste Chouteau, the headmen likened themselves to waterfowl that sought open water for rest and easy sustenance. They told Laclède that in their search, "they did not find any place more suitable ... than the place where they were."[1]

According to Chouteau's recollection, Laclède threatened the Missourias by telling them that if they were indeed like waterfowl, they would be easy prey for predators in open water. If they did not leave St.

Louis for a safer place, Laclède told them, they would likely be killed. He warned them that a force of several hundred warriors, including the Missourias' enemies the Sacs, were gathering in Illinois to attack the British as soon they arrived to take possession of Fort de Chartres. Should those men learn of the Missourias' presence at St. Louis, they would likely cross the river to annihilate them. Despite this threat, Laclède was no doubt aware that the situation called for diplomacy. While he was eager to send the Missourias on their way, he understood that they were still a force to be reckoned with and that he would need their cooperation and their business if his new trading settlement was to prosper. After much discussion, Missouria leaders agreed to return home under the condition that Laclède give them supplies and provide them with much-needed food for the trip.[2]

A Pawn in a Global Conflict

Louisiana, the French name for the region west of the Mississippi River, had become a pawn in a global conflict that, for the most part, took place hundreds of miles away. The French and Indian War, or the Seven Years' War as it was known in Europe, pitted European powers against one another in a contest to determine who would control colonies in North America, Africa, and Asia. In North America, much of the fighting took place in present-day New England and in the Great Lakes region, where France was badly beaten by the British. With New France, or Canada, already having fallen into British hands, and fearing that he was likely to lose Louisiana to the British as well, King Louis XV of France proposed a secret deal to King Charles III of Spain in 1762. To prevent the British from taking control the entire North American continent, France offered to give Spain title to all the land La Salle had claimed in the Mississippi River watershed. King Charles accepted the offer in November, and three months later, on February 10, 1763, France, Britain, Spain, and Portugal signed the Treaty of Paris, bringing an end to the war. In the treaty, France lost nearly all of its North American empire and Britain took control of most of the land between the Appalachians and the Mississippi River; while this vast swath included some of the land France had ceded to Spain in the secret agreement, the Spanish colonial leaders were content with their new holdings west of the Mississippi River and did not contest the treaty.[3] Suddenly, the great river divided two European colonial powers, with Britain in control of Illinois, east of the river, and Spain in possession of Louisiana west of it. It would be some time before the Native inhabitants of Mississippi River Valley had the opportunity to meet their new European landlords, however. British government representatives did not reach Fort de Chartres until 1765, while Spanish officials did not arrive to take formal possession of Louisiana until 1766.

News of the terms of the treaty of Paris and the pending arrival of the British quickly led many French residents to move across the river from Illinois to Louisiana. Prior to the war, the few settlements, posts, and forts established west of the Mississippi River had been short lived. It was not until the founding of Ste. Genevieve, in present-day Missouri, sometime around 1750, that Europeans settled permanently in Upper Louisiana. Ste. Genevieve had been established by residents of Kaskaskia, which was located just across the Mississippi River, on the Illinois side. Though there were substantial salt and lead deposits nearby, the town was originally created to be an agricultural community. With Britain's victory in the French and Indian War, French residents concerned about the prospect of living under British rule fled Kaskaskia and other nearby communities to settle in Ste. Genevieve. Similarly, residents living in the northern French towns around Cahokia helped the new settlement of St. Louis expand rapidly after the war. Some had even dismantled their homes, moving lumber, doors, and windows across the river along with their livestock, machinery, and personal belongings.[4]

St. Louis on the Rise

St. Louis began as a trading post constructed by a New Orleans trading firm owned by Gilbert Antoine Maxent and Pierre Laclède. In July 1763, The French colonial government in New Orleans awarded Maxent an exclusive trading license for the Mississippi River Valley. He established a warehouse at the village of Chartres in Illinois but decided to move his business west of the river in the face of the coming British government. Laclède is credited with choosing to situate the new post north of the site of the old Kaskaskia mission that had briefly been located on the River Des Peres in 1700. At the time of St. Louis's founding, the area already was, as we have seen, home to Indigenous and French people. A few French settlers had remained near the old mission site, while Clement Delor de Treget had established the village that would eventually be known as Carondelet on the Mississippi shortly before Laclède's arrival.

The post's location near the confluence of the Mississippi and Missouri Rivers made it an ideal spot from which to traffic goods between

Indigenous towns and French settlements both near and far. Despite Laclède's dismissal of the Missourias, Indigenous people became a common sight in St. Louis and were an integral part of its success. As historian Patricia Cleary has pointed out, "St. Louis was in Indian territory, its very existence as a center of fur trade dependent on the tolerance on the Indians' part of the villagers' presence as well as their willingness to engage in trade." In fact, Osages trading partners played such an indispensable part in the existence of St. Louis that historian J. Frederick Fausz labeled them "co-founders" of a "one-industry town." As word of the new French town circulated among Indigenous nations, many Native representatives visited to offer terms of kinship and seek out the prospects of trading there. Traders from the region's Native towns regularly visited St. Louis with furs to exchange for European trade goods. Because of its central location and its easy river access, the confluence region had long been an important gathering place where members of various nations came together to meet, either diplomatically or commercially. And even after the founding of St. Louis, Natives continued to gather there to conduct business unrelated to the French. Eventually, groups of Indigenous people did come to settle in the area around the town. For example, one group of Peorias who had fled Illinois settled just two miles downriver from St. Louis in 1766, apparently with Laclède's approval.[5]

The historian Patricia Cleary has referred to early St. Louis as a "place without borders." This is to say, that in its first years the settlement was one made up of many overlapping cultural, political, and geographical communities. As a riverport and administrative center, the village was visited by traders, clergy, government officials, and soldiers. As St. Louis grew, it became a place where French, Native, Métis, free people of color, enslaved people all came together to work and live. Despite the lack of borders, however, colonists had constructed a strict social order in the new community. Catholic clergy, military officers, and merchant-traders were at the top of the hierarchy. Below them were common soldiers, boatmen, hunters, trappers, and permanent settlers. At the bottom of the hierarchy were enslaved Africans and Natives. The place of Métis, persons of French and black or Indigenous heritage, in this hierarchy was largely determined by the social rank of their French—usually male—parent. By 1770, just six years after the founding of St. Louis, the town of about 257 people was home to seventy-five enslaved persons. Of those who were held in bondage, sixty-nine were Indigenous.[6]

IMAGE 6: *Painting of An Indian Woman* by Anna Maria Von Phul, 1818. Indigenous people were a common sight in Missouri towns and villages throughout the nineteenth century. In this painting of a woman in St. Louis in 1818, artist Anna Maria Von Phul recorded the manner in which Natives had adopted European-American-made goods such as trade blankets into their traditional dress. *Courtesy of the Missouri Historical Society*

On the east side of the Mississippi River, Indigenous resentment of the change from French to British colonial rule was simmering. Even before British Captain Thomas Stirling arrived at Fort de Chartres to relieve St. Ange in October 1765, the sentiments of both Natives and French citizens in the Illinois Country had become largely anti-British. While the British believed the French had intentionally turned the Indigenous population against them, much of the Native resentment toward the British had been created by the French and Indian War. The

Ottawa leader Pontiac, who had led pan-Indigenous forces against the British in the Great Lakes, had a powerful influence over many of the Natives living in Illinois. Pontiac had married an Illinois woman and visited Fort de Chartres more than once to recruit warriors from among her people. In November 1764, Pontiac sent coded wampum belts to several nations in the area. These belts expressed his anger at the British by depicting them as the "most cruel enemies around." Several Natives came to the fort confirming the widespread hatred of the British and asking for weapons to use against them. St. Ange tried to convince the Natives that the new British government was coming in peace, and not to fight against them.[7]

In April 1765, a delegation of Osages, Missourias, Peorias, Cahokias, Michigameas, and Kaskaskias met with British Lieutenant John Ross of Britain's 34th Regiment and St. Ange at Fort de Chartres. The Indigenous delegates wanted to express their concern over the imminent transfer of Illinois to Britain. The initial meeting quickly turned hostile. The Kaskaskia headman Tamarois told Ross that his people did not want the British on their land. All the Indigenous leaders in attendance agreed and vowed to continue to resist the British presence. A few days later, one of the Osages attempted to kill Ross with a hatchet. After St. Ange intervened to save the British officer, the Osage man declared that he had promised Pontiac that he would "strike at all Englishmen." He vowed that while he had been prevented from taking Ross's life on that day, he would wait patiently to have his satisfaction later.[8]

That summer, several leaders of regional Indigenous nations also met with British Colonel George Croghan. They informed him that they would tolerate British "possession of the posts in their country," only if it meant increased trade. Otherwise, they would continue to do business with the French across the river in Upper Louisiana. The leaders then reminded Croghan that since the French had not conquered the Natives, nor had they purchased any of their land, Indigenous people still controlled Illinois. The original inhabitants had given the French "liberty to settle" there only because they had generally treated them well and paid for the privilege with gifts, kinship, and trade. Croghan learned that the British, too, would be expected to give the Indigenous people "proper returns" if they wanted to remain.[9]

In October 1765, British Captain Thomas Stirling finally arrived with eight barges and one hundred soldiers from New Orleans to formally take possession of Fort de Chartres. Upon landing, the British were dismayed to discover that the fort had been emptied of anything useful, and somewhat amused to find that St. Ange and the few French soldiers who remained at the fort appeared to be little more than "old men looking like invalids without any sort of uniform." After the official transfer of the fort, St. Ange and his men retreated to St. Louis, leaving the British to fend for themselves. Almost immediately, Stirling succeeded in making a bad first impression with the Indigenous population. Representatives from several nations came to meet the commander of the fort and to establish diplomatic relations with the British but were disappointed to find there were no interpreters to help them communicate and no gifts to exchange with them.[10]

It is difficult to overstate the importance Natives placed on the ritual of exchanging gifts. Indigenous headmen viewed gift giving as an important symbol of friendship, trust, and reciprocity. The exchange of gifts reinforced kinship bonds and business ties and were an important part of Indigenous relations with European colonizers. Unlike their French predecessors, who had understood the importance of rituals of kinship and gift giving, the British had chosen to take a harder line with the Natives and, due to their depleted national treasury, were trying to control Illinois as cheaply as possible.

Kathleen DuVal has observed that the Indigenous people of Illinois and Louisiana during this time could not accurately be labeled as pro-British, pro-Spanish, or pro-French. They were, she writes, "pro-themselves." They looked after their own interests and allied themselves with the European or Indigenous powers that were most likely to help them attain their goals. For this reason, the British never enjoyed the monopoly on trade in Illinois that they may have expected. With St. Louis and Ste. Genevieve just across the river, Indigenous traders in Illinois still had easy access to French goods. Traders like Laclède and Chouteau had made strong ties to the Osages and other nations and were on their way to becoming a dominant trading force in the region. Indeed, the British began to realize that the French had moved their trade business, as well as nearly all serviceable weapons, from the Fort de Chartres garrison to St. Louis and would prevent them from controlling the region. As they would soon find out, the imminent arrival of Spanish officials in St. Louis in 1766 would do nothing to remedy that situation.[11]

Like Britain, Spain's involvement in several European wars had brought it to the brink of financial insolvency. Because of this, it was ill prepared to take control of its new colony. After turning Fort de Chartres over to the British, Captain St. Ange had become acting civil and military administrator for Upper Louisiana. His deep knowledge of the territory and four decades of governmental experience in the region, especially in Indian affairs, made him a valuable advisor to Spanish colonial officials. Even after the first Spanish governor of Louisiana, Antonio de Ulloa, arrived in New Orleans nearly three and a half years after the signing of the Treaty of Paris, Spain continued to rely on St. Ange to administer the territory. The following year, in September 1767, the first Spanish representative in Upper Louisiana, Captain Francisco Ríu, arrived in St. Louis with a contingent of forty soldiers. While St. Ange remained in charge of St. Louis, Ríu was focused on building fortifications near the confluence of the Mississippi and Missouri Rivers. The Spaniards hoped these forts would keep British traders from reaching Indigenous villages on the Missouri River and its tributaries.[12]

Osage historian Louis F. Burns has posited that French policy toward Natives was "harsh" but carried out in an "enlightened" way, while the Spaniards' policies were generally enlightened but carried out in a harsh way. A prime example of this were *The Requirements*, a long announcement which was to be read aloud each time Spanish Conquistadors encountered a group of Indigenous people for the first time. *The Requirements* explained to the Natives that the Pope had "donated" their land to the Spanish crown, which now owned it. Should the Natives accept that they were now Spanish subjects, the soldiers would receive them in "all love and charity," and they would be allowed to live "free without servitude." However, should the Indigenous people reject Spanish rule, Spaniards would "powerfully enter into [their] country, and make war against [them] in all ways and manners." Moreover, they would subject them to the "yoke and obedience" of the Church. While the Spaniards may have seen this threat as a benevolent invitation to a peaceful relationship, *The Requirements* were often simply a formality to be read aloud—in Latin—as soldiers prepared to storm into Indigenous towns to pillage and kill.[13]

While the Spaniards had used this forceful tactic to great effect in Mexico, Texas, and Florida, they lacked the military resources to implement *The Requirements* and the campaigns of terror associated with it in Upper Louisiana. Like the French and British colonial governments, Spanish officials in the Missouri River valley were severely understaffed, and the few resources at their disposal were directed at preventing

British traders from encroaching into their territory. Thus, Spanish officials were forced to rely on knowledgeable French administrators, such as St. Ange, and established French traders, like Laclède and Chouteau, to help them manage the colony through alliances and trade. The Spaniards realized that if they were to keep British traders out of Upper Louisiana and keep French traders in check, they would have to treat the region's Indigenous population more fairly and humanely than they had elsewhere. Governor Ulloa advised Ríu to, "exercise a great deal of tact and care with the Savages," and make them believe that the Spaniards are on their lands "because they want us [on it]. . . ."[14]

Spaniards attempted to create a more equitable system of trade through restrictions, licenses, price regulations, and a ban on the use of liquor in trade negotiations. Louisiana governor Ulloa quickly made a serious misstep with Indigenous nations and St. Louis merchants alike when he issued new trade policies. These protocols prohibited traders from traveling to Native towns in Upper Louisiana without a license—a license that could be obtained only in New Orleans, which was no less than a three-month round trip from St. Louis by boat. Angered by this threat to their business, St. Louis merchants, who relied on the fur trade for their livelihood, declared that they would no longer sell goods to the Spaniards and appealed to St. Ange for help.

Similarly, a delegation of Pawnees, Otoes, Kanzas, and Great and Little Osages met with Ríu in St. Louis to express their displeasure at the trade restrictions. A Kanza leader recounted for the commandant the many ways that the French had treated them well when they had controlled Louisiana. Declaring that Spanish authorities were not living up to French standards of gift giving and diplomacy, the headman walked out of the meeting and was followed by the remaining delegates. Most likely on the advice of St. Ange's, Ríu rescinded the order requiring trade licenses. Perhaps in response to this debacle, Ulloa soon removed Ríu from his post and replaced him with Captain Don Pedro Piernas, who would become Upper Louisiana's first Lieutenant Governor.[15]

With the arrival of each new Spanish administrator in St. Louis, representatives of many of the Native nations in the region came to meet with the new official and pay him a diplomatic visit. St. Ange had prepared a list of Indigenous nations that were "accustomed to receive presents" (under the French), which he gave to the Spanish leaders in 1769. Those on the list included the Ioways, Kaskaskias, Sacs, Foxes, Sioux, Kickapoos, Ojibwas, and Cahokias. Captain Piernas reported that soon after his arrival in St. Louis, delegates from these nations and others visited him. Ever conscious of keeping down expenses, Piernas held meetings with Native visitors north of town at the newly constructed Fort San Carlos. He reasoned that were he to entertain the delegates in St. Louis, they would be likely to stay longer and, in so doing, incur additional expenses for meals and lodging. Piernas and St. Ange were also careful to ration the number of gifts they presented to their visitors. Obviously disappointed, the Indigenous delegates perceived that the Spaniards' stinginess was meant to offend, and so informed their hosts that even their British competitors were more generous.[16]

Indigenous nations did not particularly care where the trade goods they wished to receive originated. They were far more concerned with the quality and cost of the merchandise, mutual bonds with traders created by gift giving, and the fairness with which Europeans treated them. For those reasons, the British had already made trade inroads with Osages and Missourias before any Spanish officials had arrived in St. Louis. This was due in part to the fact that the British had hired French Canadian coureurs de bois to transport merchandise to Indigenous towns on the Missouri River and its tributaries. To undercut the Spanish colonial government's effectiveness, the British had also gone out of their way to appease the Osages and Missourias with gifts and had even succeeded in luring them across the Mississippi River to Kaskaskia to trade on a regular basis. The fact that, as early as 1767, British Union Jacks could be seen flying over some Osage and Missouria villages bore testament to the success of their efforts.[17]

Eager not to allow the British to turn the region's Native population against them and to retain access to their main suppliers of furs, Spanish officials in St. Louis realized they needed to foment a more favorable relationship with the Missourias and Little Osages by matching the generosity of the British. However, even these overtures failed to win over the Natives. In fact, some Great and Little Osages moved their villages west and south, farther from the Spanish authorities in St. Louis but still within range of British traders. The Missourias and Little Osages also became more aggressive in displaying their displeasure with Spaniards. They captured traders on the Missouri and Des Moines Rivers and diverted the cargos toward their own towns. They also conducted raids to steal horses at St. Louis and Ste. Genevieve.[18]

After Missourias and Little Osages killed three hunters and captured two others on the Des Moines River, Spanish authorities retaliated with another trade embargo. Angered by the new restrictions, one hundred armed Missourias and Little Osages showed their strength—and highlighted the Spaniards' weakness—by forcing their way into Fort San Carlos in July 1772. They overpowered the handful of soldiers guarding the installation and commandeered the stores of ammunition and food the fleeing troops left behind. The following day, several of the Natives made their way to nearby St. Louis, where they entered the village in a threatening manner and raised the Union Jack near the river. Spanish soldiers, enlisting the help of armed French villagers, managed to take down the flag and to prevent any real violence.[19]

The Missourias and Little Osages almost immediately expressed remorse for their actions and Spanish officials chose not to punish them. This earned the Missourias and Little Osages the ire of other Indigenous nations who were allied with the Spanish government. The day following their entrance into the village, the attackers were themselves assaulted outside St. Louis by a group of Potawatomis and Ojibwas from Illinois. Two Little Osage headmen died in the attack, while the rest of the Little Osages force fell back into the village seeking refuge from their assailants. Spanish officials relished the sudden turn of events and pointed out to the Missourias and Little Osages that, without the protection they had found in the village, they would have been destroyed. The defeated Natives hurried back to the villages after promising the Spaniards they would conduct themselves better in the future.[20]

Despite Spain's periodic use of trade embargos as tools to punish the Osages, there was no shortage of traders who were eager to fill the void. This was especially true because, during periods of peace when trade was normalized, the Osages alone accounted for more than half of the Missouri fur and slave trade that came through St. Louis. In the fall of 1772, a British trade expedition, led by the French-Canadian trader Jean-Marie Ducharme, thwarted a Spanish embargo by crossing over from Illinois and making its way up the Missouri River without being detected. The expedition succeeded in reaching the villages of the Osages, where they traded throughout the winter. Upon learning of Ducharme's brazen defiance of Spanish restrictions, Lieutenant Governor Piernas sent a group of volunteers, led by Pierre Laclède, to apprehend the trader and his cargo. The party encountered Ducharme on the Missouri River as he was making his way back to Illinois. While the trader escaped arrest, Laclède's party captured many of his men and all the hides the Osages had traded him over the winters.[21]

Laclède and the Chouteaus also saw Spanish trade restrictions as opportunities to build their business. After losing their exclusive right to trade on the Missouri in 1769, Laclède and Maxent had dissolved their partnership. Laclède went into business for himself and soon employed his stepson, Auguste Chouteau, who was then in his early twenties. They also hired Laclède's son and Chouteau's younger half-brother, Pierre Chouteau. The Laclède/Chouteau family proved to be masterful in its ability to profit by creating relationships, not only with Indigenous people but also with colonial officials. As a result of their business savvy, their firm rapidly grew and prospered.[22]

Relationships between French traders and Indigenous people changed both French and Native communities a great deal from the seventeenth century onward. By the time the Spanish colonial government arrived in St. Louis, many of the citizens there and in surrounding communities were second- or third-generation Métis. Métis, who were the multicultural descendants of French and Indigenous parents, were eligible to live in higher levels of the social hierarchy in Louisiana. The boys were a much-needed source of labor, while young Christian Métis women often married men who were habitants, or permanent residents of the community. Despite their multicultural ancestry, Métis were not socially segregated and received full protection of the law.[23]

In Indigenous towns, there were generally two types of intermarriages between French men and Indigenous women. Coureurs de bois entered informal, and often temporary, marriages with widows or young women from less prominent Indigenous families. Prominent traders like the Chouteaus entered more formal marriages with women from more prestigious families. In the case of the Chouteaus, the traders' success with the Osages hinged in part on their ability to conform to Indigenous expectations as well as prove their value as good husbands and relatives. These responsibilities were not to be taken lightly. A family's status in the Osage nation was dependent on the men's ability to share wealth and distribute gifts to members of the community. By marrying men like the Chouteaus, or any wealthy man from outside the community, Osage women were able to bring status and respectability to their families. Such marriages also ensured that members of the Indigenous women's families had direct access to much sought after trade goods.[24]

While Laclède ran the business from St. Louis until his death in 1778, the two Chouteaus spent their time in the field. As they entered the complex world of Osage culture and business, the brothers first relied heavily on Métis traders to act as intermediaries between them and the Osages. Over time, however, both Auguste and Pierre Chouteau forged their own kinship ties with the nation, each marrying Osage "country wives" and becoming adopted members of the nation. Both the Chouteaus and the Osages saw marriage as a strategic way to gain wealth and status. For example, Pierre Chouteau married into the family of Noel Mongraine. Mongraine, an interpreter of Osage and French ancestry, married Marie Pawhushan, the daughter of the powerful Osage headman Pawhuska, or White Hair. The Mongraines were also linked to the biracial Osage *Hun Ka* headman Jean Lafond, who, according to Burns, was also the uncle of the future Osage headman Clermont II. As we will see, these familial connections not only gave Osages access to the most successful traders in St. Louis, but also allowed them the opportunity to exercise a great deal of influence over the city's economic wellbeing.[25]

A Struggle for Power

Trade proved to be an ongoing issue of contention between the Osages and the Spanish colonial government, especially because the Osages dictated the terms of doing business. Not only were the Spanish rulers nearly powerless to rein in the Osages, but they also had to appease them to have any hope of administering Upper Louisiana peacefully. With a strength of eight hundred fighting men in the 1770s, the Great Osages had the power to force Spain to accede to their demands.

Geography, too, played an important role in the Great Osages ability to circumvent the Spanish regulation of the terms of Osage trade. The so-called Arkansas Osages lived near the site at which the Neosho and Verdigris Rivers met the Arkansas River, in present-day Oklahoma. The remainder of the Great Osages were located on the Osage River, near the present-day border of Missouri and Kansas. From this location they had easy access to important western water routes like the Red River and the Arkansas River. The Osages could also control those routes to diminish European access to western trade.[26]

As historian Tai S. Edwards has observed, the introduction of European trade goods into the Mississippi River Valley and the central plains and prairies provided the Osages with the means to increase the power they had over Indigenous enemies. Just as they were able to prevent Europeans from free use of western rivers, the Osages could also prevent Native rivals from doing so. This allowed them essentially to deny their enemies the ability to acquire weapons and horses, two items that greatly enhanced the power of any group in the region.[27]

The Great Osages possessed enough strength to exert a limited amount of control over Spanish trade. During embargoes against them, Osages were often able to capture boats laden with goods that were headed farther north on the Missouri River to Osage rivals, the Otoes, Kanzas, Ioways, and Pawnees. The Osages would threaten, though not generally harm, the traders and divert the trade goods intended for the other groups to their own villages. These Osage blockades put Spain in a difficult position. If Spaniards could not move trade goods past the Osages, to Indigenous nations living on the upper Missouri River, the latter tribes would turn to British traders to obtain the supplies they needed. Should this happen, the Missouri River nations were likely to procure more weaponry than the Spanish traders were willing to sell them. This, in turn, could lead to even more conflict between these nations and the Osages.[28]

Spain tried to diminish the power of the Great Osages by banning the trade of livestock and enslaved Indigenous persons. Both had been highly profitable commodities and were the result of Osage raids in the West. Enslaved people generally came from the captives taken during Osage attacks on Caddoan people, while the Osages managed to rustle livestock and horses from Spanish communities in Texas and New Mexico. However, even after the ban, Great Osages used their connections to French and British traders to continue an illicit trade in both enslaved people and horses.[29]

Historian Kathleen DuVal has suggested that the Osages were, "far more successful than either France or Spain at building a mid-continental empire." Their power in numbers, advantageous location, and ability to play competing European powers off one another made it possible for them to expand their geographical sphere of influence during the Spanish regime. Osages were also able to overcome Kiowas, Pawnees, Wichitas, and Comanches to push their own territory as far west as the Oklahoma panhandle and south to the Red River. Their relatives, the Little Osages, continued to live on the Missouri River and, with their allies the Missourias, hunted well north of the Missouri. For much of the second half of the nineteenth century, the Osages were the most successful expansionist power in all of Louisiana.[30]

The arrival of Euro-Americans in the Mississippi River Valley after the American Revolution further complicated matters of trade for

Spain. In the war, the British lost control of all land between Illinois and the East Coast. Though the British were bound by the 1783 Treaty of Paris to vacate the area, their traders continued to travel south from bases in Prairie du Chien and the Great Lakes to do business with the Osages and other Indigenous Nations in Spanish Louisiana. US traders located just across the Mississippi River were also making illegal trips into the Osage territory to trade. As a result, the Osages had little difficulty getting enough guns and ammunition to make them better armed than most of their rivals.[31]

The Osages were, however, about to experience new threats to their territory. Even before the American War for Independence ended, the United States had undertaken what military historian John Grenier has termed an "unlimited war" against Native inhabitants who lived between the Appalachians and Illinois, on what was then called the Northwest Frontier. While the Kickapoos and Shawnees had allied themselves with the British, the Delawares had explicitly pledged their neutrality in the war. Nonetheless, a white American campaign to capture British forts in 1778 turned into what Grenier has called a "slaughter of innocents," as US soldiers indiscriminately attacked Kickapoo, Shawnee, and Delaware men, women, and children in what is now western Pennsylvania. The chaos reverberated west all the way to the Mississippi River, as Kickapoos, Shawnees, and Delawares fled their homes and moved west to escape the violence. Some of these Native refugees found their way to the Mississippi River Valley and, by the 1780s, into Spanish Louisiana.[32]

Spanish colonial leaders saw that it would be to their advantage to bring these Indigenous immigrants into Louisiana and settle them where they might serve as a buffer between Spanish and French settlers and the Osages. In July 1787, Lieutenant Governor François Cruzat granted one thousand two hundred Shawnees and six hundred Delawares permission to settle north of Ste. Genevieve, a village that for years had lost horses in raids conducted by the Little Osages and Missourias.[33] At the same time, Spanish authorities invited members from several nations of the Illinois Confederacy to settle in the eastern Ozarks, near the White and St. Francis Rivers, land that constituted the heart of Osage territory. This had been a region that both helped to protect the Osages from enemies and provided them with some of their most valuable resources. Farther south, near the Arkansas River, groups of Miamis requested permission to seek refuge from Euro-Americans in Spanish territory.

Although this was Quapaw land, the Spanish commandant at Arkansas Post, Joseph Valliere, approved the request.[34]

While these new settlers helped solve a problem for the Spaniards, they created new challenges for the Osages. When the Shawnees and Delawares began to encroach on Osage hunting land, the Osages violently defended their territory. The Osages' problems were, however, compounded as other immigrant Indigenous nations forced across the river by violence in the East also began encroaching on their land. The Potawatomis, Ioways, Kickapoos, Sacs, and Foxes in the north and the Cherokees, Choctaws, and Chickasaws in the south, all roamed onto Osage land to hunt and trap. Determined to protect their territory against any unwelcome interlopers, be they Indigenous or European, the Osages struck back in a wave of violence that claimed the lives of not only Natives but also several French traders. As Osages attacked homes of Spanish and French citizens and stole horses near St. Louis and Ste Genevieve, inhabitants of Louisiana clambered for the Spanish colonial government to do something to stop the violence and punish the perpetrators. Among the loudest voices for retribution was that of Louis Lorimier, a French-Canadian trader who had helped the Shawnees settle in Missouri and later became the commandant of the settlement of Cape Girardeau. In response, the lieutenant governor of Upper Louisiana, Manuel Pérez, demanded concessions from the Osages. Pérez also insisted that they execute one of their tribesmen who had killed a Euro-American. Not surprisingly, the Osages simply ignored these demands.[35]

Frustrated with the situation, Louisiana Governor Francisco Luis Héctor, the Baron de Carondelet, with the approval of King Charles IV of Spain, formally declared war on the Osages in June 1793. In trying to determine how best to conduct their offensive, the Spaniards faced some harsh realities. The first of these was the fact that Osage fighting men significantly outnumbered Spanish forces. During the late eighteenth century and early nineteenth century, the total Osage population was between eight thousand and ten thousand persons. Based on those numbers, Burns believed that they had about two thousand "prime-age warriors." In reserve, Osages could also field approximately a thousand young and aged fighters as well as an unknown number of women skilled in the use of weaponry. According to a 1771 census, the total non-Native population of Upper and Lower Louisiana comprised 11,344 men, women, and children, a number that more than matched that of the Osages. Of this total, however, more than forty-six hundred were enslaved. Burns calculated that from the remaining six thousand seven hundred or so free-persons, Spain could only muster a fighting force of eight hundred to a thousand men. And even then, few of these Spanish soldiers would have been as well trained as the Osage warriors.[36]

To overcome this disadvantage, the Spanish authorities considered employing Indigenous proxy fighters against the Osages. This, too, presented challenges, not the least of which was that few Native nations liked or trusted the Spaniards. As we have seen, over the years of Spanish control, the officials' efforts at frugality in the administration of Indian affairs had alienated several potential allies. In general, Native groups perceived Spaniards as being aloof and indifferent to Native people, so the Spanish colonists were not nearly as successful at creating kinship bonds and alliances with Indigenous people as were the French. As a result, when Spain tried to enlist Native groups to ally with or fight for them in military campaigns, they enjoyed only tepid success. As Burns described it, Spanish diplomacy followed a predictable pattern; "Speeches are made that promise support against a despised enemy; some token raids are made; powder and ball are issued, and the support fades away."[37]

Osage historian John Joseph Mathews described Spain's campaign against the Osages as a "tribal war" in which many longtime enemies of the Osage, the Potawatomis, Sacs, Foxes, Shawnees, Miamis, Caddos, and others, launched attacks against the Osages on Spain's behalf. Spanish soldiers, however, refused to leave the confines of Fort San Carlos to support their Native allies, even when Osages stood within view of the fortification and taunted them. In the end, while violent attacks did occur, there was never a proper "war." This was due in part to the Native fighters' realization that Spain was too weak to offer the assistance they had promised in either manpower or weaponry. Furthermore, Indigenous warriors from the various groups, who had their own reasons for wanting to fight the Osages, were never able to unite into a cohesive force to effectively combat them. Likewise, the Spanish leaders never succeed in coordinating their proxy fighters into anything resembling a strategic battle force.[38]

Nevertheless, the Spanish war with the Osages did have one unintended tragic consequence: the violence associated with the offensive served in some ways to affect the devastation of the Missouria nation. The Missourias had been engaged in a feud with the Sacs that dated back to their battle in Detroit in 1712. This long-running enmity had resulted in several more battles and much bloodshed over the decades. By the 1790s, the Sacs and Foxes, who were solid allies of the British, had been well-supplied with British weapons. Spain, too, had provided the Sacs and Foxes with muskets, lead, and powder in their efforts to persuade them to attack the Osages. This fire power made the Sacs a particularly deadly foe. There is some evidence to indicate that the Spaniards incited the Sacs to attack the Little Osages on the Missouri River and that Missourias, who were fighting alongside the Little Osages, bore the brunt of the attack. Other reports indicate that the violence was directed solely at the Missourias. What is known is that in 1792 or 1793, the Missourias suffered heavy losses after one or more violent encounters with the Sacs and Foxes. Historian Michael Dickey has estimated that nearly four hundred Missourias died in those battles. Those who survived dispersed to live with other nations including the Osages, Kanzas, and Ioways. Most of the remaining Missourias, however, moved west into present-day Nebraska with their Chiwere relatives, the Otoes. As Dickey laments, "The tribe that seventy years earlier had prevented French expeditions and traders from going up the Missouri River unchecked was finished as an independent nation."[39]

Finally, in 1794, Spanish Governor Carondelet in New Orleans elected to end the war against the Osages to confront a new crisis, a new war with France. France had recently undergone a revolution that had overthrown the monarchy in 1789. In 1793, as tensions between the two nations mounted, Spain declared war on revolutionary France. Concerned about the loyalty of Louisiana's large francophone population, Spanish colonial authorities began to fear the possibility of an uprising from within their own population. Such worries were not without warrant. In early 1794, France recruited US Revolutionary War hero George Rogers Clark to lead an army of French loyalists into Spanish Louisiana. Concerned about a possible "French" invasion, citizens in New Madrid, Ste. Genevieve, Cape Girardeau, and St. Louis prepared defense fortifications. Though Clark reportedly recruited two thousand Kentuckians who were willing to pledge allegiance to France and march on Louisiana, the invasion never materialized.[40]

Still determined to improve relations with the Osages, Spanish Lieutenant Governor Zenon Trudeau agreed to Auguste Chouteau's plan to build a fort near the Great Osages. With their long experience in living and trading with the Osages, Trudeau rightly believed that the Chouteaus were likely to succeed in peacefully having the installation built in Osage territory. To formalize the agreement, Chouteau traveled in the company of six Osage headmen to New Orleans in the Spring of 1794 to meet with Governor Carondelet. There, the trader laid out his plan. Chouteau offered to operate and maintain the fort, which his half-brother, Pierre Chouteau, would command. In return, he asked for a six-year monopoly on trade with the Osages and two thousand pesos per year to pay the salaries of the small detachment of soldiers who would garrison the fort. Carondelet approved the plan, and the contract with Chouteau was signed in May 1794. However, an incident occurred on the Chouteau delegation's return trip home that would have long-lasting implications for the Osages leadership structure. As Chouteau and company made their way back to St. Louis, their boat was attacked by a group of Chickasaws. In the attack, three of the Osage leaders, including Jean Lafond, one of the two most important Great Osage leaders, lost their lives.[41]

The Chickasaws' killing of Jean Lafond on the Mississippi River upset the balance of Osage power. At the time of his death, Lafond was the leader of the Osage Earth People, one of two main divisions of the nation, while Clermont I was the leader of the other division, the Sky People. Because both men lived in the Osage River villages, the Great Osages there held power and influence over Osages living elsewhere. Spain hoped that by building Chouteau's new fort on the Osage River, they could help these villages hold their strength. With Lafond's death, however, the Earth People chose a new leader, Big Track, who lived with the Arkansas River bands of the Great Osages. For the first time, Osage power was split between two groups living far apart.[42]

Even before Lafond's murder, the Chouteau brothers had been working to alter Osage leadership by helping their friend and relative, the headman Pawhuska, unseat Clermont I as leader of the Sky People. Because of their kinship bond and business ties, the Chouteaus believed they could increase their own influence over the Osages and enhance their lucrative trade endeavors by strengthening Pawhuska's position within the Osage nation. To this end, Auguste Chouteau and Pawhuska used their meeting with Carondelet to actively diminish Clermont I's position of leadership. They were aided by the fact the Clermont had not attended the meeting. Afraid for his safety, he had refused to make the trip to New Orleans, instead sending Pawhuska to represent him. In their meetings with Carondelet, Chouteau persuaded the governor that Pawhuska was by far the more powerful and capable of the two leaders. Under the false impression that Clermont I was considered to be incompetent by his own people, Carondelet awarded a large medal to Lafond, recognizing him as the "Head Chief" of the Osages and bestowed a smaller medal on Pawhuska in recognition of his position as "Second Chief" of the Osages.[43]

After the meeting, then, the Chouteaus used Lafond's death to further mold the perceptions of Spanish officials in their favor. They persuaded the governor and lieutenant governor that, considering the recent vacancy in leadership, Pawhuska was now the legitimate "Head Chief" of the Osages. Based on the Chouteaus' recommendation, Pawhuska received a large medal from the Spanish, now making him the leader of all Osages. Shortly thereafter, between 1795 and 1800, Clermont I died.[44]

The tragedy of this manipulation notwithstanding, the Great Osages were pleased with Chouteau's plans for the new fort. They did not see the installation as an extension of the Spanish empire. Instead, they believed it symbolized Spain's recognition of Osage power and strength. Even though the structure was supposed to be a military fortification protected by soldiers and arms, which could potentially be used against them, the Osages knew that any sort of defenses the fort might house would be no match for their warriors. In the end, the fort was little more than an armed government-sanctioned trading post built within eyesight of Pawhuska's village. As Lieutenant Governor Zenon Trudeau reported to Carondelet, because the fort was on Osage land, they treated it as though it was their own. Not surprisingly, other Indigenous nations in the region angrily viewed the fort as a symbol of the Spanish government's preferential treatment of the Osages. Most notable among the critics of the fort was the Miami headman Picanne, who complained that even though the Osages were responsible for a great deal of violence, they "get nothing but caresses and are supplied with everything."[45]

As the site for Fort Carondolet, the Chouteaus chose a high spot on the south bank of the Osage River called Halley's Bluff, in what is now Vernon County. Named, obviously, after the Spanish governor of Louisiana, the structure was to be solidly built according to his specifications. Plans called for a thirty-two-foot square, two-story blockhouse. The first story of the blockhouse was to be made of stone. The second story, constructed of wood, would be set diagonally on top of the first to provide the soldiers with a clear view in eight directions. As there are no known drawings or maps of Fort Carondelet, more than one historian has speculated that Auguste Chouteau may have skimped on materials and expenses during the fort's construction, while preventing Spanish officials from finding out. The fact that government representatives apparently never visited the remote fort indicates that the Spaniards had complete trust in the Chouteaus.[46]

Much to the chagrin of the Chouteaus' St. Louis competitors, Fort Carondolet proved to be a boon for the brothers' business interests. The location of their new enterprise among the Great Osage and their monopoly on Osage trade assured them nearly half of all business passing through St. Louis. More than two hundred miles west of the Mississippi River, the new post also gave them a base from which to expand trade even farther west. Pierre Chouteau and his son Auguste Pierre Chouteau set up a new trading post in present-day Oklahoma at the point where the Verdigris and Neosho Rivers meet the Arkansas. The post would cater to two new Osage villages that had been established by Clermont II, the young son of Clermont I, and Le Chenier, two Osage leaders who had broken away from the Great Osages near Fort Carondolet.[47]

Even with the new fort and trade expansion, the Chouteaus were unable to prevent certain persistent problems, chief of which was that the Osages continued to undertake violent retaliatory raids against anyone who invaded their territory. In one notable example, members of the Natchitoches Confederation attacked a semi-permanent Osage hunting camp on the Arkansas River, destroying a ceremonial lodge and killing Clermont I's father-in-law. Though Pierre Chouteau tried to dissuade the Osages from going on a mourning war, his entreaties failed to prevent a party of one hundred warriors from seeking vengeance. Two years later, as more and more violence involving the Osages kept erupting, the Chouteaus' St. Louis trade competitors attempted to use the incidents to discredit the brothers and leverage an end to their monopolistic trading practices. Auguste Chouteau defended himself to Carondelet by fixing the blame for the Osage violence on a few "insubordinate individuals who break loose from the general mass to abandon themselves to the excesses of their barbarism."[48]

By 1799, the violence still seemed to be never ending. The Kickapoos, Potawatomis, Sacs, Foxes, and various groups of Illinois hunters were crossing the Mississippi River to hunt, conduct raids to steal horses, and, when the opportunity arose, attack the Osages. The number of Euro-Americans on Osage land was increasing, too. In March 1800, Arkansas Osages were blamed for the murder of two white settlers, Adam House and his son Jacob House, on the Meramec River. Feeling the need to react forcefully, the Spanish colonial governor in New Orleans, the Marquess of Casa Calvo, sent a letter to the new lieutenant governor of Upper Louisiana, Don Carlos Dehault Delassus, urging him to dispatch Pawhuska and a group of Osage warriors from the Osage River to attack and destroy the Osages living on the Arkansas River.[49]

However, just a few days after receiving the directive, Delassus was visited in St. Louis by two hundred members of all branches of the Osages, who wished to meet with him. On August 29, with Spanish militiamen standing by, Pawhuska, the Spanish-appointed headman of all Osages, and Le Chenier, a leader of the Arkansas River band, met with the lieutenant governor and the Chouteau brothers at the government house. Spain's primary goal for the meeting was to persuade the Arkansas River Osages to move back to Pawhuska's village on the Osage River. There, Delassus and the Chouteaus were confident that the Osages could be more easily controlled and less likely to launch attacks on settlers or other Natives. For their part, the Osages had traveled to St. Louis with the intention of turning over the man accused of leading the Meramec River murders and to ask the Spaniards for forgiveness.

In council, Pawhuska declared that he was in favor of the reunification of the two Osage groups. Le Chenier claimed that he, too, believed it was a good idea for the Osages to live together once again, but stated that his young fighting men were against it and would not listen to him. Le Chenier then turned over the leader of the Meramec River attack who, accepting responsibility for the killings, was put in chains and taken to the fort for imprisonment. The events of the first day concluded at Delassus's quarters when he dined with the Chouteaus, various Spanish military officers, Pawhuska, Le Chenier, and two other Osage headsmen.[50]

On the following day, both sides spoke again to air their grievances. Delassus expressed gratitude to the Osages for bringing the murderer to him to be imprisoned. He then told Le Chenier that Governor Casa Calvo was so frustrated with the Arkansas River Osages that he had authorized him to send Pawhuska and his warriors to attack them. Casa Calvo hoped that this threat would help the two factions of the Osage understand the importance of reuniting. "Until this day," Delassus scolded the Arkansas Osages, "I had never been able to imagine that your tribe would be so deaf in hearing my words." The lieutenant governor told them that he had believed Pierre Chouteau "was the cause of the evil which you have done," and that he had considered sending this friend and relative of the Osages to New Orleans to be away from them.[51]

Cognizant that his family's trade monopoly would soon go before the Spanish government for renewal, Chouteau quickly rose to defend himself and publicly chastise the Osages. "You always lie to me," he accused them, "since you are always doing evil." Not surprisingly, Pawhuska rose in support of his friend and relative Chouteau and expressed regret for the actions of his people, stating "I bewail daily the sorrow that our young men cause thee." The Spaniards and Chouteaus concluded the talks by giving the Osages an impressive number of presents, including one hundred muskets, one hundred pounds of powder, and three hundred pounds of bullets. Also included were kettles, hatchets, knives, flints, mirrors, cloth, hats, and ribbon. At Chouteau's request, the Osages were allowed to remain in St. Louis for a few more days, during which they summoned members of the Kickapoos, Shawnees, Miamis, and "Avenakis." Upon their arrival, the representatives of these nations met with the Osages and Pierre Chouteau to discuss peace terms. With an agreement seemingly reached during this council, the group held an intertribal dance before all the Indigenous participants departed St. Louis on September 4.[52]

Increased Trade in Louisiana

If Delassus was inclined to blame the Chouteau brothers for Osage misdeeds prior to the council, his mind seems to have been changed by the traders' actions during the discussions. He wrote to Governor Casa Calvo in New Orleans to say, "I have been greatly surprised at seeing the confidence which this tribe [the Osages] places in the Messrs. Chouteau, and the manner in which they get along with them." Casa Calvo apparently accepted Delassus's observations and authorized the renewal of Auguste Chouteau's trade monopoly for four years, "because he is really worthy of it."[53]

Within a year, however, Delassus received a petition from a twenty-eight-year-old trader based in New Orleans named Manuel Lisa, asking him to end the Chouteaus' exclusive right to trade with the Osages. While St. Louis traders had long complained about the monopoly, and the secretive way in which trading licenses where issued, Lisa had joined forces with about forty other traders to challenge the status quo. Interestingly, three men who joined Lisa in the complaint, Gregory Sarpy, Charles Sanguinet, and Jacques Chauvin, all had received exclusive licenses from the Spanish colonial government to trade with Indigenous nations farther up the Missouri River. Lisa's petition essentially argued that the trade in furs was the sole resource that had "supported the commerce of Upper Louisiana," and that trade restrictions were causing a prosperous livelihood to be "forbidden to the greater part of the citizens." Consequently, claimed Lisa, "the commerce of this metropolis [St. Louis] must suffer a considerable loss."[54]

Recalling that Spain had allowed free trade in Louisiana prior to 1792, with disastrous results, Delassus quickly dismissed the idea, and forwarded Lisa's petition, with commentary, to Casa Calvo in New Orleans. Though the governor denied having responded to the petition, Lisa's request must have struck a nerve in New Orleans, because Lisa received a lengthy, though unsigned, written rebuttal. Among other points, the author lectured the petitioners that they needed to end their interest in the fur trade and "draw from the lap of agriculture," as farming was the main renewable resource that would bring real prosperity to Upper Louisiana. The writer mocked some of those who had signed the petition as "useless," and concluded that the Spanish "Government, far from having placed any obstacle in your way, has, on the contrary, favored your enterprises with all its power."[55]

Undaunted, Lisa determined that as the Spaniards planned to continue to issue exclusive trade licenses, he would work with new partners, Sarpy, Sanguinet, and François Marie Benoît, to win the Osage trade away from the Chouteaus. Lisa, Sanguinet, and representatives of the other two partners traveled to New Orleans to petition a new Spanish governor of Louisiana, Manuel de Salcedo, in June 1802. They promised Salcedo that in return for exclusive Osage trade, they would forgo the annual disbursement of two thousand pesos the crown was paying the Chouteaus and would build, at their own expense, a "water mill with two millstones with which to make flour as good as the flour of the Anglo-Americans." They claimed the mill would be of great service to Upper Louisiana because it would lessen the colony's dependence on flour made by American companies. Lisa and his partners also asserted that the mill would greatly improve the decadent state of agriculture around St. Louis.[56]

On June 12, Salcedo, believing that the offer would ultimately benefit the crown, agreed to immediately cancel the Chouteaus' exclusive trade with the Osages and award it instead to Lisa and his partners for a period of five years. Though shocked at the sudden annulment of their contract, the Chouteaus soon realized that the new deal would not entirely exclude them from Osage trade. The Chouteaus retained their contract to supply Fort Carondelet and other government installations in Louisiana, and they were also able to trade with Osages who did not live on the Missouri and Osage Rivers. This left them free to continue trade with the Arkansas River Osages. Feeling he was under no further obligation to assist Spain, Pierre Chouteau immediately reversed his previous efforts to persuade Arkansas River Osages to return north to live in Pawhuska's village. Instead, he now entreated Pawhuska's Great Osages to move south to live in the villages of either Clermont II or Big Track. Not eager to challenge Clermont II for authority, Pawhuska elected to remain on the Osage River. However, nearly three thousand, or half of all Great Osages, did make their way to the Three Forks region of the Arkansas River.[57]

The archaeologist Carl H. Chapman has written that during much of the eighteenth century, "the Osage Indians were indomitable in maintaining their position of power in the prairies on the western border of Spanish Illinois." Throughout both the French and Spanish regimes, the Osages had been the dominant power of the Osage and Arkansas Rivers. Their military strength had allowed them to protect their land from immigrant Native nations as well as from French settlers. Their economic power had allowed them to dictate the terms of trade and circumvent any draconian measures Spanish authorities might employ to control the Osage trade machine. Their partnership with the Chouteaus had helped to create the port of St. Louis, creating an international market for furs and enslaved Indigenous people. But this had all come at a cost, and by the dawn of the nineteenth century, the Osages' strength had been compromised. Burns has written that, given that their villages were now spread over a vast area and that their leadership structure had been disrupted by the Chouteaus, the nation was diminished "on the eve of their severest challenge—the coming of the Americans."[58]

Since at least 1795, the Spanish crown had concluded that it could not fully exert control over Louisiana. The cost of administering the vast colony had become prohibitive for the cash-strapped nation. In addition, Louisiana had also become difficult to defend against the British, the US (the military as well as squatters and other would-be settlers), and various Indigenous invaders. While Spain had proposed returning the colony to France several times throughout the 1790s, it was not until Napoleon Bonaparte's short-lived plan to restore a French empire in

North America that an agreement was reached. Though the Third Treaty of San Ildefonso by which Spain ceded the colony of Louisiana back to France was signed on October 1, 1800, citizens of Louisiana would not learn of the deal until the fall of 1802. By that time, the United States was just months away from signing a treaty in Paris that would make the territory part of the United States. The long period of European colonial claims in the North American heartland had come to an end, and life for Indigenous and European residents alike was, once again, on the verge of changing dramatically.[59]

Voices

The Great Spirit punishes those who deceive us, and my faith is now pledged.[1]

—*Black Hawk (Fox)*

We have beaten the enemy twice under separate commanders. We cannot expect the same good fortune always to attend us. The Americans are now led by a chief who never sleeps; the day and the night are alike to him. And, during all the time that he has been marching upon our villages, notwithstanding the watchfulness of our young men, we have never been able to surprise him. Think well of it. There is something whispers me (sic), it would be prudent to listen to his offers of peace.[2]

—*Little Turtle (Miami)*

These lands are ours. No one has a right to remove us, because we were the first owners. The Great Spirit above has appointed this place for us, on which to light our fires, and here we will remain. As to boundaries, the Great Spirit knows no boundaries, nor will his red children acknowledge any.[3]

—*Tecumseh (Shawnee)*

Do you make the writing God? The white people break the word of God;—what need of making so much of this writing?—put it into the fire.[4]

—*Mad Bear (Osage)*

You have brought poverty to us.[5]

—*Anonymous (Osage)*

Chapter Five

Invaders and Defenders

WHEN BIG TRACK FIRST LEARNED that the United States had "purchased" the Territory of Louisiana, the Osage leader refused to believe
it. He angrily threw the letter that Pierre Chouteau had sent to inform
him of the news into a fire, doubting its accuracy. The Osage told the
trader whom Chouteau had sent to deliver and read the letter to them,
that if the news were true, they would no longer be trading in St. Louis,
because they would rather trade with the British than with Americans.
Osage historian Louis F. Burns believed this was probably a bluff on the
part of the Osages, who may have believed that such a threat would lead
the United States to make concessions to them. If this was their intent,
wrote Burns, "the Osages were to be disillusioned."[1]

The Ioways and some Sacs and Foxes also learned about the land
transfer from written dispatches sent to them by Meriwether Lewis, who
was just then beginning his journey up the Missouri River with William
Clark and the Corps of Discovery. Because the trader sent to interpret
Lewis's words for the Sacs and Foxes was apparently British, their first
impression of the news was decidedly anti-American. To correct this
perception, Captain Amos Stoddard, who had come to formally take
possession of Upper Louisiana on behalf of the United States, personally
traveled to the Des Moines River to hold a council with the Ioways, Sacs,
and Foxes.[2]

Some Indigenous nations living near St. Louis, including Delawares
and another band of the Sacs, had the opportunity to learn of France's
land cession to the United States directly from Spanish Lieutenant
Governor Don Carlos Dehault Delassus. Stoddard had encouraged
Delassus to arrange the meeting on the grounds that the Natives might
find the news more palatable if they heard it first from the Spaniard.
"Your Father the Spaniard is going," Delassus told them in a council.

"His heart is happy to know that you will be protected and sustained by your new father." He continued by telling them that he prayed that the Master of Life would "shower on you all a happy destiny and prosperity in always living in good union with the whites."[3]

While it's not known how most Indigenous people reacted to the news, we do know that Americans were familiar to them. Some had helped Native allies defeat the Americans on the Wabash River a decade earlier. They had all heard how Major General "Mad" Anthony Wayne had rebuilt the American military after that loss and then went on to defeat the Indigenous confederacy at the Battle of Fallen Timbers in 1794. They also knew about the terrible atrocities Wayne's army had committed against Indigenous people after the battle, burning crops and destroying entire villages in a swath of destruction that extended for fifty miles on either side of the Miami River. Now, the US military and white American settlers would be crossing the Mississippi River and arriving on the lands of the Osages, Quapaws, Shawnees, Delawares, Ioways, Sacs, and Foxes in large numbers. Clearly, the news these nations had received troubled them.[4]

Many members of these nations were also aware that two Euro-Americans, Meriwether Lewis and William Clark, had established a camp across the Mississippi River from St. Louis, where they were pre-paring for a voyage that would take them up the Missouri River and west beyond the boundary of the Louisiana Territory. Curious Indigenous people visited the camp over the winter. Some had crossed the river simply to observe it, while others had gone there to trade for whiskey or tobacco with the soldiers. Having previously seen the French, Spaniards, and British undertake expeditions like the one Lewis and Clark read-ied for, they understood that the Americans were planning to explore natural resources as well as establish commercial ties with Indigenous nations far to the north and west.[5]

Most white Americans had been just as surprised as were Native Americans to learn about the land deal between their federal govern-ment and France that would become known as the Louisiana Purchase. Even President Thomas Jefferson had not expected his diplomats in Paris, US Minister to France Robert Livingston and former Governor of Virginia James Monroe, to negotiate a deal that would nearly dou-ble the size of the country. Jefferson's main concern in sending em-issaries to France had been to ensure that, with the pending transfer of Louisiana from Spain to France, that Americans would still enjoy

MAP 9. This map shows the general locations of Indigenous nations living in and around present-day Missouri at the time of the Louisiana Purchase in 1803. *Map by the author*

unimpeded access to the Mississippi River and the vital port of New Orleans. He had dispatched Livingston to Paris in 1801 after hearing rumors that Spain had retroceded Louisiana to France in a secret deal. The gossip, which of course turned out to be true, had been difficult to verify, in part because French diplomats refused to discuss the deal with Livingston. Some of the uncertainty centered on the fact that Spain had not yet formally turned the territory over to France and would not do so until 1803. Even so, the United States immediately became concerned that, if it did in fact again own Louisiana, the revolutionary government of France would not recognize the United States' right to navigate the critical waterway. Jefferson instructed Livingston to stop the rumored retrocession from taking place if possible. Failing that, he was to attempt to purchase "the Floridas," as the Gulf Coast colonies between New Orleans and present-day Florida were then called, for the United States.

Spain's decision to close New Orleans to all foreigners in October 1802 prompted Jefferson to send Monroe to France to help resolve the increasingly tense situation. Monroe's instructions were to negotiate for the purchase of New Orleans as well as Florida from the French. However, just prior to Monroe's arrival in Paris, French Minister Charles Maurice Talleyrand unexpectedly asked Livingston if the United States government had any interest in buying all of Louisiana. Napoleon Bonaparte's dreams of building a new empire in North America had been dashed during a disastrous French military campaign in Saint-Domingue, on the Caribbean Island of La Española. Recognizing their failure in North America and in desperate need of cash, the French were eager to unload the Louisiana Territory on the United States in an all-or-nothing deal.

Napoleon's eagerness to sell the territory led to a hasty series of meetings, giving the US envoys no time to inform Jefferson about the change in plans, let alone wait for his approval of them. Fearing that the French might change their minds and back out of the bargain, Livingston and Monroe acted quickly—and independently—to negotiate an agreement with French finance minister François Barbé-Marbois. On May 2, 1803, just two weeks after Monroe had arrived in the French capital, the three diplomats signed the Louisiana Purchase Treaty in Paris, which transferred "ownership" of eight hundred thousand square miles of land to the United States for $15 million, roughly eighteen dollars per mile.[6]

Two months later, news of the sale reached Washington. While Jefferson was pleased to learn that Livingston and Monroe had reached an agreement to keep the Mississippi River and New Orleans open to US trade, he was unsure how to handle the acquisition of the huge Territory of Louisiana. So much about the land remained unknown. No European powers, including Spain and France, seemed to have determined precisely how far west America's new possession extended. There was also much to learn about the Native nations that lived in the far reaches of the territory. And, almost immediately, new questions began to arise regarding the way the vast new territory would become part of the United States. Jefferson doubted that the constitution would allow him to simply annex Louisiana to the United States or extend citizenship to all the non-Indigenous people already living in the territory. Finally, there were also apprehensions about the way Louisiana would formally be transferred to the United States. Spain was furious to learn that Napoleon had violated the terms of the secret Treaty of Ildefonso, which prohibited France from selling Louisiana. As Spain had not yet formally transferred ownership of the territory to France, the Americans worried that they may refuse to do so.[7]

Settler Colonialism

At the time of the ceremonial raising of the US flag over St. Louis on March 10, 1804, officials were still sorting out the process by which the Louisiana Territory would be incorporated into the United States. It soon became clear that the United States intended to treat the new possession far differently than had previous colonial powers. While France and Spain had held the territory as a dependent colony, the United States planned to annex Louisiana. This would be accomplished by first establishing a territorial government with a governor and legislature. As many of the Indigenous people living in the territory already suspected, making Louisiana a part of the United States also meant carrying out an aggressive program designed to "transform Indian Country into Anglo-American homesteads."[8]

And yet, significant legal barriers remained in the United States' effort to gain outright ownership of Louisiana. Contrary to popular perception, the Louisiana Purchase did not grant the United States possession of the territory. Instead, as historian Colin G. Calloway has observed, the sale had conveyed to the young nation "not [Louisiana] itself, but the preemptive right to negotiate with the indigenous people for title to that land."[9] Adding even more complexity to the transfer was the fact that the Treaty of Paris bound the United States to honor all the agreements Indigenous nations had previously made with the Spanish colonial government. These pacts included land transfers from Native nations to individuals and to colonial powers. Some of that land, in turn, had been granted to corporations, individuals, and other Native groups by the Spanish government.[10]

Jefferson hoped to avoid a chaotic land rush by would-be American settlers by planning for the orderly settlement of Upper Louisiana, the name given to all the newly acquired land north of the Arkansas River. He wanted to prohibit whites from moving into the territory until such time as they had fully occupied the land east of the Mississippi River. In the meantime, Upper Louisiana would become an Indian Territory where those Indigenous people still living east of the Mississippi could be relocated. A prohibition of white settlement in Upper Louisiana would also allow time for the United States to negotiate with those Native nations who had land claims in the territory. However, few governmental officials supported the president's methodical plan, many viewing it as being either unnecessary or unrealistic. Rufus King, a former member of the Continental Congress and a US senator from New York, warned that "Nothing but a cordon of troops will restrain our people from going over the [Missouri] river and settling themselves down on the western bank."[11]

Before the Louisiana Purchase, the United States had already begun the process of Indian removal and making land treaties east of the Mississippi River. As the historian Francis Paul Prucha has observed, even though several Native nations may have felt they had been abandoned by Great Britain after the American War for Independence, they "did not think they had been militarily defeated." Meanwhile, the "United States looked upon itself as a conqueror and counted Indians among the conquered."[12] After the American Revolution, the newly independent United States had immediately begun to adopt British laws regarding Indigenous people and retained its use of the Doctrine of Discovery. To assert control over the settlement and sale of Indigenous land, the new government quickly began the process of making treaties with Native nations. By Prucha's count, the United States signed, and the Senate ratified, 367 such treaties between 1778 and 1868. Some were agreements in which both parties had agreed to peace and friendship. Many others were treaties in which the United States exercised its preemptive right to purchase Native land. By the time the so-called treaty era ended, during the administration of President Ulysses S. Grant, the United States is estimated to have paid $800 million in nineteenth-century dollars and confiscated one billion acres of Indigenous property.[13]

The process of making treaties was augmented by an aggressive policy of settler colonialism. Very much tied to the concepts of the Doctrine of Discovery, settler colonialism, as defined by German historian Julius Wilm, "was premised on the idea that white European settlers had a superior and ordained claim to the colonial land base for cultural and economic reasons and that the original inhabitants therefore could be displaced." More succinctly, the Australian anthropologist and ethnographer Patrick Wolfe wrote that the process of settler colonialism "destroys to replace." While the French, Spaniards, and British had been interested in extracting natural resources such as lead, animal skins, and even enslaved Natives from Louisiana, the United States brought what historian Jacob F. Lee has called "a new form of imperialism" to the territory. American settlers were driven by the acquisition and occupation of land, and inherent in the taking of land was the use of violent genocide to displace Indigenous people.[14]

Even before the United States gained its independence, Euro-American colonists had unleashed violence to force Indigenous people from their land. This form of unlimited warfare was carried out by irregular forces, or militias, to disrupt and destroy any assets Indigenous people possessed that might be utilized to wage hostility. Incredibly, this seems to have included homes, fields, livestock, and even civilian populations. The goal of such warfare was to destroy an enemy's will to fight or ability to put up any form of resistance.[15] As we have already seen, the attacks carried out against Natives by military men like Major General Wayne were not designed to bring about the defeat of an opposing army; they were intended to exterminate Native people and to deny any of those who survived both their homes and their livelihoods.[16]

Because the US army was small, settlers formed important proxy armies that carried out much of the violence necessary for removal. John Joseph Mathews has argued that, because of their heritage as European peasants, many American settlers carried with them a "tribal" or "racial memory" for violence. Historian Roxanne Dunbar-Ortiz points to the Ulster Scots, better known as Scots-Irish. Often characterized as hardy individualists, Scots-Irish had been recruited by the British to drive Indigenous farmers from a half million acres in Northern Ireland in the early seventeenth century. Nearly a quarter million of Scots-Irish arrived on the North American continent between 1717 and 1775. Most of these immigrants were from poor, landless families and had come to the American colonies as indentured servants. Scots-Irish also made up a sizable portion of westward moving settlers. Dunbar-Ortiz writes that in the Ohio and Tennessee River valleys, the Scots-Irish "cleared forests, built log cabins, and killed Indians, forming a human wall of colonization for the new United States." In Upper Louisiana, many Scots-Irish settlers would gravitate toward the rugged Ozark hill country. Ethnographer and geologist Henry Rowe Schoolcraft, who visited with some of them there in 1819, noted that "the rude pursuits and coarse enjoyment of the hunter state [is] all they know."[17]

Burns wrote that the early settlers in the Louisiana Territory were not the "noble pioneers" of American mythology:

The intruder settlers were the dregs of American Society, lawless misfits who sought the frontier to escape punishment within their own culture.... They were citizens of the United States. Loudly and persistently they proclaimed that right and broke every law of the country that protected them.[18]

Similarly, US Indian Agent G. C. Snow explained that when settlers reached present-day Kansas, they "knew they were trespassers, and had no right whatever to settle where they did." Yet they vowed to "fight for their rights," expecting the US government to give them each a quarter section of land as a reward for the work of "driving Indians from their homes and the graves of their fathers."[19]

Extinguishing Indigenous Land Claims

With Euro-American settlers eager to cross the Mississippi River, US officials wasted little time in beginning the work of removing Indigenous people living in the new territory. A delegation of fourteen Osages left St. Louis with Pierre Chouteau even before the territory was officially transferred to the United States, in February 1804, to meet with President Jefferson in Washington. Though he was unwilling to grant the Osages special concessions, Jefferson was aware of the necessity of cultivating them as allies. While the Sioux were the most formidable people north of the Missouri River, the Osages were the strongest indigenous nation south of the river. "With these two powerful nations we must stand well," the president commented, "because in their quarter we are miserably weak."[20]

While meeting with the Osage delegation, led by Pawhuska and the Little Osage headman Dog Soldier, on July 16, 1804, Jefferson laid out a lengthy set of requests. After assuring the Osages that, unlike the French and the Spanish colonial regimes, the US government was in Louisiana to stay, he asked the Osages to grant permission to US explorers to enter their land. Along with the expedition even then being led by Lewis and Clark on the Missouri River, the federal government was planning other exploratory expeditions on the Arkansas and Red Rivers. These groups would not only need consent to travel on Osage lands, but they also would need Osage assistance and support. The president's awareness that Big Track and Clermont II, the representatives who would need to give their permission for an Arkansas River expedition, were not present at the meeting, brought Jefferson to his next point. He stated that the two bands of Osages living separately on the Arkansas and Osage Rivers needed to reunite. To that end, the President offered the Osages their own federal Indian Agent and all the assistance that person could provide to bring them together. Finally, the president raised the issue of trade. He told the Osages that a successful trading partnership would benefit both nations. Apparently laying the groundwork for the formal treaty the United States would sign with the Osages four years later, as well as the construction of Fort Osage and its trading factory, Jefferson emphasized that the US trade with the Osages would be controlled and regulated fairly.[21]

By the time the Osages returned to Upper Louisiana, the territory was being administered by officials from the neighboring Indiana Territory. General William Henry Harrison, the ambitious territorial governor of Indiana, was also serving as governor of Upper Louisiana and as an agent of Indian affairs. Harrison, who had served as Major General Wayne's aide-de-camp at the Battle of Fallen Timbers, had already gained a reputation as a ruthless treaty negotiator. Beginning in May 1803, he had negotiated three treaties in five weeks, and in doing so demonstrated that he was willing to bribe, coerce, and threaten Indigenous representatives to advance the process of national expansion. His dual appointment as acting territorial governor and Indian agent endowed him with wide-ranging authority to negotiate and sign treaties with Native nations, and he began to exercise that authority soon after arriving in St. Louis.[22]

In early September 1804, reports reached St. Louis that Sac and Fox men had killed four white settlers whom they had caught encroaching on their land near the Cuivre River, fifty miles to the northwest. The Sacs and Foxes are two culturally and linguistically related nations that the United States government united for treaty purposes. The name "Sac and Fox" is an inaccurate translation of the words "Sac" (Sauk), or Thâkîwaki, which means "people coming forth," and "Fox," or Meskwâki, "people of the red earth." The US government first officially misapplied these names during treaty negotiations which would be conducted in 1804. After the Black Hawk War in 1834, the government would forcibly combine the two groups into a single nation.[23]

Settlers feared that some Indigenous nations, especially the Sacs and Foxes, were becoming increasingly anti-American and as such constituted a serious threat to their expansion of land ownership. Meanwhile, many Sacs living near St. Louis were horrified, fearful that the murders would make them the target of violence at the hands of settlers living in the region. One of the nation's headmen, Quashquame, traveled to St. Louis at the end of September to discuss with US officials how best to make amends for the crime.[24]

In October, Quashquame led a second delegation of Sac and Fox leaders to meet with General Harrison, to determine the fate of one of the murderers. When the delegates sat down with the general on November 3, Harrison did his best to keep them off guard. He plied them with presents and liquor supplied by his negotiating partner, Pierre Chouteau. The Fox leader Black Hawk would later claim the Americans had kept his representatives drunk much of the time they were in St. Louis.[25] The delegates were pleased, if a little confused, when their talks with Harrison shifted away from the murders to the topic of a land cession agreement.

The Sacs and Foxes were eager to be protected from their enemies, the Osages. At the end of the eighteenth century, white settlement east of the Mississippi River had pushed the Sacs and Foxes into northwest and central Missouri, where they had encroached onto Little Osage land and engaged in battles with them.

The Sacs and Foxes were hopeful that a closer relationship with the United States might put them on the receiving end of American gifts and goodwill. To that end, Chouteau and Harrison persuaded the five Sacs and Foxes to put their marks on what would be the first treaty involving the cession of Indigenous land in present-day Missouri. Most of the land the Sacs and Foxes had relinquished extended east of the Mississippi River into Illinois and Wisconsin, but a significant parcel extended into Upper Louisiana, between the Missouri River and the Jeffreon, or Jeffron River, now known as the North River.[26]

In his autobiography, Black Hawk relayed the report his delegates made to him upon their return.

On our arrival at St. Louis we met our American father and explained to him our business, urging the release of our friend. The American chief told us he wanted land. We agreed to give him some on the west side of the Mississippi, likewise more on the Illinois side opposite Jeffreon. When the business was all arranged we expected to have our friend released to come home with us.

About the time we were ready to start our brother was let out of the prison. He started and ran a short distance when he was SHOT DEAD![27]

Louis Burns has pointed out that US treaties had a way of "making the desires of the United States appear to be a desire for the benefit of the Indian."[28] While five men whose judgement may have been clouded by whiskey believed that many of the articles of the Sac and Fox Treaty of 1804 would benefit them, the articles were, in fact, designed to undermine the sovereignty of the Sacs and Foxes by limiting their commercial, military, and political activities. First, under the terms of the treaty, the Sacs and Foxes declared themselves to be under the sole protection the United States. This article prohibited the Sac and Fox nations from engaging in an alliance with any European power. Second, they pledged to take any conflict they might have with other Natives or white settlers to US officials for resolution. In addition, the Sacs and Foxes agreed to end their fighting with the Osages. This article was likely pushed by Chouteau, because of his long and lucrative trading relationship with the latter group.[29]

The United States had long been worried that British traders, who were still operating from posts in the north, might turn Indigenous sentiment against them and would supply Natives in the Mississippi River Valley with arms they could use to oppose the US in battle. To control relationships with British traders, the treaty forbade the Sacs and Foxes to transact with any trader who was not licensed by the US government. To further control the economic activity of the Sacs and Foxes, the United States promised to build and stock a trading post, known as a factory, for them. This article was eliminated in 1822, however, when the treaty was amended.[30] Trading factories, which were a kind of government run "company store," became an important tool in suppressing Indigenous peoples in the early nineteenth century. By forcing Native nations to buy goods only from the factory at highly inflated prices, the United States was able to keep them in debt. After struggling with chronic indebtedness and poverty, Natives were often willing to sell the only valuable commodity they possessed: their land.

If the Sacs and Foxes were confused about the United States' intention to keep their land, it was because the treaty contained language that seemingly contradicted the cession of land. "The United States will never interrupt the said tribes in the possession of the lands which they rightfully claim, but will on the contrary protect them in the quiet enjoyment of the same against their own citizens and against all other white persons who may intrude upon them," reads Article Four. Article Seven states, "As long as the lands which are now ceded to the United States remain their property, the Indians belonging to the said tribes, shall enjoy the privilege of living and hunting upon them."[31]

These articles refer to the concept, derived from the Doctrine of Discovery, which states that, while only the United States or a European power could possess the Right of Ownership over the land, Indigenous people could retain the Right of Occupancy. Articles Four and Seven of the Treaty of 1804 outline the fact that the United States believed that, as owner, it had the right and power to control who lived on the ceded land. It had the right to keep both settlers and foreign traders off the land, until the government was prepared to transfer title of the land to settlers through regulated sales at the Federal Land Office. Up to that point, only the Sacs and Foxes would be able to "enjoy" the land, this at the US government's pleasure. When the government was ready for the sale of the land to commence, the Sacs and Foxes would be removed.

Below the signatures, at the very bottom of the treaty document, as though added as an afterthought, is an important article that had far-reaching consequences in the dissemination of Indigenous land in Missouri. The additional article states, "It is agreed that nothing in this treaty contained, shall affect the claim of any individual or individuals who may have obtained grants of land from the Spanish government." French residents of Upper Louisiana, such as the Chouteaus, had worried that the new US government would not recognize their Spanish land grants. As one of the treaty negotiators, Pierre Chouteau, who likely added the article, was in an ideal position to protect the land interests of his family and associates.[32]

It is important to note that the treaty was not simply the result of a cordial meeting held between four or five members of the Sac and Fox nations and two US Indian Agents. The Indigenous delegates were purposely placed in an intimidating situation when asked to sign the agreement. During the final signing ceremony in St. Louis, there were more than twice as many men representing the US as there were representing the Sacs and Foxes. Two of the US representatives, Hypolite Bolen and Joseph Barron, were interpreters. Six others were high-ranking US officials. Aside from Harrison and Chouteau, the American delegation included three military officers. Captain Amos Stoddard and Major James Bruff had been appointed by President Jefferson to oversee the transfer of Upper Louisiana from French to American control. Joining them was a third commissioned officer in the US military, Lieutenant S. Warrel. Accompanying Harrison was John Griffin, a judge in the Indiana Territorial Court, and the treaty secretary, William Prince.[33] In many ways, the meeting followed a formula by which treaty negotiations would be held in the early nineteenth century. Placing Native delegates in intimidating circumstances and, if necessary, plying them with gifts and liquor often helped US negotiators gain the concessions they wanted.[34]

After they learned about the treaty their delegates had signed, the Sacs and Foxes were incensed by its terms. When Harrison's successor as governor of Louisiana, James Wilkinson, met with the Sacs and Foxes in the spring of 1805, they told him they deeply regretted the agreement. "We have given away a great Country to Governor Harrison for a little thing," one of the headmen told him. They asked Wilkinson to reconsider the treaty on the grounds that the men who signed it had been sent to St. Louis only to resolve the Cuivre River murders. Though Quashquame, the principal signer of the treaty, was a village leader of some standing, neither he nor any of the other delegates had been granted authority by Sac and Fox headmen to engage in treaty negotiations in the matter of land cessions. Even though they would revisit the matter of the land cession again in subsequent treaty negotiations in 1815 and 1816, the Sacs and Foxes continually contested the validity of the 1804 treaty. The matter would continue to sour US relations with the Sacs and Foxes through the War of 1812, and it directly contributed to the Black Hawk War in 1832.[35]

Harrison's tenure as administrator of Upper Louisiana was brief. Congress designated all the Louisiana Purchase north of the 33rd parallel as a new territory, to be called the Louisiana Territory. A new territorial government was to take effect on July 4, 1805. In 1806, President Jefferson appointed Wilkinson to be the first territorial governor and Pierre Chouteau as the territory's first US Indian Agent. Despite concerns about the Frenchman's loyalty to the United States, Chouteau had a long history with the Osages that Jefferson believed would make him an indispensable agent. By March 1807, however, Secretary of War Henry Dearborn had become wary of, among other things, Chouteau's habit of mixing his personal business with government business. The

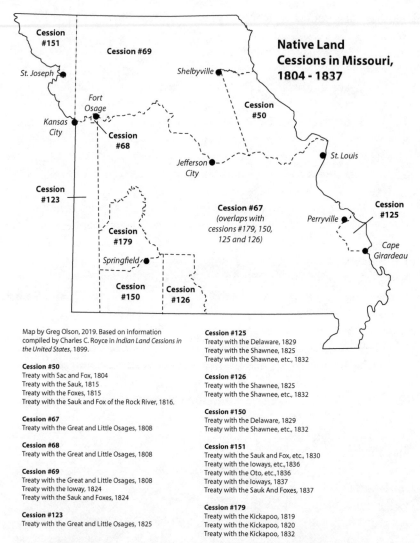

Native Land Cessions in Missouri, 1804 - 1837

Cession #151

Cession #69

St. Joseph

Shelbyville

Fort Osage

Cession #50

Kansas City

Cession #68

Jefferson City

St. Louis

Cession #123

Cession #67
(overlaps with cessions #179, 150, 125 and 126)

Perryville

Cession #125

Cession #179

Springfield

Cape Girardeau

Cession #150

Cession #126

Map by Greg Olson, 2019. Based on information compiled by Charles C. Royce in *Indian Land Cessions in the United States*, 1899.

Cession #50
Treaty with Sac and Fox, 1804
Treaty with the Sauk, 1815
Treaty with the Foxes, 1815
Treaty with the Sauk and Fox of the Rock River, 1816.

Cession #67
Treaty with the Great and Little Osages, 1808

Cession #68
Treaty with the Great and Little Osages, 1808

Cession #69
Treaty with the Great and Little Osages, 1808
Treaty with the Ioway, 1824
Treaty with the Sauk and Foxes, 1824

Cession #123
Treaty with the Great and Little Osages, 1825

Cession #125
Treaty with the Delaware, 1829
Treaty with the Shawnee, 1825
Treaty with the Shawnee, etc., 1832

Cession #126
Treaty with the Shawnee, 1825
Treaty with the Shawnee, etc., 1832

Cession #150
Treaty with the Delaware, 1829
Treaty with the Shawnee, etc., 1832

Cession #151
Treaty with the Sauk and Fox, etc., 1830
Treaty with the Ioways, etc.,1836
Treaty with the Oto, etc.,1836
Treaty with the Ioways, 1837
Treaty with the Sauk And Foxes, 1837

Cession #179
Treaty with the Kickapoo, 1819
Treaty with the Kickapoo, 1820
Treaty with the Kickapoo, 1832

MAP 10: Indigenous Land Cessions in Missouri, 1804–1837. *Map by the author based on information compiled by Charles C. Royce*

trader's duties as Indian Agent therefore were diminished, and he began working only with the Osages. President Jefferson then appointed William Clark to take Chouteau's place as US Indian Agent to Upper Louisiana. As agents, both Chouteau and Clark served as commissioners to several treaties.[36]

That same month, the president appointed Clark's partner in the Corps of Discovery, Meriwether Lewis, to succeed James Wilkinson as the territory's second governor. At the time of his appointment, Lewis was still working in the East and would not arrive in St. Louis to assume his position until March 8, 1808. In the meantime, a man who would prove to be Lewis's political nemesis, Frederick Bates, served as acting governor. As the territory's administrators, both Bates and Lewis spent a great deal of time occupied with Indian Affairs, especially in determining how to manage the Osages.

At the time of the Louisiana Purchase, the Osages were split into three main groups. The Little Osages left the Missouri River valley and had moved south, closer to the Osage River. The Great Osages lived in two main groups. Pawhuska's villages were on the Osage River west of the present-day Kansas-Missouri border. Clermont II's villages were located at the Three Forks region of the Arkansas River in present-day Oklahoma. Together, the three groups claimed large parts of present-day Missouri, Arkansas, Oklahoma, and Kansas as their hunting grounds. As white settlers began to move into Upper Louisiana, and then arrived in increasing numbers, the Osages became more vigilant in defending their homeland, often fending off intruders with violence.[37]

In the years since the Louisiana Purchase, the population in the territory had grown rapidly and in some regions would double between 1804 and 1810.[38] The influx of settlers and emigrant Natives onto land that the United States still did not own created conflict with the Osages. Governor Lewis, who believed the Osages' violence was offensive rather than defensive in nature, grew frustrated with the situation. He believed that there were "but two effectual cords by which the savage arm can be bound, the one is the love of merchandise, and the other is the fear of punishment."[39] He managed to employ both strategies by penalizing the Osages for their attacks on settlers by cutting trade with them and declaring that any Osages who did not meet in an upcoming council with William Clark in September 1808 would no longer be under the protection of the United States. Hoping to use other Native nations as a proxy military force, Lewis invited Shawnees, Delawares, Sacs, Ioways, Kickapoos, and others to attack the Osages "in their own way." However, the governor warned these nations not to undertake such aggressions unless they had a "sufficient force to destroy or drive [the Osages] from our neighborhood."[40]

In truth, several challenges had already begun to weaken the Osages. Aside from the split between Clermont II and Pawhuska, the encroachment of settlers and emigrant Indigenous nations from the East had upset the balance of Osage life. Believing that his trade sanctions alone had weakened them, Lewis gloated that, "The Osage nations . . . were reduced in the course of a few months to a state of perfect submission without bloodshed."[41] Expecting that the Osages were ready to bargain, Clark set out for the September council at Fire Prairie, near the present-day town of Buckner, Missouri, to negotiate a land cession with them.

To ensure the Osages participated in the meeting, Clark dispatched dragoon commander and the son of Daniel Boone, Nathan Boone, to bring Great and Little Osage delegates to the site of a new fort that was taking shape on the Missouri River near Fire Prairie. Pawhuska, representing the Great Osages, and Nichu Malli, or Traveling Rain, of the Little Osages accepted the invitation. They anticipated that Clark simply wanted to meet with them to chastise them for their violent tactics and to deliver a stern warning for them to end their vicious behavior. Well before the arrival of the Americans into the Missouri country, the Osages had found themselves in similar situations with French and then Spanish officials and had always been able to use declarations of friendship and promises to improve their behavior to remain amiable with whichever colonial power considered itself in charge of the region.[42]

When all the parties arrived at Fire Prairie, however, Clark laid a paper before the Indigenous delegations to sign. He persuaded the Osages present to cede a huge swath of land bounded on the north by the Missouri River, on the east by the Mississippi River, on the south by the Arkansas River, and on the west by a line drawn due south from Fire Prairie. The Osages at the council agreed to this cession of fifty thousand square miles, some of which rightfully belonged to the Quapaws, who were excluded from the negotiations. The cession was equal to nearly half the total area of the current states of Arkansas and Missouri. In return, the US delegation promised to protect the Osages with the aid of a newly built fort and to establish a trading factory for them adjacent to the fort.[43]

Pawhuska and Traveling Rain believed that the treaty to which they had just agreed had merely given the United States the right to use Osage hunting grounds. They were pleased to once again be trading with the United States for much needed items and looked forward to the protection the fort, called Fort Osage, would offer. They believed that having their own designated fort and attached trading factory was a sign of their importance to the US government. They were also pleased with Clark's declaration that by living on land owned by the United States, Osages could hunt without the worry of being attacked by either settlers or other Native nations that had immigrated from the East. The agreement, they hoped, would create a buffer between them and those who had been encroaching on their land.[44]

However, the Osage delegation soon learned that they had not correctly understood the terms of the treaty. They were appalled to find out later that the United States would not only use their land for hunting but would allow members of other Native nations to settle on it. They claimed that Clark had misled them and were deeply offended to discover that the fort would also serve the Ioways, Kanzas, and Sacs, nations with whom they were not on friendly terms. Finally, Clermont II and the Arkansas River Osages were outraged at having been excluded from the negotiations, pointing out that Pawhuska and Traveling Rain had no authority to sign the treaty on behalf of all Osages.[45]

Soon, a delegation of Osages traveled to St. Louis to express their displeasure with the treaty concluded at Fire Prairie. To save the agreement, Governor Lewis called on Pierre Chouteau. It may have been the War Department's distrust of Chouteau that led him to be omitted from the original negotiations, especially since he still served as the Osages' US Indian Agent. In any event, Chouteau and Lewis made what appear to have been minor changes to the treaty, and it was Chouteau, not Clark, who returned to Fire Prairie in November once again to present the document for Osage approval. John Joseph Mathews believed that his Osage ancestors would not have signed the revised treaty had it not been for Chouteau's presence, due to his close relationship with Pawhuska and his gentle prodding of the other delegates.[46]

The final agreement, signed by one hundred ten Great and Little Osages at Fort Osage on November 10, 1808, as well as by fifteen of Clermont II's Arkansas River Osages in St. Louis nine months later, finalized the land cession. In consideration of the land sale, the United States promised $1,200 in gifts and a yearly annuity of $1,500 in merchandise. Aside from the fort and the trading factory, the United States pledged to allow the Osages access to a blacksmith, a grist mill, and agricultural implements at that location. They also promised to build a strong block house in each of the Osage towns. As with the Sac and Fox treaty, the Osages pledged their loyalty solely to the United States and promised to turn any disagreement they had with settlers or other Indigenous people over to the US military for resolution. To further address the issue of the violence that had been directed toward settlers, the government agreed to reimburse victims for any property damages inflicted by Osages. In addition, Chouteau included an article that confirmed a Spanish land grant he had received. The land in question was on the Osage land cession, located along the Lamine River in present-day Cooper County. While the Osages agreed with Chouteau's provision, Governor Lewis struck the article before sending the final draft of the treaty to the Senate for confirmation.[47]

Curiously, Article Six of the treaty specified that, along with the land they claimed in southern Missouri and northern Arkansas, the Osages agreed to relinquish "all lands situated northwardly of the river Missouri." This was land the Osages had rarely ventured onto since the annihilation of the Missouria by the Sacs and Foxes in the 1790s had made it possible for the Sacs, Foxes, and Ioways to occupy and defend it. In fact, it appears that William Clark was trying to exaggerate the size of the Osage cession to declare it open for white settlement at the end of the War of 1812. By promoting this generous interpretation of Osage land claims, he was also attempting to deny the claims of other nations. In 1815, Clark asserted that the US had already bought the land north of the Missouri River and had no need to treat with the Sacs, Foxes and Ioways to purchase it again. Historian Robert Lee has proposed that an 1815 map recently attributed to Clark shows him extending the boundaries of the Osage cession to exclude not only the Sacs, Foxes and Ioways, but also the Quapaws, who claimed land in the Missouri Bootheel. As we will see, however, the Sacs, Foxes and Ioways asserted their claims, forcing the US to hold a treaty with them in 1824.[48]

Confusion surrounding the terms of the treaty lingered for years after its negotiation. The Senate did not ratify it for nearly a year and a half, which meant that the annuities and provisions the US had promised the Osages did not arrive until after April 1810. This long delay, in turn, led some Osages to consider the agreement as null and void.[49] There also remained confusion about Osage hunting rights on the ceded land. Burns blames both the treaty's complex wording and Chouteau's faulty translation of the treaty at Fort Osage for the problem. "It would seem," he has written, "that when a complex treaty full of concessions to the United States was involved, every possibility for misunderstanding was

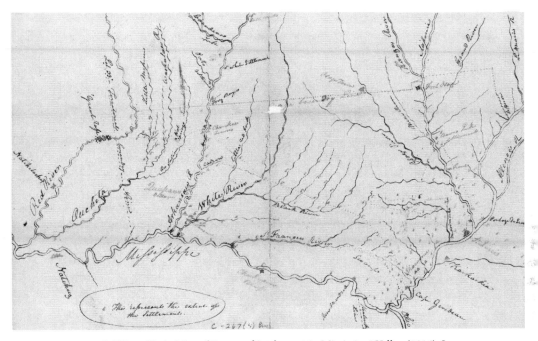

MAP 11: William Clark, Map of Extent of Settlement in Mississippi Valley (1816). In this map, Clark exaggerated the size of the land cession the Osages had made in the Treaty of 1808 to include land north of the Missouri River that is equal to the size of present-day Switzerland. This land was rightfully claimed by the Ioways, Sacs, and Foxes, who ceded it to the US in 1824. *Courtesy of the National Archives and Records Administration, Washington, DC*

present. On the other hand, simple treaties with clear provisions were clearly communicated."[50]

Article Eight of the treaty states that the Osages retain the right to hunt "on any other lands within the territory of Louisiana, without the limits of the white settlements, until the United States may think proper to assign the same as hunting grounds to other friendly Indians." Thus, Osages retaliated to defend their land when Cherokee "Old Settlers" moved onto land in Arkansas, on which they still believed they had the right to hunt.[51]

Other scholars have placed the blame for the Osages' misunderstanding of the treaty on William Clark. Historian Tai S. Edwards has shown that the way the Indian agent thrust the original treaty on a few unsuspecting representatives of the Great and Little Osages in September 1808 was coercive, and that he had purposefully deceived them about the document's provisions. Clark later told an acquaintance that the Osage treaty was "the hardest bargain against the Indians he had ever made, and that if he was to be damned hereafter, it would be for making that treaty."[52]

Burns points out that the Osages remained dissatisfied with the treaty because some of its provisions put them in a difficult position. Though they were commanded to turn any grievances or conflicts they had with settlers or other Indigenous nations over to the US military for resolution, the terms of that legal resolution at the hands of Americans were hardly fair. United States authorities were completely dismissive of the fact that the Osages had their own long-standing protocols for dealing with infractions. In addition, Osages were reluctant to engage in a system of justice that regularly found them to be guilty of violence against immigrants who were encroaching on their land. Moreover, the US failed to prevent squatters from infringing on Osage land rights. Instead of extending the treaty's promised protection to the Osages, the government protected those newcomers.[53]

The death of Louisiana Territorial Governor Meriwether Lewis in September 1809 was an unexpected blow to US officials. Lewis apparently took his own life while traveling from St. Louis to Washington on a trip he had undertaken to clear his name. Lewis had been accused of improprieties in awarding a $7,000 government contract to the Missouri Fur Company, a firm in which he was likely a silent partner. The company received a contract to return a Mandan headman named Shahaka and his family safely to their village on the upper Missouri River. The Missouri Fur Company, which had been formed largely by Manuel Lisa but included several important St. Louis trade partners, William Clark and the Chouteaus among them, was licensed to trade in the upper Missouri. Lewis promised not to issue any other trade licenses for the nations above the Platte River until the convoy returning Shahaka left St. Louis. This insured that Lisa and company would have a head start on any potential competition.[54]

Though Lewis's tenure in Louisiana had been short, his close relationship with President Jefferson had helped bring the challenges faced by the territory's settlers to the attention of officials in Washington. This was particularly important to them at a time when relations with Louisiana's Indigenous population were becoming more unsettled. As new groups of Cherokees began to move across the Mississippi River, settling near the St. Francis River on what is now the Arkansas-Missouri border, the sheer number of people, between four thousand and six thousand by 1815, created conflicts with the Osages that would only worsen.[55]

At the same time, interference by the British threatened to turn nations such as the Sac and Fox against the United States. In fact, Lewis's successor as governor, Benjamin Howard, believed that by early 1812, the threat of a British invasion of Louisiana from Canada was serious enough to warrant the construction of blockhouses and the formation of additional militia units.[56] Meanwhile, Clark was concerned about the possibility that the British might succeed in turning Indigenous people against the United States. In May 1811, he had informed Secretary of War William Eustis that an unnamed Ioway headman had warned him, "The time is drawing nigh when the murder is to begin, and all the Indians who will not join are to die with the Whites."[57] Eustis authorized Clark to assemble a delegation of Indigenous representatives from the nations living between the Great Lakes and the Arkansas River and bring them to Washington for peace talks. In early May 1812, the party of over forty Osages, Sacs, Foxes, Shawnees, Ioways, and Ho-Chunks left St. Louis bound for the US capital.

The War of 1812

During the two months the delegation spent on the road, Congress passed a bill transforming a large portion of the Territory of Louisiana into the Missouri Territory. Just two weeks later, President James Madison signed a declaration of war against Great Britain. Upon their arrival in Washington, the Indigenous delegates found US government officials preoccupied with preparations for war. While many of their meetings with these officials were cut short, the Native delegates were able to meet with Madison and dine with him at the White House. The president told them that the war with Britain was the result of unresolved resentment stemming from the War of Independence, three decades earlier. He warned the delegates that there were "bad birds" from Canada who were trying to persuade Indigenous people to help the British in a war that was between white men. "The red children must avoid this ruin."[58]

Those Native headmen who replied to the president's remarks were generally supportive of the United States in the new conflict, though they could not guarantee that all their people would follow suit. A Sac and Fox leader named The Blue confessed that his people "were in the habit of receiving presents from the English. We cannot leave them all at once," he warned the president, though he promised he would do his best. Clermont II, the Osage leader, proclaimed that his nation would not fight for the British. "I know the bad road from the good," he told Madison, "and know how to take the best."[59] Though the Osages remained true to their word, the council seems to have done little to reduce the violence taking place in Missouri.

Given their isolation, recently arrived white settlers in the Missouri Territory were particularly vulnerable to attack, not from British soldiers, but from their Native American trading partners and allies. Some of the settlers feared that the British would join Natives in an all-out attempt to chase them from Missouri. These anxieties increased when word reached the territory that at a recent meeting at the Sac villages on the Rock River in Illinois, at least five Indigenous nations, the Ho-Chunks, Potawatomis, Kickapoos, Shawnees, and Miamis, had pledged to help Britain by declaring war on the United States. While other nations, such as the Sacs and Ioways, had not formally declared war against the United States, their loyalty remained questionable.[60]

In 1812, there were only about two hundred fifty regular US soldiers stationed west of the Mississippi. Missouri Governor Howard and congressional delegate Edward Hempstead lobbied officials in Washington for a stronger military presence in the region. In the meantime, Pierre Chouteau traveled to Osage villages to raise a fighting force to counter the activities of those Natives who had allied themselves with Britain. Though he succeeded in persuading two hundred sixty Osages to join, the Department of War declined to deploy the volunteers due to concerns about their trustworthiness. William Clark appealed in vain directly to President Madison on Chouteau's behalf, "Should only half of [the Indigenous] force be turned against these Territories, the scattered population within it will not be adequate to their defense against such a herd of savages."[61]

The Osages remained loyal to the United States throughout the War of 1812. They had in part elected to support the United States because they had long resented the British for furnishing their enemies, the Sacs, Ho-Chunks, and Ioways, with weapons. They also remained loyal to the Americans because of the efforts of their long-time friend Chouteau and the operator of the trading factory at Fort Osage, George Sibley. Sibley's business relationship with the Little Osages had been extremely beneficial to both parties. Thanks to the Osages' skill in hunting and trapping, Sibley's factory had been the only one in the US system to turn a profit. It was therefore a test of Osage allegiance when US officials informed them that they could no longer spare the manpower needed to defend the remote fort and would have to abandon both it and the factory in June 1813. The Little Osages were disappointed because many of them lived near to the fort and relied heavily on the factory. But the Great Osages, who lived farther away, had found the region around fort to be dangerous. To protect themselves from being attacked by pro-British Natives, many of the Great Osages had moved farther south.[62]

Much of the violence that took place in the Missouri Territory during the War of 1812 had been the work of Sacs from the Rock River villages in Illinois and their allies. However, many nations, especially the Sacs, Foxes, and Ioways, remained split in their loyalties throughout the conflict. To protect those Natives who supported them, the United States moved them west, away from the fighting. "I have . . . thought it a correct measure to draw off these tribes, from the Mississippi; and place them on the Missouri," Clark wrote to Secretary of War John Armstrong in September 1813. The site on which Clark chose to resettle them lay on the south side of the Missouri River in present-day Moniteau County. To provide them with trade goods, Clark also sent the former factor from Fort Madison, John Johnson, to trade with them. Some Osages were upset that Clark would resettle their traditional enemies so close to their villages. A party of Osages acted on their resentment by killing a settler on the Gasconade River. Once again, Pierre Chouteau was dispatched to the Osage villages, this time to mend their strained relations with the United States. To placate the Little Osages, Clark dispatched Sibley farther upriver, to a spot near Arrow Rock, where he set up a factory meant to replace the one at Fort Osage that had closed. But as violence increased in the spring of 1814, both Johnson and Sibley were forced to abandon their factories.[63]

The violence during the spring and summer of 1814 was especially heavy in the Boone's Lick region, just east of Arrow Rock, in present-day Howard County. There, a force of about seventy anti-American Ioways, Otoes, and Ho-Chunks launched attacks against white settlers. By August, Manuel Lisa reported that violence in the region was widespread. For protection, about four hundred settlers had formed their own militia units and constructed five fortresses. In response, the United States sent Colonel Henry Dodge and a force of two hundred soldiers and fifty Shawnees to the region. Their presence helped quell the violence for a time, but as soon as they were recalled to St. Louis, the attacks resumed.[64]

William Clark was appointed as the fourth governor of the Missouri Territory in July 1813. Realizing he would need assistance in controlling the region's Native population, he appointed Pierre Chouteau's son, Auguste P. Chouteau, to serve as Subagent for the Osages on August 20, 1814. At the same time, he appointed Manuel Lisa as the Subagent of Indians above the Kansas River. These men were assigned to persuade allied Native nations to fight for the United States. In the face of the heavy violence of 1814, Clark once again asked Secretary of War Armstrong to allow Osages to fight for the Americans. While he did not receive an outright refusal, the war ended before Osages could lend a hand.[65]

It took some time for indigenous fighters in the Missouri Territory to learn that the Treaty of Ghent had officially brought an end to the war on the day before Christmas, 1814. In early 1815, Lisa, who was supposed to be informing Native nations that the war had ended, instead exploited the situation by inciting more violence. Lisa, who was married to Mitain, an Omaha woman, used his kinship ties to the Omahas to persuade them and their relatives, the Poncas, to fight those Ioways, Sacs, Foxes, and Santee Sioux who had opposed the United States during the war. Lisa then traveled up the Missouri River to meet with Lakota and Yankton Sioux at the confluence of the James River. After ensuring that they would remain US allies, he accompanied some of their headmen east to meet with Clark for a treaty council at Portage de Sioux. After Lisa's departure, several hundred Sioux marched toward the Mississippi River. While it is unclear whether Lisa had enflamed their fury against enemies of the United States, the Sioux seemed hungry for battle. On the way, they stumbled on the Chariton River villages of some of the pro-American Ioways whom Clark had moved west. The Sioux battle party killed twenty-four of the Ioways and destroyed their corn fields.[66]

Violent acts continued into the spring of 1815 in Missouri. These included the killing of four settlers at Cote Sans Dessein, in present-day Callaway County, and the so-called Battle of the Sink Hole in which Black Hawk led a group of Sacs and Foxes in the ambush of a company of US rangers at the mouth of the Cuivre River. When they finally heard the news regarding the Treaty of Ghent, however, few of those who lived in Missouri were pleased. Pro-British Indigenous nations felt abandoned by the withdrawal of their British allies, and many Native groups vowed to keep fighting. White settlers, on the other hand, were not pleased with Article Nine of the treaty, which called for the United States to cease warfare with Natives and for the restoration of all the "possessions, privileges and rights" Natives had held prior to the beginning of the war. By early summer, US officials determined it was time to end hostilities and bring all the region's Indigenous nations together for a council.[67]

The new secretary of war, James Monroe, tasked Clark, Illinois Territorial Governor Ninian Edwards, and the trader Auguste Chouteau with officially informing the Indigenous nations along the Mississippi and Missouri Rivers that the United States and Great Britain had ceased hostilities and were at peace. In accordance with the terms of the Treaty of Ghent, these commissioners were also assigned the task of signing peace agreements with the individual Indigenous nations. The commissioners chose Portage des Sioux, located midway between the mouths of the Illinois and Missouri Rivers on the west bank of the Mississippi as the site of their council. Earlier they had dispatched messengers to thirty-seven Indigenous bands and nations, summoning them to meet there. By the time Clark arrived at Portage des Sioux in early July, between two thousand and three thousand Natives were already encamped at the site. To ensure peace during the proceedings, Clark brought an estimated $20,000 worth of gifts for the Native delegations. He also ordered two fully armed gunboats to patrol the river while 275 soldiers were stationed on shore.[68]

Historian Martin Case has observed that to streamline the task at hand, the trio of commissioners assembled a "treaty-making machine" of influential military, business, and political leaders to serve as witnesses and interpreters. These included several members of the Chouteau and Clark families along with Pierre Menard and Manuel Lisa, both of whom had strong ties to the Missouri Fur Company. Also in attendance were John W. Johnson, a future St. Louis mayor; Henry S. Geyer, a future US senator from Missouri; Henry Dodge, who would become a congressman, governor, and US senator from Wisconsin; Alexander McNair and John Miller, who each served as governors of Missouri; and Robert Walsh, a future US Supreme Court justice. Between July 18 and September 16, 1815, the commissioners signed thirteen separate treaties with members of the Piankeshaw, Omaha, Kickapoo, Ioway, Osage, Sac, Fox, and Kanza, as well as with several different bands of Sioux. Many nations that had fought against the United States had signed because they believed they had no other choice. They realized they must resign themselves to the fact that the Americans would not be expelled from the trans-Mississippi West. Many, like the Ioways, who had just suffered at the hands of pro-American proxy fighters, signed the treaty because they were eager to get back on friendly terms with the United States.[69]

Burns has written that the treaties, which were drawn up in 1815, essentially "reaffirmed the *status quo ante bellum*." The thirteen documents were largely identical with each nation agreeing that all past hostilities were to be "mutually forgiven and forgot," and that "there shall be perpetual peace and friendship between all." However, the commissioners did take the opportunity to revisit some past issues that had remained unresolved. Both the Sacs and Foxes agreed to "recognize, re-establish, and confirm," the contested Treaty of 1804. Additionally, the Sacs agreed to sever all relationships with their relatives who remained on the Rock River with Black Hawk. Black Hawk's band of Sacs would meet with Clark, Edwards, and Chouteau in St. Louis to sign a treaty of friendship in May 1816.[70]

Treaties of Removal and Deportation

The violence and upheaval that took place in the region prior to and during the War of 1812 had temporarily halted treaty making in the Missouri Territory. After the war and the completion of the peace treaties of 1815, the United States resumed its vigorous efforts to negotiate with Native nations to extinguish their claims to land in the Northwest Territory, which was bounded by the Great Lakes, the Mississippi River, and the Ohio River. For the first time, Thomas Jefferson's plan to remove nations living east of the Mississippi River into the Missouri Territory was put in motion. The first nation to be removed was the Kickapoos.

Though the Algonquin-speaking Kickapoos originated east of the Great Lakes along the St. Lawrence Seaway, some members of that group had settled in present-day Missouri as early as 1765. About seventy-five families, led by the headman Serena, moved into Spanish Louisiana at the invitation of its first governor, Antonio de Ulloa. Among his first acts, Ulloa had established posts along the west bank of the Mississippi River as a defense against the British, who occupied Illinois on the opposite bank. He also made overtures of friendship with the region's Indigenous population in hopes that they would help defend the territory. Serena's Kickapoos first settled about forty miles up the Missouri River from St. Louis, though over time they moved farther west, near the Osage and Gasconade Rivers. From there, they maintained relations with the two other main groups of Kickapoos who lived near the Illinois River and the Wabash River in present-day Illinois and Indiana, respectively.[71]

These eastern Kickapoos, many of whom had fought against the United States during the War of 1812, were understandably aggravated by white settlers who were invading their land. They also remained suspicious of the white Americans and were not eager to reach an accord with them. When the war leader Little Otter failed to persuade Potawatomis and Miamis to help fight settlers, the Kickapoos undertook the campaign unilaterally, raiding surveyors' camps and destroying survey markers. Finally, unable to stop the settlers, the Kickapoos agreed to meet with treaty negotiators in the spring of 1819. Auguste Chouteau and Benjamin Stephenson held a council with the Kickapoos who lived on the Illinois River, while Benjamin Parke met with those who lived on the Wabash in Indiana. Both Stephenson and Parke were politically invested in their respective states. Stephenson had served as a US congressman from Illinois and had been appointed by President James Madison to be the Receiver of Moneys at the Federal Land Office in Edwardsville, Illinois. Parke, too, had served in Congress as the first territorial representative from Indiana. At the time he served as a treaty commissioner, he was a US district court judge.[72]

Kickapoo reluctance to sign treaties with the US forced negotiators to invest several weeks, tons of provisions, gifts of horses, and weapons to persuade them to exchange all their land east of the Mississippi for a parcel of land at the confluence of the Osage and Pomme de Terre Rivers in Missouri. The Illinois Kickapoos signed a treaty with Chouteau and Stephenson on July 30, 1819, and the Wabash Kickapoos reached an agreement with Parke one month later. Aside from promising the Kickapoos that the land in Missouri would be theirs "forever," the United States pledged "to guaranty [their] peaceable possession of the tract . . . and to restrain and prevent all white persons from hunting, settling, or otherwise intruding upon it." The United States also agreed to pay the nation $2,000 annually for fifteen years, to give them an additional one-time gift of $3,000 of merchandise, and to facilitate their deportation from their current homes to their new one in Missouri.[73]

Historian Claudio Saunt has written that the phrase "Indian removal" is unfitting "for a story about the state-sponsored expulsion of eighty-thousand people." He also points out that the phrase was devised by early-nineteenth-century proponents of the policy and is "artfully vague." It avoids any hint of coercion and violence and lacks a sense of who was removing whom. Instead, Saunt proposes that we apply the words *deportation* and *expulsion* when addressing the topic of what was essentially forced migration for the purpose of ethnic cleansing. *Deportation* depicts the act of a government driving people beyond its national borders. Expulsion carries with it a sense of the violence used to uproot people from their homeland.[74]

It should come as no surprise, then, that the Americans discovered the Kickapoos, whom William Clark had once referred to as "the most uncooperative of all tribes," were as resistant to their expulsion as they had been to treaty negotiations. Eager to make way for white settlement in Illinois and Indiana, the United States awarded Auguste Chouteau's brother-in-law, Paschal Cerré, the contract to oversee the Kickapoo deportation. In September 1819, Cerré gathered two thousand men, women, and children together for the trip west. To his surprise, the Kickapoos immediately split into smaller bands, with each making their way separately to the Osage River. This apparently happened because a group of Potawatomis had convinced some of the Kickapoos that Cerré intended to lead the entire group to St. Louis, where American soldiers would slaughter them. The one band of Kickapoos that remained with Cerré belonged to the headman Blue Eyes. Cerré reported that their trip proved to be painfully slow and that his charges were "very shy and pretty hard to deal with." Along the way, Blue Eye's band insisted on avoiding white settlements and would often stop, refusing to move further.[75]

As they neared the Osage River, Blue Eyes seemed especially reluctant to continue. Later, the Illinois Kickapoos would claim that Chouteau and Stephenson had promised them that they could choose the locations of their new villages. When the reunited bands arrived to find the land had already been surveyed, many refused to settle in the location stipulated by the treaty. This, in turn, created trouble with the Osages, who lived adjacent to the Kickapoo tract. The Osages complained that the Kickapoos were building their villages too close to their own and were infringing on their hunting land. Secretary of War John C. Calhoun reported to Governor Clark that he believed the Osages' grievances were justified, concluding, "it will be almost impossible for such near neighbors to live in peace."[76]

To avert further trouble, Chouteau and Stephenson again met with the Kickapoos in July 1820 to adjust the boundaries set in the 1819 treaty. But this second agreement, signed on July 20, did little to sooth the ongoing dispute. As historian Arrell M. Gibson has observed, the Kickapoos' time in Missouri was marked by "continued brigandage" on white settlements and "intermittent warfare" with their neighbors, the Osages. The violence, which was heaviest between 1821 and 1826, forced Clark to call Osage delegates to St. Louis for peace talks with the Kickapoos, Delawares, Shawnees, Weas, Piankeshaws, and Peorias, all emigrant nations that had been removed from their land east of the Mississippi River and had clashed with the Osages. After six days of vigorous debate, Clark was finally able to secure a signed agreement on October 7, 1826, calling for perpetual peace between the nations. The six nations agreed to pay the Osages $1,000 for the murder of several tribal members and pledged not to hunt on Osage land. While the agreement addressed past grievances, Clark was already thinking of ways to prevent future violence. He introduced the idea of another removal with each of the delegations of emigrant nations before they left St. Louis. Clark asked them to consider relocation on land in present-day Kansas. Several headsmen told him they would visit the land and take his suggestion into consideration. Thus, the ground was laid for what would become the eventual deportation of all Indigenous nations from Missouri.[77]

Voices

Some think, my father, that you have brought all these warriors here to take our land from us, but I do not believe it. For although I am but a poor, simple Indian, yet I know that this land will not suit your farmers; if I even thought your hearts bad enough to take the land, I would not fear it, as I know there is not wood enough on it for the use of whites. You might settle along this river, where timber is to be found; but we can always get wood enough in our country to make our little fires.

There is one thing I fear, my father; my nation is coming down here to hunt this winter, and if you send out your soldiers to hunt also, they will drive off all the game, and our women and children will starve. We have heard of the ascent of the troops up this river ever since last fall, and we have been told by other nations, that if they chance to meet with any [women] unprotected, they ravish them. But, my father, we shall soon know if this be true or not; because, having but little to eat, our [women] will be obliged to go out into the prairies to dig roots; I shall trust to you, and not hesitate to let them go.[1]

—*Big Elk (Ongpatonga) (Omaha)*

I know that we are not able to cope with the whites. I have seen some of your soldiers and know that they have better guns than we have, and I am told they are numerous as the sands on the riverbank or the great herds of buffalo on the prairies, but if the whites compel us to make peace with the Pawnees, we will, if we can do no better, scratch you with our toe and finger nails and gnaw you with our teeth.[2]

—*White Cloud (Maxúthka) (Ioway), 1819*

My father! My heart is glad, and I must shake hands with you.

Sioux, Sacs & Foxes, that are here! Look upon me and you look upon almost a white man. . . .

All these people you see here, who wear one of these things [pointing to his war club] think themselves very great.

. . . I have learned to plough and now I eat my own bread, and it makes me large & strong. These people eat everything, and yet are lean. They can't get fat Even by eating their own words.

. . . This, father, is what I have to say. When I was young, I used to pride myself in one of these things [warclub] but now I mean to throw it aside. I know of other things.[3]

—*White Cloud (Maxúthka) (Ioway), 1830*

Fathers! You have writings and books before you to tell the truth by. We have nothing of that kind from our ancestors.

My Fathers! When I want to speak the truth, I always look up first to the heavens, next to the earth, and then to you as the third, which enables me to do so.

Fathers! You once kindled a fire here and had my relations around it, they have broke the peace that was then made. I was not here at that time, but I heard all about it. I am here now.

Fathers! Our ancestors had nothing as a token of peace but their pipe, which they always took with them and it was held sacred. Now that I have smoked your pipe here, can I do wrong?

I have several times heard my Great Father's words. I have heard yours; I now hear them to-day and I hear my Agent's words often; He is a good father to me.

My elder brother here has spoken the truth when he said we were once as one nation, and I hope hereafter I, his younger brother, will speak the truth.

Fathers! I think I follow your advice as well as I can when any of my young men go and do any one wrong. I take my pipe and I go and settle it, but you do better than even my father here (my Agent) you come yourself and help us settle our difficulties. I have smoked out of your pipe my father—this is my medicine pipe, and I give it to you to smoke.[4]

—*Waw-ron-esaw (The Encircler) (Otoe), 1830*

Chapter Six

Land and Paper

ON SEPTEMBER 17, 1819, A group of Ioways spotted a disconcerting apparition churning the waters of the Missouri River. As they stood on the riverbank at Manuel Lisa's trading fort near the Council Bluff, they watched what appeared to be a huge smoke-belching underwater panther, struggling wildly against the river's muddy current. Seeing the Ioways' apprehension at the sight, David Meriwether, a nineteen-year-old trader, told them it was "a big snake swimming upriver with a little boat on its back." Though "this astonished the Indians very much, . . . many seemed to doubt it." Not deceived, but still wary, especially when the craft landed and howled as it let off steam, the Ioways moved back cautiously. As they continued to eye the bizarre vessel suspiciously, a handsome young white man in military uniform emerged from its belly to greet them. The officer was Major Benjamin O'Fallon, businessman, aspiring politician, newly appointed Indian Agent for the Upper Missouri, and a nephew of William Clark. The US military invasion of the Upper Missouri River had begun.[1]

The serpent was in fact the *Western Engineer*, a stern wheel steamboat designed by Major Stephen Long to carry the Yellowstone Expedition's scientific branch up the Missouri River. By all appearances, the man-made monster was no more benevolent than the underwater panther of the Ioway spirit realm. Long had apparently designed the sternwheeler with the intention of intimidating the Indigenous people he encountered on the expedition. Meriwether recalled that the *Western Engineer* featured a sheet iron bowsprit fashioned into the shape of a serpent head. "When a puff of steam escaped," wrote Meriwether, "it passed through this imitation of a snake's head, the jaws of which were fixed on hinges so as to let the steam escape through the mouth." Even without the serpent's head, the *Western Engineer* was an impressive sight.

Not only was it the first steamboat to travel beyond Fort Osage on the Missouri River, but the deck of the boat was brimming with artillery pieces. While Europeans and their armed emissaries were nothing new to the Indigenous nations of the Missouri River valley, Long, O'Fallon, and the *Western Engineer* were the harbingers of a new type of colonial presence. The boat's appearance at Lisa's fort was soon followed by the arrival of five hundred soldiers from the Sixth Infantry, led by Colonel Henry Atkinson. Such a sizable military force was surely cause for concern among the region's Indigenous residents.[2]

IMAGE 7: *Western Engineer,* by Titian Ramsay Peale, 1819. Used by Major Stephen Long as part of the Missouri Expedition in 1819, the *Western Engineer* was the first steamboat to successfully travel the Missouri River above Franklin, Missouri, and may have been the first stern-wheeler ever constructed. *Image in the collection of the American Philosophical Society. Reproduced under the Creative Commons CC0 1.0 Universal Public Domain Dedication*

Almost immediately after the Louisiana Purchase allowed white Americans to cross the Mississippi in great numbers, scenes like, though perhaps less theatrical than, the one that occurred at Council Bluff, took place throughout the US's newly acquired territory. Native Missourians began to witness a far greater number of incursions by white American military men, traders, and settlers. The first wave of the invasion was generally scientific and military in nature. Even while Lewis and Clark's Corps of Discovery was still on the Missouri River, Territorial Governor James Wilkinson sent a military expedition led by Lieutenant George Peter and accompanied by Pierre Chouteau up the Osage River, the land of the Osages, to explore, collect geographic information, and scout sites for future military installations. That same year, 1805, had also seen the construction of Fort Belle Fontaine, near the confluence of the Missouri and Mississippi Rivers. The following year, Wilkinson dispatched Lieutenant Zebulon Pike up the Arkansas River to map the Louisiana Territory's western boundary. While these expeditions were sent west to reconnoiter the territories of Indigenous nations and to assess which might be friendly to the US, the soldiers and scientists also conducted inventories of natural resources—minerals, animals, timber, waterways—that might be exploited for profit. From the start, the intent of the United States was not to share land and resources with Indigenous people, but to remove the original inhabitants in order to take full control of their natural assets.[3]

After becoming secretary of war in 1817, John C. Calhoun was determined to facilitate "the enlargement and protection of our fur trade, and the permanent peace of our North Western frontier by the establishment of a decided control over the various Indian tribes in that quarter." To accomplish these goals, he planned to construct more military installations on the Missouri River. Aside from Fort Belle Fontaine, the Americans still operated Fort Osage, which had been reopened in 1815 and would remain in service until 1822. However, Calhoun envisioned additional military installations farther upriver. As Ioway historian Lance M. Foster has written, "forts served a dual function: to establish claims to a territory" and "to try to tie the resident tribes to the interests of the contending country through trade." In the case of the US, trade became an effective mechanism for tying Indigenous nations to the market economy and debt.[4]

With these objectives in mind, Calhoun conceived of the grandiose Yellowstone Expedition. He planned to send a force of one thousand soldiers up the river on steamboats to build a fort at the confluence of the Yellowstone and Missouri Rivers near present-day Williston, North Dakota. More than a military mission, the Yellowstone Expedition would also include a corps of artists and scientists led by Major Long of the Corps of Engineers.[5]

The Yellowstone Expedition quickly became a fiasco. Richard Mentor Johnson, a Kentucky Congressman who had become something of a folk hero after claiming to have killed the Shawnee leader Tecumseh at the Battle of Thames, and his brother James Johnson, invested $267,000 in the expedition. In return for their largess, they were awarded a government contract to outfit five steamboats for the expedition and expected to receive additional contracts to supply forts once they were established on the river. Any hopes the military had of traveling to the Yellowstone River in 1818 were dashed, however, when the Johnson brothers' steamboats and supplies arrived at Fort Belle Fontaine weeks later than planned. Based on technology that had not yet been well tested on the muddy Missouri River, the boats turned out to be extremely unreliable. Two of them, the *Calhoun* and the *Exchange*, may have broken down even before reaching the fort. The First Battalion of the Rifle Regiment, which was to be the expedition's first wave, was delayed and unable to leave Fort Belle Fontaine on the remaining three steamboats until late August.[6]

Just one hundred seventy miles from St. Louis, the steamboat *Jefferson* broke down. The remaining two boats, the *Johnson* and the *Expedition*, continued crawling upriver at a pace of only slightly better than 7.5 miles a day, until reaching Cow Island, near the present-day town of Iatan, Missouri, in mid-October. There, still more than a thousand short of their destination, the two hundred sixty riflemen spent a long hungry winter at a camp they called Cantonment Martin, named after the regiment's commander, Captain Wyly Martin. Cantonment Martin became the US military's westernmost installation and remained in use for two years.[7]

The new camp quickly drew the attention of nearby Indigenous people. Within two weeks of their arrival on the island, the soldiers were joined by a large group of Kanzas who set up thirty lodges nearby. They, in turn, were soon joined by a small group of Sacs. Like the soldiers, the Kanzas and Sacs were short of food and found the cantonment to be an irresistible source of clothing and sustenance. Emboldened by the discovery that the regiment was too small and poorly equipped to police them, the Kanzas had begun stealing from the fort's hunting parties, and even stole directly from the camp itself. After being apprehended by the soldiers, a few of the Kanzas were tried in a makeshift military court on charges of the theft of private and public property and of breaking the bonds of friendship by which they had promised the soldiers they would abide.

When asked to speak on the Kanzas' behalf, one of the men told Captain Martin that while the soldiers were bound to remain in the camp under the threat of punishment, the young Kanza men were free to roam the land and do as they chose. "These woods and streams are ours," the Kanza reminded Martin.

> The beaver which inhabit this river and the buffalo which range in these forests are ours; their skins afford us clothing and shelter from the rude blasts of winter; their meat a luxurious substance. . . . Should we then who are Lords of the forests quit the pleasures and the adventures of the hunt, and like you, confine ourselves to one solitary valley, to practice discipline and subordination to live in idleness and indolence?[8]

The Kanzas begged Martin to release them so that they could find those who were responsible for the thefts and bring them to the camp for punishment. Unimpressed, Martin had five of the defendants flagellated and admonished them all to "Mend their Manners and Morals."[9]

The thefts continued, as did the punitive actions with which the military answered them. Much of the discipline was meted out by Major O'Fallon. At the time he first visited Cantonment Martin in 1818, he was a special Indian agent holding councils along the Missouri River with Kanzas, Otoes, and Omahas. Despite his complete lack of experience in diplomacy or Indian Affairs, O'Fallon had received his appointment as an Indian agent the previous year. He was originally stationed at Prairie du Chien, where he had "exhibited a tendency to be forceful, even belligerent, in his dealing with the Indians."[10]

The Indigenous people living around the camp quickly learned that, unlike the French, who had reciprocated kinship ties with them, the white Americans were not averse to meting out physical punishment. At Cantonment Martin, the arrogant O'Fallon had severely chastised those suspected of committing crimes against whites. In one incident in November 1818, he met a man of mixed Native heritage who boasted of having taken part in an attack on Fort Dearborn in 1812. Enraged, O'Fallon cut off the man's ears, gave him one hundred lashes, and threw his weapons in the river. Though this incident received the negative attention of the War Department, O'Fallon was not disciplined and, in fact, received a commission as Indian Agent for the Upper Missouri in March 1819.[11]

After returning to St. Louis for the winter, the newly commissioned Major O'Fallon returned to Cantonment Martin with the second wave of Yellowstone Expedition personnel in July 1819. Secretary Calhoun had ostensibly sent O'Fallon up the Missouri to improve relations with the Native nations. In his instructions to the major, Calhoun wrote,

> If practicable you will gain the confidence and friendship of all the Indian tribes with whom you may have any intercourse. Undoubtedly the Indians ought to be fully impressed with our capacity to avenge any injury which they may offer us; but it is no less important that they should be equally impressed with our justice and humanity. Should you succeed in convincing them of both, all difficulties will be removed. . . .[12]

Far more inclined to employ the proverbial stick rather than the carrot, O'Fallon called a council with between one hundred fifty and two hundred Kanzas at Camp Martin a few days after his return. His main objective seems to have been to exact retribution for at least two incidents that he considered punishable offenses. The first was an incident in which several Kanzas had shot at, and possibly wounded, O'Fallon while he was aboard a boat en route to St. Louis. The Kanzas were also charged with having repeatedly "insulted and plundered" Captain Martin's men. O'Fallon admonished the Kanzas to "guide their conduct," warning them that the Sixth US Infantry was at that moment making its way to the camp to relieve the rifle regiment and that they possessed enough arms to force the tribe into compliance. Captain Martin then ordered several of the Kanzas, whom he believed had robbed the cantonment, to be flogged. Some among the Kanzas expected the soldiers to exact even greater revenge, as it was rumored among them that the soldiers had buried barrels of gunpowder under the council site and intended to blow them up while they were gathered. Exploiting this fear, O'Fallon further agitated the wary delegation by concluding the council with a few ceremonial rounds from the howitzers mounted on the *Western Engineer*, which was anchored nearby. Understandably, the Kanza headmen dutifully expressed regret for their behavior.[13]

O'Fallon and other members of the Yellowstone Expedition soon left Cantonment Martin, leaving the Sixth Infantry behind to staff the camp.

Those who continued up the river again failed to reach their goal, only making it as far as the spot where Lewis and Clark had held a council with the Otoes in 1804. There, at the Council Bluff, the military established another installation called Fort Atkinson. Because of the change in plans, Stephen Long's Corps of Engineers were ordered to travel west in search of the sources of the Platte, Arkansas, and Red Rivers. On that trip, Long would famously refer to the plains of Nebraska, Colorado, Texas, and Oklahoma as the "Great American Desert."[14]

Meanwhile, those Natives left behind at Cantonment Martin would find the surrounding landscape forever changed. The soldiers had made a significant impact on the region's natural resources as they endeavored to feed themselves and construct their fortification. They had mined stones, cut timber, and left behind refuse. They had also decimated the region's wildlife. During the winter of 1818–1819 alone, Captain Martin's men are estimated to have killed two thousand to three thousand deer and uncounted numbers of bears, turkeys, and smaller animals. This led the Omaha leadman Big Elk to remark to O'Fallon, "There is one thing I fear, my father; my nation is coming down here to hunt this winter, and if you send out your soldiers to hunt also, they will drive off all the game, and our women and children will starve." The Kanzas, Ioways, Otoes, Missourias, and Omahas were left with a ravaged and diminished country on which it was difficult for them to survive without the goods provided by traders and soldiers.

The prospect of this dependence no doubt concerned them as they had seen firsthand the ruthless physical violence of which these new US invaders, or as some Natives called them, "long knives," were capable. As Big Elk had inquired of O'Fallon,

> There is one thing, my father which I wish you to inform me of. We have heard of your tying up and whipping individuals of several nations, as you ascended this river. What is the offence which will subject us to this punishment? I wish to know, that I may inform my people, that they may be on their guard.[15]

Competition for Resources

Along with the military, traders had become more numerous and moved farther up the Missouri, Kansas, and Arkansas Rivers. With the backing of prominent St. Louisans, Manuel Lisa and the Missouri Fur Company had had been a presence at Council Bluff since 1810. Nearby, another trader, Joseph Robidoux, had established a post at the mouth of the Platte River. However, the opening of the Missouri River to Americans drew new investors and traders from other parts of the United States to St. Louis. Wilson Price Hunt, a partner in John Jacob Astor's new Pacific Fur Company, created a stir in the city when he arrived to organize a trade excursion up the river in 1811. Much to the chagrin of Lisa, who was preparing his own expedition that spring, this new competitor quickly assembled a crew and supplies and succeeded in getting a three-week head start on the Missouri Fur Company. Determined not to let Hunt get to the Upper Missouri and the Mandan villages ahead of him, Lisa pushed his crew relentlessly up the river until they overtook Hunt two months later in present-day South Dakota. From there, the two parties traveled to the trading post, known as Fort Mandan, in tandem. The frantic race between the two groups was indicative of the competition that then existed as multiple trade companies struggled to get any advantage they could on the Missouri.[16]

Territorial Governor William Clark estimated that Missouri Territory's Native population that year stood at about five thousand, or just a quarter of what it had been five years earlier. Clark's estimate included thirteen hundred Shawnees, eight hundred forty Delawares, fifty Peorias, two hundred Piankeshaws, sixteen hundred Great Osages, and an unspecified number of Ioways, Sacs and Foxes.[17] Meanwhile, the Euro-American population, which had grown to 19,783 in 1810, was growing rapidly and would reach 66,586 a decade later.

One man who chronicled the changes then taking place in the Missouri Territory was geologist and ethnographer Henry Rowe Schoolcraft. Schoolcraft arrived in the town of Potosi, Missouri, in 1818 to inspect lead-mining operations there. Hearing that rich deposits of lead lay in the White River valley, Schoolcraft and his traveling companion, Levi Pettibone, traveled nine hundred miles on foot, with a pack horse, to investigate. Leaving Potosi in late fall 1818, and being, as Schoolcraft put it, "unacquainted with the hunter's art of traveling in the woods," the pair "encounter[ed] some difficulties from want of experience."[18]

While Schoolcraft may not have been a particularly savvy backwoodsman, he was observant and articulate. In the journal of his trip, which he published two years later, he recorded astute observations about plants, animals, minerals, Native people, and settlers. He also chronicled some of the changes white settlers had brought to the rugged hill country of the Ozarks. Schoolcraft noted significant differences between the groups. He wrote about the tradition of "covering the dead," a system of reparations used by Osages and other Native people. The custom called for those who had been responsible for killing a person to make some sort of restitution to the family of the victim. While the tradition did not always work to make amends, it often helped to minimize endless retaliatory feuds, which Schoolcraft noted were the preferred methods used by white pioneers to exact revenge for the killing of one of their own.[19]

Perhaps a more consequential change chronicled by Schoolcraft was the difference between the ways that Natives and white settlers used natural resources. He was impressed by the efficient way Indigenous people could build a hot fire with just a fraction of the wood that settlers would use to get the same result. Similarly, he wrote that a typical Euro-American pioneer "destroys all before him and cannot resist the opportunity of killing game, although he neither wants the meat, nor can carry the skins." A Native hunter, by comparison, "never kills more meat than he has occasion for." Schoolcraft estimated that by 1818, there were more than a thousand commercial hunters operating in the White River valley and some species, such as beaver, were already becoming scarce. The careless way settlers exploited resources had a devastating effect on the sustainable economy that natives had maintained for millennia.[20]

Establishing a State on Indigenous Land

When the Missouri Territorial legislature petitioned Congress for statehood in 1818, it did so with equal measures of moral certainty and legal ambiguity. While the US government had long believed its status as continental conqueror entitled it to encroach on Indigenous land and sovereignty with impunity, it did not yet hold legal claim to most of the territory within the proposed state's boundaries. In fact, when Missouri was admitted into the Union in 1821, only the Sacs, Foxes, and Osages had ceded rights to any property inside the state, and the validity of the Sac and Fox Treaty of 1804 still lay in dispute. In all, it would take thirty-three years to negotiate twenty treaties with thirteen different Native nations, before the United States finally established clear title to all the land inside Missouri in 1837.

The United States Supreme Court, which would codify elements of the Doctrine of Discovery into US law in the 1823 case *Johnson v. M'Intosh*, stated that Indigenous inhabitants retained what the court called the Right of Occupancy, or Aboriginal Title, to their land. However, the high court also said that the discovering or conquering nation held the exclusive right to purchase the land from them, should they choose to sell. Though Indigenous nations were almost always reluctant to sell their land rights to the United States, they could usually be "persuaded" to do so by ongoing harassment from settler colonists who encroached on it. Historian John Mack Faragher has referred to these squatters as "proxy invaders" who carried out the work of ethnic cleansing for the US government. Native nations could also be forced to sell their land, which had already been invaded by settler colonialists, to cover debts incurred from having to purchase extravagantly overpriced trade goods from government-licensed traders. In the words of President Thomas Jefferson, we shall "be glad the good and influential Indians . . . run into debt, because we observe when these debts get beyond what the individual can pay, they become willing to lop them off by a cession of land."[21]

After Missouri entered the Union as the twenty-fourth state on August 10, 1821, officials renewed their push to end all Indigenous claims within its boundaries. Negotiating with the Ioways and a branch of the Sacs and Foxes known as the Sac and Fox Nation of Missouri was a vital next step in this process. Except for the land the Sacs and Foxes had ceded under duress in 1804, the nations held claims to all the state north of the Missouri River.

The treaties signed in 1824 with these nations were notable in two important ways. First, the negotiations were not held in Missouri, but rather in Washington, DC. The fact that the government was willing to underwrite the expense of sending a delegation representing the Sacs, Foxes, and Ioways to the nation's capital city is testament to the importance it placed on the land cession it hoped to gain. Second, the treaty signed in Washington led to the first complete forced removal of an entire Native nation—or in this case three nations—from the boundaries of Missouri. Though the policy of Indian Removal is most often associated with President Andrew Jackson, it was favored by President Jefferson as early as 1803. He had written to his friend John Adams in 1812 that to deal with Indigenous nations, the United States "shall be obliged to drive them, with the beasts of the forest into the Stony Mountains." Removal continued to be a goal of government relations with Native people, well before Congress enacted the Indian Removal Act at President Jackson's request in 1830.[22]

In June 1824, William Clark accompanied the Ioways, Sacs, Foxes, and some of their family members to the council in Washington. Traveling to eastern cities was intended to be an overwhelming experience for the Native delegates. Those making the trip usually traveled first class, stayed in excellent hotels, and received gifts and new clothing, all at government expense. Besides visiting Washington, the delegation visited Baltimore, Philadelphia, and New York. While in the capital city, they were entertained at several Washington galas and dinners. Because the city's social elite viewed Indigenous people, especially women, as exotic novelties, they were quite taken with Flying Pigeon Woman, wife of the Ioway headman White Cloud. Her husband, on the other hand, made a less favorable impression during the visit to Washington. He suffered a broken arm in a fall from the window of his second-story room at the Indian Queen Hotel on Pennsylvania Avenue. The delegates met with President James Monroe and visited factories and a shipyard. Some, including Great Walker, White Cloud, and Flying Pigeon Woman, had their portraits painted by the noted Washington artist Charles Bird King. This dizzying array of activities and diversions was intended to display for the Natives the wealth, military strength, and supposed cultural superiority of the United States.[23]

IMAGE 8: This lithograph of the Ioway leader Great Walker, later known as Big Neck, is a copy of a painting made by artist Charles Bird King in 1824. King painted Great Walker, White Cloud, and Flying Pigeon Woman while the Ioways were in Washington, DC to sign the Treaty of 1824. As a symbol of his regret over signing the treaty, Great Walker routinely blackened his face with ashes. *Courtesy of the Missouri State Archives and Library of Congress*

MOA-NA-HON-GA,
Great Walker,
AN IOWAY CHIEF.

When they finally met with Clark and Superintendent of Indian Affairs Thomas McKenney in early August, the two Ioway leaders, White Cloud and Great Walker, stated that the Sacs and Foxes, who were led by Tiamah, Pah-sha-pa-ha, and Keokuk, had no claim to the land in question, nor, for that matter, did the United States. White Cloud pointed out that the Ioways had been "deceived by the Spaniards and the French for they had no right to the Country which they sold to the Americans." The Sacs and Foxes contested the Ioways' claim of ownership and further alleged that the Osages had no right to cede northern Missouri to the United States in 1808. Keokuk boasted that since they had chased the Osages out of the area, it belonged to the Sacs and Foxes by right of conquest.[24]

Clark suggested that since they had competing claims to northern Missouri, both nations—the Sacs and Foxes were treated as a single nation in this treaty—could cede the land in question. They reached an agreement that stipulated that each Nation would be paid $500 each year for ten years. The treaty also promised to provide them with blacksmiths, agricultural tools, and cattle, which the government hoped would inspire the nations to pursue agriculture and thereby become self-sufficient once again. Since the treaty called for the Sacs, Foxes, and Ioways to vacate Missouri by January 1, 1826, the government made plans for them to settle west of the state, along the Platte River in what is now Buchanan County, Missouri (on land the state would acquire some ten years later). There, the government would create an Indian agency for them and assign them an agent.[25]

By affixing their marks to the treaty, the Ioways appeared to have fully committed themselves to helping their people adjust to the settlers' world. Their sincerity seems evident in the fact that, as they made their way to Washington, White Cloud and Great Walker had visited St. Regis, a school run by Jesuits in Florissant, near St. Louis. During their stopover, the headmen agreed to send five Ioway boys, including Great Walker's son, to the school to gain a European American education.[26]

The Ioway boys arrived at the school on June 11, 1824. Writing about their arrival more than a century later, Father Gilbert J. Garraghan observed,

The Indian youths did not submit without a protest to what must have seemed to them, accustomed as they were to the freedom of the forest, as nothing short of imprisonment. As their parents prepared to depart, they began to wail in true Indian fashion, whereupon one of the scholastics took up a flute and started to play. The music had the effect of quieting the lads and making them resigned, as far as outward indications went, to their new environment.[27]

Jesuits hoped that exposing the boys to a mixture of rigorous religious instruction, academic study, and manual training, they could be assimilated into white American society. Evidence suggests however, that the students were forced to work long hours and were subjected to beatings. John O'Connor, a Jesuit who worked at the school, described seeing Jesuit priests "tie the hands of the Indian scholars like so many felons and take them to be cruelly scourged on the naked back in the open air under his own eyes." He adds that their hands "were stretched in the form of a cross fastened to a tree and a post."[28] Not surprisingly, many of the boys ran away and St. Regis closed its doors after only seven years in 1831.

After the Ioway delegation's return home, Great Walker soon expressed profound regret for his part in signing away the land on which the Ioways and their Oneota ancestors had lived for centuries, and on which many of their ancestors were buried. "I am ashamed to look at the sun," he lamented. "I have insulted the Great Spirit by selling the land and the bones of my fathers; it is right that I should mourn always." As a symbol of his grief, he routinely blackened his face with ashes.[29]

White Cloud moved west of the old Missouri state line to live near the newly created Ioway Agency. There, he made earnest attempts to live as his white neighbors did. In the fall of 1828, Great Walker, who by then had begun to call himself Big Neck, elected to move north and east to live with about sixty other Ioways on land they still held claim to north of the Missouri border. He and his followers, derisively known as the Pouting Party, lived and hunted near the Chariton River in present-day Iowa.

In June 1829, Big Neck's party discovered settlers living west of present-day Kirksville, Missouri, at a place known as The Cabins. Believing they were on their own land, the Ioways warned the settlers that they were living there illegally and that US soldiers would force them to leave. On one of the Ioways' subsequent visits to The Cabins, settlers traded cheap whiskey to them for guns and clothing. Angry at being cheated, the hungry Ioways killed one of the settlers' hogs. Soon, more hogs disappeared, and the settlers became concerned that the

Ioways would turn their violence on them. On July 17, a militia company of twenty-six men led by Fields Trammel tracked the Ioways to their camp north of The Cabins. There, a gun battled erupted in which three Ioways and three militiamen, one of whom was wounded and later tortured by Big Neck, also died.[30]

Following the incident, Big Neck and his band fled north to the Iowa River, where a small military detachment led by their Indian agent, Andrew Hughes, caught up with them in September. Many of the group were so ill and malnourished that soldiers feared they would not survive the trip to St. Louis to stand trial. In the end, they took only Big Neck, ten other Ioway men, and one Ioway woman to be jailed at Jefferson Barracks near St. Louis. After an investigation, state officials determined that, as the fight had taken place just eighteen miles south of Missouri's northern border, the Ioways were justified in believing they were on their own land when the militia caught up with them. The investigation further revealed that the militia had fired first, and that Big Neck had been holding only his ceremonial pipe when the shooting started. After some consideration, the prisoners were tried in Huntsville, Missouri, the seat of the newly created Randolph County and seat of the court which was located closest to the scene of the battle. Accordingly, the grand jury acquitted Big Neck and four other Ioways for the killings. Big Neck died a year later in a fight with some Sioux. Most of the remainder of his party eventually returned to live with the rest of the Ioways near the agency.[31]

Though the Osages had ceded their claims to nearly all the land in the state of Missouri as part of their treaty with William Clark in 1808, they still held a twenty-two-mile strip of land that ran along the state's western border from the Missouri River south to Arkansas. In the seventeen years since their first cession in Missouri, settlers and as many as eight thousand Indigenous immigrants, who had been removed from their homes east of the Mississippi River, had settled on Arkansas and Missouri land relinquished in the 1808 treaty. As these immigrants found it hard to procure enough wild game to survive, they pushed west, into Osage hunting lands. This led to violent clashes between Osages and Kickapoos, Delawares and, most notably, Cherokees. In October 1817, six hundred Cherokees, aided by Choctaws, Chickasaws, Delawares, Shawnees, Quapaws, and Caddos, attacked Clermont II's village in northeast Oklahoma while many Osages were away for a buffalo hunt. The intertribal war party killed thirty-five people, mostly old men, women, and children, and took one hundred hostages. The Osages unsuccessfully attempted to persuade an alliance of Shawnees, Delawares, Quapaws, Kanzas, and Foxes to help them retaliate against the Cherokees. "In order more effectually to extend to [the Osages] that protection of the Government so much desired by them," Clark called approximately one hundred Osage leaders and warriors into a treaty council, this time in St. Louis.[32]

While the Osages did, in fact, wish for US protection, it is unlikely that they were eager to participate in new treaty negotiations that would force them to make another land cession. Osage historian John Joseph Mathews noted that many Osages believed that they were being unfairly punished for violence that had been incited by Cherokees and white settlers. Furthermore, the timing of the council presented them with a serious dilemma. Should Osage men travel to St. Louis to meet with Clark in May, doing so would disrupt their annual summer buffalo hunt. As a result, the Osages would enter the lean winter months ahead with less food than they needed to sustain themselves. Given the situation, however, many believed they had little or no choice but to make the journey to St. Louis.[33]

The Treaty of 1825 constituted the Osages' last huge cession of land. In it, they relinquished all their remaining claims to land in Missouri and Arkansas. They also ceded nearly all the land they claimed between the Kansas River and the Canadian River in present-day Oklahoma. At the conclusion of the negotiations, all that would remain of the Osages' land was a fifty-mile-wide strip that paralleled the present southern border of Kansas and ran from the Neosho River west two hundred fifty miles to the 100th Meridian. The United States promised that the Osages could keep this land "so long as they may choose to occupy" it.[34] The treaty also included a twenty-five by fifty-mile buffer or neutral zone meant to separate Osages from settlers and other nations: this extended from the western border of Missouri west to the Neosho River.

Many articles in the treaty were meant to encourage the Osages to learn to live in the manner of white settlers. Clark had come to believe that perpetual annuities harmed the Indigenous nations that received them, because they served to disincentivize them to become "civilized." His hope was that the Osages would quickly learn to grow their own food, which Osage women had been doing in their own fashion for millennia, and that annual payments would become unnecessary. He therefore proposed to compensate the Osages $7,000 annually for a period of twenty years. To help lead the Osages toward civilization, or at least *civilization* as whites perceived it, the treaty promised them six hundred head of cattle, six hundred hogs, one thousand domestic fowls, ten yokes of oxen, six carts, and farming utensils. The treaty also included a provision by which fifty-four acres of land would be sold to pay for the Osages' education. In 1819, the federal government had created the Civilization Fund and began appropriating $10,000 annually to be passed on to assist religious organizations in establishing missions on Indigenous land. Two such organizations received land in the 1825 treaty on which to establish missions for the education and religious conversion of Osages.[35]

The treaty also included several provisions that distributed land and money to a few individuals. More than forty ethnically mixed Osages each received a square-mile section of the newly ceded land. Recipients of these 640-acre land grants included ten children and four grandchildren of Noel Mongraine, the French and Osage interpreter who was married to the headman Pawhuska's daughter. Mongraine was also related to Pierre Chouteau through marriage. When Chouteau and Pawhuska had earlier allied to usurp the power of Clermont I, both counted Mongraine as an important supporter. It is difficult not to view the giving of these land grants as anything other than a tactic intended to further divide and weaken the Osages. Not only were the grants rewards for the assistance the Mongraine family had rendered to Chouteau and the white Americans, but they also served to further split the Osages into artificially created divisions between those who were of mixed heritage and those who were not.[36]

Finally, the government paid many of those who had outstanding claims against the Osages. The Delawares received $1,000 for damages the Osages had inflicted in clashes with them. American settlers were also reimbursed for items they claimed Osages had stolen or damaged. The government also paid Osage debt to the traders Auguste P. Chouteau, Paul Balio, and William S. Williams and cancelled the Osages' outstanding bills at George Sibley's Fort Osage trading factory. In exchange for this last provision, the Osages promised to release the United States from the promise it made in the Treaty of 1808 to keep the fort staffed with soldiers and to operate the factory. This allowed the government to close both installations that same year.[37]

The Osages' removal to their new reservation caused them both practical and spiritual difficulties. In the first place, it took them five years to locate permanent sites for their new villages. The removal disrupted their hunting and farming routines, which in turn led to widespread malnutrition. It also became more difficult for Osage people to fight the diseases transmitted to them by white settlers. Some Osages believed that the root of their suffering lay in the fact that they had abandoned the animals and plants that Wah'Kon-Tah had given them to care for on their ceded land. These relatives had been gifts from the creator and had sustained them for centuries. By leaving them behind to be misused by the white newcomers, the Osages had reneged on their promise always to protect them. As a result, many Osages believed the angry Wah'Kon-Tah "threw his crooked lance of fire more frequently at them."[38]

Even as their land domain shrank, six Osages had the opportunity to explore the world beyond North America during a promotional tour of Europe. As many Indigenous delegations that had traveled to the cities in the eastern United States had discovered over the decades, urban whites were intensely fascinated by peoples they considered exotic, romantic, and picturesque. Few curiosities intrigued eighteenth- and nineteenth-century Euro-Americans more than the traditions, clothing, and physical appearances of Indigenous people. Representatives of the Osage, Missouria, Illinois, and Otoe nations had discovered this to be true in Europe as well when they traveled to France with Bourgmont in 1725.[39]

Not long after the Osages moved to their new reservation in Kansas, an enterprising, if not particularly honest, promoter named David Delaunay paid them a visit. Dressed in a US military uniform, Delaunay persuaded twelve Osages to travel with him in Europe, possibly by constructing the illusion that the trip was somehow related to official government business. His powers of persuasion were such that, according to some sources, he talked the Osages into using their own money to finance the trip. As the party traveled to St. Louis, the boat or raft on which they were traveling sank in the Missouri River. Though everyone aboard survived, they had lost all their provisions. At that point, six of the Osages declined to travel any farther. Those who chose to continue were Little Chief, his wife Hawk Woman, Black Bird, his wife Sacred Sun, Big Soldier, and a man the French called Little Soldier. Osage John Joseph Mathews has referred to these six travelers as "the gullibles" because he believes they allowed themselves to be duped by the unscrupulous Delaunay. Mathews theorizes that, because all those in the travelling party except Little Chief were under the age of forty—the two women

185

were still teenagers—they may have traveled in hopes of distinguishing themselves within the nation or their clans. It is also possible that they simply were desperate. Having just been uprooted by the provisions of the Treaty of 1825, they were impoverished. Perhaps they thought the trip would offer them the opportunity to present their plight to someone who might be inclined and able to help them.[40]

The party arrived in Le Havre, a French town on the Normandy coast of the English Channel, on July 27, 1827. Contemporary accounts reported that the streets of the town were so filled with people wishing to view the Osages, that it was difficult for them to be transported safely to their hotel. Over the next few weeks, the crowds followed them to the opera and the theater, where the Osages did not perform, but usually sat in box seats as spectators. One evening, the group left their seats to go to the theater lobby, where the gawking crowd pushed them into the railings until Little Chief became visibly angry. It appears that Delaunay had been charging the theatergoers for the chance to view the Osages and was likely receiving a portion of the ticket receipts from those theaters in which the "Missourian Majesties" appeared. According to Mathews, the Osages seemed not to have been aware of this financial arrangement.[41]

In Paris, as public interest in the Osages began to wane, Delaunay's promotions became increasingly extravagant. He advertised a program that would include the Osages performing traditional dances and a hot air balloon ascension. At the event, Little Chief, who was a member of the eagle clan, expressed his desire to ride in the balloon's basket so that he could see the earth the way the eagles viewed it. Such events failed to maintain the public's enthusiasm for long, however, and by fall 1827 the Osages were begging on the streets of Paris suburbs for assistance. The group was soon being shuttled around the European cities of Amsterdam, Dresden, Frankfurt, and Berlin, as Delaunay tried to stay one step ahead of his creditors.[42]

In February 1828, Sacred Sun gave birth to twin daughters in a hotel in Liège, Belgium. Both girls were baptized and given Christian names. Maria-Theresa was adopted by a local wealthy woman, but died the following year, while Maria-Elizabeth remained with Sacred Sun. Meanwhile, the group continued to travel and perform for money wherever they could until early 1829, when Delaunay abandoned them in the city of Breslau, in present-day Poland, never to be heard from again. It took the Osages a year to raise the money and to arrange the return trip home. Hearing about their abandonment, church and government officials stepped in to aid the group in their preparations. In April, Black Bird, Sacred Sun, and Young Soldier sailed from Bordeaux.

IMAGE 9: This lithograph of the Osage woman Sacred Sun and her daughter Maria-Elizabeth is a copy of a painting made by artist Charles Bird King in 1829. The two had just returned from a trip to Europe, where Maria-Elizabeth was born. Six Osages had made the trip at the coaxing of promoter David Delaunay, who abandoned them in present-day Poland. It took the Osages a year to raise money for their return trip home. Sacred Sun's husband Black Bird and another man known as Young Soldier died on the sea voyage home from Europe and were buried at sea. *Courtesy of the Missouri State Archives and Library of Congress*

The remaining three sailed out of Le Havre sometime later, after having had their belongings confiscated on the dock by Delaunay's creditors.[43]

Black Bird and Little Soldier died on the voyage home and were buried at sea. On their journey back to the Osage reservation, Sacred Sun with Maria-Elizabeth stopped in Washington, where Charles Bird King painted a portrait of the mother and young daughter. Big Soldier, who had been the oldest member of the entourage, lived into his seventies and met the writer Washington Irving and the painter John Mix Stanley, both of whom used him as a subject for their work. Little Chief, the leader of the delegation, continued to represent the Osages in treaty negotiations in 1833 and 1839. Little is known about Hawk Woman's life after she returned from her trip to Europe.[44]

Deporting Missouri's Indigenous People

Back in Missouri, public opinion of Indigenous people was far less positive than it had been in Europe. German immigrant Gottfried Duden, who lived in what is now Warren County, Missouri, from 1824 until 1827, vividly documented the depth of ignorance many Missouri settlers had regarding Native people. Duden wrote that in the mid-1820s, Natives were rarely seen in his part of the state, except for those traveling the river to trade or receive annuities in St. Louis. "One often sees Indians in St. Louis," Duden observed in 1826, "sometimes Osage, sometimes [Kanza], sometimes members of the Fox tribe, sometimes Sioux, and others. They molest no one in any way, as little as do Negroes and whites."[45]

Lambasting whites who opposed the expulsion of Natives from the land, Duden warned that "the person who looks for virtue among undeveloped people connects entirely erroneous ideas with this word and introduces vague images of biased imagination into a field that should be reserved for rational thinking."[46] He supported these wildly inaccurate claims with tropes that were common at the time. He claimed that while Indigenous people were childlike, they were not innocent, and he posited that any harm the United States was causing them was far outweighed by the benefits they received. "If the Indians are constantly decreasing in number, the United States has no cause to blame itself. The real reason can be found in their way of life and in their constant feuds."[47]

Of course, Duden was hardly an impartial observer of Indigenous people and their various cultures. His purpose in writing his influential report on life in Missouri in 1829 was to encourage settler colonialism:

urging his countrymen to come to North America and replace the settlements of Indigenous Americans with those of Germans. His descriptions of the state's land and climate were overly sanguine and his estimation of its Native inhabitants exceedingly racist. Both were meant to ease settlers' concerns about relocating to a "new land" on another continent. "Here," he seemed to be saying, "one can escape the problems of modern Germany and start over again in a land that is without history or culture." The success of his invitation can be seen in the fact that thirty-eight thousand "followers of Duden" had settled in Missouri by 1840.[48]

Given the public eagerness to flood Missouri with colonizers, it comes as little surprise that settlers were applying increasing pressure on the Missouri legislature to remove the Shawnees and Delawares from their home near Cape Girardeau. During their early years in Missouri, the Shawnees had enjoyed living on what Finnish historian Sami Lakomäki has referred to as a "frontier of inclusion." While maintaining their heritage, Western Shawnees, as they were called, proved highly adaptable in their new home. They learned traditions of house design and town platting from their French neighbors, and they adopted European ways of farming and animal husbandry. Their white neighbors were impressed with the organized, well-constructed, and prosperous villages the Shawnees built along Apple Creek, north of Cape Girardeau, and the two groups generally mixed well, both commercially and socially.[49]

This mutual accommodation between cultures ended, however, with the Louisiana Purchase and the arrival of white American settlers. While the French had been content to live with the Shawnees, the white Americans demanded their complete removal, and by 1807 they had begun to intrude on Shawnee land. The population of white settlers in Cape Girardeau mushroomed after the Louisiana Purchase, from 1,996 people in 1804 to 4,620 just six years later. In the decade that followed, whites initiated an all-out campaign to force the Shawnees out of southeast Missouri. Settlers killed the Shawnees' livestock, ransacked and destroyed homesteads, and even assaulted village residents. The federal government failed to step in to protect the Shawnee land grant, let alone the Shawnee people, and local law enforcement officials refused to prosecute settlers for assault, vandalism, or squatting on Shawnee land.[50]

As a result, many Shawnees decided to move west to the White River, on the Missouri-Arkansas border, or south to the Arkansas River. Between 1815 and 1819, the Shawnee population in southeast Missouri dropped from one thousand two hundred to four hundred. Hoping to offer the Shawnees some measure of protection from settlers, William Clark herded them onto a reservation which they were to share with the Delawares in the extreme southwest corner of the state in 1820. Located adjacent to land the Osages still claimed, the Shawnees and Delawares maintained their previous military alliances with other emigrant nations in the region, such as the Cherokees, Peorias, Piankeshaws, and Kickapoos. However, Clark's Shawnee and Delaware reservation never received the federal government's approval, and after Alexander McNair, head of the territorial militia and firm supporter of squatters' rights, defeated Clark in the 1820 election to become Missouri's first governor, it became clear that the new state government wanted Natives removed to make way for settlers.[51]

By 1823, twenty-five hundred Shawnees had settled in the White River settlements, though their alliance with the other Native emigrant nations in the region made them appear to be larger in number. In February 1825, three headmen from the White River Shawnees, Kishkalwa, Mayesweskaka, and Petecaussa, also known as Captain Reed, met with Secretary of War John Calhoun to request compensation for the Spanish land grant in southeast Missouri from which they had been driven off by white settlers. Calhoun agreed to reimburse them with new reservation land west of the state of Missouri. Because the Shawnees preferred to remain close to the land that they had been forced to move to five years earlier, Clark considered relocating them in what is now northeastern Oklahoma, on land the Osages had ceded in 1825. In fact, Article Two of the treaty signed by fourteen Shawnee headmen who met with Clark in St. Louis in November 1825, describes a one-hundred-mile by twenty-five-mile reservation in that location. However, Article Three of the same treaty states that if the Oklahoma land was not suitable to the Shawnees, they would be given a reservation along the south bank of the Kansas River, just west of the Missouri state line. For reasons that are not entirely clear, the Shawnees settled on the Kansas land.[52]

The 1825 Shawnee treaty is somewhat unusual in that, instead of providing a litany of atrocities committed upon settlers by Natives, it acknowledges the losses, injuries, and "spoliations" the Shawnees had suffered at the hands of white settlers. Even though the Shawnees had not documented claims of their material losses to the satisfaction of the government, they received $11,000 in compensation. For the cession of their land grant in Missouri, the Shawnees received $9,000 in annuities and an additional $5,000 worth of domestic livestock and farm implements.[53]

The Kansas reservation was not, however, intended for the White River Shawnees alone. It was also intended for the few Shawnees still living in eastern Missouri, as well as those who remained east of the Mississippi River along the Ohio. Some White River Shawnees were disappointed in the quality of the land on their new Kansas reservation and uneasy about living near Plains Nations with whom they had little in common. They were also uncomfortable about being reunited with the Ohio River Shawnees. Led by the Shawnee Prophet, Tenskwatawa, the Ohio River arm of the nation had been less accommodating to the United States. For this reason, several hundred White River Shawnees refused to leave their land in southwestern Missouri and northwestern Arkansas until 1832.[54]

In October of that year, at least ten headmen representing Cape Girardeau Delawares and White River Shawnees met with US representatives Frank J. Allen and Nathan Kouns on William Clark's farm, Castor Hill, located outside St. Louis. Both treaty commissioners were well-connected Missouri Democrats. In 1834, Allen would be appointed the Registrar of the Federal Land Office in the mineral-rich region near Jackson, Missouri. A physician, Kouns was a staunch Callaway County Democrat who had campaigned in Missouri for the presidency of Andrew Jackson and had been appointed postmaster of the town of Fulton.[55]

The Delawares' portion of the treaty is discussed below, but for their part, the Shawnees received $1,600 in cash, clothing, and supplies necessary for their removal to Kansas to join those members of their nation who had removed in 1828. In addition, they would receive provisions for one year after their removal.[56] While this removed most Shawnees living in Missouri and Arkansas, there remained yet another group of Shawnees who had moved into Spanish territory near present-day Texas. Like their ancestors who had moved into Missouri, they, too, were determined to retain their cultural identity. These Absentee Shawnees, as they were known, remained separate and eventually received federal recognition separate from the rest of their nation.[57]

The Delawares, who had been deported from their original homeland in what is now Delaware Bay in New Jersey to Indiana by 1801, had already been a party in eleven treaties with the United States before 1818. In that year they had ceded their land in Indiana. Though the treaty allowed them three years to vacate their cession, it did not specify where the Delawares would be resettled, stating only that the United States agreed to "provide a country [for them] to reside in, upon the west side of the Mississippi."[58] Slowly, the Delawares made their way to Missouri, under the guidance of their Indian agent, the trader Pierre Menard. In 1820, 1,346 Delawares crossed the Mississippi River at Kaskaskia with nearly fifteen hundred head of livestock. For the next two years, many members of the nation camped along the Current River, where they suffered because the removal had disrupted their hunting and agricultural routines, resulting in a great deal of hunger and sickness.

Over time, the Delawares made their way to the reservation William Clark wanted them to share with the Shawnees in southwest Missouri. There they established their main village—called Anderson's Village after the Delaware leader Chief William Anderson—along the James Fork of the White River, in what is now northwest Christian County. The scarcity of wild game that had made it so difficult for other emigrant nations to survive in southwest Missouri forced Delaware hunters west into Osage territory, which predictably, led to violence.[59]

After the expulsion of the Shawnees in 1825, the government revisited the issue of the Delawares' removal from Missouri and their need for a formal reservation. The treaty that Indian Agent George Vashon negotiated with the Delawares in late September 1829 became an addendum to the Treaty of 1818, the one that had forced them into Missouri. Vashon, who was an agent for the Cherokees and later the Shawnees, conducted the negotiation for the relatively simple agreement at Anderson's Village. The treaty addendum states that the Delawares agree to give up any claims to land they have anywhere in Missouri and to move to a new home in Kansas. The land that the United States promised the Delawares, "the quiet and peaceable possession and undisturbed enjoyment of," was located on the north bank of the Kansas River, opposite the reservation granted to the Shawnees four years earlier. The United States agreed to provide the Delawares with horses, ox teams, and wagons for the more than one-hundred-seventy-five-mile journey. In addition, for extinguishing their claims to land in Missouri, they were provided with a perpetual annual annuity of $1,000. For the education of Delaware children, thirty-six square miles of the ceded Missouri land would be sold to establish a school fund. Six men were selected to travel to Kansas to make sure the roughly two million acres of land designated as their new reservation was agreeable to the Delawares. On October 19, they returned to formally agree that they approved of the reservation and were prepared to move onto it.[60]

In the fall of 1830, Isaac McCoy, a Baptist minister who had worked with the Delawares in Indiana, was hired to survey the new reservation. To ensure that the Delawares were satisfied with the survey, the nation sent a delegate named John Quick to work with McCoy. Quick was so impressed with the Kansas land that he returned before the survey was complete to inform his nation that they should move as quickly as possible. Chief Anderson, who lamented that the Delawares had never been happy in Missouri, led about one hundred people and a herd of horses to the reservation while McCoy was still laying out the boundaries. The remainder of the nation followed the next spring.[61]

The Cape Girardeau Delawares, however, remained dissatisfied with the treaty, claiming that they still had never been compensated for their Spanish land grant. In addition, they claimed not to have received a share of the annuities and gifts given to Anderson's Delawares. A group of the Cape Girardeau Delawares traveled with White River Shawnees when they met with Allen and Kouns in October 1832. The commissioners addressed grievances and claims of the Delawares and Shawnees in the same treaty. For their part, the Cape Girardeau Delawares received $2,000 worth of livestock as a replacement for the cattle they had lost to white settlers. The treaty also gave them funds to hire a grist mill operator, to break up farm fields near their new homes, and to support a school. The government paid $12,000 in the Delawares' debt to William Gillis and William Marshall, both traders married to Delaware women. Finally, the Delawares received $5,000 in gifts. In return, the nation agreed to give up all claims to land in Missouri.

Four days after the Shawnees and Delawares signed the Castor Hill treaty, William Clark, Kouns, and Allen signed a brief addendum that provided lifetime annual annuity payments of $100 each to three of the Delaware headmen who had signed the treaty, Tah-whee-lalen, also known as Captain Ketchum, Natcoming, and Meshe Kowhay, who was also known as Patterson.[62]

After the signing of the treaty, the Cape Girardeau Delawares split into two main groups. Many joined Chief Anderson in Kansas, where they adapted well to the new landscape and became farmers and cattle ranchers. Other Delawares, those determined to pursue a more traditional lifestyle, migrated into Texas.[63]

On Wednesday, July 7, 1830, William Clark and his treaty co-commissioner Colonel Willoughby Morgan stood under a clear summer sky on a council ground at Fort Crawford, near the Mississippi River town of Prairie du Chien. At age sixty-nine, Clark was nearing the end of his long career and seemed content to allow Morgan, the fort's commander who was in his mid-forties, to take the lead in addressing the hundreds of Native delegates assembled before them. Given his age, it is also possible that Clark would have preferred to be home in St. Louis, but the council negotiations before him and Morgan were of such importance that he believed his presence was necessary to reach an agreement of the desired terms. After four decades of building relationships with the region's Indigenous nations, Clark wrote, "Had I not attended the treaty meeting, [neither] Sauks nor Foxes would have attended."[64]

Clark had ostensibly called the treaty council, which included members of the Ioways, Otoes, Missourias, Omahas, Menominees, Sacs, Foxes, as well as the Mdewakanton, Wahpekute, Yankton, and Santee bands of Sioux, to establish a "lasting" peace in present-day Iowa and Minnesota, where violence with settlers had become an ongoing problem. "Chiefs and Warriors," Morgan addressed the delegates. "I am commanded by your Great Father to say to you that you must make peace with each other, and here in this council bury the tomahawk forever." He continued in a more threatening tone.

Your Great Father the President commands me to say to you, if you continue your wars, he will march an army into your country and take sides with those who regard his admonitions and chastise those who refuse to regard his council, and more especially will he do this, if in your wars your young men should kill any of his white children, Your Great Father warns you beforehand of your danger.

If you should hereafter disregard the counsels of your Great Father the President, and continue, or even attempt to continue your wars, it will be my duty, however I may regret it, to seize upon your Chiefs and Principal Men, and hold them until those who shed blood shall be surrendered to me. All the troops in this country are at my disposal for this purpose; and you know how soon more could be had if more were required.[65]

Many of the headmen present rose to speak in favor of making peace with their enemies, though they pointed out the difficulty in doing so. The Omaha headman Big Elk expressed impatience with the behavior of some of those in attendance.

> You my brothers look at me; I am tired sitting; my back and my legs ache. If I could divide my body between you, I would give half to one and half to the other. You have been at war; I wish you would do like me and be at peace and in quiet. I do not speak of the Menominies or the Winnebagoes, but of the Sioux & Sacs & Foxes, and wish they would have pity on me, and keep quiet.
>
> My Father! The first words you spoke are yet in my head. If I had eaten them, they would have went out again, but they entered in my head, and there they remain.
>
> Why, my father, do your Children not listen to you? Why is it that they have no ears? You must have spoken falsehoods to them. You never have yet to me. I wish they would do as I do.[66]

The council showed that various tribes were not even in agreement among themselves. The Sac warrior Amoway even chastised members of his own nation when he admitted,

> All the old Chiefs are dead who used to listen to you, the young ones who are now here are just coming in the world, and will also listen to you. I am glad at what you have told all the people. To myself it does not apply because I have always kept your words.
>
> My Fathers! I have helped the Otoes, Omahas, and my own people here to make a strong peace this time, but I fear they do not listen very attentively. Although they are my own people, I am afraid of them. I feel like a wolf on the prairies.[67]

After four days of discussion, the peace portion of the treaty was read and signed on July 10. When the council reconvened two days later, Clark and Morgan pushed the delegates one step farther by arguing that ceding the land in question to the United States was the only way to forge an everlasting peace. To help prevent the Dakota from fighting with the Sacs and Foxes, Clark proposed the creation of a 40-mile-wide neutral zone to run from the Upper Iowa River in northeast Iowa to the Des Moines River in central Iowa. He then suggested that all nations present agree to a cession that would extend into present-day Missouri and affect the Ioways, Sacs, and Foxes.

> My Children! I therefore propose, as a means of obviating further difficulties between yourselves, that you all relinquish to the United States that portion of the country between the Des Moines and Missouri; which you all assent a right to hunt upon; to be allotted as a common hunting ground to the Sacs, Foxes, and others who may be designated, or located upon it by the President of the U. States.[68]

This proposed cession included the land between the old Missouri state line and the Missouri River on which the agency for the Sacs, Foxes, and Ioways had been created as part of the Treaty of 1824. For this cession, the Ioways were promised $2,500, necessary funds to hire an assistant blacksmith, and some agricultural tools. Their neighbors the Sacs and Foxes, who in the treaty are referred to as the Sacs of the Missouri River, to distinguish them from Black Hawk's people on the Mississippi, were to be paid $5,000. The treaty also established two "half-breed tracts," one located on the west bank of the Missouri River in present-day Nebraska and the other one across the Des Moines River from the State of Missouri, in what is now Lee County, Iowa.[69]

The Ioway headman Crane said his people were in favor of the cessions, if everyone was treated equally.

> Fathers! I have nothing more to say than your other children. I hope they have ears and will attend to your words. When you say anything 'tis the truth. I also have but one tongue.
>
> Fathers! Our Great Father has been speaking to us through you. I don't think 'tis fear of us that induces him to buy our lands; but 'tis for our peace and comfort.
>
> . . . We only wish to have an equal portion with the rest. You have given to some of the tribes more than others of us.
>
> Fathers! That part of the country which my tribe now disposes of us, is perhaps the only part where there is now two animals left alive; and that is the reason why I claim more . . .
>
> Fathers! You know we are not like the white people to lay up money. We lay out our annuity for things that are necessary to our existence.

Fathers! I now feel disposed to remain at one place and be settled . . .[70]

One wonders what liberties the government interpreter may have taken in translating Crane's words. Even though he had asserted that his nation deserved to be paid more for their land cession than their Sac and Fox neighbors, the Ioway delegation later claimed that they had not understood that they were ceding the land in question. The Ioways did not have their own interpreter, and as the government did not provide them with one, a faulty or incomplete translation of the treaty seems likely to have been the cause of the misunderstanding. For this reason, the Ioways contested the validity of the treaty and refused to vacate the land until they finally agreed to cede it years later as part of the Platte Purchase Treaty of 1836.[71]

Having already pushed the Ioways, Sacs, Foxes, Osages, Shawnees, and Delawares west of the Missouri border, state officials next set their sights on removing the Kickapoos. Not only had the passage of the Indian Removal Act of 1830 stepped up the making of land cession treaties, but a general hysteria among white settlers caused by the 1832 Black Hawk War put additional pressure on the government to complete the removal process.

For their part, the Missouri Kickapoos had never been satisfied with the land the US government had assigned to them along the Osage River in southwest Missouri as part of the Treaty of 1819. Disgruntled, they traveled to St. Louis on more than one occasion to complain to William Clark about the poor quality of the property, which the headman Kishko derisively referred to as a "small hole." Though the United States had promised to guarantee the Kickapoos' "peaceable possession" of their land in Missouri, Clark had spoken to them about moving to Kansas as early as 1826, and he was reasonably certain they now were amenable to the offer.

However, the Kickapoos' ability legally to cede their Missouri land was wrapped up in federal red tape. Nations indigenous to Missouri had ceded land they claimed by Right of Occupancy, and emigrant Native nations, like the Shawnees and Delawares, had ceded land that had been granted to them by Spain. The Kickapoos, however, were living on Missouri land that already had been assigned to them by the US government as part of a Senate-ratified treaty. While the Indian Removal Act had created a general policy for extinguishing title to treaty-assigned

Native land east of the Mississippi River, the law did not include Missouri or other states west of the Mississippi. Therefore, Clark could not negotiate a new land cession with the Kickapoos until Congress approved a similar policy for Missouri, which it did in late 1831.[72]

In the meantime, Kishko informed Clark that the Kickapoos had traveled to Kansas and found the land there acceptable. Clark called them to his home at Castor Hill to negotiate the cession treaty. He had also summoned the Vermillion Kickapoos, who had remained in Illinois after the 1819 treaty, to negotiate their removal to the Kansas reservation as well.[73]

In October, eighteen headmen representing the two Kickapoo bands met with Clark and commissioners Frank Allen and Nathan Kouns to sign an agreement in which the Kickapoos ceded their claim to all land in Illinois and Missouri and agreed to resettlement in a twenty-mile by sixty-mile plot of land adjacent to the Delaware reservation, near Fort Leavenworth. The details of the treaty indicate that because the Kickapoos were forced to buy goods at highly inflated prices from the government licensed traders, they were placed in the position of having to sell their Missouri land to be relieved of their debt. For their cessions, the Kickapoos received $18,000, two-thirds of which was withheld to pay the nation's debts to the government traders. In addition, the United States agreed to pay them an annual annuity of $5,000 for nineteen years. The United States also would pay for a blacksmith, tools, farm equipment, a mill, a church, and a school for the relocated people.[74]

Members of both bands of the Kickapoo Nation began to arrive on the Kansas land in the spring of 1833. The Illinois Kickapoos, under the leadership of the headman Kennekuk, also known as the Kickapoo Prophet, seemed fairly content with their new home. They took advantage of the equipment and tools provided by the treaty and began to make progress in adapting to the ways of white farmers. The Missouri band, led by Kishko, resisted acculturation and generally avoided contact with their Illinois relatives. Upon arriving in Kansas, Kishko directed the four hundred Missouri Kickapoos to build their village separate from the one Kennekuk's people had built. Though Edward A. Ellsworth, a commissioner from the Bureau of Indian Affairs, met with Kishko and other Prairie Kickapoos, he was unable to reconcile the two bands. In late 1833 or early 1834, Kishko led about a dozen families south, into the Indian Territory, where he hoped they would be able to maintain a life more rooted in Kickapoo traditions.[75]

The Platte Purchase and the
Quest for an Indigenous-Free Missouri

Missouri officials had considered annexing the land between the state's western border and the Missouri River as early as 1829. That year, Missouri Senator Thomas Hart Benton and Congressman Spencer Pettis asked Secretary of War John Eaton to meet with the necessary Native nations to cede the 3,125 square-mile triangle-shaped piece of land, known as the Platte Country, to the United States. William Clark had included the cession in the complex Prairie du Chien Treaty of 1830, but the Ioways had contested that agreement with their claim that the treaty had not been adequately explained to them.[76]

Though the Platte Country had been set aside solely for the use of Native people in 1824, it had been overrun by white settlers almost from the beginning. Part of the problem was that the border between Missouri and the Indigenous land was an imaginary line that ran north from the confluence of the Kansas and Missouri Rivers. Squatters caught living on the western side of the line could easily claim ignorance about its location. In July of 1835, the Ioways' agent Andrew S. Hughes distributed fliers to more than eighty squatters living in the Platte Country, informing them that they must vacate the region. "Should there be found among the Settlers any who are so reckless of consequence to refuse a compliance with this order," the flier read in part, "then it will be my disagreeable duty to request of Col. [Henry] Dodge a sufficient Military force to cause their removal."[77]

For their part, many of the Natives living in the Platte Country were tired of being harassed by whites. Unscrupulous traders sold them cheap whiskey and stole or cheated them out of their food and clothing. Some Natives had their cornfields destroyed by settlers' cattle. One Sac man told Indian Agent John Dougherty:

> We wish to move, but not in the direction of the Mississippi, we want to travel towards the setting sun, we would like to have that (pointing to the Missouri) rapid muddy stream running between us and the white settlements, we are at war with no nation white or red, we wish for a home to ourselves in exchange for which we are willing to enter into a treaty with our Great Father and to give up all claim to any unsold lands we may have between the Mississippi and Missouri rivers, or anywhere else on the face of this earth, we are desirous to live at home, quit hunting, work and raise stock like white men do.[78]

However, even as Clark was trying to remove the Ioways and the Missouri River Sacs and Foxes out of the Platte region, the United States conducted a treaty in Chicago with the Potawatomis that would have moved them from Illinois and Wisconsin *into* the Platte Country. When that treaty, which was signed in 1833, arrived in the Senate for ratification, Missouri Senators Benton and Lewis Linn succeeded in having the agreement amended. They removed the Platte land as a resettlement option and instead offered the Potawatomis land along the Little Sioux River, in what is now northwest Iowa. After seeing the apportioned land's treeless, slough-riddled prairies, the Potawatomis rejected the Iowa land, with some moving south and west to live near the Kickapoos in Kansas. However, by December 1835, many of the Potawatomis had begun crossing the Missouri River from Kansas into the Platte Country.[79]

Occasionally, unscrupulous white settlers chose to exploit their proximity to the Ioways and Potawatomis. Such was the case with events that led to the so-called Heatherly War in 1836. George Heatherly, his wife Jenny, and their four sons were living in what is now Mercer County, Missouri. Stories recounting the genesis of the trouble vary. One version claims that the Heatherlys attempted to sell whiskey to a group of Potawatomis. When, however, the Natives refused to buy the liquor, the Heatherlys stole their horses. A second account reported that James Dunbar, Alfred Hawkins, and a man named Thomas succeeded in raiding an Ioway camp near what is now the Thompson River, stealing some of their horses. Most accounts agree that either the Ioways or Potawatomis chased the horse thieves south until they caught up with them near the present-day town of Chillicothe, Missouri. There, a confrontation between the two groups turned violent, with Thomas dying in the ensuing gun battle. The Ioways retrieved their horses, while the surviving members of the Heatherly party fled the scene.

After returning to their home, the Heatherlys and their partners told local authorities that they had been attacked without cause by "thousands of Indians on the warpath."[80] Fearful that James Dunbar would expose their lie, the other members of the gang killed him and hid his body. Fear of an Indigenous uprising spread quickly throughout northwest Missouri. In response, General B. M. Thompson led a group of militiamen from Ray and Carroll Counties directly to the scene of the fight, while Colonel Shubael Allen led more than one hundred fifty men from Clay County north along Missouri's western border to intercept any Natives who might be trying to return to their agency on the Platte River.

General Thompson quickly found the group of men who had traded shots with the Heatherly gang and determined that they had acted in self-defense when they killed Thomas. Thompson disbanded the militia, and the incident ended without further violence. In mid-July the Carroll County Sheriff apprehended the Heatherlys, who, along with their accomplice Alfred Hawkins, stood trial for the murder of James Dunbar. Only Hawkins was convicted of the crime.[81]

Difficulties in the Platte region were compounded later in the summer of 1836 as the government prepared to expel even more Potawatomis from Illinois. In this event, about seven hundred fifty men, women, and children from the Fox River valley were corralled into a detention camp on the Des Plaines River. Because they had to deport the Potawatomis, who had not yet selected the land in Iowa, the government elected to move them temporarily to the Platte Country. By the time the government's removal agent had led the group to the Mississippi River at Quincy, Illinois, on October 17, 1836, measles had broken out among them and at least one child had died. On October 20, during a snowstorm, the exhausted band crossed the Mississippi. They slowly made their way across northern Missouri, reaching the Platte Country in mid-November. With the addition of the new group, one thousand six hundred Potawatomis now lived in the region. Tensions between Missourians and the Potawatomis increased dramatically. Missouri Governor Daniel Dunklin threatened to drive the Natives across the Missouri River with a force of six hundred volunteers and was thwarted only after federal troops from Fort Leavenworth arrived to turn the Missourians back.[82]

Meanwhile, the United States needed to negotiate with eight other Indigenous nations to gain clear title to the Platte Country. In the first of two treaties, Colonel Stephen Watts Kearny, William Clark's son-in-law and commander of the First Regiment US Dragoons, met with the Ioways and the Missouri River band of the Sacs and Foxes at Fort Leavenworth in September 1836. It is worth mentioning here the nature of the bonds that connected four of the participants in this treaty negotiation. Eugene Joseph Robidoux, also known as Joseph E. Robidoux or "Indian Joe," and who signed the document as a witness, had close ties to at least three other participants in the treaty council. He also had a filial interest in the treaty's outcome. Robidoux's father, the well-known trader Joseph Robidoux IV, stood to profit handsomely from Missouri's annexation of the Platte Country. The elder Robidoux had established a Missouri River trading post at the Blacksnake Hills, and in 1843 he would plat and sell the first town lots for St. Joseph, Missouri, on that site.[83]

Like his father, Indian Joe Robidoux had a long trading and family relationship with the Ioways and was the brother-in-law of the Ioways' lead treaty negotiator, Francis White Cloud. Like many traders, Joseph Robidoux IV had taken at least one Ioway "country wife." Such relationships created kinship bonds that were good for business. The marriage of Mary Many Days, the elder Robidoux's half-Ioway daughter, to White Cloud strengthened those bonds and may have had some bearing on the negotiations at hand.[84]

Indian Joe Robidoux's father had also once enslaved the Ioways' interpreter, thirty-year-old Jeffrey Deroine. While still a teenager, Deroine, who was of mixed African and European ancestry, unsuccessfully sued the elder Robidoux for his freedom. However, the Ioways, with the help of their Indian agent Andrew S. Hughes, bought Deroine from the trader for $600 in 1832. Thereafter, Deroine became a free man, and the Ioways hired him as their interpreter. Deroine also became a trader who, in 1836, formed a business partnership with Indian Joe Robidoux and one of Andrew Hughes's nephews. The partnership infuriated Joseph Robidoux IV because it competed directly with his own trading business. It is difficult to believe that the interpersonal dynamic between these men did not in some way affect the nature of the treaty negotiations.[85]

Even in negotiating with the aid of their interpreter, the Ioways, along with the Sacs and Foxes, could do little to prevent their second forced removal in a dozen years. In the negotiations, the Missouri River Sacs and Foxes were again treated as a single nation, together receiving the same compensation as the Ioways. In return for ceding all claims to the Platte Country, the two groups were sent to live on what would become their first reservation. They would share four hundred square miles located between the Kickapoo Reservation and the Half Breed Tract that had been established by the Treaty of 1830. In return for the land, the Ioways would receive one half of the reservation and $7,500; the Sacs and Foxes would inhabit the other half of the reservation and be paid $7,500. Much of the compensation came in the form of tools and services that the US hoped would help lead the Natives to embrace "civilization," such as farming implements, livestock, a gristmill, and a small number of "comfortable houses." The United States would also establish a subagency on the reservation that would include a blacksmith, farmer, schoolteacher, interpreters for each nation, and a US Indian agent.[86]

The following month, the Otoes, Missourias, Omahas, and the Yankton and Santee bands of Sioux met with Indian Agents Joshua Pilcher and John Dougherty at Dougherty's Bellevue Agency near the site of present-day Omaha, Nebraska. Like the Ioways, Sacs, and Foxes, the five nations ceded all claims to the Platte Country. As compensation, they shared $4,520 in merchandise. Each nation also received cash payments, ranging from $1,250 for the Otoes to $1,000 for the Sioux. Having already been removed to present-day Nebraska, the Otoes, Missourias, and Omahas were also promised assistance in preparing ground on their reservations for farming. The Senate ratified both treaties in early 1837, and President Martin Van Buren proclaimed the Platte Country as part of the State of Missouri on March 28.[87]

Thereafter, most Ioways, Sacs, and Foxes removed across the Missouri River in the spring of 1837, hoping to arrive in time to plant crops for the new year. Meanwhile, the federal government focused on removing the Potawatomis, who held no legal claim to the land on which they were living in the Platte Country. Since the members of the nation were still technically in the process of moving from Illinois to their assigned spot near what is now Council Bluffs, Iowa, the government was providing them with food and supplies. To persuade the Potawatomis to move on, the government began to withhold those provisions at the end of June 1837. This action had such a devastating impact on the people that Major General Edmund Gaines, then in charge of the army's Western Department, undercut his superiors in Washington and reinstated the supplies. By then, however, the Potawatomis were prepared to willingly relocate to Iowa.[88]

For all practical purposes, with the Platte Purchase the state of Missouri had successfully extinguished all Indigenous titles to its land. However, because the state's newly annexed land was technically tied to the cession of western Iowa, which several nations had disputed after the Treaty of 1830, the government summoned the Ioways to Washington to negotiate yet another treaty, this time with the Mississippi River Sacs and Foxes. Though its deliberations had little to do directly with Missouri land, the council was notable for the hostility the Ioways and the Sacs and Foxes displayed toward each other during the negotiations. The

Ioway leader No Heart and the Sac leader Keokuk traded barbs with one another over which nation had the legitimate right to cede the land in question. The council became so heated that the Ioways left Washington without signing the agreement. It was only when they stopped in St. Louis on their way home that William Clark persuaded them to agree to the pact.[89]

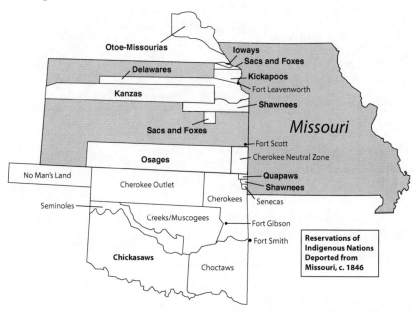

MAP 12: Reservations of Indigenous nations removed from Missouri, c. 1846. *Map by the author*

As historian Robert Lee has shown, it is extremely difficult to determine how much the United States actually paid Native people for their Missouri land claims, as compensation came in various forms. If annual annuities listed in the treaties were in fact paid as promised, the amount paid for Missouri totals roughly $300,000 outright in cash or goods. That is equivalent to approximately $6.8 million today.[90] Add to that sum the untold amounts of money spent on provisions, livestock, instructors, equipment, and buildings, and the figure is far greater. Of course, it is certain that not all that money made it into the hands of Native people. The Bureau of Indian Affairs was a notoriously corrupt and inefficient government agency, and some of the money, especially that which the government held in trust, was never paid out as promised. A significant amount of the money was lost in bad government investments. For example, $55,000 belonging to the Ioways had been invested in bonds issued by the states of Florida, Louisiana, North Carolina, and South Carolina before the Civil War. Not only were Ioways unable to draw interest on these bonds after those states joined the Confederacy, but it is also unclear whether even the principal was recovered after the war.[91]

Most of the cash annuities paid to Native nations in the years following their treaty negotiations ended up in the hands of traders who had claims of debt against them. Similarly, contracts for goods and services meant to better the lives of Indigenous people were often insufficient because of graft and fraud. In many cases, the nations received goods of inferior quality or surplus from government stores. In just one example, in December 1839, the Missouri Sacs and Foxes were expecting a promised shipment of hunting rifles from the government. What they received instead were small Derringer pistols, which the recipients loudly ridiculed. According to the Indian agent in charge, the guns were a "mockery of the article they were intended to represent."[92]

Voices

"The Indians will vanish" has been the talk of the older Indians ever since the white people first came to mingle among them. They seemed to prophecy that the coming of the white man would not be for their good and when the steps toward their removal to the country to the West was just beginning, it was the older Indians that remarked and talked about themselves by saying, "Now, the Indian is now on the road to disappearance." The elders feared that removal from ancestral home-lands would result in "their leaving of their ways."[1]

Siah Hicks (Cherokee)

Many Indian people have been strong enough and fortunate enough to cling to family, community, clan, and tribe through this half millennium of deliberate, orchestrated, colonially, and federally designed physical and cultural genocide. But many have not. These mixed white-and-Indian families, or white-Indian-and-African American, with children sometimes resembling a Rainbow Coalition, assembled for somber photos in front of blanket-doored cabins, represent a crucial period in the histories of America and of mixedblood people in this country, a period that is often unknown or misunderstood by Americans, Indian and non-Indian alike . . . .

They were people simply surviving together—Indian and white—and they deserve to be honored. . . . It is as human beings who loved one another while crossing borders and erasing boundaries and, de-spite immeasurable odds, *surviving* that they deserve our recognition and utmost respect.[2]

Louis Owens (Choctaw/Cherokee)

I learned that generations of our people had to be closed concerning their Indian blood, or suffer the consequences of severe prejudice, persecution, and sometimes death.

. . . As much as possible, we lived in close proximity to one another and rarely associated with those outside our Indian circle.[3]

Beverly Baker Northup (Cherokee)

My Grandmother refused to talk about it and didn't want anyone else in the family to speak of it.[4]

Harvey Wyatt (Cherokee)

Chapter Seven

Crossing Borders and Erasing Boundaries

THOUGH THE STATE HAD MADE a substantial effort to deport its Indigenous population by 1837, Missouri would continue to be the scene of several more years of untold suffering as Native people were marched, often at gunpoint, across the state's hills and prairies to the Indian Territory. When Congress passed the Indian Removal Act in 1830, it committed the United States to a massive program that would systematically displace at least 123,000 people from land east of the Mississippi and move them to land west of Missouri. As we have already seen, "Old Settler" Cherokees had crossed the Mississippi before 1800, to be followed by at least one thousand more Cherokees in the 1810s. Many had settled in present-day Arkansas and Missouri, while some others moved farther west. In their wake, nations such as the Kickapoos, Shawnees, Delawares, and Senecas were forcibly pushed through Missouri by 1832.[1]

Trails of Death
The process of deporting Indigenous people from the organized United States into the unorganized US-owned western territories had been presented as a project of mercy and compassion. Proponents of the policy had argued that Natives were a vanishing people and needed to be removed from the decadence of white society to be saved. At the same time, many whites believed that Indigenous people needed to be civilized so that they might eventually be absorbed into the American melting pot. The Cherokees had proven the fallacy of these arguments. Not only had they refused to vanish, but also they had increased in number after 1800. They also became savvy enough in the US legal system to oppose their forced removal from Georgia, Alabama, Tennessee, Kentucky, and the Carolinas, for nearly a decade.[2]

After members of the Cherokee "Treaty Party" signed the controversial Treaty of New Echota in December 1835, however, that nation ran out of legal options. The treaty stipulated that the Cherokees had to leave their land in Georgia by May 23, 1838. As the deadline grew near, the federal government sent General Winfield Scott and thirty-five hundred troops to round up Cherokee people and place them in internment camps in Alabama and Tennessee to await deportation. The following month, about twenty-seven hundred Cherokees left by boat to travel the Tennessee, Ohio, Mississippi, and Arkansas Rivers to Fort Gibson, near the present-day site of Tulsa, Oklahoma. At least seven hundred to eight hundred people died en route, most of them from disease. Fearing a similar fate, the remaining Cherokees petitioned Scott to allow them to stay in their camps until the weather cooled and "the sickly time" had passed. This left sixteen thousand men, women, and children stranded without sufficient food, water, or sanitation for four months. By October, when they finally began their journey west, disease had dwindled the number of Cherokee travelers to 13,948.[3]

These Cherokees were divided into thirteen groups, twelve of which traveled the so-called Northern Route to the Indian Territory. This took them through Nashville, where they passed just ten miles west of Andrew Jackson's plantation, the Hermitage. They proceeded to walk through western Kentucky, southern Illinois, and crossed the Mississippi River just north of Cape Girardeau, Missouri. From there, most groups marched generally northwest until they reached Rolla, where they joined what would later be called the Telegraph Road linking St. Louis and Springfield. Some took the slightly shorter Hildebrand Route, which cut south of Rolla, connecting to the Telegraph Road near Springfield. In Springfield, they turned south toward Fayetteville, Arkansas, and finally west toward the town of Tahlequah, their destination in the Indian Territory. In all, the roughly twelve thousand Cherokees who were forced to walk through Missouri traveled a minimum of six hundred fifty miles during the coldest four months of the year. By the time they reached their destination, at least six hundred of them had died, mostly of "chills and fever from exposure." Though the US sent white physicians with the Cherokees, it was the traditional healers who were most invested in caring for those who fell ill. Yet, as a descendant of one of the Cherokee deportees recalled, "Indian doctors couldn't find the herbs they were used to and didn't know the ones they did find, so they could not doctor them as they would have at home."[4]

At about the same time that the Cherokee "Trail of Tears" was taking place in southern Missouri, another "Trail of Death" was under way in the northern half of the state. As we have seen, seven hundred Potawatomis had already been marched across Missouri in 1836. At that time, the leader Menominee had refused to leave his village in north-central Indiana, stating flatly, "I have not sold my lands. I will not sell them. I have not signed any treaty and will not sign any. I am not going to leave my lands."[5]

However, younger Potawatomi leaders who hoped to get some compensation before their entire land base was invaded by white squatters, had been persuaded to cede Menominee's land to the United States. On August 29, one hundred volunteer militiamen surrounded Menominee's village and forced eight hundred fifty Potawatomis to leave at gun point. As they made their way through Indiana and Illinois, the deportees were exposed to typhoid, and three hundred of them contracted the illness. Many were further weakened because they were unable to eat the spoiled rations they received. They crossed the Mississippi River at Quincy, Illinois, on October 8, 1838. As the Potawatomis marched through the Missouri villages of Palmyra, Paris, Huntsville, Keytesville, Carrollton, Richmond, Lexington, and Independence, so many fell by the wayside because of illness that some stayed behind to round them up. By the time they reached their new land in Kansas, forty-two Potawatomis had died.[6]

Additional bands of Potawatomis soon followed. A group of 524 was marched across the Missouri in October 1840, while 439 more boarded steamboats at Peru, Illinois, and sailed up the Missouri River to Westport, Missouri. In all cases, US officials prioritized the removal of Natives over the health of those being deported. The historian R. David Edmunds has observed, "Subjected to fraud and chaotic planning, the Potawatomis were often marched west under the supervision of political hacks more interested in making money than in the welfare of their charges." Such corrupt carelessness understandably persuaded many Natives that the federal government placed little value on their lives.[7]

During the early 1840s, members of other nations crossed Missouri on their own paths of deportation. In July 1843, 664 Wyandots traveled up the Missouri River on their way to new homes in present day Kansas City, Kansas. One hundred of them died before reaching their destination. A group of 337 Miamis traveled the Osage River to homes in northeast Indian Territory in 1846. Along the way, two-thirds of the group became ill and sixteen died. In June 1846, about two hundred fifty Senecas, Oneidas, and Tuscaroras from New York arrived in St. Louis while on their way to reservation land beyond Missouri's western border. Curious white observers noted that some of these people were "dressed entirely after the fashion of the whites; Though a great majority of them still retained the Indian costume in part." The whites were intrigued by the degree to which the New York Natives had been assimilated. Most spoke English fluently and many were interested in modern agricultural topics and the latest crop prices. "But what surprised us most," wrote one correspondent, "was that the majority of them seemed to have lost all desire for hunting, the real delight of the true Indian."[8]

With the long series of deportations complete, Missouri was seemingly an "Indian free" state. During the campaign leading up to the 1840 general election, Missouri's all-Democratic Congressional delegation, which consisted of senators Thomas Hart Benton and Lewis Linn and Congressmen John Miller and John Jameson, ran partly on the success of the expulsion of Indigenous people from the state. "Every vestige of Indian title has been extinguished," and the white settler "population has advanced to the outside limit of the State," they bragged to their constituents. Land, which had only recently been "encumbered with Indian title" was "now enlivened and animated by the meritorious industry of a happy, tranquil, free, and prosperous population."[9]

Even though many Indigenous nations had been forced into the territory just west of Missouri, the potential for conflict between them and white settlers continued. All that stood between the two groups was a state border marked either by an imaginary line in the south, or by the Missouri River in the north. In some ways the marked border was irrelevant for both Natives and settlers. Traffic over the imaginary line continued as hunters crossed to pursue wild game, farmers searched for runaway horses or enslaved persons, and traders conducted business.

By the spring of 1840, the porous nature of the border led many Missouri settlers to believe a war with their Indigenous neighbors was imminent. Ioways and Otoes, who lived on reservations in southeast Nebraska and northeast Kansas, had been crossing into the newly annexed Platte Country, where they "impudently and forcibly levied contributions from all of the whites that they met with—killing their stock, and taking away whatever of grain and other thing they might want." Captain Nathan Boone, the son of Daniel Boone, led two companies of the mounted First Regiment US Dragoons from Fort Leavenworth to "remove all hostile Indians from the limits of the state and punish in a summary manner, such of the depredators as they may be able to reach." Residents lobbied their representatives to build a military post in their corner of the state. They also asked that the military presence in the region's only installation, Fort Leavenworth, be strengthened.[10]

By 1841, there were some 235,000 Indigenous people living in the region of the Indian Territory, which at that time included present-day Oklahoma, Kansas, and Nebraska. As many as fifty thousand of these were believed to be Native men of fighting age. The Missouri State Legislature petitioned Congress for increased protection in the form of a chain of US forts stretching from Iowa to Arkansas that would be connected by a military road. There were also calls for the Office of the Superintendent of Indian Affairs to be relocated to western Missouri, where it could better monitor the situation. William Clark, who died in 1838, had held the post in St. Louis since the Jefferson administration. With the election of Whig presidential candidate William Henry Harrison in 1840, Missouri Whigs hoped to have John Dougherty, a former Indian agent and newly elected Missouri State representative from Clay County, appointed to take Clark's place. Harrison, they reasoned, was a man of the frontier and "well acquainted with the embittered spirit of the Indians against the whites, and he will see that the frontiers are properly placed under the care of the Government without a moment's delay."[11] However, after Harrison died just one month into his term as president, Dougherty was passed over in favor of his political rival, Joshua Pilcher, who kept the office in St. Louis.[12]

In April 1842, rumors from Barry County, Missouri, claimed that a grand council had taken place between at least fifteen Indigenous nations, including the Osages, Sacs, Foxes, Shawnees, Choctaws, and Chickasaws. The meeting was said to have been organized by the Cherokee leader John Ross for the purpose of forming a Native confederacy that would oppose white settlement and the construction of any more US military forts in the Indian Territory. Though these rumors were unverified, they served the settlers' purpose of exerting further pressure on Indigenous groups and were enough to justify a response from the military. The United States sent the Sixth Regiment US Infantry and five companies from the First Regiment US Dragoons—perhaps one thousand to one thousand two hundred men in all—to Fort Smith,

Arkansas. That same year, the federal government established Fort Scott, located at a point roughly halfway between Fort Leavenworth and Fort Gibson, which was in the Cherokee Nation, and just five miles west of the Missouri Line.[13]

Indian Removal and Ethnic Cleansing

Less than three years after the Ioways, Sacs, and Foxes were removed from the Platte Purchase, the Missouri legislature passed a law that essentially made it illegal for Indigenous people to be in Missouri. "An Act to Suppress Intercourse with Indians," which was approved on February 9, 1839, and took effect four months later, stated, "if any Indian or Indians, shall be found hunting or roaming within the limits of this State, without a written permit from their properly authorized agent, they shall be deemed guilty of a breach of this act, and, on conviction thereof, shall be sentenced to a fine of not less than ten dollars, or imprisonment of not less than ten days, or both." The act also prohibited Missourians from selling items to or trading with Natives. The law was later revised to give militia leaders the authority to remove Indigenous people from the state at their own discretion.[14]

While it is difficult to determine how vigorously Missouri's 1839 act was enforced, there was at least one instance of an individual being charged with violating the law. John W. Kelly was an Oregon, Missouri, attorney who would go on to represent Holt County in the Missouri State Legislature in the early 1850s. After the Ioways' removal from Missouri in 1836, Kelly had become acquainted with several members of the tribe, whose reservation was just across the Missouri River from his home. Kelly sometimes assisted the Ioways with legal matters and would occasionally write correspondence to government officials at their request.[15] On July 5, 1841, a white man named Thomas Page asked Kelly if he could issue a permit to authorize five Ioway men to cross the Missouri River into Holt County to search for a lost horse. Two days later, Congrave Jackson, who was then the Ioways' Indian Agent, saw a man named Pohaunie and other Ioways on the Missouri side of the river and asked if they had a permit to be there. Because agent Jackson was the only person properly authorized to give Ioways permission to enter Missouri, Kelly was charged with illegally allowing Ioways into the state in violation of the 1839 law. Kelly was tried in Holt County Circuit Court in 1842, but it appears he was able to have the charges dismissed on the grounds that two members of the Grand Jury who had prepared his indictment were not qualified to serve because they did not meet residency and land ownership requirements.[16]

Yet, even with these legal and military measures in place, many Native people continued to enter and remain in the state, with or without permission. Throughout the 1840s, Indigenous people remained a common sight in Missouri towns, especially in cities like St. Louis, Neosho, and St. Joseph, which were adjacent to state boundaries or major waterways. In 1848, the Swiss artist Rudolph Friedrich Kurz noted that in St. Joseph, "one sees constantly . . . Indians of various tribes—the Potawatomi, the Foxes (Musquakee), Kickapoo, Iowa, and Oto. . . . They conduct themselves in a very dignified manner."[17] Travelers on the Oregon Trail often had their first encounters with Indigenous people in St. Joseph, where they were required to wait for a ferry to cross the Missouri River into present-day Kansas. "We proceeded to the ferry, but could not cross for 2 hours for the crowd of teams which were in before us," wrote traveler Lodisa Frizzell in her journal. "While waiting there, some 200 Indians of the Pawtawattimees [sic] and Winewbagoes [sic] came down the street."[18]

Early settlers to Harrison County in Northwest Missouri found that there were still some five hundred Cherokees living just north of the site of the present-day town of Bethany. There were also many Potawatomis living just across the border in the Iowa Territory who camped and hunted in Harrison County. Wary of living so near members of these two nations, residents of Harrison County formed a militia to handle any emergency that might arise. For the most part, whites and Natives seemed to coexist peacefully, and the militia was never called into action.[19]

The 1830s were a time of conflict between Missourians and members of the Church of Jesus Christ of Latter-Day Saints, or Mormons. Groups of Mormons had migrated into Jackson County, Missouri, from Ohio in 1830 and 1831. Because they held what some believed to be controversial religious and social views, Mormons quickly became the victims of persecution, which erupted into a violent "Mormon War." Missouri Governor Lilburn Boggs directed that Mormons should be removed from the state and signed Executive Order 44, which made it legal to kill Mormons and to use violence to expel them. By 1843, Boggs's successor, Thomas Reynolds, had offered a reward for the capture of Mormon founder and leader, Joseph Smith. In August 1843, Reynolds received word from L. B. Fleak, the justice of the peace and postmaster of Keokuk, Iowa Territory. Fleak warned that Smith, who was then living in Nauvoo, Illinois, was "smoking the pipe of peace" with two hundred Potawatomis living in Iowa. He claimed that Smith had met with three Potawatomi headmen to enlist their help in launching a military campaign in Missouri. Fleak, who seemed obsessed with Joseph Smith and had been sending the governor letters related to him for over a year, implied that there were also Sacs, Foxes, and Kanzas involved in the plot to invade the state. "If those Mormons do not give you trouble on your western and northern borders this fall," Fleak warned Reynolds, "it will be because they cannot get enough of the Indians to fall in with their diabolical schemes." He continued:

They have a number of emissaries among the Indians at this time who represent to the Indians that they are Englishmen. They are also scattering English medals among the Indians and represent to them that Smith holds a commission under the British government. This may all look like a hoax to you, but the time will come when it will not feel like a hoax.[20]

Because the *Book of Mormon* identified Indigenous people as the lost Lamanites who would slaughter all unrepentant gentiles, and because the two groups shared the bond of displacement and disenfranchisement, Missourians were especially fearful of an alliance between Indigenous people and Mormons. "It is not my wish to create any . . . alarm," wrote Fleak, "But I do think that the inhabitants of the border of the state should know what facts there are in the case." Fleak vowed to capture Joseph Smith and collect the reward Reynolds had offered for him, but neither Fleak's promise nor the alleged plot between Smith and the Potawatomis ever materialized.[21]

The Myth of the Vanishing Indian

Almost as soon as Americans believed they had succeeded in removing all Indigenous people west of Missouri, they began to express a romantic nostalgia about the "vanishing" of Native people. Despite evidence to the contrary, most white Americans believed that Natives, like bison and the "virgin wilderness," were doomed to disappear in the wake of "progress." Hoping to capitalize on this national melancholy for the picturesque West, two enterprising men from Boonville, Missouri, launched an early version of a Wild West show in the spring and summer of 1844. The pair led an entourage of twelve Osage men, two Osage women, and a small herd of bison, on a tour of performances through Missouri, Illinois, and Indiana. A correspondent for the *Boon's Lick Times* who saw the show in Glasgow, Missouri, reported that while the people of the state were used to seeing Native people and bison, the War dance they performed was "amusing and entertaining, and will well repay any person for the time and money it costs to witness it."[22]

That same year, fourteen Ioways traveled to Europe to perform as part of artist George Catlin's Indian Gallery. Catlin had spent time with the Ioways and members of many other Indigenous nations living along the Missouri River in the 1830s. Along the way, he had painted hundreds of portraits of Native individuals. In France, England, and Belgium he displayed many of these paintings as a backdrop for the Ioways' dances. The Ioways had accepted Catlin's invitation in hopes of bringing attention to their poverty and of making enough money to relieve their situation. When they returned in 1846, however, they brought home only trunks full of worthless trinkets, medals, and 105 Bibles, gifts from European clergy who had tried to convert them to Christianity.[23]

Of course, not all Natives were removed from Missouri in the 1830s. In fact, it is likely that hundreds—perhaps thousands—of Indigenous people remained in the state after the period of deportation. The reasons for the disparity between those who were deported and those who remained are complex and draw on several factors. Among these were white settlers' perceptions regarding Native identity. If Indigenous people seemed to have vanished from Missouri after the 1830s, it is largely because centuries of colonization had forced Natives to adapt to survive. Coupled with these adaptations was the inability of European Americans to "see" Indigenous people who had acculturated.[24] Anishinaabe novelist and scholar Gerald Vizenor has written that "the absence of Natives as an *Indian* presence is a situation that serves the spurious history of dominance."[25] In other words, while the stereotypical savage, buckskin-clad, tomahawk-wielding "Indian" is easily identifiable to whites, acculturated and multiracial Native people are not.[26]

As has been mentioned earlier, the state's western border with "Indian Country" was a porous one. Rare court cases like *State v. John Kelly* notwithstanding, Indigenous people found ways to cross the state border just as they found ways to shift their identities. As a result of these changes and adaptations, there was often no clear boundary between who was and who was not Native, just as the boundary between Missouri and "Indian Country" was sometimes vague.[27]

The state of Missouri did attempt to differentiate between "full blooded Indians" and "half-breeds" in enforcing some of its laws. For instance, even before the 1839 law against intercourse with Indians, it had been illegal to sell liquor to Natives. The law did not, however, apply to Indigenous people who were multi-racial. In February 1839, Henry D. Spear was indicted by a grand jury for allegedly selling whiskey to an unidentified Indigenous man at his grocery in Cape Girardeau, Missouri. When Spear's case went to trial, the judge instructed the jury that, even though the prosecution had failed to present the man who allegedly bought whiskey from Spear, they "must be satisfied" that he was a "full blooded Indian." Perhaps because of this lack of evidence, Spear was acquitted. The State appealed the verdict, in part, because the Cape Girardeau Circuit Court had not allowed the jurors to know the identity of the recipient of the alcohol. The State's appeal was apparently based on its contention that, when being tried for breaking a law that only applies to one ethnic group, ethnicity must be a central point of agreement to determine guilt or innocence. Nonetheless, the Supreme Court of Missouri remained skeptical and upheld Spear's acquittal.[28]

Legal efforts to deal with the shifting boundaries of Indigenous identity are illustrated by the case of settler William Banks, who married and had children with two Indigenous women in the 1840s. A native of the Isle of Man, Banks had first visited the future site of Holt County, Missouri, in 1832 while working for the American Fur Company aboard the steamboat *Yellowstone*. While on shore to cut wood for the boat's boilers, Banks came upon a site to which he would return in 1841 with his business partner John McIntosh to establish a trading post. While Banks famously bears the distinction of being the first white settler of Holt County, the land on which he planned to establish his business was already occupied by the person who was likely the county's first non-Native resident, Jeffrey Deroine, the formerly enslaved trader who had become an interpreter for the Ioways in 1832. Deroine sold his property to Banks and McIntosh who, with Deroine's help, set up their trading post in Missouri, along with a ferry to transport goods to a landing on the west side of the river, which Banks named Iowa Point.[29]

In about 1844, Banks began living with an Ioway woman named Waru'skami, or Giant Woman. Though she was only eighteen or nineteen years old at the time of their marriage, Waru'skami was already a widow and had a young son. According to the later recollections of Banks's employee Frank Dupuis, Banks married Waru'skami in the tradition of the Ioways by giving her family "ponies, blankets, cloth, etc." Dupuis said there had been no formal Christian wedding ceremony. Waru'skami's parents simply brought her to Banks's home in Holt County. Waru'skami continued to live with and keep house for Banks for about four years, and the couple had a son named Joseph William sometime around 1847. Shortly thereafter, Waru'skami left Banks and returned to the Ioway reservation, where she soon died. Reasons for her departure remain sketchy, but some believed she had returned home to receive traditional Ioway treatment for an illness.[30]

Young Joseph Banks continued to live with his father in Missouri after Waru'skami left. Not long after she died, Banks married Jane Newasha, a Sac and Fox woman from the tribe's reservation, which was adjacent to the Ioway reservation. She, too, lived with Banks in Missouri, and on August 24, 1849, they had a son named William Jr. Jane Newasha Banks died in about 1854, reportedly of blood poisoning. The elder Banks never remarried and after Jane's death, turned the care of his sons over to his enslaved housekeeper, Sarah. In 1865, Banks asked his niece, Catherine Galbraith, to come to Missouri from the Isle of Man to live with him and keep house, which she did until his death.[31]

As Joseph Banks and William Banks Jr. grew, their lives sometimes reflected their multi-ethnic heritage. Because the local school district considered them to be Native children, they were discouraged—though not expressly forbidden—from attending the white school. As a result, Joe attended the Presbyterian Ioway, Sac, and Fox Mission School, located between the Iowa and Sac and Fox reservations near Highland, Kansas. After some pushback from the elder Banks, William Jr. was allowed to attend public school in Holt County. While Joseph does not appear on any available Ioway census, he collected at least one annual annuity payment as an Ioway citizen in 1889. All four of his children who survived infancy, Oscar, William Joseph, Ada, and Bessie, appear as enrolled Ioways in the 1891 census of the Great Nemaha Agency and each received an allotment of land when the Ioway reservation was divided up under the Dawes Act that same year. William Jr. appeared as an enrolled member of the Sac and Fox Tribe of Kansas and Nebraska in 1898, though none of his nine children appear to have been listed on the rolls.[32]

For the most part, however, both Joseph and William Jr. were able to live as "white" citizens in Missouri. Both married white women and lived most of their lives working as farmers in Holt County. William Jr.'s wife, Sarah Helen Wake, was born in Gentry County, Missouri, while Joseph married Elizabeth Ellen Simmons from Holt County. It is likely that their status as the only sons of the prominent local pioneer who came to be affectionally known late in life as "Uncle Billy" Banks, helped them gain acceptance from their neighbors.

The vague definition of who was Indigenous in Missouri became a legal issue in 1895, when William Banks Sr. died, and his heirs fought over his estate in court. Banks left his all his property and other assets to his niece Catherine, his son William Jr., and to William Jr.'s descendants. Neither Joseph Banks, who had died in 1890 in a wagon accident, nor members of his family received any inheritance from the elder Banks's estate. It is unclear why Joseph's family was disinherited. William Jr. claimed that his half-brother and his father had a falling out sometime around 1866, not long after Catherine Galbraith came to live with them. Some insinuated that she may have had something to do with the split, though William Jr. said it was related to a disagreement over farming.[33]

Soon after discovering they had been left out of their grandfather's will, Joseph's children, Oscar, Willie, Ada, and Bessie, sued Catherine Galbraith and the family of William Banks Jr. for a just percentage of the inheritance they had been denied.[34] In order to win their case, Joseph's children and their attorney had to persuade the court that they were William Banks Sr.'s legal heirs. While no one denied that Joseph Banks was the son of William Banks Sr., the court focused on the legitimacy of William Banks Sr.'s marriage to Waru'skami. Though three Ioway witnesses had testified that the couple had wed according to Ioway custom, the Holt County Circuit Court did not accept the marriage as legal in Missouri. After losing the first trial, Oscar and his siblings appealed the case to the Supreme Court of Missouri. Though that court had previously recognized traditional marriages between whites and Indigenous people, those unions were deemed valid because they had taken place in "Indian Country." Because the arrangement between Banks and Waru'skami's parents had happened in Holt County, the court did not recognize it as a lawful marriage. Instead, the majority opinion cast the relationship as an arrangement "for the prostitution of the woman for such time as Banks chose to use her."[35] Because the status of William Banks Jr.'s children as heirs to William Sr.'s estate was not a matter that had been placed before the court, they rendered no opinion as to whether the marriage between Banks and Jane Newasha was any more or less valid than his marriage to Waru'skami.

Another Missourian who crossed the boundaries of both geography and race was Joseph Robidoux IV's son, Joseph E. Robidoux or "Indian Joe." Born in 1806, Joseph E. is generally accepted to have been the son of the elder Robidoux, the founder of St. Joseph, Missouri, and his first wife, Eugenie DeLisle Robidoux, though some speculated Joseph E. may have been multi-racial. Whatever his true ethnicity, he had earned the nickname "Indian Joe" through his adopted lifestyle. He chose to self-identify as a French Métis, becoming the embodiment of what Robidoux's biographer, Hugh M. Lewis, has called a "Frenchman gone Native." Joseph E. lived much of his life with Native people, appropriated their mode of dress, and married and had children with two Ioway women. He also had a reputation for violent and antisocial behavior, alcoholism, and an inability to adapt to white society. Because whites closely associated such behavior with Indigenous people, this only enhanced his notoriety as an "Indian."[36]

Joseph E. Robidoux's business partnership with Jeffrey Deroine had initiated a feud with his father, who viewed Joseph E.'s behavior as an embarrassment to the rest of the family. In one instance, the artist Rudolph Kurz recounted that Indian Joe attended Catholic Mass "dressed like an Indian, i.e., practically naked."[37] Finally, the elder Joseph Robidoux, who was known to have a violent temper of his own, locked his son in a cellar for several weeks without liquor and refused to let him out until Joseph E. agreed to give his father a parcel of land he had inherited from his mother.[38]

The city of St. Joseph and much of northwest Missouri also appears to have been the home of many multiethnic people of Indigenous and African descent in the mid-nineteenth century. Mary Alicia Owen, a white woman who was born in St. Joseph in 1850 and lived there until her death in 1935, grew up in a slaveholding household. A writer and collector of folk tales, Owen noticed that many of the stories she heard from the enslaved women who cared for her as a child were very similar to those she heard from the Indigenous people she interviewed years later. She also recalled that her enslaved nannie, Mymee Whitehead, was a practitioner of hoodoo or conjure. Conjure seems to have been a uniquely American practice originally brought to this continent by enslaved Africans. British historian Jeffrey E. Anderson has observed that even though conjure was built on an African foundation, "European and American Indian elements were as important in the practice of conjure as those originating in Africa." Through cultural interaction with Indigenous people, the practice of conjure developed into a unique expression of an individual's relationship with the supernatural. Perhaps because of the state's high population of enslaved Blacks, conjure appears to have been common in Missouri during the mid to late nineteenth century.[39]

In 1893, Owen published *Old Rabbit, the Voodoo, and Other Sorcerers*, a collection of African American and Native American stories and folklore. As a literary device to connect the stories in the book, she devised five characters, whom she called the Aunties, who gathered in the evenings to swap stories and folk wisdom. These women, likely modeled after real people, illustrate the familial ties that existed between Natives and African Americans and portray bits of the culture they shared. Of the five Aunties, four are of mixed African and Indigenous descent. Among them were Granny, who was born in Culpepper County, Virginia, and of African and Delaware ancestry. Big Angy, was the daughter of a French trapper and a woman whose father had been "the big chief of the Ioways." Along with a rosary and various conjure charms, Big Angy kept a sacred pipe and eagle-bone whistle as part of the bundle that she called her "Key to Heaven." Aunt Em'ly, was the child of a black mother and a Fox father, while Aunt Mary was described as part African American and part "Injun."[40]

These multiracial women represent the intermarriage that had long taken place between blacks and Indigenous people throughout the United States. While the kinships that developed between African Americans and slaveholding Indigenous peoples like the Cherokees, Choctaws, and Chickasaws are well represented in the historical record, the history of Indigenous people who helped enslaved people find their way to freedom is far less well documented. While evidence of such efforts existed among Native communities in present day Michigan, Ohio, and Indiana, it has also been suggested that Natives sheltered African Americans just outside of Missouri's western border before the Civil War. Some enslaved people likely passed through the reservations as they tried to make their way north, while others may have stayed for longer periods of time and married. During the 1840s, the Ioway reservation appears to have harbored a large enough African American population to have raised the concern of Superintendent of Indian Affairs in St. Louis Thomas Harvey. At a council with the Ioways in 1846, Harvey told them "You are red birds. Black Birds have no business among you. . . . You must now think how this country was reserved for Indians, not Negroes."[41] A decade later, the Ioway reservation's location on the easternmost part of the border between the Kansas and Nebraska territories made it the terminus of abolitionist James Henry Lane's "Lane Trail," which took those fleeing enslavement through the state of Iowa to Chicago.[42]

Accordingly, some of the stories Owen included in *Old Rabbit, the Voodoo, and Other Sorcerers* reflect this mixture of African and Indigenous cultures. In just one example, Big Angy tells a folk tale about how Ol' Woodpecker tricked Bear out of his claws and tusks, which Ol' Woodpecker then used to make a fine bear claw necklace. These necklaces were symbols of authority worn by leaders of the Ioways and other Indigenous people.[43]

Another story in *Old Rabbit* includes bits of folkways and a description of how a conjurer named King Alexander made a "luck ball" for Owen. While the Aunties may have been fictional characters, King Alexander was an actual person of mixed Cherokee and African American ancestry. He was well known throughout Missouri as a conjurer and became one of Owen's principal informants. While many multiethnic conjurers lived as African Americans, and although the practice is most closely associated with African culture, the Indigenous heritage and knowledge of herbology and spirituality the conjurers possessed were critical to their trade. Even the famous Boonville, Missouri, conjurer Guinea Sam Nightingale, who was born in Africa, gathered much of his knowledge about medicinal plants from Native people in Louisiana.[44]

As Native Americans, African Americans, and French Métis were forming new cultural identities through kinship and exchange in northwest Missouri, something similar was happening in the Ozarks. Historian Kent Blansett has written about the process of "intertribalism" that took place in the region in the decades before the Civil War. He points out that policy of Indian Removal succeeded in dividing people, noting that both the Cherokees and Delawares were fractured into several smaller groups as a result. At a time when the Osages were in the process of being forced out of the Ozarks, various waves of

Cherokee, Shawnee, Delaware, Kickapoo, Scots-Irish, and German im-migrants began to take their place. The result, writes historian Brooks Blevins, was that the remote and secluded backwoods area became a "cultural crucible."[45]

Just as the historian Richard White has explored the concept of a "Middle Ground," where whites and Natives relied on cooperation and exchange to survive, Blansett sees Ozark intertribalism as a process of cultural adaptation between various groups or "tribes" that occupied the region. "Identity for Native Ozarkian nations was formed out of interde-pendence, trade, violence, warfare, and a host of influences that both ab-sorbed and deflected acculturation," writes Blansett. "Cultural exchange, therefore, did not take place in a vacuum; more specifically it was shaped by the reciprocity of cultural exchange."[46] Not only did Indigenous tribes band together through kinship and alliances in the Ozarks, but Both German and Scots-Irish settlers were also "tribalized" by intermarriage, kinship, and economic ties with the Cherokees, Delawares, Kickapoos, and Shawnees.

As Blansett points out, just as the Cherokees did not become any less Cherokee when they adopted European-style agriculture and log homes, the Scots-Irish retained many of their cultural traits at the same time they adopted "Native clothing, trade and cultural customs." These changes, writes Blansett, created an intertribal community able to adapt to the region "while simultaneously absorbing cultural traits or tools from other nations for its own political and cultural survival." Through the process of intertribalism, many Indigenous people remained in Missouri after "removal" because they did not readily fall into the racial and cultural category of "Indian."[47]

Indigenous Missourians Hiding in Plain Sight

Missouri has long been the home of many people who maintain their Indigenous ancestors were able to remain in the state after escaping from forced removal caravans, hiding from authorities, or passing as white or African American. Beverly Baker Northup, chief of the Northern Cherokee Nation of Old Louisiana Territory, has pointed out that many Cherokees have lived in Missouri and Arkansas since the mid-eighteenth century. As Missouri became a territory in 1812 and then a state in 1821, many Cherokees remained in the region, mixing as best they could into the emerging white society while rarely talking about their heritage."[48]

Some Indigenous people claim that their ancestors had successfully escaped from forced removal caravans that crossed the state. Others returned to Missouri after having been forced into the Indian Territory. The story of writer David Edward Walker's ancestors is representative of those who tell of Cherokees intermarrying and hiding in plain sight after removal. Walker's "3rd generation paternal grandmother, Elizabeth Gibson, walked the Trail of Tears from Murfreesboro, Tennessee, with her husband, Alfred Hirton Barlow." At the end of the forced removal, Gibson, who was Cherokee, and Barlow, who was apparently white, left the Indian Territory and settled in the town of Pineville, Missouri, just thirteen miles from the Indian Territory. There, they became members of the local Presbyterian Church and generally kept low profiles for fear of being forced to move back to the reservation. Though she was considered an "intermarried white," Gibson was eligible to remain on the Cherokee census rolls. However, she did not register for fear that doing so while living in Missouri would make her a fugitive.[49]

While some historians have scoffed at the possibility of Cherokees, Potawatomis, or other Natives escaping forced removal, there is evidence that it did occur. The WPA oral histories collected from descendants of those who were removed mention occasional instances of people being lost or abandoned during the removals, even though they were supposedly being monitored by soldiers. Lilian Anderson recounted that her grandfather, Washington Lee, lost his parents and sister during the removals, "and never saw them again. He did not know whether they died or got lost." Jennie McCoy Chambers recalled hearing that while her mother and grandparents were on the Trail of Tears, they picked up two children: a boy whose parents had died of disease and a girl who apparently did not know what had become of her family.[50]

Some Cherokees were apparently able to take advantage of moments of chaos and confusion, or the intemperance of guards, to escape during removal. In 1838, two thousand eight hundred Cherokees received permission to supervise their own removal while accompanied only by a small military and medical escort. The group was divided into three detachments and sent west on steamboats that departed from Ross Landing, Tennessee. In the confusion caused by dangerously overcrowded boats and the subsequent transfer of the Cherokees from boats to rail cars, as many as one hundred of the deportees escaped. By the time they reached Paducah, Kentucky, up to two hundred more Cherokees were found to be missing from the group.[51]

Confusion about the number of deportees who were included in any given detachment seems to have been standard. "On the march there were many deaths, a few desertions and accessions and occasional exchanges from one party to another," wrote historian Grant Foremen, "so that an accurate statement of the number removed and of those who perished on the way became impossible."[52] Historian Ralph Jenkins has calculated that 11,949 Cherokees traveled on the Trail of Tears routes that went through Missouri. According to his findings, sixty-eight children were born while 414 Cherokees of all ages are listed as having died during the removal. Because mortality figures for four of the twelve groups that traveled through Missouri are not available, the number of casualties is more likely to be at least six hundred. There were also 182 reported deserters among these groups. Jenkins points out, however, that when the arrivals were finally tallied in the Indian Territory, 1,263 additional Cherokees were unaccounted for. While it is likely that some were unrecorded deaths, many of that total number likely escaped, either to return to their homes in the Southeast, or to remain in states along the trail. As we will see, the desertion and assimilation of Natives during this time has ramifications that continue in the twenty-first century.[53]

One well-known Cherokee citizen was able to find temporary refuge in Missouri around 1849. John Rollin Ridge was the son of Cherokee Treaty Party leader John Ridge and the grandson of Major Ridge. Because the Ridges had signed the Treaty of New Echota, they became targets of the Cherokee faction led by John Ross that had resisted removal. On June 22, 1839, Ross supporters launched a coordinated attack that killed Major Ridge, John Ridge, and John Rollin Ridge's cousin Elias Boudinot. Boudinot's brother Stand Watie was also a target of the attack, but he survived. Members of the family, including twelve-year-old John Rollin Ridge, witnessed his father's murder. Fearing for their safety, Ridge's widow, Sara Bird Northup Ridge, moved the family out of the Cherokee Nation to Fayetteville, Arkansas.[54]

Ridge lived in Arkansas for a time and attended school in the East before returning to the Cherokee Nation in the late 1840s. In 1849, when he was twenty-two years old, John Rollin Ridge killed a man named David Kell in an argument over a horse. Kell was a Ross supporter, and some speculated that he had initiated the dispute to kill Ridge. Ridge was again forced to flee the Cherokee Nation, this time landing in Springfield, and later Independence, Missouri. From Missouri, he tried to raise money and wrote to Stand Watie about raising a force large enough to return to the Nation and kill Chief John Ross and his supporters. Though he was certain that he would not be convicted of murder in a trial that was to take place in 1850, Ridge took the advice of his family, who begged him not to return to the home of his enemies. Eventually, he followed the throng of gold seekers who were heading to California, where he quickly realized that he was not suited to gold prospecting. Instead, he worked as a newspaper man, and, with the publication of *The Life and Adventures of Joaquin Murieta* in 1854, became what many consider to be the first Native American novelist.[55]

By and large, Native people who attempted to acculturate, or who succeeded in keeping a low profile, were allowed to remain in Missouri. Though some Natives who stayed were subject to discrimination and even violence, the white settler population was far more concerned with the removal of sizable groups of Indigenous people whom they believed constituted a threat to their livelihoods. Perhaps ironically, those who were not perceived as threatening to white sensibilities were embraced by northerners and southerners alike as the nation entered the Civil War.

Voices

The Little Ones were confused. They had not known just what they ought to do when the Metal Maker and the Black Robe talked to them, and now with the Black Robe gone and Metal Maker Killed by Heavy Eyebrows soldiers, they were more confused, and they "held the feather" because this man Pike and Cherokee John Ross persuaded them to do so.

Inspired by their own importance, indicated by the attention they received, they signed the Treaty with Albert Pike, representative of the Confederacy.[1]

—John Joseph Mathews (Osage)

We have responded to your call for volunteers and have therefore enlisted in the United States Army to give a hand as true patriots to put down this rebellion. Some of us have been in battles, as your honor will see by the Officers certificates, and have done our duty to the best of our ability. But we must very much complain about our Agent John A. Burbank. He has promised us he would be careful for the interest of our families and our friends at home; but he has not done anything since we are in the service, which would be in any way taken care, or protecting our families and friends at home. We have been informed and have had experience of his character; when we was at home on a furlough. We was sneered at by the Chiefs of our Nation, and was made fun of by those leading Indians, and our complaint to Mr. John A. Burbank did get no hearing.[2]

—Ioway men serving in the 13th and 14th
Regiments of Kansas Volunteers

Chapter Eight

On the Front and Out of Sight

BECAUSE MANY INDIGENOUS PEOPLE LIVING in Missouri at the start of the Civil War had been forced to acculturate into the mainstream culture, it is extremely difficult to determine how many of them enlisted in the military. According to Civil War historian Mary Jane Warde, an estimated twenty thousand Indigenous men fought for both the Union and the Confederacy, "for reasons that had less to do with the issues dividing the states, than with their own leaders, history, conditions and fears." We know that hundreds of soldiers were members of nations that had been removed from Missouri; Chickasaws, Delawares, Ioways, Osages, Otoes, Kickapoos and more, all took up arms in the war fought between white men.[1]

In the trans-Mississippi West, Indigenous soldiers played an important role in the fighting on Missouri's southern and western borders with Arkansas, Kansas, and the Indian Territory. The first Native recruits in the region joined the Confederacy, though largely out of necessity rather than by choice. In April 1861, just five days after Confederate forces opened fire on Fort Sumter in South Carolina, the opening salvo in the conflict, the federal government abandoned four isolated military installations in the Indian Territory. This left the Cherokees, Muscogees, Seminoles, Chickasaws, and Choctaws vulnerable to attack from Confederate forces located just south of the territory in Texas. The fact that the federal government had forced these nations to move to the Indian Territory just twenty-five years earlier, only to abandon them, understandably led many Natives to resent the Union cause.[2]

Sensing an opportunity to exploit this resentment, President of the Confederacy Jefferson Davis sent two trusted negotiators, Brigadier General Benjamin McCulloch, a former Texas Ranger who became the Confederate commander in the Indian Territory, and Albert Pike, a large and eccentric man who had worked as a lawyer representing the Choctaws, Chickasaws, and Muscogees in litigation against the US government, to meet with representatives of each of the Five Civilized Tribes, the Choctaws, Chickasaws, Muscogees, Seminoles, and Cherokees. The agents promised Native leaders that the Confederacy was willing to annex the Indian Territory, guarantee the practice of slavery inside its borders, protect the Native nations from invasion by federal troops, and assume the responsibility of paying the annuities the federal government had promised them as part of the treaty process. In return, the nations agreed to raise home guard units that would be armed and paid by the Confederate government but would be reserved only for defense inside territorial boundaries.[3]

Internal factions within the Cherokee and Muscogee nations made negotiations difficult for the Confederacy's emissaries. However, Stand Watie agreed to raise a mounted regiment of Cherokee soldiers. In return, McCullough commissioned him as a colonel and appointed him to lead the regiment. After attempting neutrality, Watie's adversary, Cherokee leader John Ross, reluctantly agreed to allow the Confederacy to recruit a second Cherokee regiment. The Muscogees were also divided on the issue of loyalty to the Confederacy, but a group led by Daniel Newman McIntosh signed an agreement with Pike and McCullough to recruit the First Creek Mounted Rifles, while his half-brother, Chilly McIntosh, organized the First Battalion Creek Cavalry. The Seminoles, Choctaws, and Chickasaws were more eager to work with the Confederacy and quickly recruited two additional regiments, the First Choctaw and Chickasaw Mounted Rifles and the First Battalion Seminole Mounted Rifles. The Confederates organized these four regiments into a single brigade, which Pike, who received a commission as brigadier general, then commanded.[4]

Though several Great Osage leaders signed a treaty with Albert Pike to support the Confederacy, the Little Osages refused to do so. The treaty required the Osages to furnish five hundred men to form a Confederate battalion. After they were unable to meet their enlistment quota, the Osages were absorbed into other Confederate units. Meanwhile, a group of pro-Union Little Osages, led by We-He-Sa-Ki, or Hard Rope, were forced into a running fire fight on their own reservation in southern Kansas. They had intercepted a group of Confederate horsemen who were trying to sneak into Kansas to incite Indigenous violence against the Union. A force of about two hundred Osages killed twenty of the Confederates and foiled their plot. By the end of the war, Osage loyalty would shift toward the Union and four hundred Osages would ultimately fight in the Union army.[5]

In February 1862, Confederate forces planned a campaign into Missouri. Though Pike's brigade had been organized as a protective home guard, they were quickly ordered to become part of the offensive. Major General Earl Van Dorn, commander of the Confederacy's Trans-Mississippi District, ordered Pike to move his troops into Arkansas as soon as possible. Logistical problems forced Pike to march with only two of his regiments, John Drew's First Cherokee Mounted Rifles and Stand Watie's Second Cherokee Mounted Rifles. Pike, dressed in a Plains-style feather headdress, leggings, and beaded moccasins, led eight hundred Native soldiers toward Pea Ridge, Arkansas. One bystander recorded that the soldiers rode small Indian ponies while, "yelling forth their wild whoop. . . . Their faces were painted and their long strait hair, tied in a queue, hung down behind. Their dress was chiefly in the Indian costume—buckskin hunting shirts, dyed of almost every color, leggings, and Moccasins of the same material, with little bells, rattles, earrings, and similar paraphernalia. Many of them were bareheaded and about half carried only bows and arrows, tomahawks and war clubs."[6]

Upon their arrival at Pea Ridge, Pike's men were immediately drawn into the battle, which had already begun. Watie's Cherokee soldiers charged the Union cavalry, overwhelming Captain Gustavus M. Elbert's First Missouri artillerymen, who fled, leaving their cannons behind. The Cherokees pursued the federal troops and succeeded in taking the battery. As Union reinforcements unleashed artillery fire on the Cherokees, they retreated into the woods, where they were reported to have stayed for the remainder of the battle.[7] Union commanders later alleged that Watie's Cherokees had scalped and mutilated the bodies of at least eight—some claimed as many as forty-five—of Elbert's dead and wounded artillerymen.[8]

While the Confederate Indian Home Guards had shown that Native soldiers could perform well in battle, McCullough's opponent at Pea Ridge, Major General Samuel Curtis, commander of the Union's Army of the Southwest, stated, "I cannot expect Indian regiments to practice civilized warfare."[9] Many in the US War Department, including Secretary of War Edwin M. Stanton, similarly believed that Native troops could not be trusted or controlled.[10]

Since the beginning of the war, thousands of pro-Union Indigenous refugees had flooded into Kansas from the Indian Territory. Kansas Senator James Henry Lane had been lobbying the War Department to allow him to form Native home guard regiments to protect the southern border of Kansas from a Confederate attack. By recruiting regiments from this refugee population, Lane hoped to organize an expedition that would use Native troops, armed by the federal government, to escort their fellow refugees back to their homes in the Indian Territory. Just days after Pea Ridge, the War Department agreed to allow Native Americans to enlist in Kansas regiments if they fought only other Natives and were engaged solely in the defense of the state. Lane received permission to recruit loyal Native American volunteers from Kansas to fill two new regiments. In a matter of months, about two thousand Muscogees, Seminoles, Delawares, Kickapoos, Osages, Senecas, Cherokees, Chickasaws, and Choctaws had enlisted in the First and Second Kansas Indian Home Guard Regiments. Later, a group made up mostly of Cherokee defectors from the Confederacy enlisted in a Third Kansas Indian Home Guard Regiment.[11]

In 1862 and 1863, Indigenous men were allowed to join regular Kansas Volunteer Regiments, in which they served alongside white soldiers. Ioways and Delawares sent the greatest percentage of their men to fight for the Union. Of the 201 Delaware men between the ages of eighteen and forty-five, 170 enlisted, many serving in the Sixth and Fifteenth Kansas Volunteer Cavalries. Of the seventy-eight Ioway men who were of military age, fifty volunteered to serve in the Thirteenth Kansas Volunteer Infantry and the Fourteenth Kansas Volunteer Cavalry. Because both the Ioways and Delawares were small, weak nations, those who enlisted may have believed that aligning themselves with Washington was the only way to ensure their and their people's survival.[12]

For the most part, Indigenous troops fought outside the borders of Missouri. One notable exception was the first Battle of Newtonia, Missouri, in September 1862. About four thousand men, including Confederate General Joseph O. Shelby's Missouri Cavalry and the First Cherokee Battalion, the First Choctaw Regiment, and Brigadier General Douglas Cooper's First Choctaw and Chickasaw Mounted Rifles, were occupying the region around Joplin, Missouri. To challenge this presence, Brigadier General Frederick Salomon moved from Fort Scott, Kansas, into Missouri with a force that included the Third Regiment of Indian Home Guards.

On September 30, a federal detachment attacked Confederate troops occupying the town of Newtonia. For some time, the Union troops held the advantage, until Cooper's Choctaw and Chickasaw Mounted Rifles galloped through the town "singing their war songs and giving the war-whoop" as they rode straight into the Union line. The heaviest fighting took place between the mounted rifles and the Third Indian Home Guard. Overwhelmed by the charge, the Union home guard was forced to retreat. Despite the defeat, the Native soldiers fighting for the Union had proven "not only their loyalty but their ability to fight."[13]

The presence of Confederate forces in southwest Missouri also created a refugee problem in Newton County, Missouri. On Christmas Day 1862, more than a thousand Cherokees arrived in the partially deserted town of Neosho. The road weary group of refugees was escorted by four companies of the Third Indian Regiment, many of whom were also Cherokees, under the command of Union Major John A. Foreman. Slightly more than a week later, a second group of Cherokees reached the seat of Newton County. This group too traveled with a military escort under the watchful eyes of Indian Agents A. G. Procter and Justin Harlan. In all, 2,250 Cherokees would inhabit the town, which had numbered less than one thousand residents before the war. There, the refugees spent the frigid winter months occupying abandoned houses and any other available shelters while the members of Foreman's Indian Regiment occupied the Newton County court-house.[14] Memoirist and Union veteran Wiley Britton, who grew up in Neosho, wrote that because many in Newton County were considered to be Confederate sympathizers, "it was regarded as no more than right that the secessionists of the country should contribute some of the supplies for subsisting the troops and Indian families at Neosho during the winter." The following April, the refugees were escorted back to the Indian Territory by three hundred Indian soldiers under Captain A. C. Spillman. A train of wagons a mile long slowly made the eighty-mile journey from Neosho to Park Hill, just south of the Cherokee capitol of Tahlequah.[15]

The presence of Indigenous soldiers serving in Missouri or with Missouri regiments is largely anecdotal. This is in large part because by the middle of the nineteenth century, many Native people had adopted European names. This was especially true of younger Natives, many of whom had been educated in Christian-run mission schools. There, children were often given "Christian" names by the missionaries. For this reason, it is only possible to determine a soldier's ethnicity if it is listed on muster rolls.

However, Indigenous soldiers in Missouri units do occasionally appear in the historical record. One instance was twenty-year-old Jefferson Whitecloud. Whitecloud was the son of the Ioway leader Francis White Cloud, the Grandson of Joseph Robidoux IV, and brother of long-time Ioway chief and fellow Civil War veteran, James Whitecloud. On September 1, 1864, Jefferson Whitecloud left the Ioway Reservation in Kansas and crossed the Missouri River to St. Joseph, Missouri, where he enlisted in Company K of the Forty-Eighth Missouri Volunteer Infantry. He was mustered in on September 24 and served in Missouri, Tennessee, and Illinois, until he was mustered out at Benton Barracks in St. Louis on June 29, 1865.[16]

In other anecdotes, Indigenous soldiers serving in Missouri are mentioned only in passing. There is, for example, a reference to the band of Delawares who rode with Major Frank J. White's "Prairie Scouts" and performed duty as part of General John Fremont's Bodyguard. Ozark historian Elmo Ingenthron remarks that Confederate Brigadier General Jeff Thompson, also known as the Swamp Fox, traveled with an Indigenous aide-de-camp named Ajax. Prior to the war, Ajax apparently worked as a member of a performing showboat troop.[17]

That these tidbits border on the folkloric seems somehow to make sense in an age when many Missourians believed that the only "real Indians" were those who resembled caricatures in the imagination of whites. This might explain why, less than thirty years after removal and during the so called "Indian Wars" in Minnesota and in the American West, Indigenous men were allowed to serve in the military. It is possible that many believed that Natives living in Missouri, Kansas, and the Indian Territory had become acculturated enough to be accepted by some whites as something other than "savage" Indians. How Native men were treated by their fellow soldiers is open to question. Historian Mathew Stith has maintained that the vicious nature of the war in the Trans-Mississippi West forced both soldiers and civilians alike to abandon their traditional cultural roles. Because all soldiers fighting in the region around the Missouri, Kansas, and Arkansas border were living outside of what Stith calls their "cultural comfort zone," everyone was in unfamiliar territory and had to adapt to the new realities of military life. Therefore, Indigenous men may not have been any more out of place than their white comrades who were also fighting far from home on strange terrain against a common enemy. In battle, members of the same company often fought shoulder to shoulder, their arms sometimes touching, as they advanced toward the enemy. As Civil War historian Earl Hess has observed, the men learned to rely on one another and to trust their fellow company members with their lives.[18]

For most of those who lived through it, the Civil War had been the defining event of their lives, one that likely led many to question the assumptions they had previously held about themselves, their neighbors, and the Union. Missouri had not only been the scene of hundreds of military battles and skirmishes, but it also had witnessed years of border violence and guerrilla warfare before the war began. In short, violence born of the struggle over slavery had torn the social fabric. Contributing to the general postwar sense of disorder was the abolition of slavery, a marked increase in immigration, and the changing characteristics of Missouri itself.

Indigenous Life in a Growing State

After the Civil War, Missouri no longer was considered as the edge of the frontier. Instead, it became the self-proclaimed "Gateway to the West." Towns like St. Joseph, St. Louis, and Kansas City, which had recently been home to settlers, trappers, and traders, were now thriving commercial centers that profited by outfitting those who were moving even farther west on the Oregon and Santa Fe Trails. At the same time, Jefferson Barracks, just south of St. Louis, became a staging ground for the military campaign that was to make the West "safe" for these waves of white settlers and for the expansion of the railroads. An important part of this crusade that some saw as the last phase of the United States' "Manifest Destiny," was the annihilation of the great many Indigenous people still living off reservations and in their traditional manner on the Great Plains. At Jefferson Barracks, the African American "Buffalo Soldiers" of the Ninth and Tenth Cavalries, which fought Native people, received their training. "The pathway to freedom in the late nineteenth-century United States," writes historian Walter Johnson, "was through Indian killing." The fact that African Americans would risk their lives to further white America's settler colonialism is, according to historian Quintard Taylor, "a painful paradox."[19]

This "new" Missouri was growing quickly. The population of Kansas City, a town barely a decade old when the Civil War started, exploded by 630 percent between 1860 and 1870, to reach a population of over

33,000 people, surpassing St. Joseph, which was home to just under 20,000 people in 1870. The state's largest city, St. Louis, nearly doubled in size during that same decade, swelling to a population of 310,000. Over the same period, the state gained more than a half million people to reach a total population of 1.7 million by 1870. The increase was due largely to the coordinated efforts of state officials, railroad companies, and immigrant societies to encourage immigrants to move into the state. In the first four months of 1866 alone, the General Land Office reported that nearly one-quarter of a million acres of land, which had been taken from Indigenous people just a generation or two earlier, had passed into private, white, hands.[20]

Rapid change and unhealed wounds from wartime violence were just two causes that underlay the unease, uncertainty, and strong desire to restore a sense of order that had seemingly been lost. Some sought to reclaim social order through legislative means. In the decade after the Civil War, Missouri held two constitutional conventions. After the adoption of the 1865 Drake Constitution, named for Charles Drake, the man largely responsible for its ratification, the radical faction of the Republican Party had disenfranchised many white male supporters of the Confederacy by administering a loyalty oath as a precondition for voting. Only those who could swear that they had never taken up arms against the federal government or had never lent support to the Southern cause could cast a ballot. Men who could not truthfully take the oath also were barred from becoming teachers or ministers and were unable to hold political office. The oath was short lived, but the psychological scars that it caused among many former Confederates led to years of political, social, and economic upheaval. By 1875, the Democratic Party was back in charge in Missouri and a new convention replaced the Drake Constitution with a document that was far less trusting of centralized government's ability to control the lives of citizens.[21]

Some Missourians looked to the court system for compensation for acts of wartime violence and loss of property. After prosperous farmer and Missouri state representative Obadiah Smith was killed by bushwhackers near his home in Cedar County in April 1863, the executor of his estate sued thirteen confederate sympathizers and bushwhackers for killing Smith, stealing between $800 and $900, and destroying property. In 1866, the Cedar County Circuit awarded Smith's estate $12,000 in damages, in part because the defendants were found to have participated in a rebellion against the US Government.[22]

Others enacted revenge for Civil War grudges through acts of violence. Frank James, from Clay County, Missouri, had ridden with renowned bushwhacker William Quantrill during the war, and both he and his younger brother Jesse participated in "Bloody" Bill Anderson's massacre of Union soldiers in Centralia, Missouri, in 1864. After the war, the James robbed Northern institutions such as railroads and banks.

Whitewashing the Historical Narrative

While seeking redress for past wrongs, Missourians also began the long process of reevaluating and reconstructing their shared historical narrative. Central to this new postwar narrative was the physical and cultural possession of the state for whites, and the continued erasure of the Indigenous people who had lived there before them. As Patricia Cleary has observed about St. Louis in the 1860s, "settler colonialism in the form of nineteenth-century . . . narratives of civilization and modernity constituted powerful vehicles for attacks on Indian peoples, both historic and contemporary."[23]

While white Missourians had done their best to deport all Indigenous people from the state in the 1830s, the next phase of "owning" Missouri was the destruction of signs of Native presence. Perhaps the most visible example of the colonization of the Indigenous past was the claiming and destruction of mounds related to the Mississippian-era Cahokia complex. A prime example of the erasure of the Indigenous past is demonstrated by the fact that we now know the largest mound in central Cahokia as Monks' Mound. The name has no connection to the original builders or functions of the structure. Instead, it refers to the white Trappist monks who lived on it in the early nineteenth century. After the abandonment of Cahokia, the mound had also been occupied by Indigenous members of the Illinois Confederacy, Missionaries, and a white farmer named Amos Hill. Another example of cultural erasure is the repurposing and ultimate destruction of Big Mound in St. Louis. Before the Civil War, the earthwork had been crowned with Mound Pavilion, an entertainment facility that burned in 1848. Two decades later, the North Missouri Railroad leveled the mound, using the dirt to build roadbeds for new tracks. The evisceration of Big Mound was recorded in part by artist and amateur archaeologist, Alban Jasper Conant, and in a stunning series of photographs taken by St. Louis photographer Thomas Easterly.[24]

IMAGE 10: Big Mound, Fifth and Mound Streets, St. Louis, c. 1854. Daguerreotype by Thomas M. Easterly. Though the destruction of St. Louis' largest Mississippian was complete by 1869, it appears to have been severely damaged by the date of this photograph. *Courtesy of the Missouri Historical Society*

When Europeans arrived in St. Louis, they were generally confounded by the Mississippian mounds that dotted the banks of the Mississippi River. As they colonized the region around St. Louis, settlers found these earthworks, the largest of which was 319 feet long, 158 feet wide, and 34 feet high, to be both alluring and mysterious. As early as 1819, developer William Long used the mounds as a marketing tool for the town lots he was selling in the nearby town of Fenton. Long pointed out that even in ancient times the St. Louis vicinity had been a desirable place to settle. He and his contemporaries were, however, unable to conceive of any connection between those early mound-building inhabitants and the Native people who were their contemporaries. To European Americans, it was unimaginable that the ancestors of the "primitive" and "uncivilized" Indigenous people of their own era could have possibly been capable of such a massive undertaking.[25]

To address this mystery, Euro-American settlers concocted elaborate theories to explain the mounds' existence. One popular explanation involved a supposed Lost Race of mound builders who were believed to have been either Hebrews, Greeks, Persians, Romans, Vikings, Hindus, or Phoenicians. In 1774, an amateur archaeologist named John Rozée Payton speculated that "This continent was inhabited by people of an advanced civilization, as compared to the Red Skins today."[26] In the early 1830s, Josiah Priest, writing in his book *American Antiquities and Discoveries in the West*, which sold more than twenty thousand copies, envisioned "great armies of white, warrior Moundbuilders" marching across the plains with trumpets blaring, as they fulfilled their chosen tasks. In an 1848 report, even the Smithsonian Institution denied that the mounds were the work of Indigenous Americans. The anthropologists there believed that the mounds had been built for defense purposes by an unspecified people seeking protection from "hostile savage hordes." Native people, the Smithsonian's report concluded, could not have built the mounds, as it was well known they were "averse to Labor."[27]

Seven years later, the Smithsonian published Samuel Haven's *Archaeology of the United States*. Haven's 1855 book was a complete reversal of the 1848 report. After the careful study of work being carried out by archaeologists around the globe, Haven concluded that the ancestors of Native people did, in fact, build the impressive mounds and that they were the makers of stone tools found throughout the country. He also theorized that America's Indigenous people had originated in Asia and come to North America via the Bering Strait, the narrow waterway between Russia and Alaska.[28]

In 1881, John Wesley Powell hired Cyrus Thomas to investigate the mounds for the Smithsonian's newly created Bureau of Ethnology. Only after years of research was Thomas able to lay the myth of the Lost Race of Moundbuilders to rest. In 1894, Thomas systematically debunked the Lost Race theory in a lengthy report in the Bureau of Ethnology's twelfth annual report. At the heart of his argument was his finding that the mounds in the United States were not built by a single group, but by several different Indigenous cultures.[29]

On a far broader scale, Indigenous land that had been transferred to the United States through treaties—both ratified and unratified—and outright seizures, went through a process of being "whitewashed" to erase its Indigenous past. Much of the land acquired through treaties was declared to be in the "public domain." Millions of acres of public land were then offered at no, or greatly reduced, cost to individuals, railroads, and land-grant universities. In its quest to complete a transcontinental railroad, Congress passed a package of legislation called the Pacific

Railroad Acts of 1862. The bills, introduced by Missouri Congressman James Rollins, provided private railroad companies with $6 million in government bonds and twenty million acres of public land. In general, railroads received alternating square-mile sections of land that extended ten miles on either side their right of way. This allowed them to sell the land for one hundred percent profit to finance their companies. Because much of the public domain in Missouri had been purchased by 1862, the square-mile checkerboard pattern of land grants was not possible inside the state. Still, both the Hannibal and St. Joseph Railroad and the Atlantic and Pacific Railroad, which extended from St. Louis to Joplin, received significant land grants.[30]

Land was also granted to individual settlers by the Homestead Act of 1862. The law allowed loyal citizens over the age of twenty-one to file for up to 160 acres of land held in the public domain. Homesteaders then had five years to make improvements on the land, or "prove up," their property by building a home on it and preparing part of it for agricultural production. Once that was complete, the homesteader was given a patent on the land by the General Land Office. In Missouri more than 3.6 million acres of land, or about 8% of the total state land mass, were granted to homesteaders in this manner.[31]

Finally, public land, acquired by "violence-backed treaties," was made available to public educational institutions through Seminary Land laws and later the 1862 Morrill Act. The laws allowed states to claim so many acres of public land based on its apportionment figures. The grants were to be used to fund public schools for agricultural and manual training. Across the country, fifty-two land grant universities received 10.7 million acres of land that had previously belonged to 245 Indigenous nations in what historian Robert Lee and journalist Tristan Ahtone have called "a massive wealth transfer masquerading as a donation." Their research has shown that the United States paid less than $400,000 for all the land claimed through the Morrill Act, yet by the beginning of the twentieth century, the land grants had funded $17.7 million in university endowments. Between 1839 and 1855, The University of Missouri in Columbia, then a struggling institution that sorely needed an influx of capital, made over $700,000 (or $2.1 million in 2021 dollars) from the sale of Seminary lands it had been granted in 1839. After the passage of the Morrill Act the university was allowed to claim at least 270,613 acres of land, all of which had been ceded to the United States in William Clark's treaties with the Osages in 1808 and 1825. By 1914, the university had used the grants to raise an endowment worth $363,441 ($10.1 million in 2021 dollars). Today, the university still owns 14,787 acres of their original granted lands.[32]

However, the erasure of Missouri's Indigenous past went beyond whitewashing the Native landscape and removing burials and artifacts from their original contexts. The myth of the "Vanishing Indian" became the dominant narrative regarding Indigenous people in Missouri history books. In her book *Firsting and Lasting*, historian Jean O'Brien has analyzed the ways in which Natives were written out of local histories in nineteenth-century New England. She noted that local histories tended to fleetingly mention the "last" of the region's original inhabitants, while enumerating white "firsts." These firsts typically included such things as the birth of the first white baby, the meeting of the first Christian church, and the construction of the first white school. Similar narratives were a mainstay in Missouri histories published after the Civil War.[33]

Two such histories were published by William Switzler, a Columbia, Missouri, lawyer and newspaper publisher who had been appointed to serve as provost marshal for Missouri's ninth district during the Civil War. In 1881, he published a *History of Missouri*, followed by a *History of Boone County, Missouri* the following year. In his *History of Missouri*, Switzler allowed Alban Conant, the amateur excavator of St. Louis's Big Mound, over one hundred pages to cover the state's archaeology in a section he called "Mounds and their Builders, or Traces of Prehistoric Man in Missouri." Conant's romantic musings about the state's antiquities focused on Missouri's Mississippian people. Conant was in the camp of archaeologists who believed that the mounds had been built by a vanished race of Mound Builders. He was also fixated on the crania of ancient people and took pains to point out that the study of skulls had proven that the Mound Builders were a distinct race who were separate from the Indigenous people of the nineteenth century. "The idea that there once existed on this continent a race anterior to, and entirely distinct from, that which immediately preceded the red men, is no new and fanciful conjecture," claimed Conant. It is "one which was held by the earliest and most cautious observers of the antiquities of America."[34] Conant was also a proponent of the theory that the ancient Ozark Bluff Dwellers were also a distinct race of people who were unrelated to contemporary Native people. He based this contention almost solely on the belief that nineteenth-century Indigenous people viewed "these gloomy caverns with superstitious fear, for in them they believed the great

Manitou dwelt. In view of this fact, so well attested by early writers, the idea that they were the occupants becomes a matter of grave doubt."[35]

In his subsequent section of Missouri's history, Switzler generally fails to recognize Native people, and instead revels in a long list of white and European firsts: Hernando de Soto's "marvelous" expedition was the first to "discover" the Mississippi River, and its members may have been the first white men to set foot in Missouri in 1541; La Salle was the first white man to see the mouth of the Mississippi River; Ste. Genevieve was the first white Settlement in Missouri. While these firsts deny Indigenous people of their historical agency, Switzler was far more direct in his *History of Boone County, Missouri*, in which he stated that the title of Missouri's land had belonged to those who had originally inhabited it, "But the Indians, being savages, possessed but few rights that civilized nations considered themselves bound to respect." Soon, the land was claimed for the King of France.[36]

By the 1880s, many of the state's earliest white settlers had reached the age at which they became nostalgic for their younger days, which had coincided with what they believed to be the state's early history. At about the same time that Switzler published his histories, reminiscences written by some of these early white settler colonialists began to appear in Missouri newspapers. One of these was "Early Days in Missouri," a series of twenty letters published in the *Liberty Tribune* from June to November 1883 by Joseph Thorp. Thorp was a second-generation Missourian. His father, William Thorp, was a Scots-Irish settler who had lived in what would become Howard County, Missouri, during the violence that marked the War of 1812.[37]

Though the younger Thorp expressed some compassion for his "wily foes," the region's Indigenous people, he also employed several familiar tropes when remembering them. He recounted attacks on settlers by Ioways, Sacs, Foxes, and Osages in 1811, "just when all [white] hands were enjoying themselves in a land that flowed with milk and honey, each enjoying the right to use whatever his taste and appetite called for."[38] Thorp did not seem to comprehend that the reason for these attacks was the settlers' very act of taking whatever they wanted. He also expressed the settlers' concerns about the Natives' savageness, which exposed white women and children to the danger of being murdered, or of enduring a "worse fate" than death.[39]

Thorp's reminiscences are a good example of Jean O'Brien's "Firsting," as he recalls the first steamboat on the Missouri River and the establishment of the General Land Office in New Franklin, Missouri, in 1818, and the coming of statehood. He also laments that by around 1820, "the old pioneers began to get restless, feeling themselves a little too crowded, they began to look out for a place where they could have space to breath in, and there being only one direction for them, which was still westward towards the setting sun."[40]

These revisionist local histories proved to be a useful tool in the process of creating a "white" Missouri. They employ the misty lens of melancholia and memory to soften the violent settler colonialism that forced Native people from Missouri. They also served to disconnect the ancient people of Missouri from nineteenth-century Indigenous people. Thorp, Switzler, and Conant, like thousands of other regional historians across the country, created a master narrative that robbed Natives of their culture, innovations, history, and as it turned out, future. As O'Brien has observed, "These obscure, largely forgotten authors engaged in an ideological project that involved working out a vision of American Indians that continues to shape, limit, and inhibit Indians even today."[41]

They accomplished this is at least two ways. First, they portrayed contemporary Natives as being ignorant, superstitious, and savage. Surely, men like Conant believed, these crude people were incapable of the technical and spiritual expertise needed to build Big Mound or create the artifacts found in its center. Blinded by their racism, they were forced to contend that the mounds and their contents were the work of another, more sophisticated, race of people who had since completely vanished. Second, these writers placed Indigenous people in an unwinnable dichotomy of identity. On the one hand, Thorp, Switzler, and Conant believed that, because their culture was anachronistic and full of superstition, Natives must vanish because they could never be a part of a modern America. On the other hand, as soon as Native people became acculturated and adapted to European culture, these writers ceased to recognize them as "authentic" Indians. In the end, these constructed settler colonialist narratives made no place for contemporary Indigenous people to exist.[42]

Missouri's Unrecognized Minority

If we were to believe the census figures for the late nineteenth century, we might assume these local historians were correct in their assessment that that Natives had largely be eradicated from the state. The 1870 census was the first in which enumerators had the option of recording

"Indian" under the category of race. In the entire state of Missouri, only fifty-six Indians were counted in the census that year.[43] The City of St. Louis was home to thirty, or over half of those counted. The remaining twenty-six were spread out over twelve counties. There are two likely reasons for this extremely low count. The first reason has already been discussed: those who could do so, generally tried to pass as something other than Native. When census takers arrived at Indigenous households, they were likely given false information by those who wanted to protect themselves and their families. Second, census takers were instructed to exclude "Indians not taxed" from their count. Indians not taxed referred to those who were living on reservations or otherwise under the care of the Bureau of Indian Affairs. These people also were not included in the count that determined apportionment or representation. Otherwise, enumerators were instructed to count all "Indians not in tribal relations, whether full-bloods or half-breeds, who are found mingled with the white population, residing in white families, engaged as servants or laborers, or living in huts or wigwams on the outskirts of towns or settlements." Because Indian agents made separate counts of Natives living on their reservation, the Census Bureau was able to estimate that only about 8% of the Nation's Indigenous population appeared in the US Census in 1870.[44]

The extremely small sample size of Indigenous Missourians listed in the 1870 census does, however, provide an opportunity to take a quick look at who some of the state's Indigenous people were and how they lived. This cross section shows that Missouri Natives defied conventional "Indian" stereotypes. For example, thirty-nine-year-old James Perry and his thirty-six-year-old wife Elizabeth Perry lived with their five children, all of whom were listed in the census as being "Indian," on a farm outside Shelbina in Shelby County. The Perrys, who were from Rhode Island, must have been new to the area because all their small children had been born in Canada. Despite their recent arrival, the family did possess some means. Their real estate was valued at $1,000 and they held personal property valued at $200. According to the census, the seven members of the Perry family accounted for 100% of Shelby County's Indigenous population.[45]

Many of Missouri's Natives lived in what we would now call blended households. Thomas Culvin was an Indigenous man from Mexico who worked as a teamster in St. Louis. He married Selena, a black woman who was born in Missouri. Their children, eleven-year-old Thomas Jr. and five-year-old Rebecca, were listed in the census as "mulatto."[46] A fifty-one-year-old single white woman named Eliza Elban was the well-to-do head of a household that included two Indigenous washerwomen—forty-six-year-old Eliza Minor, whose four indigenous children were between the ages of ten and twenty-one, and twenty-three-year-old Delia Heite, a Native woman with two small children, one of whom was listed as "Indian," and one who was listed as "mulatto."[47] William Pennington was an Indigenous physician living in the town of Logan in Reynolds County. Originally from Tennessee, he married Jane, a white woman, with whom he had three children who were all listed as white in the census.[48]

Many Natives seem to have been single or orphaned and were living with employers or guardians. Forty-two-year-old Mary Ward was a single Indigenous woman from Texas living with a white family, possibly as a boarder or domestic worker, in St. Joseph. Even though Mary Alicia Owen had written about several multiracial people with black and Native heritage in the region, Ward was the only Native person listed in all of Buchanan County in 1870.[49] Ten-year-old Native Eliza Dinhmete, who lived in the St. Louis home of sixty-nine-year-old Pierse Lacrois, was listed as a "mulatto." The pair lived in a segregated area of the city with black and "mulatto" neighbors.[50] Two Indigenous sisters who also lived in St. Louis, Emma Lambert, age ten, and Sophia Lambert, age twelve, were wards of the state, living "at the Asylum" with other teenage girls, most of whom were white.[51]

One individual who stands out in the Missouri census is Joseph "Injun Joe" Douglass, a man who may have been the inspiration for one of the state's most notorious Indigenous villains. Born around 1821, Douglass was a man of mixed Osage and African heritage who had settled in Hannibal, Missouri, by at least the 1840s. For years, Hannibal boosters claimed that Douglass was the model for Mark Twain's character Injun Joe. Even today, the words "Injun Joe" are inscribed in large letters on Douglass's tombstone in Hannibal's Mount Olivette Cemetery. In *The Adventures of Tom Sayer*, the character Injun Joe is portrayed as a "half-breed" thief and murderer. In reality, Joseph Douglass was a hard-working and frugal handyman who saved enough money to invest in real estate. He divided his land into town lots, which he then sold to former slaves. Douglasville, as the subdivision he created was called, grew to include eighty families and the city's first African American church and school. When Douglass died in 1923—of ptomaine poisoning he got after eating pickled pigs' feet—his death certificate listed his age as one-hundred and one.[52]

The apparent undercount of Indigenous Missourians in the US Census continued through the remainder of the nineteenth century and into the first half of the twentieth century. Even after the 1839 *Act to Suppress Intercourse with Indians* quietly disappeared from the laws of Missouri around 1905, the census count of Natives remained low. In fact, as late as 1940, the census would still show fewer than a thousand Natives living in the state. For the most part, trends showed the Native population slowly growing and becoming heaviest in Kansas City and St. Louis. Indigenous people also made up a larger percentage of the population of Jasper, Newton, and McDonald Counties, the three Missouri counties located closest to the Indian Territory. One irregularity in the census figures reveals the fact that in 1900, Cooper County had the second highest Indigenous population in the state, second only to Jackson County, the home of Kansas City. The reason for this high number was that the Missouri Reform School for Boys, located in Boonville, housed twenty-eight Native inmates. The school had opened in 1887 as a state training school for wayward boys. With a total capacity for six hundred fifty inmates, the Indigenous boys constituted only about 4% of the school's overall population. Nonetheless, the boys made up more than 12% of the state's entire recorded Indigenous population. The boys' names did not appear at the same location ten years later in the 1910 Census.[53]

Given that this was the era during which the federal government operated boarding schools for Native children, it is possible that the boys were placed in the school as a means of assimilation. For the most part, boarding schools functioned as places of indoctrination in which Indigenous children were forced to cut their hair and wear Euro-American style clothing and were forbidden from speaking their own languages. There have been 367 such schools operating in the United States between the 1820s and the present day—seventy-three are still open, fifteen of them still board students. Though there were no federal boarding schools in Missouri, there were two religious schools for Natives that received some federal funding. St. Regis School in Florissant was operated by Jesuits, while the Presbyterians' Harmony Mission School was located in Papinville on Osage land. Other Indigenous children from Missouri had been sent to far-away schools, such as the Choctaw Academy, a school operated by Richard Mentor Johnson.[54]

Another set of early-twentieth-century records provides a fuller picture of Natives living in Missouri in the nineteenth and early twentieth centuries. In 1905, the US Court of Claims ruled that so-called Eastern Cherokees were entitled to compensation for treaty violations that had occurred because of the Treaty of New Echota in 1835, and Special Commissioner Guion Miller was assigned to draw up a list of all Cherokees eligible to receive payments. Claimants did not have to be living in the Indian Territory; they only had to be alive as of May 28, 1906, to establish that they were descendants of members of the Ross Party and were not enrolled with another Native nation. The commission received nearly forty-six thousand applications that listed a total of ninety thousand claimants. Of those, only about thirty thousand seven hundred were listed on what is now known as the Guion Miller Roll. Although the 1910 US Census listed only 271 Indigenous people living in Missouri, 2,265 Missourians claiming Cherokee ancestry applied to receive payments in 1908. It is difficult to determine exactly how many Missourians succeeded in being enrolled, but if about one-third all applicants were approved, it is likely that fewer than one thousand people in Missouri were approved to receive individual payments of $133.33.[55]

Among the fascinating Guion Miller documents are the affidavits some claimants submitted as part of the application process. Even though the majority of those who applied were not approved for the rolls, their brief statements give us a rare look into the lives of Indigenous Missourians who were not listed as "Indians" on US Census reports. Nearly all the applicants were multiracial, usually having one white parent. While most of them passed as white, many claimed that their Cherokee heritage was known to most of their friends and neighbors. Many were born in Missouri, and some were from families that had lived in Missouri prior to the removals of the 1830s.

Seventy-five-year-old Missouri A. Fleetwood was born in Miller County, Missouri, before the Cherokees were removed from their homelands. His "full blood" Cherokee grandfather had been born in Georgia and moved to Tennessee, where Fleetwood's mother was born in 1804. The family moved to Missouri in 1832, the year before Fleetwood was born. "I am generally regarded in the community in which I live as being of white and Indian parentage," Fleetwood testified in August 1908. Missouri Fleetwood's application to the Guion Miller rolls was denied because his family had left Georgia before the Treaty of New Echota was signed and "though very old, [he] has never associated with Indians."[56]

Adaniza C. Cotter Lisenby was a white woman who applied on behalf of her children. She testified that her husband's family, though part-Cherokee, never lived with other members of the nation. "They simply lived as white settlers with Indian blood. My children have always been regarded as being one sixteenth Cherokee." Grant Gooch was born in Christian County, Missouri, in 1858 to a part Cherokee father who was from North Carolina. "It has always been handed down in my family that I had Cherokee blood," he testified. James Bruten, also born in Christian County, claimed that "none of my people ever went West with the Indians. My mother told me that my grandfather . . . married a white woman. During the latter part of his life he went as a white man." Seventy-year-old Louisa Ketchum, a resident of Moberly, had lived in Missouri her entire life. Her father, James Green, had come to the state in about 1832 from Tennessee with a caravan of twenty-five wagons.[57] Clearly, the reality of Indigenous people in Missouri after the period of removal was far more nuanced than many in the state cared to admit.

Historian C. Joseph Genetin-Pilawa has characterized the post-Civil war era as one during which US Indian policy succeeded in confining Indigenous nations in space, time, politics, and in the law. Native people were confined in space by being corralled on ever-shrinking reservations that would eventually be further divided through allotment. After Congress stopped the process of treaty making in 1871, Genetin-Pilawa says Nations were frozen in time. Political relations between the United States and Native nations had been confined by a series of trade and intercourse laws passed between 1790 and 1834. Finally, US law confined Natives by chipping away at tribal sovereignty, by asserting unrestrained plenary power over them.[58]

However, Genetin-Pilawa points out that confinement is a "*limited* as well as a *limiting* process." Because, in the words of historian Jacki Thompson Rand, colonialism is the process by which both the colonizer and the colonized "do the work of creating a new set of conditions in which they both exist, albeit in unequal relations," Indigenous people found new ways to live within confinement, even as they pushed against it.[59] Indigenous nations and individuals made decisions that they hoped would ensure the survival of their descendants. Perhaps this explains why we see Native families and individuals doing their best to survive away from their Native communities and inside the state that had tried to abolish their presence.

Voices

They had their own land of so many acres apiece that they must go and live on. They were living down in the village there, my mother's father, uncle's people, and the other chiefs. They, they were trying to find the locations where their land was, their allotments. My grandfather doesn't feel very good over that. No, he did not feel that it should have been such a thing as allotment act. He feels it should have been reservation. With allotment they only have so many acres that each one is allotted during that time. That leaves all the younger generations without land, without a home. If it was in reservation they would go out and establish their home. And still the land belongs to the tribe and the folks. There the generations could come along and would have a place to go, and live and try to make a living.[1]

—Blaine N. Kent (Ioway)

When I was a boy I saw much game and buffalo, and the animals my forefathers used to live upon, but now all are gone. Where I once saw the animals I now see houses and white men cultivating the land; and I see that this is better. I ought long ago to have tried to work like the white man; but for several years I have been trying, and perhaps in the future I can do much better for myself and my friends. . . . I want title to my land. I am troubled about it, for I am not sure I can have the land if I do not get the title. . . . In the morning I get up and look at my fields, and I wish that God may help me to do better with my land and let it be my own.[2]

—Anonymous (Omaha)

Chapter Nine

"Peaceful Red Men and Satisfied White Ones"

LATE ON THE AFTERNOON OF Saturday, December 16, 1866, several Ioways including Kihega (also known as Henry Lee), James Whitewater, Sandy Reed, George Washington, Henry Washburn, along with a handful of Sac and Fox men, unexpectedly barged into the office of their US Indian Agent John Burbank. Burbank asked them if they had come to meet with him in council. Kihega replied that they had heard some disturbing news and needed to talk to him. Whitewater added that the men had come to tell him "things their chiefs were afraid to say."

The Ioways, who were all recent Civil War veterans, told Burbank that they were unhappy with all of the agency employees. They made it clear that they intended to throw him out of the office and take charge of the agency themselves. Eager to look over the agency financial records, George Washington forced the agent to give him the keys to the office and the safe. Certain that they intended to murder him, Burbank made an excuse to go to the agency house, some four hundred yards away. He heard gunfire behind him as he bolted for the door with Washington on his heels repeatedly snapping the trigger of a revolver that failed to fire. Burbank made it safely to the house only to discover that his own revolver was rusted and useless. As he tried to find a place to hide, the Ioways broke into the house, firing at least two more shots in the agent's direction. Miraculously, Burbank was uninjured and managed to calm his assailants enough to persuade them to return peacefully with him to the council house.[1]

By 1871, the Ioways, Sacs and Foxes, Delawares, Kickapoos, and Osages, all Indigenous nations that had been deported from Missouri to Kansas, had seen their reservation lands dwindle. The four hundred square mile reservation that the Ioways split with the Sacs and Foxes of Missouri in 1836 had been decreased by three fourths in the Treaty of

1854, signed the year Kansas became a territory. In 1861, the reservation was cut one final time, this time by half. Each of the nations was left with fifty square miles, or one eighth of their original reservation land.[2]

This new generation of Ioways, many of whom had been educated in a Presbyterian mission school and some of whom had experience in the military, had tried to grapple with the long history of Ioway dispossession. Having failed to solve their deprivation by violence, a group of Ioways, which included Kihega, subsequently sought a solution through the treaty process. The Ioways' Treaty of 1854 had contained an article authorizing the President of the United States to order their land to be allotted to them in severalty. Beginning in 1871, the group repeatedly requested to receive allotments of land from the reservation. Given the long history of the government taking the Ioways' lands, those requesting allotments believed it was their only way to prevent having it taken away from them entirely. To the frustration of the Ioways and Sacs and Foxes, their agent stalled the request. This led many of them to contemplate moving to the Indian Territory, where they believed they would be more likely to retain land.[3]

While the Ioways may not have realized it at the time, individual allotment of reservation land was on the horizon and one of its most ardent supporters would be the Missouri Senator, George Graham Vest. If Missourians recall anything about Vest, it is most likely to be the fact that he once brought a jury of twelve men to the verge of tears with his eloquent eulogy of a dog. Born in Kentucky, Vest was elected to represent Missouri in the Confederate Senate, and became famous when he represented Charles Burden in a court case in Johnson County in 1870. Burden had sued his brother-in-law Leonidas Hornsby for $150 in damages after Hornsby shot and killed Burden's hunting dog, Old Drum. In his closing argument, Vest, who possessed a talent for dramatic oratory, delivered an impassioned speech that persuaded the teary-eyed jury to award his client $50 in damages. "The one absolutely unselfish friend that a man can have in this selfish world," Vest eulogized, "the one that never deserts him and the one that never proves ungrateful or treacherous is his dog." Because of the eulogy, Vest is often credited for coining the phrase "a dog is a man's best friend."[4]

Perhaps not coincidentally, the phrase "history is written by the victors" is also attributed to Vest. He was elected to the US Senate in 1878 and served in that body until ill health forced him to retire in 1903. The historian Jeffrey Pasley has characterized Vest as a Jeffersonian Democrat who "tried to combine a certain earnest humanism and racially selective egalitarianism with a fierce resistance to change."[5] A protector of Yellowstone National Park, a defender of Mormons in Missouri, and a foe of US imperialist expansion abroad, Vest also had a strong interest in Indian policy. As a member of the Senate Committee on Territories and the Indian Commission, he had the opportunity to tour various Indigenous communities. In that capacity, he was a proponent of ending the US system of making treaties with Indigenous nations, granting Natives US citizenship, and forcing the allotment of land to individual Natives to open additional land to non-Native ownership. Vest was also one of the Senate's leading supporters of opening the Indian Territory to white settlement. Vest's assault on Indigenous land, sovereignty, and collective identity would have dire consequences for Native people across the country for decades to come.[6]

To be sure, other Missourians had expressed their desire to see Indian reservation land opened up to the general public, especially in cases where the land was found to hold or lay atop valuable resources. Former Missouri Governor Thomas Fletcher had publicly called for the removal of the Sioux from the gold-rich Black Hills in 1875. This put him at odds with the Missouri State Legislature, which sent a joint resolution to Congress two years later asking it to prevent removal of the Sioux. Their plea was based on the belief that moving the Sioux out of the Dakota Territory and into the Indian Territory would do "great injustice and injury" to the cause of civilization. Not only would it remove fertile land from "settlement or occupation by any useful class of citizens," it would convert the Indian Territory, which lay at the doorstep of the State of Missouri, into a "haunt of marauders and outlaws."[7]

Residents of northwest Missouri expressed support for opening up reservation land that was located just across the Missouri River. A Holt County resident argued that the Ioways had been "entirely civilized" by 1875 and ought to be "thrown on their own resources the same as the rest of mankind."[8] Many white settlers seemed to have conveniently forgotten that the annual annuities Natives received from the government were payments for land ceded to the United States and not cash handouts. A St. Joseph journalist who visited the Sac and Fox reservation complained,

> I don't believe there is hardly a red cuss on this reserve but would steal or commit murder to-day if he thought he would not be

detected and punished. And yet here they own a very large reserve in the very heart of civilization which they will never improve, and which, being underlaid with excellent coal, as it has been positively ascertained it is, would be of immense value to the white settlers of the west.[9]

In the second half of the nineteenth century, land-hungry settlers and railroad companies had begun to eye Indigenous lands with new interest, and a large portion of the Western citizenry had become tired of government support for Indigenous people. "The dusky rascals are well fixed," opined the St. Joseph newspaper correspondent, and "walk around, dressed and fed by the Government."[10]

Missourians Working to Assimilate Indigenous People

The decades after the Civil War were a time of great national expansion that coincided with a dramatic growth in the size of the federal government. Both factors contributed to an accelerated push to reform US Indian policy. Much of the campaign was led by Christian organizations made up of white East Coast elites. As historian C. Joseph Genetin-Pilawa has observed, these reformers tended to believe that they "understood the best interests of Indian peoples, better than Indian peoples themselves."[11] Reformers trusted that Indigenous people would benefit from being forced to assimilate to the dominant white society. Of course, this misguided policy assumed that Indigenous people were inherently inferior and in need of uplift. They argued that by doing away with anything that separated Natives from the rest of the US population, there would be fewer obstacles for them to overcome on their road to improvement. Paramount among the obstacles that supposedly stood in the way of Natives was what Francis Paul Prucha referred to as the "tribalism of Indians." Many believed that tribalism, or cohesive Indigenous cultural identity, was protected by treaty rights and the communal ownership of land. "Unless tribalism and its remnants were destroyed," wrote Prucha, "[reformers] believed there was little chance that the Indians as individuals could be completely absorbed into mainstream society." In this way, this brand of reform neatly fit Patrick Wolfe's previously mentioned axiom that settler colonialism "destroys to replace."[12]

Reformers referred to these efforts at assimilation as the "Vanishing Policy." "What better way for American society to ease the Native's march into oblivion," writes historian Tom Holm, "than to have them vanish into it."[13] In a sense, Vest and other reformers seem to have been trying to recreate in the Indian Territory what they imagined themselves to have successfully accomplished in Missouri—the "disappearance" of Indigenous people. Having failed to annihilate them, assimilationists focused instead on forcing Indigenous people to become something other than "Indians." They planned to accomplish this by breaking up communal Indian reservations and forcing Indigenous people to live on individual plots of land. They would send Native children to government-run boarding schools to be indoctrinated in the ways of European American culture. Along the way, Native land and natural resources would be opened to white-owned companies and individuals for development.

Even though they often worked toward the same goals as Vest, wealthy Eastern philanthropists and Congressional reformers, many of whom were New England Republicans, greatly annoyed the Missouri Democrat and his sense of pragmatism. "The last three generations in New England have had no Indian war," Vest charged in 1880. "They view the [Indian] question by the light of the domestic lamp and not by that of the burning house. For us in the West, it is a living, practical and real question."[14] In a similar vein, a St. Joseph newspaper declared in 1875 that most Natives were "lazy cusses which our eastern friends delight in styling 'the noble red men.'"[15]

However, one of the most powerful Republicans working toward the Vanishing Policy was Vest's fellow Missourian, Carl Schurz. Born in Germany, Schurz had been active there in the Revolution of 1848 and was forced to flee his homeland after the revolutionaries were defeated by the royal government. He moved to the United States in 1852 and became a newspaper reporter. A skilled orator and political tactician, Schurz supported Abraham Lincoln's 1860 presidential bid and briefly served as a diplomat in Spain before persuading the president to appoint him as a brigadier general in the Union Army. Schurz settled in St. Louis in 1867 and was elected US senator from Missouri two years later. Appalled by the Radical Republicans' draconian political agenda for Reconstruction, Schurz broke with President Ulysses S. Grant and helped form a liberal branch of the Republican Party. While the Liberal Republicans were able to elect B. Gratz Brown as Missouri's governor, Schurz lost his own reelection to the Senate in 1874.[16]

After supporting Rutherford B. Hayes for the presidency in 1876, Hayes rewarded Schurz by appointing him as Secretary of the Interior.

In that position, he oversaw the Department of Indian Affairs and successfully thwarted an attempt led by Generals William T. Sherman and Phillip Sheridan to have the Indian Office once again become part of the Department of War. During his eleven years at Interior, Schurz worked to clean up the notoriously corrupt Department of Indian Affairs. Like Vest, the secretary advocated the allotment of reservation land to individual natives. Unlike Vest, Schurz saw the destruction of reservations as an important move in desegregating the Indigenous population and assimilating them into American society.[17]

Vest's motives for supporting Indian policy reform and wanting to open the Indian Territory for settlement seem to have been based on practical rather than noble or humanitarian interests. Vest biographer Marian Elaine Dawes has written that during the second half of the nineteenth century, "peaceful red men and satisfied white ones were an asset to any Western Senator" hoping to retain his seat in Washington.[18] Vest worked to keep his white constituents satisfied by nurturing his long-time friendships with railroads and the Kansas City and St. Louis business interests who backed them. Prior to being elected to the Senate, Vest had been an attorney for the Missouri-Kansas-Texas Railroad, also known as the Katy. Even after his election, members of the Cherokee Nation suspected that he remained on the company's payroll and, indeed, the stakes for both the Katy and the Cherokees were high. If Indigenous title to rights-of-way through the Indian Territory could be extinguished, the railroad stood to receive a land grant of two million acres.[19]

Legally, the railroad rights-of-way could be made available only with the consent of the Indigenous nations that owned the land on which the tracks would be laid. However, by 1882, many in the Senate began to argue that previous US treaties with Indigenous nations should be deemed null and void if these nations denied the government the ability to take land for the railroads by eminent domain. When natives objected on both legal and ethical grounds, Vest blustered that it was foolish to seek consent from an ungrateful Indigenous population. "All this aesthetic talk and constitutional argument amounts to nothing in the face the great fact that the people of the United States today are stopped on their imperial course toward the Southwest."[20]

In January 1882, Congress approved a right-of-way for the Frisco Railroad through the Choctaw Nation. Because the bill did not have the approval of the Choctaw legislature and had been altered by Congress without the Choctaws' consent, it set an ominous precedent. More railroad rights-of-way were requested and approved during the 1880s. The result was that Indigenous nations lost all control over the encroachment of railroads on their land.[21]

Having made incursions onto Indigenous land and struck a serious blow to Native sovereignty, the Senate was ready to codify the settler colonial policy of land allotment. Henry Laurens Dawes, a Republican senator from Massachusetts and chair of the Senate Committee on Indian Affairs, took advantage of broad bipartisan support for the measure by ushering the General Allotment Act through Congress in the mid-1880s. Though the act, which President Grover Cleveland signed in February 1887, did not initially include the Osages, Muscogees, Cherokees, Chickasaws, Choctaws, or Seminoles—all of whom held fee simple ownership over their reservation lands—it was considered by most Indian policy reformers as a triumph. "It was," declared George Vest, "not only heroic, but the proper treatment" of Indigenous people.[22]

The Dawes Act, as it is often called, stipulated that Indigenous families would receive individual plots of reservation land—usually one hundred sixty acres—while orphans and single adults would each receive eighty-acre plots. These plots would be held in trust by the government for a period of twenty-five years, or until the government declared the holder of the land patent to be competent to own the land outright. Once all eligible Natives received their land allotments, any reservation land that had not been allotted would be declared "surplus" and made available to white settlers.[23]

Congress created a number of panels to negotiate with Indigenous nations in the Indian Territory for the implementation of allotment. One of the best known was the Cherokee Commission, later known as the Jerome Commission for its chairman, former Michigan governor David Jerome. From 1890 to 1892, the Jerome Commission negotiated, cajoled, and threatened at least fifteen reluctant Indigenous nations, including one-time Missouri residents the Ioways, Sacs, Foxes, Kickapoos, and Absentee Shawnees, to accept allotment. "We are *Indians*, and whenever we own anything, someone comes along and takes it," Ioway delegate Joe Vetter protested when Ioways met with the Jerome Commission on May 8, 1890. "It is nature for everyone to keep everything that he has." Indeed, the process of allotment was devastating for all of the nations forced to go through it. On the Ioway Reservation in Oklahoma, 109 families and individuals received a total of about eight thousand six hundred acres of allotted land. However, more than twenty times that amount, at least two hundred twenty thousand acres, were declared as surplus by the federal government and thereafter claimed by white settlers in the so-called second Oklahoma Land Run on September 21, 1891.[24]

The work of the Jerome Commission also included the dissolution of tribal governments, many of which had recently been forced to model themselves after that of the United States. Like communal land holdings, tribal governments were considered to be holdovers of the sort of tribalism that would prevent Natives from assimilating. In November 1891, the Sacs and Foxes in the Indian Territory were forced to give up their constitution and their supreme court. Their government was reduced to an eight-member council led by two headmen. Seven years later, even that modest form of tribal government was abolished by federal authorities.[25]

In 1893, Congress created the Dawes Commission to facilitate allotment with the Cherokees, Muscogees, Chickasaws, Seminoles, and Choctaws. In 1895, a survey of the Indian Territory was initiated, and the following year the Dawes Commission began to draw up citizenship rolls, or Final Rolls, of eligible allottees for the five nations. Though the leaders of these nations resisted and attempted to formulate alternative plans, the Curtis Act, passed by Congress in 1898, a decade after the Dawes Commission convened, forced all of them into allotment; the Curtis Act also helped clear the way for the Indian Territory to be admitted to the Union as the state of Oklahoma in 1907.[26]

While it ostensibly extended the right of land ownership to Indigenous people, the Dawes Act, contained built-in provisions that, in practice, prevented Natives from improving their property and exercising the rights of land ownership. Because the government held allotments in trust status for at least twenty-five years, allottees were unable to use their property as collateral to secure home mortgages. This greatly hampered their efforts to improve their property. It also made it very difficult for Natives to pull themselves out of poverty or to leave accumulated wealth to their descendants. This was true even after Congress granted US citizenship to Indigenous people in 1924. Thus, as historian K. Tsianina Lomawaima has pointed out, "Native individuals have simultaneously been invited into the fold of citizenship but held at arm's length [and] marked as different."[27]

Government Rolls and Indigenous Identity

Census listings, or tribal rolls were a vital part of the Dawes Act. Definitive lists of those persons belonging to each Indigenous nation were needed to ensure that only legitimate tribal members received land allotments. As might be expected, the process of compiling these rolls was fraught with corruption. The Dawes Commission was, as mentioned, charged with compiling rolls for the Cherokees, Choctaws, Chickasaws, Seminoles, and Muscogees, while other task forces, like the Jerome Commission, worked with the remaining nations.

Commissioners were authorized to enroll tribal members based on three criteria: enrollees must physically reside within the boundaries of their particular nation; they must have been alive at the time of their enrollment; and finally, enrollees must have appeared on either the 1896 or 1880 census made by their particular tribe *and* had to be recognized by that tribe as being a citizen of the nation. Commissioners used a combination of written records and oral testimonies to determine not only who was "Indian," but what amount of "Indian Blood," known as blood quantum, an individual possessed. This was further complicated by the fact that individuals were only permitted to enroll in one tribe. In cases in which persons had direct ancestors from more than one tribe, they were only allowed to count their blood quantum for the tribe in which they were trying to enroll. This led to cases in which, for example, a person may have a "full blood" Cherokee father and a "full blood" Choctaw mother, but could only be listed as a "half-blood" if they enrolled with either tribe.[28]

Under these guidelines, Indigenous sovereignty was usurped because commissioners had the final say in approving who would be included on the lists. In short, the process of determining eligibility for enrollment was haphazard and racially biased. While compiling the Choctaw rolls, members of the Dawes Commission often resorted to deciding a person's enrollment status and blood quantum by a simple visual inspection. Historian Katherine Osburn has written about instances in which persons who displayed "prominence of Choctaw blood and characteristics" did not have to produce documentation of their ancestry, whereas those who looked "less" Choctaw did have to provide documents. "For some claimants," writes Osburn, "an Indian identity could be established if one's neighbors perceived the defendants to be Indian."[29]

The process was slowed dramatically by the large number of ineligible people requesting placement on the rolls. Overall, the Dawes

Commission received a total of two hundred fifty thousand applications for membership in all the Five Civilized Tribes. Of those, they approved about 101,000 applicants. The Choctaws alone received nearly twenty-five thousand applications for enrollment; when the registration period ended in 1907, only 1,634 people claiming membership in the Choctaw Nation had their requests accepted. The large number of applicants was attributed to the fact that enrolled tribal members would receive benefits of land and money, said to be worth between $5,000 and $8,000. Several whites submitted fraudulent claims. The Choctaws were especially watchful of the claims of white men who had wedded Choctaw woman in "sham marriages," and charges of so-called "five-dollar Indians" bribing commissioners to gain enrollment ran rampant, although it is impossible to determine how many of these false claims succeeded.[30]

At the same time, there were many legitimate tribal members who protested allotment by refusing to be entered onto the rolls. Cherokee resistance to allotment was led by National Councilman Redbird Smith, who worked tirelessly to persuade Cherokees to return to a more traditional lifestyle. To this end, he helped resurrect the Nighthawk Keetoowah Society and led a community of resisters in the Cookson Hills region of the Cherokee Nation. At its height, Smith's resistance movement had 5,500 supporters. At the same time, more than five thousand Muscogees opposed allotment. They were led by Chitto Harjo, also known as Crazy Snake, who helped to create an alternate Muscogee government located in the Hickory Ground settlement. In the end, both leaders were arrested and forced to enroll. Harjo was shot and later died while in hiding.[31]

The allotment work of the government commissions broke up collective land holdings and struck serious blows to the viability of Native communities and culture in the Indian Territory. Its effect on Indigenous people living in Missouri, while less direct, was no less devastating. Because many Missourians were left out of the enrollment process, they became disenfranchised and lost official ties to their tribes. Unenrolled Natives were left "scattered and landless" and, as historian Katherine Ellinghaus has pointed out, were more likely to experience poverty and a myriad of health and social problems that went with it. She has also suggested that those who were left off of the tribal rolls often struggled with identity. The prevalence of unflattering stereotypes that cast those persons left off tribal rolls as "shrewd inauthentic wannabes," led to even stricter controls over the process of determining just who was eligible for enrollment and receipt of land and government support. By inadvertently instituting a category of Indigenous person that Ellinghaus refers to as undeserving mixed-descent Indians, the allotment and assimilation process created long-lasting problems for generations of Indigenous people. In the words of journalist Alysa Landry, the institution of tribal rolls "forever changed the way the federal government defined Indians—and, in many cases, the way Indians still define themselves."[32]

The apparent success of allotment and enrollment led reformers and politicians to proclaim that Indians had been "forced to succumb," and that the end of Indian tribes had arrived. In 1910, Secretary of the Interior Richard A. Ballinger said that "he believed the day had come when tribal relations should cease and the Indian take his place by the side of the white man in the obligations and privileges of [US] citizenship." Among these obligations was the expectation that the United States would no longer be guardians of Indigenous people.[33]

Imperialist Nostalgia

Ironically, just as the Vanishing Policy was put in place, the American public began to undergo a renewed interest—albeit profoundly romanticized—in Indigenous people, knowledge, and traditions. Anthropologist Renato Rosaldo has labeled this "imperialist nostalgia." The rapid industrialization of the United States, the increase in immigration and urbanization, and the class inequities of the Gilded Age left many Americans longing for more authentic connections to the myths of the nation's founding. "It is indeed ironic and perhaps fateful," writes historian Tom Holm, "that the white man became more and more interested in conservation, environmentalism, and a collective world order at the precise point in time when he had all but destroyed Native American peoplehood and the Indian knowledge of the environment."[34]

At that point, many white Americans, who had been appropriating Indigenous culture for their own purposes since at least the 1773 Boston Tea Party, began to see themselves as the custodians of Native material culture, folklore, and knowledge. They reasoned that it was up to them to ensure that Native cultures would not pass from memory and therefore be lost forever. Anthropologist Jacob W. Gruber has written that this bid to "salvage" Indigenous cultures reflected the belief of many whites that they were in danger of disappearing forever.[35] Much of this work came in the form of whites playing the roles of Native people in organizations and in performances that perpetuated the myths regarding the role of Indigenous people in that nation's history. In 1910, for example, one hundred grammar school students from Columbia, Missouri, staged a two-hour production of Henry Wadsworth Longfellow's *Song of Hiawatha* as part of their graduation exercises. The 1855 play, in which Hiawatha eventually moves west into the vapors of the "purple distance," seemed to provide whites with a potent reminder of the supposed passing of Native culture. Productions of the play were common, as were those of similarly melodramatic productions such as John Augustus Stone's *Metamora; or, The Last of the Wampanoags*. Missouri folklorist Mary Alicia Owen, who studied Indigenous people in the late nineteenth century, wrote a play in this genre to be performed by St. Joseph High School students in 1909. *The Sacred Council Hills: A Folklore Drama* takes place among the Sacs and Foxes, during their removal from Missouri to their reservation in Kansas.[36]

A number of newly created outdoor scouting organizations for youth also appropriated the perceived folklore, teachings, and regalia of Indigenous people. "Those live longest who live nearest to the ground," wrote artist Ernest Thompson Seton, who founded the League of Woodcraft Indians in 1902. "That is, who live the simple life of primitive times, divested, however, of the evils that ignorance in those times begot."[37] Longing for a "simpler time," many whites extolled the virtues of teaching a generation of young men primitive, outdoor life skills. The popularity of the outdoor scouting movement led to the creation of the Boy Scouts of America, which Seton would help found in 1910.

Scouting officially came to St. Joseph, Missouri, in 1916, when a local scout council was formally organized. In the early 1920s, the St. Joseph Council formed Manhawka, a scouting society based on Indigenous lore. Inductees were required to spend a night alone in the woods located on the society's property. Those who gained membership received "Indian names" and were offered a mysterious "black drink" as part of their induction ceremony. In 1925, twenty-six-year-old H. Roe Bartle became the leader of the St. Joseph Council of Manhawka. Fresh from a similar job in Wyoming, where he claimed to have been given the name Chief Lone Bear by an Arapahoe headman, Bartle immediately revamped the Manhawka Society, creating a new one he called the Tribe of Mic O Say.[38]

Mic-O-Say flourished under Bartle's watchful guidance. A large gregarious man with a booming voice, he ensured the organization's financial stability and social cachet by enlisting several prominent St. Joseph businessmen to serve as his Mic-O-Say "Chieftains." In 1928, Bartle became the Scout Executive of the Greater Kansas City Area Council. He established a second chapter of Mic-O-Say in Noel, Missouri, which moved to Osceola, Missouri, in 1929. In the first five years of its existence, the organization's membership grew from thirty-five to one hundred sixty boys. By 1940, Mic-O-Say had six hundred members, and the organization, which continues to this day and includes both adult and youth members, now claims a membership of seventeen thousand.[39]

Mic-O-Say members participate in rituals orchestrated by white leaders and only loosely based on Indigenous ceremonies. (Bartle himself originated some of these ceremonies.) Mic-O-Say scouts dressed in Native-themed regalia, in which they performed dances that they claimed were meant to teach participants to appreciate Indigenous culture. "Leaders and members [of Mic-O-Say] have a list of Native-themed titles," writes journalist Vincent Schilling, "such as chief, chieftain, foxman, brave, warrior honorary, warrior hard-way, re builder, tom-tom beater, runner, Keeper of the sacred bundle, shaman, sachem, keeper of the wampum, sagamore and medicine man depending on their level of achievement and status in the Mic-O-Say."

The Mic-O-Say's own website once declared, "By blending the spirit and pride of the American Indian with the ideals and objectives of the Boy Scouts of America, the Tribe of Mic-O-Say endeavors to prolong the Scouting adventure with a historical theme that has held the attention and captured the imagination of boys and men alike for many generations." Besides Bartle, who went on to become mayor of Kansas City in the late 1950s and early 1960s, prominent past members have included Missouri Congressmen Ike Skelton from Lexington and Sam Graves from Tarkio.[40]

Another organization that saw itself as the "acknowledged conservators of the history, the customs, and the virtues of the original American people" was the Improved Order of Red Men (IORM). Formed in the late 1840s, the IORM is a secret fraternal order which denied membership to Indigenous men until the 1970s. The IORM claims to be America's oldest fraternal organization, with ties to the sons of Liberty in the 1770s and had half a million members by the 1920s. At least four US presidents, Thomas Jefferson, Theodore Roosevelt, Franklin Roosevelt, and Richard Nixon, were "Red Men." The late historian James W. Loewen suggested that the organization enjoyed popularity at the turn of the twentieth century because, "White Americans wanted to inherit the aura and spiritual strength of the American Indian," and to "feel a closer kinship with the land and with nature."[41]

The IORM was never as popular in Missouri as it was in other parts of the nation. The state's first local chapter, Hiawatha Tribe No. 1 of St. Louis, was formed in 1856. By 1898, the state had just eight local IORM tribes and could claim a total of fewer than three hundred members. The club was, however, popular in the Pemiscot County town of Hayti, where IORM news appeared on the front page of the local paper almost weekly in the early twentieth century. In August 1909, the town's Wakarusa Tribe No. 171 held a two-day "Scalp Dance and Picnic." Aside from foot races, ball games, and barbeques, event organizers promised an "Indian Raid" in which Indians, played by whites, would capture a prairie schooner.[42]

The Red Men seemed to value patriotism above all else and are perhaps best remembered today for the bronze statues they erected to commemorate the Indigenous people they believed to be vanishing. They were particularly fond of life-sized bronze likenesses of Natives who had either supported or capitulated to white settlers and the US government. The IORM dedicated a sculpture of the Ioway headman White Cloud, or Maxùthka, in Oskaloosa, Iowa, in 1909. The bronze plaque on the stone base of the monument points out that White Cloud was a friend of the white man. Similarly, a statue of an unnamed Mascouten man dedicated by the Red Men in Muscatine, Iowa, in 1926, depicts a non-threatening warrior who appears to be contemplating his destiny as a member of a vanishing race. At least one tribe of the IORM also participated in the dedication of the new Missouri State Capitol on October 6, 1924. At the time, few present at the ceremony seemed bothered by the fact that the IORM and Tribe of Mic-O-Say haphazardly appropriated elements of Indigenous culture. Afterall, most members of the organizations likely believed that "real Indians" no longer existed and that the work of the clubs was honoring their memory.[43]

IMAGE 11: The Improved Order of Red Men was a popular fraternal organization open only to white men. The "Red Men" appropriated Indigenous imagery into their rituals, symbols, and regalia. Here, an unknown local lodge, or tribe, of Red Men participates in New Capitol Day festivities in Jefferson City on October 6, 1924. *Courtesy of the Missouri State Archives*

Salvage Anthropologists

At the same time, white collectors, believing that they too were preserving the vestiges of a dying culture, began amassing large assemblages of Native material culture. Mary Alicia Owen and Harry L. George of St. Joseph, and Patrick "Patsy" Ryan of Oregon, Missouri, were just three of the Missourians known for the large number of items they had gathered. The three were heavily involved in what has come to be known as "salvage anthropology," as they steadfastly worked for decades to collect artifacts from Indigenous people. They were of a generation that had seen the toll settler colonialism had taken on Indigenous people. While Owen believed that Native people were inferior and that the "progress" of Euro-American civilization was necessary, she and other salvage anthropologists, ethnographers, and folklorists hoped to mitigate the damage that had already been done by attempting to preserve what they could from threatened cultures.[44]

Harry L. George was a textile broker who is said to have accumulated one of the most "encyclopedic" collections of Indigenous artifacts in the Midwest. His collection of about four thousand items became the centerpiece of the St. Joseph Museum when it opened in the 1940s.[45] A native of Ireland, Patsy Ryan emigrated to Holt County, Missouri, with his parents in the 1850s. As a young man, his work for various railroad companies gave him the opportunity to travel widely through the American West. Around 1900, he exhibited his collection of artifacts in St. Joseph. By then, Ryan's fame as a collector had led him to be selected in 1901 as the organizer of the American Indian Congress at the Pan-American Exposition at Buffalo, New York. As part of the Congress, Ryan transported six train carloads of Indigenous performers from Chadron, Nebraska, to Buffalo.[46]

By her own count, Owen made one hundred trips to the Ioway, Sac and Fox, Kickapoo, Pottawatomi, and other reservations in Kansas, Oklahoma, and Iowa between 1881 and 1898. She claimed to have had an "Indian Spirit" and to have been adopted by the Sacs and Foxes. In truth, Owen was a ruthless collector who was not above exploiting impoverished informants to get the artifacts she desired. She complained to her mentor, the folklorist Charles Godfrey Leland, that she was an impatient collector who felt that she had to unfairly wait longer than others to get what she wanted. "Go about [your collecting] earnestly, be among the first," Leland advised. "For I foresee that sooner or later, every scrap, good or bad, will be studied and admired . . . and men will wonder that among all the scholars of our age, so few cared for such a marvelous record of the vanishing race. . . . Don't lose time."[47] Many of the items Owen collected were donated to the Museum of Archaeology and Anthropology at the University of Cambridge in England. She also donated nearly one hundred artifacts to the Missouri State Museum in Jefferson City in 1931.[48]

In the meantime, the entrepreneur Fred Harvey exploited the public's growing interest in Indigenous culture to create what we now call cultural tourism. A native of England and long-time resident of Leavenworth, Kansas, Harvey opened his first restaurant in St. Louis on the eve of the Civil War. After the conflict forced the restaurant to close, Harvey went to work for the Hannibal and St. Joseph Railroad. Putting his experience to good use, Harvey opened a "railroad lunchroom" at the Santa Fe Railroad depot in Topeka, Kansas in 1876. Harvey's partnership with the Santa Fe flourished, and they collaborated to open a chain of restaurants, dining cars, and hotels that stretched from Kansas City to New Mexico.[49]

Harvey died in 1901, but the company he founded continued to build an empire to satisfy the public's appetite for exotic travel experiences. In the 1920s, the Fred Harvey Company created "Indian Detours," which offered tourists the opportunity to experience "authentic" indigenous culture and history. Small busses, called Harveycars, took tourists on multi-day trips through New Mexico to visit ruins, pueblos, and art markets, all the while adhering to a reliable railroad-like schedule. The partnership between travel, tourism, and commerce not only took curiosity seekers to New Mexico, but it turned the Indigenous culture and art of the American Southwest into a commodity, one that was brought to and sold in Missouri. Harvey House Restaurant gift shops sold Indigenous art, helping to create a class of collectors across the nation. When curators at Kansas City's Nelson Art Gallery, now the Nelson-Atkins Museum of Art, prepared for the museum's opening in 1933, they purchased 415 Indigenous art objects from the Harvey Company. Some of the artwork was displayed in two dioramas specifically built for the museum's inaugural exhibitions. The two displays showed the figures of artists at work on their craft. Modeled by artist John Prasuhn, one featured a Navajo weaver, modeled after a woman named Bah-Mary. The second displayed the likeness of Maria Martinez, a potter from the San Ildefonso Pueblo who was perhaps the most famous Indigenous artist of the time. Situated in the ground floor "Indian Room," the Nelson Gallery's dioramas remained in situ for over four decades and became the favorite displays of many museum visitors.[50]

Part of the tragic legacy of salvage anthropologists and collector hobbyists is that they further exploited a desperate population. The fact that collectors, museum curators, archaeologists, and souvenir hunters were combing the country for Native artifacts to add to museum and personal collections meant that, much like Indigenous land, thousands of culturally significant pieces of material culture passed out of the hands of those who had made and used them and into the homes and museums of whites. This caused articles of Indigenous culture to become disconnected from their original contexts, ceremonial functions, and traditions, which in turn led to the erasure of the indigenous knowledge that the objects embodied. Archaeologist Paulette F. C. Steeves has pointed out that this separation and erasure was aided by the development of the professional disciplines of archaeology and anthropology during the first two decades of the twentieth century. "Histories of Indigenous people

IMAGE 12: Indian Room installation, date unknown (1933–1975), William Rockhill Nelson Gallery of Art and the Mary Atkins Museum of Fine Arts, Kansas City, Missouri. *Photo courtesy of the Nelson-Atkins Museum of Art*

of the Western Hemisphere were equally assailed and erased through the knowledge production of newly sanctified archaeological experts," writes Steeves. "Dominant archaeological discourses buried Indigenous histories in a colonial terra nullius, a land devoid of civilization." This was largely because prominent scholars such as Lewis Henry Morgan, Aleš Hrdlička, and Earnest Hooton adhered to ideas of social evolution, or Social Darwinism, which led whites to view Natives as inherently inferior persons. Seen thorough this lens, the influential theories and professional impact of this new wave of social scientists could not help but discount or displace the validity of Indigenous knowledge in the perception of the wider public.[51]

Perhaps the most extravagant display of the theory of Social Darwinism and the erasure of Indigenous histories took place in 1904 at the Louisiana Purchase Exposition, better known as the St. Louis World's Fair. Meant to commemorate the centennial of the Louisiana Purchase, the fair was also intended to celebrate the conquering of the

American West and the civilization of the Indigenous people who lived there. As former Missouri governor and fair organizer David R. Francis put it, human history had reached its "apotheosis" on the fairgrounds.[52]

To drive home this point, organizers hired William J. McGee, former head of the US Bureau of Ethnography, and Samuel M. McCowan, the superintendent of the Chilocco Indian Training School in Oklahoma, and others to create what has been called the largest human zoo in history. It is estimated that as many as five hundred Indigenous people from twenty-nine different societies from all over the globe were transported to St. Louis to live on the fairgrounds for the event's duration in reconstructed versions of their Native habitats. People from the Philippines, Japan, South America, and Africa were put on display at the "zoo" in order to illustrate "the development of man from his primitive condition to the present height of achievement."[53]

Many of the Native Americans at the fair appeared in an "Indian School," organized by McGowan, that showed the "positive assimilation" of Indigenous people during the previous century. On one side of the school building were older Natives engaged in making traditional crafts such as blankets, baskets, and pottery. These activities of the past were offset by the other side of the building in which younger, more "progressive," Natives attended school. According to McGee, the hope was that visitors would see the transformation of Indigenous people and the effort of whites to prepare them for a future as assimilated Americans.[54]

The most famous "exhibit" in the Indian School was the Apache warrior popularly known as Geronimo. Though he was seventy-five years old at the time of the fair and had essentially been a prisoner of the US government for two decades, an estimated four million people passed by his booth at the fair, each trying to get a view of the once fearless resistance fighter. Organizers had originally invited several of the old "surviving chiefs" to the fair. In particular, they hoped to entice Quanah Parker, "the last great Comanche chief," and Chief Joseph, the Nez Perce headman who was known as "one of the greatest Indians who ever lived." On display, these famed warriors of the resistance would have been "trophies or bodies won by conquest." They were men who had fought the US government in the so-called Indian Wars of the 1870s and 1880s but who had been defeated. As historian James Swensen has pointed out, the implied message behind the display of the chiefs in St. Louis was clear: "even the most savage person could be brought under the spell of civilization."[55]

Scholars have debated whether Parker or Chief Joseph ever attended the fair. If they did, their visits would have been brief and inconspicuous. In the end, only Geronimo appeared for an extended period, living in the Apache village for six months and manning his booth in the Indian School to make bows and arrows. By the time of his appearance, Geronimo was no stranger to large fairs and expositions. He had visited the 1898 Trans-Mississippi Exposition in Omaha and been part of Patsy Ryan's American Indian Congress at the Pan-American Exposition in Buffalo in 1901. Since his capture, Geronimo had become conscious of his public image. Swensen explains that he came to realize his name had monetary value and that his appearance in St. Louis was important to the overall success of the anthropological displays. Because of this, Geronimo understood that he had some power in negotiating the terms of his part in the fair. He was allowed to keep a portion of the money he made from the sale of his bows and arrows. He also made additional money by selling his hats and buttons from his jackets to fairgoers and posing for numerous photographs.[56]

IMAGE 13: The caption on this stereoscope card reads "Geronimo the Great Apache Chieftain, 70 Years Old But Still Erect and Haughty. Worlds Fair, St. Louis, 1904." *Photograph by William H. Rau. Courtesy of the Missouri Historical Society*

When I was at first asked to attend the St. Louis World's Fair I did not wish to go. Later, when I was told that I would receive good attention and protection, and that the President of the United States said that it would be all right, I consented. I was kept by parties in charge of the Indian Department, who had obtained permission from the President. I stayed in this place for six months. I sold my photographs for twenty-five cents, and was allowed to keep ten cents of this for myself. I also wrote my name for ten, fifteen, or twenty-five cents, as the case might be, and kept all of that money. I often made as much as two dollars a day, and when I returned I had plenty of money—more than I had ever owned before.[57]

Many visitors were disappointed that the Indigenous people on exhibit, such as Geronimo, did not live up to the ideal Indians of popular culture. Those who had hoped to catch a glimpse of a savage warrior instead encountered an old man who was long past his fighting days. One fairgoer whose romantic notions of the American West were shattered by meeting Geronimo was the painter Thomas Hart Benton. Fifteen years old when he traveled from his home in Neosho, Missouri, Benton had hoped to see an Indigenous person who possessed more exotic features than those he was used to seeing in his hometown.

I went with an excited heart to gaze at this red warrior who had so recently held all the United States soldiers at bay and put a scare into a good portion of the West. When I faced him, all my imaginative world fell down. He was just like the Indians . . . I had seen since earliest childhood. Only he was sadder looking, a kind of tired old man who gave bored answers to questions. . . . If there was any bitterness in his heart, it was not marked. There was only apathy.[58]

One of the strangest events involving the fair's aboriginal people was a sort of pseudo-scientific anthropological Olympic games. The fair had hosted the 1904 Olympics and, perhaps inspired by that competition, held a two-day athletic contest they called Anthropology Days on August 12 and 13 in which about one hundred Indigenous people from around the world participated. McGee expected these contests to prove the racial superiority of whites over Indigenous people. Instead, the games turned into a fiasco. The first day's contest included Olympic sports such as the shot put, long jump, high jump, basketball, and various races—water polo matches were apparently scrapped at the last minute. These events went poorly, in part because the participants spoke so many different languages that it was difficult for officials to explain the rules of contests with which most of the participants were completely unfamiliar. The second day featured an event that organizers hoped would appeal more to Natives, such as tree climbing, archery, fighting, javelin, and a lacrosse match between teams of Mohawks and Senecas. The program proved to be poorly organized, sparsely attended, and too haphazard to provide McGee with any data that would prove the superiority of the white race.[59]

It should be noted that, McGee's racist theories of white supremacy notwithstanding, Indigenous people represented the United States by participating and performing well in some of the official Olympic Games. A Seneca man from New York named Franklin Pierce may have been the first Indigenous American to participate in an Olympic marathon, though he did not finish the race. Peter Deer, a Mohawk runner from Quebec, qualified for the finals of the 800- and 1,500-meter races, and an Iroquois lacrosse team from Ontario placed third out of the three teams that participated in the games, winning a bronze medal for their effort.[60]

The Progressive Era and the Pan-Indian Movement

By the beginning of the third decade of the twentieth century, it became clear that for all the damage it had done, the US Vanishing Policy and efforts to force Native people to assimilate were not working as planned. As Tom Holm has pointed out, the policy had failed because "it had not transformed the Indian identity into an American one."[61] The "vanishing race" refused to vanish. Natives, even those who had attended draconian federal boarding schools or other European-American educational institutions, often retained an affiliation—damaged though it may have been—with their own people, and many of them used their education to further Native causes.

Just as they always had, Indigenous people adapted to the changing conditions and challenges they faced. Even as tribal connections had been weakened by allotment, enrollment, and assimilation, a broader Pan-Indian movement began to gather strength. Pan-Indian coalitions were not new. Since at least the eighteenth century, groups of diverse Indigenous nations had formed confederacies to fight against common enemies—most often European colonizers. By the beginning of the twentieth century, as many Natives saw their individual nations weakened by government policies, they realized that, despite their cultural and geographical differences, they were bound to other Indigenous groups by the fact that their relationships with the US government were unlike that of any other ethnic group. By working together, many twentieth-century Natives believed they could create an Indigenous identity that would be more meaningful to them than a simple racial category. Some, like Charles Eastman, Carlos Montezuma, and Laura Cornelius, to name just three of the "new" or "progressive" Indians, became culture brokers working between Indigenous people and whites. They undertook efforts to educate whites about their heritage while trying to dispel myths of Native savagery. They also worked tirelessly to advocate for Indigenous causes and to help usher Native people into the new era.[62]

In 1911, Eastman worked with Montezuma, Cornelius, Henry Standing Bear, and several other Indigenous reformers to create the Society of American Indians (SAI), an organization founded to monitor legislation of importance to Native people and to cooperate with the Office of Indian Affairs for the benefit of Indigenous people.[63] The SAI was important in that it was an all-Indigenous organization—non-Natives were allowed to join as "associates," but had no voting power—that set itself apart from white-run Christian societies that had been doing similar work for decades. Their goal was to help Indigenous people transition from tribal life into mainstream American society. One of the points that made SAI different from previous reform-minded organizations was their recognition of the virtues of Native life. One of SAI's founders, Arthur C. Parker, stated that "All of the best things in the old Indian life . . . must be brought into and developed higher in the new civilization."[64]

Yet from the outset, the organization was beset with difficulties including lack of funding and disagreement among board members over policy issues, which led to factionalism. By 1923, the SAI had become largely inactive. Undeterred, by the dissolution of the SAI, Eastman continued to advocate Indigenous issues. As a physician, he was a strong proponent of the benefits of outdoor exercise, clean air, pure water, and healthy living. Tapping into the same movement that inspired groups like the Tribe of Mic-O-Say, he campaigned for conservation, the creation of national parks, and stricter regulations on industries that contributed to poor health by polluting the environment. He also became a preservationist for traditional Native arts and crafts. He and his wife Elaine Goodale Eastman, who was white, started a summer camp, first for girls and later for boys, which they called the "School of the Woods."

The couple separated in 1921, and the camp was disbanded. However, he continued to advocate for its principles and supported the organization of the Boy Scouts and the Camp Fire Girls.[65]

Interestingly, one of the issues that led to the disintegration of the SAI in 1923 was the members' disagreement over the growing popularity of another Pan-Indian movement, the Peyote Church, later called the Native American Church. The small peyote cactus had been used in spiritual ceremonies in Mesoamerica for centuries. The top of the plant, called the peyote button, contains mescaline. It is ingested during ceremonies and brings on visions that enhance the spiritual experience of the participants. The Kiowas and Comanches incorporated peyote into a ceremony that is similar to that which is still practiced today. The ceremony, which mixes elements of Christianity and Indigenous spirituality, spread from the Southwest in the late nineteenth century and was adopted by numerous tribes. SAI members were deeply divided over the church. On one side were SAI members who saw peyote as a dangerous intoxicant that, like alcohol, would hinder Natives in their efforts to improve themselves. On the other side, were those who extolled the benefits of the peyote ceremony. An Osage member of the SAI, Reverend Joseph K. Griffis, noted that some of the worst characters on the reservation had been changed in a positive way by "peyote worship."[66]

While Pan-Indian organizations such as the SAI represented "top down" movements which had been orchestrated by elite, well-educated intellectuals and tended to flourish in cities, the Peyote Church was a grassroots movement popular on reservations. The peyote church had abandoned earlier, more messianic, Pan-Indian movements like the Ghost Dance and sought to accommodate the realities of everyday life for Indigenous people. "While strongly rooted in traditions of the past," wrote historian Hazel Hertzberg, "the peyote religion was also a religious reform movement which sought to come to terms with the present." Part of the movement's success also hinged on the fact that it was neither a white man's religion nor a tradition belonging to a single Indigenous nation.[67]

While short-lived, the popularity of the Ghost Dance during the late 1880s and early 1890s helped set the stage for the peyote religion to spread from reservation to reservation. The Ghost Dance and its prophet Jack Wilson, also known as Wovoka, carried the promise of a world without white people. While the dance was violently suppressed by US troops, its prophecy eventually proved to be a disappointment, and the dance died out in the 1890s. Nevertheless, it had opened what Hertzberg called "channels of friendship" between Indigenous reservations and settlements. As the Ghost Dance subsided, the peyote church used these same social networks to spread.

While the peyote religion was not commonly practiced in Missouri, it was popular in the surrounding states of Oklahoma, Nebraska, and Iowa by 1910. Still, attacks against peyote became swept up in the overall movement toward the national prohibition of alcohol. In February 1918, Congressman Carl Hayden of Arizona proposed legislation that would prohibit the use of the drug. To place themselves in a position to protect their religious liberty, members of the religion chartered a Native American Church (NAC) in Oklahoma. Omahas and Winnebagos in Nebraska soon chartered their own NACs and others followed until, by 1925, there were incorporated versions of the church in at least seven states. The strategy proved successful, and by the 1930s the Native American Church had become an important institution that enabled Native people to express themselves spiritually with other Indigenous people.[68]

Having been separated and distanced from their tribal nations, many Missourians adopted Pan-Indian activities, especially dances. As has been noted earlier, white promoters organized touring troupes of Indigenous dancers to perform for white audiences at least as early as the 1820s. These traveling shows remained popular for a century and culminated with large extravaganzas like William "Buffalo Bill" Cody's Wild West Show. Indigenous dancers and actors in these shows were often much more than exploited victims. "Native performers should be credited for navigating a difficult and often hostile environment in a society that openly anticipated (and sometimes facilitated) their extinction," writes historian Isaias McCaffery. Indigenous performers exercised power over which dances they were willing to perform, and while some of the white audience members may have viewed them with mockery and derision, Native performers walked away with their money.[69]

With the assimilation policy and the rise of various other Pan-Indian efforts in the 1880s, Indigenous people began to organize their own dances for their own purposes. These dances were not usually intended for the entertainment of whites, but rather served as community gatherings and expressions of "Indianness" amid the new social realities of assimilation. Such dances not only helped preserve cultural traditions, but they also helped to fill cultural gaps for Natives that had lost old rituals. The Quapaws, who had been removed to a small reservation in extreme northeast Oklahoma, began organizing early annual dances in 1873. These dances, now called powwows, continue on the Quapaw Nation today. In the 1880s, the Osages' adopted the annual In-Lon-Shka dance. The Osages had put away many of their ceremonies that no longer served them. In 1885, their relatives from the Kaw nation gifted them the In-Lon-Shka, which means "Playground of the Eldest Son." The dance continues to this day and has become an important part of Osage life. Each June, In-Lon-Shka dances take place in the communities of Pawhuska, Gray Horse, and Hominy on the Osage Nation.[70]

Perhaps because of the general alarm caused by the spread of the Ghost Dance in the 1880s, government agents actively suppressed dances, which often sent Indigenous dancers deeper into secluded spaces. "How I hate the silly agents who suppressed [the dances]," wrote Mary Alicia Owen in 1931. Owen, who had attended dances in Iowa, Kansas, and the Indian Territory during the 1880s, remembered, "We were always dodging those white idiots the government sent out. They seemed to think Dancing was devil worship."[71]

By the beginning of the twentieth century, there were signs that dances were becoming more acceptable to whites and occurred more openly, sometimes even with white support. In 1905, the *Kansas City Journal* reported on a Sac and Fox dance taking place outside the city of Shawnee (presumably Shawnee, Indian Territory) that had been interrupted, likely by Christians who disapproved of the ceremony. Because of "disturbers who had interfered with the dance for several days," tribal leaders had invited the US deputy marshal and undersheriff to attend. Law enforcement officials took them up on their invitation and the harassment stopped. Sac and Fox headman Billy Tucho "was so pleased with the result of the white officers' visit that he made a speech of welcome," explaining to them that this was their religious festival and thanking the men for their protection.[72]

In the years that followed, Native-organized dances became a part of Fourth of July Celebrations and annual town picnics and fairs. An October Sunday in 1920 found dozens of people gathered at Big Lake, in Holt County, Missouri, for a variety of diversions including a baseball game between Ioway Indians from nearby White Cloud, Kansas, and the Regulars from Craig, Missouri. The day's events also included bronco riding, an exhibit of Ioway regalia and crafts, and Ioway dances. The celebration is notable in that it seems to have included camaraderie and good-natured competition involving people from neighboring towns in which both whites and Indigenous people participated on equal terms. After the Ioways defeated the Craig Regulars 7 to 3 on the diamond, Ioway Dave Ogden won the bronco riding prize in a competition that was "equal to anything they had in the St. Joseph Round Up." Lillian Eckley and Rachel Campbell were mentioned for their displays of a traditional Native dress and children's clothing. Finally, Ioway headman Tom Lightfoot was joined by Frank Deroin and seven unnamed Ioway women in a traditional dance. The event proved so popular that organizers planned to repeat it two weeks later.[73]

Despite decades of assimilation efforts by reformers and the US government, Natives had proven their resilience. In the first decades of the twentieth century, Indigenous people proved they had maintained control of their own spirituality and cultural traditions. While these new traditions may not have been wholly Ioway, Osage, or Kickapoo, they remained Indigenous at heart. Even in Missouri, where most Natives found themselves disconnected from tribal support, these traditions allowed them to gather with others and express their heritage in order to feel a much-needed sense of community. While the remainder of the new century and many challenges lay ahead, Indigenous people had shown that they intended to remain who they were and had always been.

Voices

We will determine what our culture is. It has been pointed out that culture constantly changes. It is not the same today as it was a hundred years ago. We are still a vital active Indian society. We are not going to be put in a museum or accept your interpretation of our culture.[1]

—Oren Lyons (Onodaga)

Indians did not discover they were Indians in the early 1970s. We were not reborn; we were simply noticed. . . .

Ironically, it is most unfair to Indians themselves to idealize them. There must have been at one point in history at least one Indian who did not know what he was talking about. There must have been at least one person who worked for the Bureau of Indian Affairs who had a good idea. Why do all old Indians have to be wise? Not all old non-Indians are wise.[2]

—Philip S. Deloria (Lakota)

I am part Indian, and I will not see my people so robbed of their rights and the bodies of their dead taken from the sacred burying ground of the tribe in defiance of the treaty because there is now no one to stand up for the rights of the Indians. I have tried to save the cemetery from being desecrated by law, and now I will take care of it myself, law or no law.[3]

—Lyda Conley (Wyandot)

The earth itself is our grandmother . . . our people have been ripped from her, and I don't know if that means anything to you, but it means a great deal to us. . . . It's ugly, it's obscene, it's unnatural. . . . We are a continuum of those people. . . . I don't have to have known them personally. I don't even have to say I am directly descended from them, because they are our people. . . .[4]

—Sandra K. Massey (Sac and Fox)

Chapter Ten

Relocation and Repatriation

ON APRIL 23, 1921, A delegation of Osages, accompanied by newly appointed Commissioner of Indian Affairs Charles H. Burke, visited President Warren G. Harding at the White House in Washington, DC. While a few wore traditional Osage clothing for their meeting, many of the delegates were dressed in business suits, a reflection perhaps of their status as members of one of the wealthiest Indigenous nations in the United States. In 1872, the Osages had moved to a new 1.47-million-acre reservation which they purchased from the Cherokees. Before the end of the nineteenth century, oil was discovered on the Osage reservation, and by 1906, the nation was receiving between $10 million and $30 million dollars in oil revenue annually.[1]

One of the topics likely to have been on the agenda for their April 23 meeting with the president was the fact that just six weeks earlier, on March 3, Congress had passed sweeping legislation that would alter Osage life for decades. A portion of the law granted the Osages US citizenship. By the 1920s, 125,000, or about one-third, of all Indigenous people had not received the status of citizenship. Many of the other 225,000 Natives had been granted citizenship under provisions of the Dawes Act. The pressure to grant the remaining Indigenous people citizenship had increased after more than twelve thousand Natives fought for the US in the first world war.[2]

Unfortunately, the law, officially called "An act for the division of the lands and funds of the Osage Indians in Oklahoma," also stipulated that in order for Osages to be paid their share of the nation's quarterly oil revenues, they had to pass a "measure of competency." Those who were unable to do so and those under the age of twenty-one were assigned guardians. It was the job of the guardians to receive and manage the oil income paid to their wards. This arrangement made it easy for

IMAGE 14: A delegation of Osages stand at the White House in Washington, DC with Commissioner of Indian Affairs Charles H. Burke (far left in overcoat and hat) on April 23, 1921. The previous month, congress had passed a bill that extended the status of Osage trust land and granted US citizenship to all Osages. *Courtesy of the Library of Congress*

unscrupulous lawyers and businessmen to use the guardianship system to steal funds from Osage citizens. Some white men married into wealthy Osage families to obtain oil and guardianship rights. Some guardians even murdered Osages to petition to inherit their oil rights. Many of the deaths were initially ruled as accidents or suicides and it was not until 1925 that the Osages asked the FBI to investigate the crimes.[3]

The Indian New Deal

Citizenship had been one of the goals of the Dawes Act and had long been seen as the ultimate step in assimilation. Three years after the Osages became US citizens, Congress passed the Indian Citizenship Act on June 2, 1924. Up to that time Indigenous people were treated as wards of the state, and tribes were seen as domestic dependent nations. While proponents saw citizenship as the only way Natives could enjoy the full benefits of individual freedom and self-determination, opponents feared that accepting US citizenship would mean the end of Indigenous tribal sovereignty. Others worried that with citizenship, they would lose all protections on tribal lands and treaty rights. As writer and historian David Treuer has observed, in the end, "Indians—enjoying tribal and American citizenship—became a legally unique kind of American, both Indian and American."[4]

Roxanne Dunbar-Ortiz considers the 1920s to be a time when Native people were at their "lowest point." Events such as the Osage murders, forced assimilation, attempts at tribal termination through allotment, the theft of Indian trust money, and the residual devastation left over from the so-called Indian Wars of the late nineteenth century had threatened the very survival of many Indigenous people. "It was a boom time for the national economy," writes Dunbar-Ortiz, "but life threatening for Native Americans everywhere."[5]

John Collier wanted to change all of that. A romantic at heart, Collier believed that Indigenous peoples were special, and that Native cultures and traditional ways of life offered a much-needed antidote to the harmful and destructive tendencies of Western culture. Worried by the growing commercial and individualistic nature of American society, Collier argued that we had much to learn from the traditional Native values of community and mutual responsibility.[6]

In 1933, Collier put his ideas into practice when the newly elected President Franklin Roosevelt appointed him to lead the then dysfunctional Bureau of Indian Affairs. For at least the previous two decades, there had been no coherent Indian policy and the work of the bureau had devolved into responding to crises as they appeared. In addition, the lack of an underlying philosophy and any clear direction had made the bureau unpopular with many Natives and whites alike. In 1928, the Interior Department issued a report compiled by Lewis Meriam titled "The Problem of Indian Administration." Commonly known as the "Meriam Report," it deepened concern over the ineffectiveness of the bureau and the present and future well-being of Native people across the country. The Meriam Report was highly critical of the BIA's Vanishing Policy, allotment, and federally operated boarding schools. The Meriam Commission found that the policy of allotment had been largely responsible for the extreme poverty in which many Natives lived. It further argued that the government's suppression of Indigenous culture had been a failure that had only served to demoralize Native people.[7]

As Roosevelt took office on March 4, 1933, the nation was in the throes of the Great Depression. As part of the "New Deal" package of reforms and relief programs the new president introduced to address the financial disaster, Collier worked with Congress to introduce the Wheeler-Howard Bill, which was part of the so-called Indian New Deal. As Collier conceived of it, the Indian New Deal would make sweeping changes to Indian policy that would be as broad and significant as those achieved by the Dawes Act more than thirty years earlier. The new act would not only put an end to allotment, but it also would enable tribes to regain ownership of government land that had been declared surplus under the Dawes Act. It also created a revolving fund that was available to tribes for economic development and provided money for education that allowed Indigenous students to transfer from federal boarding schools to public schools. To restore the sovereignty taken away under the Dawes Act, the Indian New Deal allowed tribes either to adopt home rule constitutions or to form business charters for economic development. In all, the Indian New Deal recognized the importance of Indigenous communities, values, religions, and traditional arts and crafts.[8]

Perhaps because of the sheer magnitude of the bill, neither Natives nor Congress universally supported Collier's grand vision. Liberal Pan-Indian organizations, or Red Progressives, tended to view the proposed legislation as a step backward for Indigenous individuals. They believed the provisions to rebuild tribal governments and repatriate communal land were an effort to segregate Natives on reservations. Meanwhile, some conservative organizations, like the American Indian Federation, were generally opposed to anything related to Roosevelt's New Deal on the grounds that it was a form of socialism and therefore "un-American." Additionally, some tribal leaders believed Collier's romantic interpretation of the relationship between the Bureau of Indian Affairs (BIA) and Indigenous nations to be paternalistic and domineering, while others were simply put off by his personal demeanor, which some considered to be "abrasive and obnoxious."[9]

As the Wheeler-Howard Bill made its way through Congress, opposition forced it to undergo considerable alteration. The terms of the policy package that Collier had proposed to Indigenous people during his 1934 travels throughout the nation matched those of the bill that emerged from the Senate Committee on Indian Affairs. The language in the final version of the Indian Reorganization Act (IRA), however, did not. Collier chose to accept the compromise as something both whites and Natives could support, even though it was not the bold legislation he had envisioned. Because public perception closely linked Collier with the IRA, the discrepancy between what had been promised and what had been delivered created conflict between Collier and some Native leaders who felt the commissioner had manipulated and lied to them.[10]

Urban Natives and the Termination Period

World War II drastically altered the environment under which the IRA had been enacted. Wartime Washington, DC had little energy to devote to Indian Affairs, and the entire BIA was moved to Chicago to make room in the capital city for the rapidly growing War Department. The conflict also changed attitudes toward Native people among both politicians and the public. In the face of massive defense spending, Congress began to lose patience with the BIA's budget and large bureaucracy, believing that the agency's resources should be directed toward the war effort. At the same time, the general public had adopted a wartime attitude of patriotism and unity unconducive to an appreciation of Indigenous cultures.[11]

The war also dramatically altered the face of "Indian Country," as thousands of Natives left reservations and moved into cities to join the war effort, either by enlisting in the military or working in the defense industry. Despite their often-antagonistic relation with the US government and the fact that they were members of Indigenous nations as well as the Unites States, a higher percentage of Natives joined the military during the war than any other ethnic group. The reasons for this are complex, but as one Diné, or Navajo, Viet Nam veteran has stated, "We serve this country because it's our land. We have a sacred purpose to protect this place."[12]

During World War II, twenty-two thousand Indigenous people joined the Army, two thousand joined the Navy, seven hundred thirty served in the Marines, and one hundred twenty were with the Coast Guard. An additional fifteen thousand to twenty-five thousand Natives found jobs in munitions factories and other occupations related to the war effort. Some schools for Indigenous students, such as Haskell Institute in Lawrence, Kansas, and the Chilocco Indian School, located near Newkirk, Oklahoma, developed special programs to prepare Native students for jobs in the defense industry. During the war, a small number of Haskell students even worked in Kansas City at the Standard and the Columbia Steel Works. Even after the war, many Natives elected to remain in cities, and by the late 1940s, one-quarter of all Indigenous people in the United States lived in urban areas. Thus, Indigenous people participated in a nationwide population shift that saw more people leaving rural areas for cities.[13]

Despite prevalent stereotypes depicting Natives as rural people, urban life was nothing new to them. As we have already seen, Indigenous people built one of the planet's largest cities when they constructed Cahokia one thousand years ago. Colin G. Calloway and others have convincingly argued that throughout the colonial history of the continent Natives have participated in urban life for reasons that were both commercial and diplomatic. Additionally, the experience of attending federally operated boarding schools, which often sent students far away from home and family, had acquainted twentieth-century Indigenous people with off-reservation life. The war effort allowed Natives an even greater opportunity to gain familiarity with living and working away from reservations, something that made a return to life on the reservation undesirable and in some cases impossible.[14]

Meanwhile, as World War II drew to a close, the lofty hopes for the Indian Reorganization Act crumbled. President Roosevelt died less than three months into his fourth term in office, and shortly thereafter his vice-president, Missouri native Harry Truman, assumed the presidency in April 1945. Collier, under pressure for not having done enough to solve the "Indian Problem," soon resigned. While Truman believed in civil rights for all citizens and a "Fair Deal" for all Americans, any plans his administration had to continue the Indian New Deal were thwarted by an uncooperative Congress that drastically cut the BIA's budget. In addition, Truman was wary of the bureau, regarding it as "unmanageable," and was unwilling to exert valuable time and resources to fix it. As the son of a state that had actively deported Indigenous people a century earlier, it is likely Truman had little interest in Indigenous issues. He once told Philleo Nash, who would later become Commissioner of Indian Affairs under John F. Kennedy, "I do not have that many good bureau chiefs that I can spare one" to oversee the BIA. For years the bureau would remain, in Nash's words, "non-managed." Truman's first commissioner of Indian affairs, William Brophy, suffered from acute respiratory disease. Washington DC's humid climate and the stress of being commissioner led to his physical deterioration and resignation before the end of Truman's first term in office. In 1949, Brophy was succeeded by John Nichols, who remained in office less than one year. This lack of continuity and the resulting "intellectual vacuum" it created in the bureau, coupled with a general postwar reaction against the Indian

New Deal, led to a policy shift that reverted the BIA's focus back to policies of assimilation.[15]

One strong proponent of this new wave of assimilation was journalist and former Missouri state legislator Orland Kay Armstrong. Even though he was a Republican who had helped investigate Truman supporter and Kansas City machine boss Tom Prendergast in the late 1930s, Armstrong had been appointed by the Roosevelt and Truman administrations to a variety of government positions in the years immediately following the war. In 1950, Armstrong was elected to the US Congress, where he represented southeast Missouri for one term. In Washington, Armstrong joined those who were intent on terminating all government engagement with Indigenous nations. Comparing Indian reservations to the concentration camps German Nazis had employed to exterminate Jews during the war, Armstrong called for disbanding reservations and all IRA-created tribal governments, terminating all treaty rights granted to tribes by the US government, and eliminating the BIA. "They can keep all the 'Indian-ness' that is worth a whoop," Armstrong challenged, "and still hold productive jobs and send their kids to integrated schools." He, like many other "terminationists" in Congress, wanted Indigenous people to embrace the concepts of private property and private enterprise without government interference. They also hoped that termination would free the government of treaty responsibilities. "They should have been brought into . . . the white man's way of life . . . half a century ago," Armstrong proclaimed. Despite his professed love for freedom, there was one right that Armstrong was unwilling to grant to Indigenous people. That was the right of religious freedom. Like nineteenth-century assimilationists before him, Armstrong believed Indigenous spiritual practices had to be replaced by Protestant Christianity.[16]

The seeds of the BIA's new policy of termination were planted during the Truman administration in 1947. Congress asked the bureau to prepare a report outlining plans to terminate Indigenous tribal governments and to list those tribes it felt were ready to end their trust status. The task fell to Deputy Commissioner of Indian Affairs William Zimmerman, who was overseeing the bureau during Brophy's prolonged illness. The Zimmerman Report became a blueprint that Congress used to begin the process of terminating Indigenous tribal governments. Zimmerman's report ranked Indigenous tribes' readiness for termination based on four criteria. These were a tribe's degree of acculturation, economic condition, willingness to cut ties with the federal government, and the ability of state governments to pick up any programs that the federal government planned to discontinue. Under the process of termination, tribes would close their rolls to include only those members who already had been listed. They could then sell off all of their tribal assets and disburse the proceeds to enrolled members. Congress also established the Indian Claims Commission in hopes of quickly settling any outstanding land disputes various tribes had with the federal government, thus ending the government's responsibility for tribal lands. The policy of termination reached full stride in 1953 with the passage of House Concurrent Resolution 108, which ended Native people's status as wards of the state and forced them to "assume their full responsibilities as American citizens." In all, termination proceedings were initiated against 109 tribes. Of those, sixty-one had their status terminated by Congress between 1954 and 1960. Many regained their federally recognized status in the 1960s and 1970s, but only after long and expensive court challenges.[17]

The Voluntary Relocation Program

Meanwhile, another initiative related to the policy of termination, one that would have a direct impact on the state of Missouri, was taking shape. The goal of the Voluntary Relocation Program was to encourage the continued migration of Indigenous populations from reservations to cities. The formal program was born out of a disaster that took place during the late 1940s when a series of brutal winters ravaged the Navajo and Hopi reservations in the Four Corners region of Arizona, New Mexico, Colorado, and Utah. Unusually cold and snowy weather made it extremely difficult for tribes to keep their members fed and warm. To avoid a catastrophic loss of life, the federal government was forced to step in and airlift aid into the region.[18]

The disaster led government officials to conclude that the Navajo and Hopi reservations had a surplus population that was straining the area's available natural resources. While Congress allocated $88.5 million in aid to the two nations, it also approved a relocation program to move Navajos away from their home reservation and into cities where they could find educational and employment opportunities. The idea of relocation fit neatly into the overall goal of termination in that it helped to disband Indigenous communities and emptied Indian reservations of valuable human resources and talent. Along the way, terminationists believed that urban Natives would become assimilated by blending into metropolitan communities. In addition, the federal government hoped relocation would relieve them of some of their fiscal responsibilities to tribes.[19]

The Truman administration signaled its full support for expanding the Relocation and Termination Programs on March 22, 1950, when it appointed Dillon S. Myer to become the next commissioner of Indian affairs. Though Myer lacked experience in Indian policy, he was chosen because he had been responsible for relocating thousands of Japanese Americans to internment camps as the director of the War Relocation Authority during World War II. "Unbending and tyrannical," Myer wanted to completely undo all of Collier's Indian Reorganization Act programs and end the federal supervision of tribes. Discontinuing such support would, he believed, allow Native people to become self-made Americans.[20]

Under Dillon Myer's direction, the Relocation Program quickly expanded. During the summer of 1951, the Bureau of Indian Affairs sent relocation officers to reservations in several US states to recruit Natives willing to move to urban areas. In November, it opened its first relocation office in Chicago. Three months later, the first group of Native relocatees reached their new homes in the Windy City. Relocation offices were designed to help integrate Natives into their new urban environments. They arranged for housing, paid for relocatees' first month's rent, assisted in finding employment, and helped relocatees locate churches, stores, and essential services. Relocation offices soon opened in Los Angeles, Denver, Salt Lake City, and Portland, Oregon. By the end 1953, two thousand six hundred Indigenous people had been relocated to these urban areas. One year later, the number had increased to six thousand two hundred. It is estimated that between 1952 and 1972, more than one hundred thousand Natives had relocated from reservation to cities.[21]

In 1954 and 1955, San Francisco and San Jose, California, opened relocation offices, and the following year, St. Louis was added to the list of BIA relocation centers. The bureau opened the St. Louis office in the Federal Building on Market Street in late July 1956. Field Relocation Officer Eudora Reed assured those who might have been concerned about the well-being of transplants living in an unfamiliar city that Indians would not simply be "dumped" in St. Louis, but that they would be carefully supervised and integrated into the community. The office planned to transplant three hundred fifty Native "units" to the city in the first fiscal year. The term *unit* was used to refer either to a single person, usually a man, who relocated, or to a family with a male head of household. Likely recruits for relocation to St. Louis came mostly from the Southwest and were predominantly Navajo, Sioux, Comanche, and Apache, though Choctaws and Cherokees from Oklahoma were also considered. The bureau made a general practice of transplanting Natives to cities that were far away from the home reservations. This, they believed, would lessen the temptation for them to abandon the program and return home. The practice also attempted to break up tribal cultural and family cohesiveness. Reed emphasized that finding employment for transplants was not expected to be difficult, as relocatees in other cities had proven to "have an inherent aptitude for work which is done with the hands."[22]

The first two Native families relocated to St. Louis by the BIA arrived on October 7, 1956. Joseph Martime, his wife, and eighteen-month-old daughter were Navajos from New Mexico. Clifton Tongkeamah and his wife were Kiowas from Oklahoma. Within a day of their arrival, both men were interviewed for jobs at a local aircraft manufacturing plant. Both Tongkeamah, who was a printer by trade, and Martime were veterans of the Korean conflict and had experience living away from their home reservations. The young families explained that they were drawn to St. Louis by the desire for better lives. They had likely seen the brochures the city had distributed to tribal relocation offices, which extolled the virtues of St. Louis shopping centers, the Muny Opera, Forest Park, Busch Stadium, and the Missouri Botanical Garden. Yet the two families seemed to be drawn by more basic needs. Mrs. Tongkeamah, who had previous manufacturing experience, cited the availability of jobs as one of the reasons she and her husband moved to St. Louis, while Mrs. Martime expressed the hope that she and her husband might find a small house with a yard for their daughter.[23]

By April 1957, the BIA had relocated 278 Indigenous people to St. Louis. Though the bureau's Eudora Reed proudly pointed out that only twenty of the transplants had returned home due to "discouragement" or "homesickness," there were signs that the transitioning had not always gone as well as planned. While the relocatees were given a small housing and clothing allowance for four weeks, securing long-term housing proved to be a challenge. The BIA initially settled families in hotels, while single men and women were directed to either the YMCA or YWCA. Many of those who remained in St. Louis had difficulty finding permanent homes, and more than half were eventually forced to live in public housing projects. Finding work seems to have been less difficult, even though many of the transplants possessed minimal job skills and education. Most found work in factories or in the service industry, and by early 1957, less than 5% still needed to find employment. That same year, Congress created the Adult Vocational Training program to help relocatees gain the skills they need to fit more readily in the job market.[24]

One of the barriers the newly arrived Indigenous people faced in St. Louis and other relocation cities, was discrimination. During orientation sessions, Reed reminded Native people that "everyone will be judging American Indians by their conduct and their attitude." Employers and landlords often held negative stereotypes about Native people and were reluctant to hire or rent to them. This was especially true once the BIA's assistance lapsed and the relocatees were left on their own.[25]

By February 1958, the Relocation Program had settled 375 Natives in St. Louis, and Charles Coffee, the new field relocation officer, was candid about some of the missteps the bureau had made during its first fifteen months in operation. "One of the biggest mistakes we made was in trying to bring too many [relocatees] in at one time," he admitted. "We lacked facilities to assimilate them, and some went back to the reservation disappointed."[26] A second mistake had been the practice of spreading Native relocatees across the city rather than relocating them into a single neighborhood. This forced the new arrivals to live in relative isolation without access to valuable support and encouragement from fellow Natives who had been in the city for some time. Many of the newly relocated persons felt disconnected from their communities and their culture.

To address the loneliness and homesickness they felt while living in strange urban areas, Indigenous people formed dozens of Pan-Indian clubs and centers in cities across the United States during the 1950s and 1960s. In St. Louis, relocated Natives had founded their own social club by early 1958. What began as a series of meals and informal gatherings held in individuals' apartments soon moved to a facility furnished by Kingdom House, a community agency. Members of the group came from fifteen different Indigenous tribes and called themselves the All-American Indian Club. They met regularly, and despite the various indigenous cultures they represented, the members found a sense of community in the company of other Natives. Soon, local church organizations recognized the needs of their Indigenous neighbors and jointly offered additional support to the members of what was essentially a new group of immigrants in their community.[27]

Despite these efforts, the Relocation Program in St. Louis continued to falter, and the BIA closed its relocation office there in the summer of 1960. Of the eighteen hundred Natives who had been transplanted to the city between 1956 and 1960, only about four hundred fifty had chosen to stay. The main obstacle seems to have been the simple fact that Native people did not feel accepted or comfortable in the city. There were a wide variety of reasons for this. Some cited the city's crime rate, while others, used to the arid climate of the West, blamed their discomfort, in part, on the high summer humidity. Most, however, felt the constant sting of discrimination. Mae Roberts, a Meskwaki woman from Tama, Iowa, reported that St. Louisans were "sometimes afraid to give Indians a chance." She and her husband Elmer, who lived in a ninth-floor apartment at the Darst-Webbe Public Housing Project, felt that the city was too big and they did not have enough personal space. They worried about their children always being "cooped up." The couple had tried to lease a house with more space but found landlords reluctant to rent to them. Though another transplant, Alex Hosey, an Apache from New Mexico, was earning twice as much money in St. Louis as he had been at home, he too wondered about the long-term consequence of raising children in the city. "We are ruining our kids," he explained.[28]

Others pointed out that the BIA had done a poor job placing potential relocatees into employment situations in which they were likely to succeed. Ellis Hummingbird, who worked as a shipping clerk at Standard Pipe Protection, believed they could have done a better job of screening candidates prior to relocation. Frank Tongkeamah, a Kiowa from Oklahoma who worked as a technician in the metallurgical lab at Carondolet Foundries, supposed that many Natives who moved to the city were ill prepared for both employment and urban life. Those who had returned home were, in Tongkeamah's estimation, "pretty backward" and had depended too much on the government for assistance to make the transition.[29]

Urban Indian Centers, Activism, and Powwows

Meanwhile, across the state, Kansas City experienced a similar increase in Native population, though its history was quite different from that of St. Louis. Kansas City had been founded on land adjacent to the reservations of the Shawnees and Delawares. Wyandotte County, Kansas, located next to Missouri's Jackson County, was also the site of a settlement of Wyandots, or Hurons, in the 1840s. Having been deported from their homes in Ontario, the Wyandots eventually purchased land on the Delaware reservation along the Missouri and Kansas River in 1843. In the 1850s, the government allotted land to the Wyandots, granted them US citizenship, and terminated all of their treaty rights. While some accepted the terms of termination, may chose instead to move to the Indian Territory.[30]

During the late nineteenth century, the settlement of Kansas City, Kansas, quickly grew around one of the last remnants of Wyandot occupation, a cemetery containing between four hundred and eight hundred sets of human remains. The cemetery, officially known as the Wyandot National Burying Ground, became a site of conflict between settlers and Wyandots. Located in what is now downtown Kansas City, Kansas, the property, which many saw as a "vacant lot" became a prime piece of real estate. After developers attempted to buy it in 1890, three sisters of mixed Wyandot heritage, Lyda, Helena, and Ida Conley, began a fifty-year vigil to protect the graves of their ancestors. Lyda and Helena both attended Park College in Parkville, Missouri, at the turn to the twentieth century. Lyda then attended the Kansas City (Missouri) School of Law, graduating in 1902, with the intent of using her legal education to save the burying grounds.[31]

In 1906, Congress passed legislation that abrogated previous Wyandot treaties and allowed the cemetery to be sold. The Conley sisters acted quickly. They locked the cemetery gate and posted a sign that read, "Trespass at your Peril." They erected a small cabin, which they called Fort Conley and began a twenty-four-hour armed vigil of the property. Aside from taking turns watching over the cemetery, the sisters also tended to the grounds and worked on a legal case to overturn the 1906 act of Congress. After a series of legal maneuvers aimed at fighting the law in court, Lyda Conley became the first Indigenous woman, and only the third woman, to argue a case before the United States Supreme Court in 1910.[32]

Though Conley lost her court case, she and her sisters continued their around-the-clock watch of the site. On at least three occasions, law enforcement officials moved in to tear down Fort Conley, only to see the sisters rebuild it. Historian Samantha Rae Dean has written that the Conleys also spent time behind bars for their actions. "In 1922, Helena spent a night in jail after using foul language and 'damning' a trespasser's soul to hell. During the same year, Lyda was detained for preventing city employees from mowing the cemetery. She also spent ten days in jail in

1937, after chasing people off cemetery grounds with a broomstick."[33] In 1913, legislation proposed by Kansas Senator Charles Curtis, a citizen of the Kaw Nation, protected the site by making it a national park. The cemetery was eventually placed on the National Register of Historic Places in 1977 and received more protection with the passage of the Native American Grave Protection and Repatriation Act in 1990.

Because of its proximity to Haskell Institute, Kansas reservations belonging to the Kickapoos, Ioways, Potawatomis, Sacs and Foxes, and to the reservations of Oklahoma, Kansas City became a natural destination for Indigenous people looking for opportunities. Just as they had in St. Louis, Native transplants living in Kansas City found they missed their communities and their cultures. To alleviate this sense of isolation and help form a support network, several Indigenous families in the city formed the Council Fire of Greater Kansas City in 1963.

Two of the driving forces behind the council were Bobby Joe Blue and his wife Nancy McCracken Blue. Bobby Blue was a Choctaw, born in Oklahoma in 1939. After being unable to adjust to life in a federally operated boarding school, he migrated to Kansas City with his father in 1950. Blue's father strongly urged his son to do his best to assimilate in their new home. "It was a white man's world," the elder Blue advised, "and you had better forget any of your Indian ways if you want to make it in this place." Life for the father and son was difficult as they tried to make ends meet while fitting in to their new urban surroundings. Bobby did his best to forget his Indigenous heritage and associated mostly with the Latinx teenagers who were his neighbors on the city's west side. In 1956, Blue met Nancy McCracken, a white woman from Belleville, Kansas, and the two married in 1957. Soon after their marriage, the couple encountered Kenneth Powlas, a member of the Oneida nation who had moved to Kansas City from Wisconsin. Powlas encouraged Bobby to rediscover his Indigenous heritage and introduced the couple to other members of Kansas City's growing Native community.[34]

In the early days, the Council Fire of Greater Kansas City served as an ad hoc service agency, informally performing many of the same functions the BIA's relocation offices had been designed to serve. Both Bobby and Nancy Blue were heavily involved in the council, even though, as a white woman, Nancy was technically ineligible for membership. On a volunteer basis, they helped relatives and friends resettle in the city, assisted them with gas money, car repairs, housing, and helped new arrivals navigate urban life. The council also became a social club that

IMAGE 15: Bob Blue and Nancy McCracken Blue (center) are surrounded by family members at a powwow in an undated photograph. The Blues were instrumental in forming the Council Fire of Greater Kansas City and the Heart of America Indian Center. *Photograph courtesy of Nancy McCracken Blue*

provided a place for Natives to come together to learn and preserve Indigenous knowledge, crafts, dances, and songs. By the early 1960s, Bobby Blue, Powlas, and others began performing dances at events throughout the community. Through these appearances and his long-standing activism for Native causes, Blue would become one of the city's most recognizable cultural ambassadors.

In the early 1960s, the Council Fire of Greater Kansas City became one of the first groups in the state to organize powwows. As we have seen, Indian dances first reemerged among Native people during the government's efforts to assimilate them in the late 1880s. Like the Ghost Dance and the Peyote Religion, early powwows, first known as Omaha Dances, Grass Dances, or Crow Dances, were Pan-Indian efforts at maintaining Indigenous culture in an era when Natives were being forced to assimilate to the dominant white culture. In the post-WWII era of termination, Native veterans helped reinvigorate warrior societies and dance traditions. These efforts gave birth to the secular social dances we know as powwows today. By the 1950s, powwows were regularly taking place on the Kickapoo and Pottawatomi reservations in Kansas.

From there, the dances quickly moved seventy miles east to the Kansas City area. Even before the Council Fire of Greater Kansas City was officially organized, members sponsored a Labor Day weekend powwow in Wyandotte County, Kansas, in 1962. The event drew one hundred fifty people representing eight tribes from at least five states. Soon, the council's powwow had become a popular annual event.[35]

At the same time, powwows began to take place throughout the state. The town of Cassville, in extreme southwest Missouri, held a large Labor Day weekend powwow in 1964. Billing itself as the first powwow ever held in Missouri, the All-American Pow-Wow was sponsored by the local Optimist Club and organized by Perry LeClair, chief of the Ponca Nation from Ponca City, Oklahoma. Organizers claimed that the event drew as many as one thousand five hundred people representing at least fifteen different tribes to the small Ozark town. In fact, they had to turn representatives from an additional thirteen tribes away from the event due to limited space.[36]

In June 1967, the Will Rogers Indian Club of Springfield, Missouri, organized the first of what would be more than four decades of annual powwows at the Ozark Empire Fairgrounds. The club, which was organized in January 1964, admitted anyone who could document they were at least one-sixteenth Native. Organizers estimated there were about three hundred participants in that first powwow. That number included many of the club's sixty members, plus dancers and singers from most of the adjoining states. "This will be the biggest aggregation of Indians in Springfield since the Kickapoo roamed the prairies in 1821," boasted one of the event organizers.[37]

As the scholar Gloria Alese Young has pointed out, powwows are built on the expression of "Indianness." As such, they integrate Natives from various tribes and cultures into a single Pan-Indian identity. Along the way, powwows enhance the quality of participants' lives through increased social contacts which are beneficial to mental health.[38]

Aside from dances, the growing communities of urban Natives across the country also sparked a new era of Pan-Indian social activism. The Red Power movement was born out of the frustration many city-dwelling Natives felt as the challenges they faced were not being heard or taken seriously by those in a position to help them. Inspired in part by the Civil Rights Movement, groups like the American Indian Movement (AIM), which was organized in Minneapolis in 1968, helped raise awareness of Indigenous issues across the country. "A.I.M. did a world of good for the urban Indian," Patricia Mangiaracina of Gladstone, Missouri, told a newspaper reporter in 1975. "People learned that Indians weren't dead yet, nor were they all on reservations and taken care of" by the government. AIM did, in fact, make efforts to recruit members from the reservations of northeast Kansas and the Kansas City metro area, but opinions over the movement's appeal became mixed after its increased involvement in militant actions in South Dakota, California, and Washington, DC.[39]

One of the causes for which the Red Power Movement had advocated was that of religious freedom for Native people. Since the late nineteenth century, government officials had prohibited or disrupted many Indigenous spiritual ceremonies and dances. While the dances and ceremonies had continued, those who practiced them were forced to do so in secret. Groups like AIM encouraged Indigenous people to forgo Christianity, embrace sobriety, and revive their spiritual traditions. Through the efforts of the Red Power Movement, Congress passed the American Indian Religious Freedom Act (AIRFA) in 1978. Since that time, Native American Church, sweat lodge, and even sundance ceremonies have been held openly within Missouri's borders.

By the early 1970s, the number of urban Indians continued to increase throughout the nation. The 1970 census calculated that nearly 40% of all Indigenous people in the United States lived in cities. Though the census showed that about two thousand five hundred Native people lived in the eight Missouri and Kansas counties that made up the Kansas City metro area, local leaders believed the actual number was perhaps twice as high. Native organizers in St. Louis estimated that about six thousand Indigenous people lived there. Compiling an accurate count was difficult because, as we have already seen, Natives have traditionally been reluctant to respond to the census and were thus routinely undercounted. The task was further complicated by the fact that many urban Natives still thought of their reservations as their permanent homes and lived in cities only for seasonal or temporary employment. Harrison Cornelius, former president of Region VII American Indian Council in Kansas City, likened this mobility to the days when Indigenous hunters would travel hundreds of miles in search of bison, returning to their villages with meat and hides after the hunt. "Most [urban] Indians are only on a long hunting trip," said Cornelius. "A majority would move back if only it could be proven they could survive economically on the reservations."[40]

At the same time, there was a growing recognition that Natives living in cities were more likely to struggle with a variety of economic and health-related issues. They were, for instance, more likely than whites to die in an accident or to suffer from diabetes or liver disease. Urban Indians were less likely to graduate from high school, own their own homes, or to be employed than whites. And even though Indigenous people were seen as the responsibility of the federal government, such programs did not cover many Natives living away from their home reservations or those who were not members of a federally recognized tribe. During the 1970s there were few state or local programs to provide much needed assistance.[41]

To address the needs of this growing and vulnerable population, Indigenous leaders in St. Louis, Kansas City, and Springfield worked to establish formal Indian Centers. The Council Fire of Greater Kansas City chartered the Heart of American Indian Center in 1971. Funding for the center was made possible by policy changes the Bureau of Indian Affairs had initiated after the period of Termination. Beginning with the administration of President John Kennedy in 1961, American Indian Policy began an era of Indian Self-Determination in which Natives were given power to exert more control over their own affairs. Part of this new power came through better access to public funding. Prior to 1960, Indian tribes were forced to go to the BIA or the Indian Health Service to request funding for all programs. With the advent of Self-Determination, tribes were given the same status as state, county, or municipal governments and therefore could apply to other government and private agencies for grants or loans. Even though states like Missouri had no federally recognized tribal entities through which to apply for funding, government officials encouraged Indigenous non-profit organizations to do so on their own.[42]

Initial funding for the Heart of America Indian Center in Kansas City came in large part from a $32,000 grant from the Office of Economic Opportunity (OEO). An initiative begun as part of President Lyndon Johnson's War on Poverty, the OEO gave Indigenous people direct access to program funding. The OEO allowed Indigenous-run organizations the freedom to define their own needs, set their own priorities, and operate their own programs, without the oversight of the BIA. Additional funding for the Indian center came from the National Indian Lutheran Board, who granted the center $4,500. Faith-based organizations would prove to be important partners in providing seed money and other assistance to start the centers in both Kansas City and St. Louis.[43]

The Heart of America Indian Center quickly started programs to help Indigenous clients obtain substance abuse treatment, employment, housing, transportation, legal aid, tuition for job training, family counseling, and food and clothing. Because the center was only able to assist Natives in Missouri, similar support agencies sprang up in Kansas City, Kansas. With funding from the OEO, groups offered services to the estimated one thousand Native people living in Wyandotte County and were eventually able to open the Wy-Kan Indian Center there. "I wouldn't say all [Indigenous people in the county] are in poverty but I would say there are an awful lot of them who are," reflected Georgia Jimenez, who worked as an organizer of Native programs for the regional OEO Foundation. "I know some families who live in conditions that are deplorable."[44]

In January 1974, a small group of Natives in St. Louis opened that city's first Indian Center. Brenda Underwood, the director and one of the founders of the new Indian Cultural Center of Mid-America, envisioned that it would fill much the same role in her community as the Heart of America Indian Center did in Kansas City. However, the St. Louis center was beset with difficulties from the beginning. Soon after opening, the center's space on South Vandeventer Street was vandalized, and employees were threatened with racially-motivated physical violence. Grant money, which had been expected to help start the new venture, did not get disbursed because of "funding foul ups." All of this hampered the center's ability to serve Native people living in the St. Louis area, a group Underwood called an "Invisible Minority."[45]

In late 1975, the center received much-needed assistance from the regional office of the Anti-Defamation League (ADL) of B'nai B'rith. Underwood had unsuccessfully applied for funding for the center from the federal Office of Native American Programs (ONAP), a housing and community development program then operated by the Office of Health, Education and Welfare. With the help of the ADL's James Klaber, leaders from St. Louis's Native community traveled to Washington, DC to directly lobby members of the city's Congressional delegation and ONAP staff members. As a result, the center received a $65,000 grant to help pay for rent, staff, and programing. According to Klaber, the ADL's assistance was part of their ongoing efforts to fight for the human rights of all people. Both the Jewish people and Native Americans "came from a tribal history," noted Klaber. "Both were uprooted from their Native lands by conquering armies." Over the next few months, the Archway Lodge of B'nai B'rith helped support the American Indian Cultural Center with donations of food, clothing, and shoes.[46]

IMAGE 16: James N. Klaber (left), regional director of the Anti-Defamation League of B'nai B'rith, participates in a press conference with Brenda Underwood (center), executive director of the St. Louis American Indian Cultural Center of Mid-America and Mary Goodvoice, the cultural center's manpower specialist in December 1975. Underwood stated at the meeting that without the help of Klaber and the ADL, "I doubt if the American Indian Cultural Center of Mid-America would have been funded by the federal government." *Photograph by David Henschel, St. Louis Jewish Light*

Indian centers were established in smaller Missouri cities as well. The Southwest Missouri Indian Center was incorporated in Springfield in September 1976. The center, still in operation, began as an affiliate of a national organization called the National Urban Indian Council. Not only did the new center serve the approximately one thousand Natives living in Springfield and Greene County, but it also provided services for an estimated six thousand Indigenous people in twenty-one counties in the southwest part of the state. While the Southwest Missouri Indian Center provided many of the same programs as those provided by centers in Kansas City and St. Louis, it also had the additional task of helping Native people get access to health care at the nearest Indian Health center, some ninety miles away in Miami, Oklahoma. Another, short-lived Indian center, the American Indian Center of Springfield, was chartered in June 1986 but appears to have closed in the early 1990s. In 2020, the center was reactivated by a group hoping to assist Natives who resettled in Springfield.[47]

Even as the population of urban Indians in Missouri increased and the need for social services grew, public money for these vitally necessary programs diminished due to government fiscal cutbacks, making the 1980s and 1990s hard decades for urban Indian centers. The National Urban Indian Council estimated that during the early 1980s, about half of the nation's seventy-one Indian centers lost their core operating funding. Of those, the council estimated that eighteen would close. The Heart of America Indian Center in Kansas City lost more than one-third of its total operating budget in 1982. Hit especially hard were the center's food and nutritional programs. In 1993, the Missouri Department of Mental Health discontinued a $30,000 annual grant to the Southwest Missouri Indian Center for drug and alcohol treatment programs. Three years later, the center lost an additional $38,000 grant. While the centers in Springfield and Kansas City suffered crippling budget cuts, they managed to survive. The American Indian Center in St. Louis, however, was operating on its "last legs" by 2002. Despite efforts to resuscitate the organization at the time, it has since become inactive.[48]

Indigenous Nations Return to Missouri
After nearly 170 years of having no cause to interact on a legal or statutory basis with Indigenous nations, the state of Missouri appears to have been caught somewhat off guard when two new laws drew Native economic and cultural attention back to the state. The first law to affect relations between Native tribes and the state of Missouri was the Indian Gaming Regulatory Act (IGRA). Gambling, in the form of such activities as hand games, dice games, and horse racing, has long been a part of many Indigenous cultures. After the advent of Self-Determination, Native nations saw gaming as a potentially lucrative tool of economic development. In the 1970s and 1980s, some nations began to operate bingo halls and card rooms on their tribal land. Since state laws did not apply to operations on Indian land, tribes were able to offer more attractive games and prizes than state-controlled non-Native gambling businesses. Not surprisingly, state governments sued tribes to try to stop their gambling operations. As these lawsuits worked their way through litigation, Federal district courts ruled that state control over gaming was regulatory rather than criminal in nature. For this reason,

they affirmed that states had no jurisdiction over gambling that took place on sovereign tribal land. In an attempt to codify several court opinions into a coherent law, Congress passed the IGRA in 1988. At that time, tribal gaming in the US was a $171 million enterprise. Just twelve years after the passage of the IGRA, it would become a $10.6 billion industry.[49]

In the early 1990s, Missouri voters approved a constitutional amendment that allowed games of chance to be played on gambling "boats" located on or within one thousand feet of the Missouri or Mississippi Rivers. A number of gaming companies quickly proposed casino projects in Missouri. Among them was the Eastern Shawnee Tribe of Oklahoma. Situated on land adjacent to the Missouri border in West Seneca, Oklahoma, the Shawnees filed a petition with the BIA to have land on the Missouri side of the state line given trust status. Trust land is property the federal government holds in title for the benefit of federally recognized Indigenous nations, in this case the Shawnees. Had the BIA approved the application, the Missouri land would have become part of the tribe's reservation, the first such land inside the state since the 1830s. The Shawnees proposed to build a fifty-three thousand square-foot casino that would straddle the border. On the Oklahoma side, they planned to offer Class II gaming such as bingo and non-banked card games, while on the Missouri side they proposed to operate full casino-style Class III gambling. Missouri Senator Christopher "Kit" Bond successfully appealed to Secretary of the Interior Bruce Babbitt to have the Shawnees' petition denied. In his letter to the secretary, Bond claimed that a Shawnee gambling operation would "defy the state constitution, mock the public will and degrade one of the country's most livable areas." "We do not believe someone should be able to bring more gambling into Missouri through the back door," Bond commented. "They are in effect circumventing the popular vote of the people." Today the Shawnees operate a casino on the Oklahoma side of the state line.[50]

In 1999, the Modoc Tribe of Oklahoma, a nation with no historical ties to Missouri, nearly succeeded in having sixty-eight acres of land near Seneca, Missouri, classified as trust land. Like the Eastern Shawnees, the Modoc Tribe's reservation was adjacent to the Missouri state line. When the BIA notified Newton County officials that it intended to grant the Modocs' request, Missouri Attorney General Jay Nixon sued the Department of the Interior to prevent the designation. The Modocs subsequently withdrew their application, claiming that they had only intended to use the land for grazing buffalo.[51]

That same year, the Eastern Shawnees and a band of Chippewa, or Ojibwa, separately expressed interest in building facilities near the resort town of Branson, Missouri. The Ojibwa proposed a resort, complete with a convention center and amusement park in Kimberling City, ten miles west of Branson. After a consortium of Branson entertainers and local politicians rallied against the proposals, both tribes withdrew their proposals.

The state's campaign to keep Native owned casinos out of its borders adversely affected several local Indigenous groups. In 2002, eight Indigenous groups in Missouri were in the process of applying for federal recognition. Because of the state's fear that such recognition would open the doors to Indigenous gaming operations, the state government pressured the BIA to deny the eight applications. "Let's not kid ourselves," declared Nixon, "Missouri is a prime target for the expansion of Indian gaming, and I will fight to prevent this expansion." This strong reaction came in spite of the fact that only one of the eight bands, the Northern Tribe of Cherokee, had publicly expressed any interest in gaming, saying that they would consider it only if it made fiscal sense. "There is something hypocritical in seeing state officials oppose recognition of Missouri Indian Tribes because they don't want to see casino gambling spread," noted the editors of the *Springfield News-Leader*. "To argue against tribal recognition because it could lead to the spread of gambling is disingenuous—particularly in a state that once made it a crime to be an Indian."[52]

The second law to have a significant impact on the manner in which Missouri state officials interacted with Indigenous groups was the Native American Graves Protection and Repatriation Act (NAGPRA). Passed in 1990, NAGPRA stipulated that those institutions receiving federal funding and in possession of Indigenous artifacts or human remains must inventory all such items, inform lineal descendants of those to whom the remains and artifacts originally belonged about its holdings, and repatriate the items to the appropriate parties. Affected institutions included museums, research facilities, universities, local governments, and state agencies. Prior to the law's passage, "it was perfectly legal to dig up an Indian and call him or her a relic," said Richard Black, a repatriation specialist for both the Iowa Tribe of Oklahoma and the Sac and Fox Nation of Oklahoma. Though Missouri did have a law covering unmarked graves, there were no clear legal guidelines regarding the handling or possession of Indigenous remains, which were often misused and exploited.[53]

As states worked to comply with the new law, determining exactly who were the lineal descendants of the many sets of human remains and artifacts stored throughout the state became an immediate challenge. Because of the state's long history of Native habitation and the forced removal of Indigenous people in the 1830s, establishing a clear linkage between present tribes and ancient remains sometimes proved difficult. NAGPRA drew renewed attention to Missouri institutions by representatives of such tribes as the Osages, Ioways, Sacs, and Foxes, and confrontations sometimes ensued. Some institutions, such as the University of Missouri's Department of Anthropology, were initially reluctant to repatriate remains, maintaining they could not establish a solid link between the remains and the tribes that claimed them. MU's initial refusal to comply with NAGPRA led to protests outside the facility that housed the remains.

In 1997, university officials reversed their decision and agreed to return parts of one thousand eight hundred skeletons to Indigenous officials. To facilitate this repatriation and subsequent ones, the Iowa Tribe of Oklahoma established a tribal historic preservation office in a refurbished American Legion hall in Princeton, Missouri. They also purchased a five-acre site near the town on which they reinterred repatriated remains. Though not all of the remains were those of Ioways, several tribes with historical ties to Missouri had signed an agreement allowing the Ioways to act on their behalf. According to press accounts, MU's repatriation of remains to the Ioways was the first made by a major US university.[54]

Initially, the repatriation process did not proceed smoothly. In the late 1990s, the Department of Natural Resources (DNR) and the Missouri Department of Transportation (MoDOT) both came under the scrutiny of the Sac and Fox Nation of Oklahoma. In its role as administrators of the Missouri State Museum and the Missouri State Historic Preservation Office (MoSHPO), the Missouri DNR possessed artifacts that fell under the purview of NAGPRA. Similarly, MoDOT held human remains and artifacts that had been uncovered during highway construction projects. The Sac and Fox Nation, with historical ties to northern Missouri and burials in the region, alleged that these state institutions were negligent in handling and storing human remains.[55]

The Sacs' and Foxes' grievances with the state were exacerbated in 1995 and 1996, when archaeologists working for the state took possession of the remains of at least twenty-two individuals and placed them in storage. The bones had become exposed by the erosion of a Late Woodland Period burial mound on a blufftop overlooking the Mississippi River town of Clarksville, Missouri. The deterioration of the mound was caused by the construction of an observation deck for a chair lift in 1962. Sac and Fox preservation officials objected to the fact that the remains had been removed from the mound without their knowledge or permission. Their stated policy on burials maintained that remains that had been uncovered through construction or excavation should "be returned to the earth at, or as near as possible to, the place where they were originally buried." They also maintained that "the institutions or agencies holding these remains were also responsible for violating the sanctity of the cemeteries where the human remains and funerary objects were located." Based on these allegations, the tribe sued the state of Missouri.[56]

In 2002 and 2006, additional remains that had been taken from the Clarksville site when the chair lift was originally constructed were added to those taken in the 1990s. In all, there were twenty-nine sets of remains and two funerary objects. In 2013, a confederacy of all three Sac and Fox Nations filed a claim for the remains so that repatriation could take place. These plans came to a halt, however, when the Osage Nation filed a competing claim with MoSHPO on the basis that Osages had lived in Missouri during the Late Woodland Period, while the Sac and Fox had arrived in the region after European contact. According to the Osage Tribal Historic Preservation officer, Andrea Hunter, MoSHPO still had not determined the validity of the Osage claim two years after it was filed. In November 2015, the national NAGPRA Review Committee sided with the Osages in a finding of fact, ruling that they were culturally affiliated with the Clarksville mound remains. The committee asked the MoSHPO to decide the proper recipient of the remains within six months.[57]

In their response to the review committee, MoSHPO pointed out that it had already accepted the affiliation claim of the Sac and Fox Nation, and despite the committee's finding of fact, they still believed the Sac and Fox Nation was the most appropriate claimant and planned to proceed with plans to repatriate the remains to them. By early 2017, the issue remained unresolved, despite a meeting between Osage officials and administrators of the Missouri DNR. Finally, in June 2019, MoSHPO officials reversed their decision and agreed that the Osages had a valid cultural affiliation with the Clarksville Mound group and stated that they planned to return the remains to them. This marked only the second time in NAGPRA's history that a state's affiliation decision had been successfully reversed.[58]

NAGRA forced accountability onto most museums with Native American artifacts in their collections. Prior to 1990, many museums had no comprehensive inventory of their Indigenous objects, and Native tribes had little idea which museums held any remains or artifacts that once had belonged to their ancestors. In some cases, museums suffered growing pains as they struggled to comply with the new law. Such was the case with the St. Joseph Museum. Though the museum held a number of Indigenous artifacts, it took the governing board of directors more than a decade after the passage of NAGPRA to comply with the law. In the summer of 2002, the museum had been the recipient of a huge collection of Native artifacts belonging to the late J. Mett Shippee, who died in 1985 after a seventy-year career as an archaeologist. Though he was an amateur, Shippee had worked extensively with Carl H. Chapman at the University of Missouri and had participated in several important Missouri archaeological excavations, particularly in the Kansas City area. Portions of Shippee's collection of forty thousand artifacts were donated to several area museums, including the Kansas City Museum. The 2002 donation to the St. Joseph Museum included an estimated twenty-thousand artifacts.[59]

A few months after accepting the Shippee family's donation, the museum's board of directors decided to apply for federal funding to help museum staff learn how to comply with NAGPRA. The receipt of the federal money also made the St. Joseph Museum legally liable to follow the law's guidelines. Even though they had relinquished control over the collection when they donated it to the museum, members of the Shippee family objected to its being subjected to NAGPRA rules, as well as to the possibility that some of the artifacts could be returned to Native tribes. In November 2002, the museum board voted to return all twenty thousand artifacts to the Shippee family so that they could be held privately. Not long thereafter, the museum and Shippee's descendants agreed that the collection would remain in the museum through a fifty-year loan. Both parties apparently hoped that because the collection would remain privately owned, it would be exempt from NAGPRA.[60]

In the meantime, public concern over the condition and care of the museum's collection prompted St. Joseph's mayor and city council to ask the museum for a partial inventory of the collection. The apprehension appears to have been largely related to a separate issue. In 2005, the board had decided to sell the museum's original building, the Wyeth-Tootle mansion. The museum's Friends organization had successfully sued to prevent the sale but doubts over the museum's operation lingered. "This is by no means a complete audit," remarked Harrison Hartley, a former St. Joseph Museum staff member who had been one of the people asked to conduct the inventory. "We just want to have an initial look to see that the mass of [the collection] is there."[61]

In April 2007, the St. Joseph Museum's board of directors discovered that they were being investigated by the Department of the Interior for possible violation of NAGPRA in their handling of the Shippee collection. The department had apparently been tipped off by a museum board member who alleged that the museum was remiss in creating a collection inventory of remains and had failed to complete a summary of cultural items. Investigators informed the board's legal counsel that a possible violation may have occurred because they had accepted federal money one month prior to turning the collection back over to the Shippee family. The board's lawyer advised the museum to accept full ownership of the collection, which was still in their possession under the terms of the fifty-year loan agreement. In doing so, the board would undo their 2002 deaccession of the collection, and while they would still need to adhere to the NAGPRA statute, they hoped to avoid being fined by the Department of the Interior.[62]

In May 2007, the museum's board did indeed vote to accept the collection to prevent the museum from future punishment under the law. In January 2008, the Department of the Interior found that the St. Joseph Museum had not violated the law and gave them five years to complete the necessary inventories that would put them in compliance with it.[63]

In many important ways, Missouri once again appeared to be part of "Indian Country," even though the state had long believed there were no Indigenous people within its borders. Today, Missouri is home to about twenty-seven thousand Indigenous people, and as new generations of Natives assert their rights over their identity, heritage, culture, and land, Missouri is likely to be altered by a new era of Indigenous sovereignty.[64]

Voices

I think what happened to us in Missouri, was terrible. Terrible. Our trek through Missouri, from there to Kansas, we lost 90 percent of our people. Those of us who survived, we have to stick together. There's only 23,000 of us so far that we can count. And, you take half of those folks and they have chosen to be outside of Oklahoma and you see who's left locally and who can work with us here. . . . You take away the elders, the children, the disabled and you're at 4,000 people or less. There are high schools in Tulsa that have more than that. We have got to realize that we are a pretty tight group.[1]

—Geoffrey Standing Bear (Osage)

We've been here for a thousand years now and, unlike other people who can buy and sell land and move away, we can never move away. This is our land forever. And we'll be here for another 1,000 years.[2]

—Lance Foster (Ioway)

Chapter Eleven

Sovereignty and Identity

FROM OUR VANTAGE POINT AT the beginning of the third decade of the twenty-first century, it appears that two of the most pressing issues now facing Missouri's Indigenous people are tribal sovereignty and Indigenous identity. Both sovereignty and identity have been under attack by settler colonialism during the past five centuries, yet Natives now appear to be in a strong position to reassert authority over them. While the issue of Indigenous identity might be the more difficult of the two issues to quantify, that has not prevented it from becoming a hotly debated subject among European Americans and Natives alike. Core questions include the following: What is Indigenous identity? Who are allowed to identify themselves as Indigenous? Who has the right to determine who is Indigenous and who is not Indigenous?

Too often, representations of Natives have been informed by more than a century and a half of popular culture in the form of dime novels, "penny dreadfuls," animated cartoons, and Western movies. Because of this, images of Native Americans are largely stuck in a mythical past, leaving little place in the American popular imagination for Indigenous people in the contemporary world. Thus, Missouri's Indigenous citizens often find themselves defined by stereotypical representations that have little, if anything, to do with the reality of their twenty-first-century lives. Crystal Echo Hawk, executive director of IllumiNative, an organization that works to promote Indigenous voices in all media, points out that many public schools do not teach the history of Native people after the nineteenth century. "This lack of representation . . . can lead to an erasure of Native American people and experiences," she says. "It serves to dehumanize native people . . . . [The American public] cannot see us as fully-formed, multidimensional human beings."[1]

Stephanie A. Fryberg, a Tulalip scholar at Stanford University, has argued that the limited representation of Indigenous people has had an adverse effect on their self-esteem and mental health. "American Indian representations were relatively scarce and fairly limited in scope, with very few contemporary, progressive images," writes Fryberg. Because minority groups have less control over the ways in which they are portrayed in popular culture, they are constrained in their ability to form their own identities. "When stereotypes, like the stereotypes of Indians in the cartoon are projected in the media, they too become powerful social representations. They say, 'this is what an Indian is' and if you want to refer to Indians or communicate about them or even be one, you have to use the available representations." Research shows that, as a result of being pigeonholed by representations that do not accurately represent them, Indigenous people can develop an inferior opinion of themselves and their communities. This, in turn, leads to lower expectations about their own potential in life. Conversely, says Fryberg, studies have shown that European Americans experience a "psychological boost" from seeing other ethnic groups represented less realistically. Consider the issue of Native-themed sports mascots. Research indicates that cartoonish Indigenous mascots, logos, and derogatory team names help "European Americans feel better about themselves."[2]

While professional sports team owners and public school administrators maintain that such team names as "Indians," "Braves," "Chiefs," and "Savages" either do not refer directly to Indigenous people or are meant to honor them, Natives feel the names diminish their humanity and mock their heritage. Nationwide, the controversy over mascots has led to protests, petitions, and litigation by Indigenous people demanding that sports teams stop using images of Natives as logos and stereotypical phrases for Natives as team names. This campaign has recently forced Washington DC's professional football team to retire its racist "Redskins" name and logo in 2020 and adopt the new name Washington Commanders in 2022. Under intense public pressure, the Cleveland Indians professional baseball team dropped its Chief Wahoo logo in 2018 and announced in 2021 that it would change the team's name to the Cleveland Guardians.[3]

In Missouri, for at least three decades Indigenous people have launched a similar campaign against the Kansas City Chiefs professional football team. The team has long maintained that its name does not refer to Indigenous Americans, but rather to former Kansas City

Mayor and Tribe of Mic-O-Say founder H. Roe Bartle, whose nickname was "Chief." The moniker was based on Bartle's claim that he had been given the name Chief Lone Bear by an Arapaho headman. Bartle was instrumental in persuading team owner Lamar Hunt to move his Dallas Texans football franchise to Kansas City in 1963. However, this version of the origin of the team's name has been overshadowed by its use of Native imagery, including its arrowhead logo, Chiefs fans' adoption of "war" paint and feathered headdresses, and the infamous "Tomahawk Chop" arm gesture as a form of cheering for the home team. This imagery appears to have been no accident. Less than a decade after moving the team to Kansas City, Hunt, a marketing genius who coined the term "Super Bowl," hired a man, who may or may not have been Indigenous, to dress in Native regalia and ride a horse named Warpaint around the field after every Chiefs touchdown. Clearly, "Chief" Bartle had become a footnote in the team's story and was replaced by a carefully crafted faux-Native brand.[4]

As early as 1991, a member of the Seminole Nation of Oklahoma filed a complaint against the Chiefs organization with the Missouri Commission on Human Rights. Michael S. Haney said he felt threatened by Kansas City fans who "were hostile [in] their right to mimic Indian dress and customs. . . . Through their Chiefs mascot image, stadium cheers, and sale of Indian related items, the Chiefs caused me to feel embarrassed and humiliated."[5]

By 2005, a group of Indigenous students from the University of Kansas and Haskell Indian Nations University in Lawrence, Kansas, had formed the Not in Our Honor Coalition to "advocate against the use of Native American imagery in sports." Since that time, members of the group have staged protests outside Arrowhead Stadium at Chiefs home games. "I just wish people would understand from our perspective why this is so hurtful to us, to have that constant chop and the drum and everything out there," says Rhonda LeValdo, one of the group's founders. "I hear it on TV, on the radio, on billboards, walking down the street, people are saying 'Chiefs!'"[6]

Well aware of the controversy surrounding its brand, the Kansas City Chiefs organization has made some effort to meet with representatives of the Indigenous community to "gain a better understanding of the issues facing American Indian communities in our region." To that end, the team has prohibited fans from wearing headdresses inside Arrowhead Stadium. Face paint is still allowed, though fans will not be allowed to wear Native-themed paint in the stadium. However, the team has yet to ban The Chop. One commentator has observed, "The Chop has become one of the most stubborn relics of the sports world's blithe attitude towards appropriating and caricaturing Indigenous culture." As of August 2020, the team was reviewing the gesture, which it refers to as the "Arrowhead Chop," and planned "additional discussion in the future."[7]

In Missouri, as in most areas of the country, Native-themed mascots are not limited to professional sports teams. A 2021 investigation by the *Columbia Missourian* found that twenty-eight high schools in the state have mascots such as "Warriors," "Indians," "Savages," and "Braves." The website *American Indian Sports Team Mascots* estimates that when grade schools and middle schools are included, the number of teams with Native mascots in Missouri jumps to ninety-seven.[8]

Some communities have undertaken efforts to change the names of local mascots, but the process has often been slow and painful. In 2020, Savannah, Missouri, whose high school mascot is the "Savages," debated the merits of changing the team's name and logo. Savannah High School alumnus and enrolled member of the Cheyenne Arapaho Tribe, Michaela Lent, helped lead the fight for the name change. As a child growing up in Savannah, she struggled with her identity as one of the only Indigenous students in the school. She said the experience "set the foundation in my way of thinking and my outlook on society." In regard to the mascot, she expressed frustration that "this is how they are depicting me and my people, my family, and everyone's just OK with it." In April 2021, the Savannah school board voted four to three to phase out all Native sports imagery and the team's logo but decided to keep the name "Savages."[9]

Indigenous people have also had to confront the ongoing issue of non-Natives appropriating Indigenous culture, traditions, and ceremonies for their own purposes. Historians such as Philip J. Deloria have skillfully shown that non-Natives have usurped Indigenous identity since before the United States won independence from Britain. From colonists dressed as Natives at the Boston Tea Party in 1773 to the twenty-first century "New Age" shaman exploiting Native ceremonies.[10]

In Missouri, appropriation of Indigenous culture has taken many forms. As we saw in an earlier chapter, H. Roe Bartle founded the Tribe of Mic-O-Say scout group in the 1920s and based it on his romanticized understanding of Indigenous traditions. While this and other similar organizations were founded at a time when many assumed Native people were vanishing, Mic-O-Say has recently become a contentious organization as Indigenous people have begun to exert more control over how they are represented. The scouts in Mic-O-Say, most of whom are non-Native, dress in powwow regalia and perform dances, which Indigenous people often see as stereotypical caricatures of their culture. Many scout leaders claim that these dances and ceremonies are meant to honor and preserve Native traditions. "Who asked the [Boy Scouts of America] to 'preserve' Native American traditions, and why can't Native peoples do that for themselves?" asks Misha Maynerick Blaise, a writer whose son is a scout. "Dancing, donning Native regalia, or utilizing sacred symbols (like eagle feathers or sacred pipes) are not things that should be divorced from their particular tribal reality and religious meaning."[11] In 2020, after a long summer of racial upheaval and the increased visibility of the Black Lives Matter movement, the editorial board of the *Kansas City Star* declared that the "Mic-O-Say program demeans Native Americans . . . [and] is long past due for a major overhaul."[12]

But the program is not without its defenders. In a rebuttal to the *Star* editorial, Mark L. Willens, an attorney and former Mic-O-Say member, claimed that "Honoring and sharing a heritage through emulation and imitation, done in a respectful, non-demeaning way and for good purposes, should not be considered cultural appropriation or even cultural mimicry. Borrowing good things with attribution and using them for good purposes is not stealing."[13] While this issue currently seems to be at a stalemate, most observers agree that at the very least, Mic-O-Say needs to consult Native advisors about their ceremonies if the program is to continue.

Indigenous Missourians have also had to protect their cultural traditions from those who have appropriated them, often for profit. Of particular concern has been the ongoing problem of non-Native artists selling ceremonies, works of art, and music, which they claim to be authentically Native American. The problem was addressed as early as the 1930s when the Department of the Interior established the Indian Arts and Crafts Board (IACB) as part of John Collier's Indian New Deal. The mission of the IACB is to "promote the economic development of federally recognized American Indians and Alaska Natives (Indians) through the expansion of the Indian arts and crafts market." The act was originally passed by Congress to protect Indigenous artistic traditions from being exploited by non-Natives. The Indian Arts and Crafts Act of 1990 strengthened that protection by making it illegal to "offer or display for sale or sell any art or craft product in a manner that falsely suggests it is Indian produced."[14]

In 2015, an Odessa, Missouri, man pleaded guilty to violating the Indian Arts and Crafts Act of 1990. Terry Lee Whetstone was sentenced to three years of probation for using a fraudulent Cherokee Nation of Oklahoma enrollment card to sell work he claimed was genuinely Native American. Whetstone, a musician and artist, claims Cherokee ancestry, but is not a member of a federally recognized tribe. Under the terms of his plea agreement in Federal Court in the Western District of Missouri, Whetstone may not sell art or perform flute music without informing buyers and audience members that he is not a member of an Indigenous nation. Since Whetstone's plea agreement, the state of Missouri has passed a bill making it illegal for anyone who is not a member of a federally recognized tribe to sell Native American art. The bill was sponsored by Rocky Miller, a Republican state representative from Lake Ozark and a member of the federally recognized Cherokee Nation of Oklahoma.[15]

Kathy Dickerson, an enrolled member of the Kiowa Tribe, has spent the better part of the last two decades protecting the sanctity of Indigenous identity, arts, and traditions. A resident of St. Louis, Dickerson is also an artist who sells her work online and at fairs and powwows. More than fifteen years ago, she began using her website to expose those whom she believes "distort the true heritage of Native Americans and rob them of what little income they can generate by selling craftwork." On her website she warns consumers that they "have the right to ask if the American Indian you are purchasing from or hiring as a performer is properly documented."[16]

In 2005, Dickerson founded a group called the St. Louis American Indian Consortium to monitor individuals and groups who were exploiting Indigenous culture. High on the group's list was a non-profit called the Thunderbird Society based in St. Charles, Missouri. The society was incorporated in 1994 for the purpose of teaching the history, culture, and arts and crafts of Native Americans and helping schools on Indian Reservations. Members of the Thunderbird Society performed ceremonies, published books, held educational dances and demonstrations, and sponsored at least one powwow in 1996. Members of the group were not required to be Indigenous and some joined chapters, or "lodges," throughout Missouri by completing an application on the group's website. "If they called themselves hobbyists, I wouldn't have a problem," commented John White Antelope, a member of the St. Louis American Indian Consortium. "But they try to pass themselves off as real Indians. In my mind they're perpetuating fraud."[17]

In 2006, the consortium succeeded in stopping the Thunderbird Society from performing at an event at Fort Leonard Wood. Mark Pashia, an "elder" with the Thunderbird Society, responded, "What we have here, is a group of card-carrying Native Americans who think the Thunderbird Society interferes with their ability to make money."[18] Under pressure from the consortium and other Indigenous groups, the society disbanded, and the state of Missouri revoked its status as a non-profit corporation due to its failure to file annual reports in 2007.[19]

Government Regulated Identity

The cases of Whetstone and the Thunderbird Society point to a broader issue of contention among Indigenous people concerning who is and who is not "authentically Native." This tension is created almost entirely by the fact that no other ethnic group has its identity regulated by the federal government. As of 2022, there are currently 574 federally recognized Indigenous nations in the United States. "These federally recognized tribes are eligible for funding and services from the Bureau of Indian Affairs, either directly or through contracts, grants, or compacts." To achieve federal recognition, a tribe must first prove that it has existed as a group continuously since 1900. Members of tribes that are not federally recognized are ineligible to participate in most federal programs created for Indigenous people.[20]

Since at least the 1880s, when the Dawes Allotment Act led to the implementation of tribal rolls, there has been a widening division between those Indigenous people enrolled in tribes that have received federal recognition and those who are either not enrolled in any tribe or are enrolled in tribes that are not federally recognized. Often, tribes have legitimate cases for seeking federal recognition, and some are in the process of working with the Bureau of Indian Affairs to achieve it. There are also groups that simply form as a way of celebrating their Indigenous heritage. Other factions, however, form illegitimate tribes that accept as members anyone willing to pay an enrollment fee. Such organizations often attract people who may believe they have Indigenous heritage but are unable to connect it to a particular Native nation. Others join in hopes of qualifying for certain minority-owned business benefits.

Federally recognized tribes see these groups as threats because they not only appropriate Native culture, but they also may use their status to receive federal and state resources meant for legitimate indigenous nations.

The Cherokee Nation of Oklahoma has been concerned about the proliferation of "wannabe" tribes and formed an ad hoc task force to monitor them in 2007. The group "looks at protecting our sovereignty," said Dr. Richard Allen, a member of the task force. "We have so many individuals and groups who are using the Cherokee name and a lot of times it's in a manner that is very inappropriate. They scam people. They charge for genealogy. They charge for DNA tests that might suggest that people could be Indian. In essence, we are looking at groups that claim to be Cherokee but have no real status and who are just distorting the culture and history." The same year that the task force was formed, the tribe attempted to expel two thousand eight hundred Cherokee Freedman from the tribal rolls. Freedman are the descendants of enslaved people owned by Cherokees. Many of these enslaved persons were forced to travel to Oklahoma with the Cherokees on the Trail of Tears. In 2017, a US federal district court ruled that the Freedmen should be allowed to remain in the tribe, a decision the Cherokees have accepted.[21]

As of 2007, there were approximately two hundred Cherokee tribes nationwide, only three of which, the Cherokee Nation of Oklahoma, the Eastern Band of Cherokee, and the United Keetoowah Band of Cherokee Indians, are federally recognized. In 2010, it was estimated that in Missouri alone, there were twenty-four unrecognized Cherokee groups spread throughout the state. Some of these tribes have claimed to be recognized by the state of Missouri, even though the state currently has no legal mechanism with which to bestow such status. Some have based their claims on the fact that, like the Thunderbird Society, they have registered as a non-profit corporation with the Missouri Secretary of State's Office. Others base their claim of recognition on the fact that they have received proclamations issued by the state legislature or by past governors.

Applicants who wish to enroll in one of the three federally recognized Cherokee nations must be able to prove that they are a direct descendant of someone listed on the Dawes Rolls. Applicants also must prove that they have a specified amount of Cherokee "blood quantum" to qualify as a tribal member. Some of the unrecognized tribes claim their ancestors do not appear on the rolls because they had moved to Missouri long before the Trail of Tears or had refused to sign treaties that would have forced them to move to Oklahoma. "The Dawes Roll is one of the most flawed documents in the world," claimed Kenn "Grey Elk" Descombes, chief of the unrecognized Northern Cherokee Nation, headquartered in Clinton, Missouri. "Its main thing was to destroy the reservation, which it did." The Northern Cherokees claim to have a secret ancestry roll, which Descombes says is "not for white people" to see until such time as the tribe is ready to prove its legitimacy. In the meantime, like many other unrecognized tribal entities, this group admits those who identify as Cherokee, without proof of ancestry.[22]

This enrollment process led to a scandal that has brought unwanted national attention on the Northern Cherokees and other Missouri groups. In 2019, an investigation launched by the *Los Angeles Times* discovered that the owners of twelve contracting companies located across the nation had enrolled in either the Northern Cherokee tribe, the Western Cherokee Nation of Arkansas and Missouri, based in Mansfield, Missouri, or in the Northern Cherokee Nation of the Old Louisiana Territory, based in Columbia, Missouri, in order to qualify to bid for minority business contracts. In all, these companies received $300 million in contracts by claiming to be members of one of these three Missouri tribes. Soon after the revelation, the City of St. Louis removed five companies from their list of minority-owned business. The companies responded by suing the city for discrimination on the basis that they were being held to a different standard than companies owned by non-Native minorities.[23]

This has brought the Missouri groups into conflict with the three federally recognized Cherokee tribes. Cherokee Nation of Oklahoma citizen and genealogist Twila Barnes has blogged for years about those who declare themselves to be Cherokee. In 2012, she worked to debunk Massachusetts Senator Elizabeth Warren's claim of Cherokee heritage. Since then, Barnes has used exhaustive genealogical research to discredit a dozen Cherokee groups in Missouri, nine of which she has labeled as "fraudulent."[24]

However, the fact remains that thousands of Missourians are the unenrolled descendants of Cherokees or of ancestors from other Indigenous tribes. In many cases, the federally initiated system of tribal enrollment has left unenrolled Indigenous people feeling like second-class outsiders. "I am tired of our Cherokee brothers accusing me of being a wannabe and making me feel diminished," writes Grey Fox, a chief elder of the Northern Cherokees, on the group's website. "My

Cherokee identity is precious to me and I am determined to no longer allow mean-spirited detractors to diminish it." Unenrolled Indigenous people who practice their culture not only run the risk of being labeled "wannabes," "pretendians," or "generokees," but they do not qualify for federal relief for Indigenous people such as health care, food distribution for the poor, and assistance for low-income homeowners.[25]

In recent years, enrollment requirements, which are established by individual tribes, have changed. As historian Kyle Powys Whyte has observed, this makes it possible for "someone who has always been Indigenous [to] be enrolled, unenrolled and disenrolled at various times during their life." Some Indigenous tribes have disenrolled members or changed their criteria to make enrollment more difficult. This is done in order to ensure that those who remain enrolled will receive a greater percentage of the tribe's economic revenue. Other tribes have taken the opposite strategy and made their enrollment criteria less strict. Some feel that increased enrollment will lend a tribe more political and economic clout. Others believe it is a way to honor the ancient tradition of accepting members into a tribe through adoption and kinship.[26]

Whyte points out that in the end, however, racial definitions that are imposed on Indigenous people are a product of US settler colonialism. While federally recognized tribes may have the authority to determine who is and who is not eligible for enrollment, it is ultimately the federal government that decides which tribes qualify for recognition. Furthermore, the metrics used to make enrollment decisions—family lineage, tribal rolls, and blood quantum—are antithetical to traditional Indigenous ways of affirming self-identity. Whyte adds that such metrics "involve impositions of choices on Indigenous peoples in which each decision option will produce [their eventual] erasure." As many Indigenous scholars have observed, erasure of Indigenous people is a necessary goal of a settler state. Citing the work of scholar Kim TallBear and others, Whyte calls for Indigenous people to assert their own identity criteria. Discussions of Indigenous identity, he writes, should begin with "self-governance and the land." "Indigenous peoples understand themselves to have emerged as coherent groups and cultures in intimate relationship with particular places," points out TallBear. Because settler colonialism so drastically altered the landscape in order to facilitate the extraction of natural resources, Whyte suggests that Indigenous identity could be tied to group actions that "challenge the ecological aspects of colonialism and their impact on Indigenous self-determination."[27] In other words, instead of appraising Indigenous identity through biology, what if it was gauged by cultural affiliation and an attachment to homeland that included efforts to reverse the environmental damage of colonialism?

Self-Governance and Sovereignty

This vision of Indigenous identity, by necessity, encompasses the second major issue faced by Missouri's Native population in the twenty-first century, that of self-governance and sovereignty over culture and land. Many nations might find it easier to assert sovereignty on their own reservation land. In recent years, for example, the Iowa Tribe of Kansas and Nebraska has begun to practice the principles of regenerative agriculture in their farming operations on land they have inhabited since 1837. By implementing more crop diversity, the minimum disturbance of soil, and the integration of livestock into their operations, the Ioways hope to make their crops more resilient to climate change, protect their water supply, and achieve food security for tribal members. These practices conform less to modern methods of large-scale agriculture and more to traditions of Ioway community and identity.[28]

However, we might see more tribes that once lived in Missouri reach outside of their traditional reservation land to exert sovereignty over lands within the state. The Osage Nation is already engaged in this process. As has been mentioned in an earlier chapter, in 2007 the Osages purchased Sugarloaf Mound in St. Louis, the last mound in the city known to have been a part of the Cahokia mound complex. In September 2021, the Native American Rights Fund (NARF) donated twenty acres of land in Lafayette County, Missouri, to the Osage Nation. The land is important to the nation because it contains burials that they wish to protect. That same month, the Osages attempted to purchase Picture Cave in Warren County, Missouri. The cave contains the largest collection of Indigenous polychrome paintings in the state and is, according to researcher James Duncan, the womb of the Osage universe. While the Osages attempted to work with landowners to purchase the cave property, it was sold at auction to an unnamed buyer for $2.2 million.[29]

In October 2021, the Osage Nation announced a plan to build a casino at the Lake of the Ozarks on a twenty-eight-acre parcel of land not far from Bagnall Dam. Principal Chief Geoffrey Standing Bear stated that the Osages expected the landmark US Supreme Court decision in the 2020 *McGirt v. Oklahoma* would make it possible for the property in Missouri to be recognized as a part of the Osage reservation.[30] On its face, the McGirt case dealt with the narrow issue of authority in the prosecution of crimes committed by Natives on the former reservation land of the Five Civilized Tribes in eastern Oklahoma. The Supreme Court majority opinion stated that such crimes fall under the jurisdiction of tribal and federal police. However, some legal observers foresee the case opening the door for the larger issue of territorial rights. This is because the majority ruled in the McGirt case that, because Congress had never "disestablished" the reservations of the Five Civilized Tribes, they still held their historic sovereign authority and will do so until and unless Congress specifically divests them of that sovereignty. Given this interpretation, one might assume that the Osages will claim sovereignty over land they once held in Missouri on the grounds that, even though they relinquished the land by treaty, Congress never explicitly revoked their sovereignty over it.[31]

Unlike the 1990s, when Missouri officials forcefully blocked efforts by the Absentee Shawnees, Modocs, and Ojibwas to build casinos in the state, the Osages already have the backing of at least two state legislators, the Lake of the Ozarks Convention and Visitors Bureau, and the Missouri Hotel and Lodging Association. This support has been garnered through a four-year lobbying campaign led by former Missouri House speaker Steve Tilley and a $52,000 donation to the inaugural fund of former Governor Eric Greitens.[32]

It is difficult to imagine a time when Missouri would again be the domain of Indigenous people. Though there is a sizeable and still-growing "LANDBACK" movement among Natives and their allies, it is unlikely that non-Native people need to worry about having their property confiscated and returned to the state's Indigenous inhabitants. And that is not necessarily the goal of proponents of LANDBACK. In their manifesto, the group demands the end of white supremacy and the return of all public land held by the Bureau of Land Management (BLM) and the National Park Service to Indigenous people.[33] In Missouri, this would amount to a little over fifty-four thousand acres of land. If land owned by the US Fish and Wildlife Service, the US Forest Service, and the US Department of Defense were added to the list, the number of acres would be 1,675,400, approximately 3.79 percent of the total land in the state. LANDBACK also demands to have control over mining, pipelines, and intrusions that take place on land over which they have a sovereign claim.[34]

These are contentious issues, perhaps especially so in Missouri because the state has not acknowledged itself as the home of Indigenous nations since 1836. However, it is not hard to picture a future in which Osages, Ioways, Sacs, Foxes, Otoes-Missourias, Quapaws, Shawnees, Delawares, Kickapoos, and members of the Illinois Confederacy once again have at least a presence in the state. As we have seen, this is already taking place. Through this presence, local and state officials will work with the Indigenous Missourians to protect the remains of their ancestors and their sacred sites. In this era of climate change, they could conceivably also have a say in the way resources are extracted from their ancestral lands. Perhaps they could once again assert their identity and sovereignty in a way that allows them to reconnect with the land here in the Show-Me State.

Voices

Long, long ago, the Ioways were bears, elk, buffalo, wolves, beavers, eagles . . . then there was change and those Ioways became humans, they lost their fur, their horns, their wings, their claws and became Indians. Not having horns or wings or claws did not stop them from being Ioways.

Not so long ago, there was further change, and those Ioway Indians transformed again, and most lost their braids, their shiny black hair, their coppery skin and flint eyes. Now through that change we are still Ioways, but our skins are often pale, eyes blue or green, our hair red, blonde or brown.

The same ear of Indian corn has white kernels, red kernels, blue kernels, brown kernels, yellow kernels.[1]

—Lance Foster (Ioway)

I speak about traditional values and culture and how to incorporate that into modern life. . . . Something we have lost in America, especially in politics, is simple human kindness. Our [Indigenous] sense of responsibility is different than a lot of the Euro-Christian sense of responsibility, which centers around power and control. With us, it is just something you do for the whole. Each individual has a responsibility to live their life as a good human being.[2]

—Larry Sellers (Osage)

Postscript

Points, Pipes, and Powwows

IN SEPTEMBER 2019, WHILE THIS book was in its infancy, I attended a gallery talk by Ioway artist Sydney Pursel and Osage artist Ryan RedCorn at the University of Missouri's Bingham Art Gallery. During the question-and-answer session that followed, the discussion turned toward David Grann's 2017 bestseller *Killers of the Flower Moon*, a book about the Osage oil murders of the 1920s. RedCorn critiqued Grann for his overriding concern with writing about the ways in which Osage people died. RedCorn said, and I am paraphrasing here, "The question should not be 'Tell me how your people died.' It should be 'Tell me how your people survived.'"

Every Memorial Day weekend for the last dozen years, our sundance family has sponsored an intertribal powwow, and for the last five years, I have been the chair of the powwow committee. The For the People Powwow is a small event and a far cry from huge events like the Gathering of Nations Powwow which draws three thousand dancers and singers each year in Albuquerque, New Mexico. There are no high stakes dance contests, and rather than meeting in an indoor stadium, we get together in a spacious metal building on the Jaycee Fairgrounds in Jefferson City, Missouri.

Despite its small size, the event has remained popular with many Indigenous Missourians; regulars expressed genuine sadness during those years when COVID-19 had made it unsafe to gather for the dance. Our powwow attracts flintknappers, who demonstrate the ancient art of creating arrowheads and projectile points. The outer walls of the pavilion are lined with Indigenous vendors selling everything from jewelry to blankets, to t-shirts, to wooden flutes. Members of a nearby county historical society have displayed small dioramas that illustrate ancient scenes of everyday Indigenous life. And then there are the dancers themselves. During the two days of the powwow, dancers of all ages, from toddlers to elders, enter the circle in the colorful regalia that they have lovingly spent countless hours and untold amounts of money preparing. For some dancers, it is an opportunity to wear regalia that has been handed down from generation to generation.

For Indigenous people, powwows—even small ones like ours—serve a number of important social and cultural functions. Powwows offer participants a forum in which to publicly honor veterans and mourn deceased family members. At the same time, they provide a place to introduce children to traditions by including them in the dance circle or to create new kinship ties with others through socializing. Powwows are also events in which Natives can express the traditional virtues of respect and generosity through community giveaways. They provide opportunities for visiting with friends and relatives, for sharing crafts and food, for competing with other singers and dancers, and for simply being Indigenous.

Especially in locations like Missouri, where there are no centralized Native reservations or settlements, intertribal powwows are lifelines that help Indigenous people retain ties to their culture, tribes, and even to their families. In fact, attending a Missouri powwow can be a lot like going to a family reunion. Like most family reunions, there are moments of reminiscing, grieving, and laughing as Indigenous people come together to participate in something that expresses ancient traditions while being entirely contemporary. Above all else, however, powwows are celebrations. While watching dancers circle in their regalia to the beat of the drum, we are called upon to celebrate the ways in which Indigenous people have survived rather than to dwell on the ways in which they died.

While working on this history, I have tried to keep Ryan RedCorn's observations about the survival of Indigenous people foremost in my mind. Throughout the narrative, I have emphasized the various ways in which Natives have met each challenge to their existence with adaptability and resilience. This means that Natives have constantly evolved over the millennia. As we have seen, when faced with a changing environment at the end of the last Ice Age, about 10,900 years ago, Archaic Missourians adapted their large Clovis projectile points to the new conditions by creating smaller, more slender Dalton points that were better suited to the new, smaller types of game they hunted.

Another adaptation was the use of the sacred pipe. Late Woodland and Oneota people learned to use the pipe to help them navigate the peripheries of the hierarchical Cahokian world adopting the best Mississippian innovations while maintaining their own decentralized societies. Through the pipe ceremony, they made relatives, created alliances, and agreed to pacts. The more egalitarian way of forming civic and military relationships helped the Oneota survive and contend with the arrival of Europeans.

And, twentieth century Indigenous Missourians have learned to overcome the challenge of living in a state with no Indigenous population center by creating community through intertribal powwows and ceremonies. In the end, there is every reason to believe that Indigenous vibrancy, resilience, and adaptability will continue.

Notes

Preface

1. "Elinor Fields," *Find a Grave.* https://www.findagrave.com/memorial/257492 84/elinor-fields; "About Us," *Indian Women's Pocahontas Club.* https://www.indian-wpc.org/about-us; Elinor Fields, "Indian News," *Pawnee Chief,* May 17, 1962, 4.

2. Robert K. Sanford, "A Hero to Home Folks," *The Kansas City Star,* May 13, 1962, 1A, 2A; Austin C. Wehrwein, "Thomas Hart Benton Welcomed at Ozark Birthplace," *The New York Times,* May 13, 1962, 1, 87.

3. Reginald Horsman, *Expansion and American Indian Policy, 1783–1812,* 113; "An act to suppress intercourse with Indians," Feb. 9, 1838, *Missouri Session Laws,* 1838, Version 2 (Jefferson City: Calvin Gunn, 1841): 66–67; "An Act to Restrain intercourse with the Indians," Feb. 27, 1845, *Revised Statutes of the State of Missouri,* 1845 (St. Louis: J. W. Dougherty, 1845): 576–77.

4. Paulette F. C. Steeves, *The Indigenous Paleolithic of the Western Hemisphere,* 48.

5. Stephen Aron, *American Confluence: The Missouri Frontier from Borderland to Border State,* 1–2.

6. Colin G. Calloway, *One Vast Winter Count: The Native American West Before Lewis and Clark,* xiii.

7. Damon B. Akins and William J. Bauer Jr., *We are the Land: A History of Native California,* 3.

8. Calloway quoted in *New Books in American Indian Studies,* a podcast hosted by Marshall Poe and produced by the New Books Network, Jun. 15, 2021.

Voices

1. "The Story of the Twelve Boys," is an oral history by Francis (Chibe) Scott and Grover Foster, edited by Henrietta Massey (Sac and Fox) and Sandra Massey (Sac and Fox), 2007. A slightly different version of this story appears in the Missouri Humanities exhibit Homeland: Northeast Missouri and the Sac and Fox Journey Home, 2007, curated by Sandra Massey, Greg Olson, and J. Frederick Fausz.

2. Adapted from John Joseph Mathews (Osage), *The Osages: Children of the Middle Waters,* 8–15.

3. Adapted from Jimm Goodtracks, "Clan Stories: Ioway, Otoe, Missouria Dictionary," *The Ioway, Otoe, Missouria Language Project.* http://www.iowayotoelang.

nativeweb.org/pdf/c_engtobax2008aug18.pdf; In many of the stories Alanson Skinner documented, he has shown that the phrase "that's when I came home," or some variation thereof, is the traditional way Ioway storytellers end their tales. Alanson Skinner, "Traditions of the Iowa Indians," 456, 458.

Chapter One

1. M. F. Ashley Montagu, "An Indian Tradition Relating to the Mastodon," 568–71.

2. Gary Haynes, "How to Kill a Mammoth: The Brutal Art of the Hunt—and an Alternative," 42; Gary Haynes, *The Early Settlement of North America: The Clovis Era*, 186–89, 193.

3. Michael J. O'Brien, *Paradigms of the Past: The Story of Missouri Archaeology*, 77–87; Elmo Ingenthron, *Indians of the Ozark Plateau*, 12.

4. Koch quoted in Gesa Mackenthun, "Albert C. Koch," *Institut für Anglistik/Amerikanistik*, Univerität Rostock. https://www.iaa.uni-rostock.de/forschung/laufende-forschungsprojekte/american-antiquities-prof-mackenthun/project/agents/albert-c-koch/): about page 2; Susan Flader, ed., *Missouri State Parks and Historic Sites: Exploring Our Legacy*, 157.

5. J. M. Adovasio and David Pedler, *Strangers in a New Land: What Archaeology Reveals About the First Americans*, 90; R. Bruce McMillan, "Objects of Curiosity: Albert Koch's 1840 St. Louis Museum," 35–36; Carl H. Chapman and Eleanor F. Chapman, *Indians and Archaeology of Missouri*, 25.

6. Adovasio and Pedler, *Strangers in a New Land*, 7; Jennifer Raff, *Origin: A Genetic History of the Americas*, 189.

7. Brian M. Fagan, *The Great Journey: The Peopling of Ancient America*, 11; Fen Montaigne, "The Fertile Shore," about page 6; Michelle Z. Donahue, "Lost Native American Ancestor Revealed in Ancient Child's DNA"; Craig Childs, *Atlas of a Lost World: Travels in Ice Age America*, xiv, 11, 20; David J. Meltzer, *First People in a New World: Colonizing Ice Age America*, 20; Haynes, *The Early Settlement of North America*, 22; Raff, *Origin*, 181–85.

8. Meltzer, *First Peoples in a New World*, 33, 34; Fagan, *The Great Journey*, 104; Adovasio and Pedler, *Strangers in a New Land*, 19; E. James Dixon, *Bones, Boats and Bison: Archeology and the First Colonization of Western North America*, 19.

9. Vine Deloria, Jr., *Red Earth, White Lies: Native Americans and the Myth of Scientific Fact*, 31; Haynes, *The Early Settlement of North America*, 10.

10. Meltzer, *First Peoples in a New World*, 35; Fagan, *The Great Journey*, 109.

11. Dixon, *Bones, Boats and Bison*, 29; Meltzer, *First Peoples in a New World*, 198.

12. Paulette F. C. Steeves, *The Indigenous Paleolithic of the Western Hemisphere*, xxii, 61–69; also see Thomas D. Dillehay, *The Settlement of the Americas: A New Prehistory*, 2–4.

13. Raff, *Origin: A Genetic History of the Americas*, 191–92; Jennifer Raff, "How People First Arrived in the Americas," *The Book Review*, Mar. 11, 2022, a podcast of *The New York Times*.

14. Todd J. Braje, et al. "Fladmark + 40: What Have We Learned About a Potential Pacific Coast Peopling of the Americas?" 2–5; Montaigne, "The Fertile Shore," about page 1.

15. Braje, et al. "Fladmark + 40," 3; Adovasio and Pedler, *Strangers in a New Land*, 30.

16. Dillehay, *The Settlement of the Americas*, xiv.

17. Abbott quoted in Herbert C. Kraft, "Paleoindians In New Jersey," 264.

18. Michael J. O'Brien, et al., "On Thin Ice: Problems with Stanford and Bradley's Proposed Solutrean Colonisation of North America," 606; Dennis Stanford and Bruce Bradley, "Reply to O'Brien et al.," 614–21; Meltzer, *First Peoples in a New World*, 185–88.

19. O'Brien quoted in University of Missouri-Columbia, "Alternate theory of inhabitation of North America disproven," *ScienceDaily.* www.sciencedaily.com/releases/2015/04/150427145121.htm; O'Brien, et al., "On Thin Ice," 607–9; Metin I. Eren, et al., "The *Cinmar* Discovery and the Proposed Pre-late Glacial Maxim Occupation of North America," 708–13; K. Kris Hirst, "Is There a Solutrean-Clovis Connection in the American Colonization?" 1–2.

20. Bradley quoted in Joseph Brean, "CBC Under Fire for Documentary that Says First Humans to Colonize New World Sailed from Europe," *National Post*, Jan. 12, 2018. https://nationalpost.com/news/canada/cbc-under-fire-for-documentary-that-says-first-humans-to-colonize-new-world-sailed-from-europe; Jennifer Raff, "Rejecting the Solutrean Hypothesis: The First Peoples in the Americas Were not from Europe," *The Guardian*, Feb. 21, 2018. https://www.theguardian.com/science/2018/feb/21/rejecting-the-solutrean-hypothesis-the-first-peoples-in-the-americas-were-not-from-europe.

21. Carl H. Chapman, *The Archaeology of Missouri*, 1: 27; Chapman and Chapman, *Indians and Archaeology of Missouri*, 15–16.

22. Michael J. O'Brien and W. Raymond Wood, *The Prehistory of Missouri*, 72.

23. Chapman, *The Archaeology of Missouri* 1: 26; O'Brien and Wood, *The Prehistory of Missouri*, 39–40; Adovasio and Pedler, *Strangers in a New Land*, 96; Haynes, *The Early Settlement of North America*, 12, 49.

24. Dillehay, *The Settlement of the Americas*, xvi, 27; Steeves, *The Indigenous Paleolithic of the Western Hemisphere*, 12.

25. Brian Fagan, *The First North Americans*, 26; Adovasio and Pedler, *Strangers in a New Land*, 24; Haynes, *The Early Settlement of North America*, xi–xii, 1–3; O'Brien and Wood, *The Prehistory of Missouri*, 55.

26. O'Brien and Wood, *The Prehistory of Missouri*, 45–53, 60–65, 154–55.

27. O'Brien and Wood, *The Prehistory of Missouri*, 60–65; Shepard Krech III, *The Ecological Indian: Myth and Mystery*, 34–36; Haynes, *The Early Settlement of North America*, 31; Dixon, *Bones, Boats and Bison*, 35.

28. O'Brien and Wood, *The Prehistory of Missouri*, 60–65; Dixon, *Bones, Boats and Bison*, 35–37.

29. Dixon, *Bones, Boats and Bison*, 38–40; Nicole M. Waguespack, "The Organization of Male and Female Labor in Foraging Societies: Implications for Early

Paleoindian Archaeology," 671–72; Steeves, *The Indigenous Paleolithic of the Western Hemisphere*, 73–74; For more on the foraging habits of Clovis people, see Haynes, *The Early Settlement of North America*, especially 170–238.

30. Raff, *Origins: A Genetic History of the Americas*, 101–5.

31. Waguespack, "The Organization of Male and Female Labor in Foraging Societies," 667, 671, 673–74; Dixon, *Bones, Boats and Bison*, 23; James Gorman, "Ancient Remains in Peru Reveal Young, Female Big-Game Hunter," *New York Times*, Nov. 4, 2020. https://www.nytimes.com/2020/11/04/science/ancient-female-hunter.html; Ed Whelan, "Discovery of a 9,000-Year-Old Female Hunter in Peru Is Rewriting History," *Ancient Origins*, Nov. 5, 2020. https://www.ancient-origins.net/news-history-archaeology/female-hunter-0014498

32. Some Indigenous scholars have pointed out the problematic nature of the term "Paleoindian." Though it is helpful in distinguishing the Western Hemisphere's first people from the Paleolithic people of Europe, "Indian" perpetuates Christopher Columbus's misidentification of Indigenous people of the Americas as being Asian. Similarly, the term "paleo" refers to a technology used to create stone and bone tools in the Eastern Hemisphere. Steeves, *The Indigenous Paleolithic of the Western Hemisphere*, 102–3.

33. O'Brien and Wood, *The Prehistory of Missouri*, 73–75; Chapman, *The Archaeology of Missouri* 1: 96, 100–102.

34. O'Brien and Wood, *The Prehistory of Missouri*, 89–91; Chapman, *The Archaeology of Missouri* 1: 96–97.

35. O'Brien and Wood, *The Prehistory of Missouri*, 89–90.

36. O'Brien and Wood, *The Prehistory of Missouri*, 102–9; Richard W Yerkes, "The Woodland and Mississippian Traditions in the Prehistory of Midwestern North America," 309–11.

37. O'Brien and Wood, *The Prehistory of Missouri*, 105, 157; Krech, *The Ecological Indian*, 105–6; Chapman, *The Archaeology of Missouri*, 1: 128.

38. O'Brien and Wood, *The Prehistory of Missouri*, 12, 157; Chapman, *The Archaeology of Missouri*, 1: 158–65; Candace Sall, "Shoes Older than the Pyramids."

39. Fagan, *The First North Americans*, 44, 136.

40. Brian Fagan writes that domestic food cultivation among Eastern Woodland people, which would have included those living in eastern portions of Missouri, began sometime after 4,000 years ago. O'Brien and Wood, using what seems to be a definition of plant domestication that is more advanced than what I described here, place the date at some time after 2,500 years ago. Fagan, *The First North Americans*, 128–29, 131; O'Brien and Wood, *The Prehistory of Missouri*, 159, 210–11, 215; Chapman, *The Archaeology of Missouri*, 1: 217, 228.

41. O'Brien and Wood, *The Prehistory of Missouri*, 159; Chapman, *The Archaeology of Missouri*, 1: 184–85, 205; Yerkes, "The Woodland and Mississippian Traditions," 313–14.

42. Gayle J. Fritz, *Feeding Cahokia: Early Agriculture in the North American Heartland*, 11–14, 20–24, 29.

43. O'Brien and Wood, *The Prehistory of Missouri*, 162; Chapman, *The Archaeology of Missouri*, 1: 219; Yerkes, "The Woodland and Mississippian Traditions," 315.

44. James L. Theler and Robert F. Boszhardt, *Twelve Millennia: Archaeology of the Upper Mississippi River Valley*, 97–98; O'Brien and Wood, *The Prehistory of Missouri*, 180–83; Chapman, *The Archaeology of Missouri*, 2: 18–20.

45. Lynn M. Alex, *Iowa's Archaeological Past*, 87–88, 91; O'Brien and Wood, *The Prehistory of Missouri*, 183–86.

46. O'Brien and Wood, *The Prehistory of Missouri*, 188–89; Chapman, *The Archaeology of Missouri*, 2: 24–61; Theler and Boszhardt, *Twelve Millennia*, 110–11.

47. Chapman, *The Archaeology of Missouri*, 2: 4; O'Brien and Wood, *The Prehistory of Missouri*, 209–12.

48. O'Brien and Wood, *The Prehistory of Missouri*, 215–16; Theler and Boszhardt, *Twelve Millennia*, 106; Mark F. Seeman, "Hopewell Art in Hopewell Spaces," in *Hero, Hawk, and Open Hand: American Indian Art of the Ancient Midwest and South*, ed. Richard F. Townsend, 65.

49. Robert L. Hall, *An Archaeology of the Soul: North American Indian Belief and Ritual*, 155.

50. Yerkes, "The Woodland and Mississippian Traditions," 321, 24.

51. O'Brien and Wood, *The Prehistory of Missouri*, 215–18; Theler and Boszhardt, *Twelve Millennia*, 108–9; Chapman, *The Archaeology of Missouri*, 2: 22–23.

52. Chapman, *The Archaeology of Missouri*, 2: 23, 61, 63. 69; Yerkes, "The Woodland and Mississippian Traditions," 321–22.

53. Chapman, *The Archaeology of Missouri*, 2: 21; O'Brien and Wood, *The Prehistory of Missouri*, 217–18.

54. O'Brien and Wood, *The Prehistory of Missouri*, 219.

55. Brooks Blevins, *A History of the Ozarks*, 1: 16–17; Lydia I. Rees and Jamie C. Brandon, "Beyond the 'Bluff Dweller': Excavating the History of an Ozark Myth," 130.

56. Blevins, *A History of the Ozarks*, 1: 17; Ingenthron, *Indians of the Ozark Plateau*, 31–32; Rees and Brandon, "Beyond the 'Bluff Dweller,'" 135–36.

57. *Arkansas: A Guide to the State* quoted in Rees and Brandon, "Beyond the 'Bluff Dweller,'" 137; Ingenthron, *Indians of the Ozark Plateau*, 44; Blevins, *A History of the Ozarks*, 1: 17.

58. Rees and Brandon, "Beyond the 'Bluff Dweller,'" 137–42; O'Brien and Wood's statement, "Trade continued to flourish during the Woodland period, even among groups in the most remote parts the Ozark Highland," seems to be specifically directed at Harrington and Dellinger's Bluff Dweller thesis. O'Brien and Wood, *The Prehistory of Missouri*, 224.

59. Theler and Boszhardt, *Twelve Millennia*, 121; Yerkes, "The Woodland and Mississippian Traditions," 328.

60. Chapman, *The Archaeology of Missouri*, 2: 78, 262–63.

61. O'Brien and Wood, *The Prehistory of Missouri*, 224; Yerkes, "The Woodland and Mississippian Traditions," 329.

62. Dale L. McElrath, et al., "Social Evolution or Social Response?" *in Late Woodland Societies: Tradition and Transformation Across the Midcontinent*, ed. Thomas E. Emerson, et al., 13–21; Gayle Fritz, *Feeding Cahokia*, 59.

63. McElrath, et al., "Social Evolution or Social Response?," 3; O'Brien and Wood, *The Prehistory of Missouri*, 225–26.

Voices

1. Katharine Berry Judson, "Old-Woman-Who-Never-Dies," *Myths and Legends of the Great Plains*, 98–99. Mandan oral tradition is used here because it is one of the best surviving examples of this Mississippian tradition. See Matthew H. Colvin, "Old-Woman-Who-Never-Dies: A Mississippian Survival in The Hidatsa World," 89.

2. Robert Small (Otoe, Wolf Clan), and Julia Small (Otoe), "6. Wankx!istowi, the Man with the Human Head Earrings" in Alanson Skinner, "Traditions of the Iowa Indians," 427–506.

3. Mathews, *The Osages: Children of the Middle Waters*, 450.

Chapter 2

1. Douglas J. Kennett, et al. "Early Isotopic Evidence of Maize as a Staple Grain in the Americas," 1; O'Brien and Wood, *The Prehistory of Missouri*, 231; Roxanne Dunbar-Ortiz, *An Indigenous Peoples' History of the United States*, 16–18; Charles C. Mann, *1491: New Revelations of the Americas Before Columbus*, 194.

2. Timothy R. Pauketat and Susan M. Alt, "Medieval Life in America's Heartland," in *Medieval Mississippians: The Cahokian World*, ed. Timothy R. Pauketat and Susan M. Alt, 3; O'Brien and Wood, *The Prehistory of Missouri*, 231–32; Yerkes, "Woodland and Mississippian Traditions," 330.

3. Amber M. VanDerwarker, "Mississippians and Maize," in *Medieval Mississippians*, ed. Pauketat and Alt, 50–51; Yerkes, "Woodland and Mississippian Traditions," 331; Dale L. McElrath and Andrew C. Fortier, "The Early Late Woodland Occupation of the American Bottom," in *Late Woodland Societies: Tradition and Transformation Across the Midcontinent*, ed. Thomas E. Emerson, et al., 108–9; Jeffrey S. Alvey, "Paleodemographic Modeling in The Lower Mississippi River Valley," 28.

4. Yerkes, "Woodland and Mississippian Traditions," 331–32.

5. Vincas P. Steponaitis, et al., "Cahokia's Coles Creek Predecessors," *Medieval Mississippians, ed. Pauketat and Alt*, 13–15; Pauketat and Alt, "Medieval Life in America's Heartland," 3–5; Timothy R. Pauketat, "The Caddo Conundrum," in *Medieval Mississippians*, ed. Pauketat and Alt, 14.

6. Michael C. Meinkoth, et al., "Late Woodland Archaeology in Missouri," in *Late Woodland Societies*, ed. Emerson, et al., 180, 212–13, 228–29; O'Brien and Wood, *The Prehistory of Missouri*, 61–62, 270–71.

7. Robert L. Reeder, "The Maramec Spring Phase," *Late Woodland Societies*, ed. Emerson, et al. 193–95, 198.

8. Chapman, *Archaeology of Missouri* 2: 139; O'Brien and Wood, *The Prehistory of Missouri*, 265; W. Raymond Wood, et al., *Holocene Human Adaptations in the Missouri Prairie-Timberlands*, 67.

9. O'Brien and Wood, *The Prehistory of Missouri*, 271–74; Meinkoth, "The Late Woodland Period in Northeast Missouri," 242, 254; Alvey, "Paleodemographic Modeling in The Lower Mississippi River Valley," 30.

10. Terrell L. Martin, "Prehistoric Settlement of Western Missouri during the Mississippian Period," 11.

11. Chapman, *Archaeology of Missouri*, 2: 184; Yerkes, "Woodland and Mississippian Traditions," 334.

12. O'Brien and Wood, *The Prehistory of Missouri*, 251–52; Yerkes, "Woodland and Mississippian Traditions," 335–36.

13. Timothy R. Pauketat, *Cahokia: Ancient America's Great City on the Mississippi*, 15–16.

14. Mark W. Leach, *The Great Pyramids of St. Louis: An Ancient Metropolis*, 25; Pauketat, *Cahokia*, 6.

15. Pauketat, *Cahokia*, 21–22.

16. The axis on which Cahokia is laid out is oriented five degrees east of true north. Timothy R. Pauketat, et al., "An American City," in *Medieval Mississippians*, ed. Pauketat and Alt, 24–25; Leach, *The Great Pyramids of St. Louis*, 61; Timothy Schilling, "The Chronology of Monks Mound," 14, 26.

17. Schilling, "The Chronology of Monks Mound," 18–19, 24.

18. Leach, *The Great Pyramids of St. Louis*, 70; Pauketat, *Cahokia*, 73–80; Susan M. Alt, "Human Sacrifice at Cahokia," in *Medieval Mississippians*, ed. Pauketat and Alt,, 27.

19. Pauketat, et al., "An American City," 28–29; Larry Benson, et al., "Cahokia's Boom and Bust in the Context of Climate Change," 468–70; Timothy R. Pauketat, et al., "A Mississippian Conflagration at East. St. Louis and Its Political-Historical Implications," 211; Fritz, *Feeding Cahokia*, 46–47, 87–88.

20. Pauketat, *Cahokia*, 120–23; Fritz, *Feeding Cahokia*, 89.

21. Thomas J. Zych, "The Game of Chunkey," *Medieval Mississippians*, ed. Pauketat and Alt, 71; Pauketat, *Cahokia*, 165–66.

22. Pauketat, *Cahokia*, 62–63; Robert L. Hall, "The Cahokia Site and Its People," *Hero, Hawk, and Open Hand*, ed. Townsend, 96–97.

23. Pauketat, *Cahokia*, 26; Leach, *The Great Pyramids of St. Louis*, 73, 75; Pauketat, et al., "An American City," 22.

24. Pauketat, et al., "A Mississippian Conflagration at East St. Louis and Its Political-Historical Implications," 210, 211, 213; Leach, *The Great Pyramids of St. Louis*, 84–85.

25. Leach, *The Great Pyramids of St. Louis*, 98–101, 109–11, 236–42; Benson, et al., "Cahokia's Boom and Bust in the Context of Climate Change," 472.

26. Duane C. Anderson, "A Long-Nosed God Mask from Northwest Iowa," 327.

27. Pauketat, *Cahokia*, 138: Hall, "The Cahokia Site and Its People," 98; Melissa R. Baltus, "Unraveling Entanglements: Reverberations of Cahokia's Big Bang," in *Tracing the Relational: The Archaeology of Worlds, Spirits, and Temporalities*, ed. Meghan E. Buchanan and B. Jacob Skousen, 149.

28. VanDerwarker, "Mississippians and Maize," 51.

29. VanDerwarker, "Mississippians and Maize," 53.

30. William F. Romain, "Moonwatchers of Cahokia," in *Medieval Mississippians*, ed. Pauketat and Alt, 34–37.

31. Thomas E. Emerson, "The Earth Goddess Cult at Cahokia," in *Medieval Mississippians*, ed. Pauketat and Alt, 58–60.

32. Romain, "Moonwatchers of Cahokia," 38–39; Pauketat, *Cahokia*, 82–84, 102–5.

33. Fritz, *Feeding Cahokia*, 112–13; Fritz quoted in Gerry Everding, "Women shaped cuisine, culture of ancient Cahokia," *Phys.Org*, Mar. 21, 2019. https://phys.org/news/2019-03-women-cuisine-culture-ancient-cahokia.html

34. Emerson, "The Earth Goddess Cult at Cahokia," 57–58; Fritz, *Feeding Cahokia*, 104–5, 109–11; Alvey, "Paleodemographic Modeling in the Lower Mississippi River Valley," 31.

35. F. Kent Reilly III, "People of the Earth, People of the Sky: Visualizing the Sacred in Native American Art of the Mississippian Period," in *Hero, Hawk, and Open Hand*, ed. Townsend, 127; George E. Lankford, "World on a String: Some Cosmological Components of the Southeastern Ceremonial Complex," in *Hero, Hawk, and Open Hand*, ed. Townsend, 208.

36. Reilly, "People of the Earth, People of the Sky," 127–28; David H. Dye, "He-Who-Wears-Human-Heads-As-Earrings: Mississippian Culture Heroes, Reincarnation, and Warfare," 91; B. Jacob Skousen, "Moonbeams, Water, and Smoke: Tracing Otherworldly Relationships at the Emerald Site," in *Tracing the Relational*, ed. Buchanan and Skousen, 47.

37. Dye, "He-Who-Wears-Human-Heads-As-Earrings," 97–98.

38. Hall, *An Archaeology of the Soul*, 148–51.

39. Dye, "He-Who-Wears-Human-Heads-As-Earrings," 93.

40. Carol Diaz-Granados and James R. Duncan, *The Petroglyphs and Pictographs of Missouri*, 208; Pauketat, *Cahokia*, 89–91.

41. Anderson, "A Long-Nosed God Mask from Northwest Iowa," 327; Pauketat, *Cahokia*, 117; Hall, *An Archaeology of the Soul*, 147–48.

42. Hall, *An Archaeology of the Soul*, 151.

43. James R. Duncan and Carol Diaz-Granados, "Of Masks and Myths," 3.

44. Michael Fuller, "Picture Cave 1," *Michael Fuller Rock Art*.

45. Pauketat, *Cahokia*, 109, 128; Fritz, *Feeding Cahokia*, 75–77.

46. Benson, et al., "Cahokia's Boom and Bust in the Context of Climate Change," 472–73, 476; O'Brien and Wood, *The Prehistory of Missouri*, 296; Chapman, *Archaeology of Missouri* 2: 263.

47. Samuel E. Munoz, et al. "Cahokia's Emergence and Decline Coincided with Shifts of Flood Frequency on the Mississippi River," 6319, 6321.

48. Lopinot and Woods quoted in Caitlin G. Rankin, et al., "Evaluating Narratives of Ecocide with the Stratigraphic Record at Cahokia Mounds State Historic Site, Illinois, USA," 378.

49. Asher Elbein, "What Doomed a Sprawling City Near St. Louis 1,000 Years Ago?" *The New York Times*, Apr. 24, 2021. (updated May 3, 2021); Caitlin Gail

Rankin, "Testing Assumptions on the Relationship between Humans and their Environment: Case Studies from Cahokia Mounds, Illinois."

50. Munoz, et al., "Cahokia's Emergence and Decline Coincided with Shifts of Flood Frequency on the Mississippi River," 6322; Alvey, "Paleodemographic Modeling in The Lower Mississippi River Valley," 56.

51. Benson, et al., "Cahokia's Boom and Bust in the Context of Climate Change," 473; VanDerwarker, "Mississippians and Maize," 53; Pauketat, et al., "A Mississippian Conflagration at East St. Louis and Its Political-Historical Implications," 218–19; Greg D. Wilson, "Incinerated Villages in the North," in *Medieval Mississippians*, ed. Pauketat and Alt, 99.

52. Hall, "The Cahokia Site and Its People," 98.

53. Annalee Newitz, *Four Lost Cities: A Secret History of the Urban Age*, 240, 250–251; Rankin quoted in Elbein, "What Doomed a Sprawling City Near St. Louis 1,000 Years Ago?"

54. Henning quoted in Martin, "Prehistoric Settlement of Western Missouri during the Mississippian Period," 10; Pauketat and Alt, "Medieval Life in America's Heartland," 1.

55. Pauketat, *Cahokia*,, 124–25; Hall, "The Cahokia Site and Its People," 100–101.

56. Louis F. Burns, *A History of the Osage People*, 3–7.

57. Michael Dickey, *The People of the River's Mouth: In Search of the Missouria Indians*, 4, 13–14; Jacob F. Lee, *Masters of the Middle Waters: Indian Nations and Colonial Ambitions along the Mississippi*, 27–29; Carl Waldman, *Encyclopedia of Native American Tribes*, 166; Hall, "The Cahokia Site and Its People," 100–101.

58. Andrea A. Hunter, "Ancestral Osage Geography," in Andrea A. Hunter, James Munkres, and Barker Fariss, *Osage Nation NAGPRA Claim for Human Remains Removed from the Clarksville Mound Group (23PI6), Pike County, Missouri* (Pawhuska, OK: Osage Nation Historic Preservation Office, 2013). https://www.osagenation-nsn.gov/who-we-are/historic-preservation/osage-cultural-history, 1–2; Hall, "The Cahokia Site and Its People," 102.

59. O'Brien and Wood, *The Prehistory of Missouri*, 347–48.

60. Burns writes that the Osages were part of what he labels the Mississippian phase of Woodland culture. From his discussion, it seems that he is referring to what we now call Mississippians. Burns, *A History of the Osage People*, 6–10.

61. Hunter, "Ancestral Osage Geography," 1–2; Shannon Shaw Duty, "National NAGPRA Review Confirms Osages Were Part of Mound Culture," *Osage News*, Dec. 4, 2015. osagenews.orgnatl-nagpra-review-committee-confirms-osages-were-part-mound-culture

62. Francis La Flesche, *The Osage and the Invisible World*, 3.

63. Alice Beck Kehoe, "Osage Texts and Cahokia Data," in *Ancient Objects and Sacred Realms: Interpretation of Mississippian Iconography*, ed. Kent Reilly III and James F. Garber, 260.

64. Pauketat, *Cahokia*, 38.

65. O'Brien and Wood, *The Prehistory of Missouri*, 288–91, 295; Charles H. McNutt, "The Central Mississippi Valley: A Summary," in *Prehistory of the Central*

Mississippi Valley, ed. Charles H. McNutt, 231, 232; Flader, ed., *Missouri State Parks and Historic Sites*, 221; Robert H. Lafferty III and James E. Price, "Southeast Missouri," in *Prehistory of the Central Mississippi Valley*, ed. McNutt, 13.

66. Michael J. O'Brien, *Cat Monsters and Head Pots: The Archaeology of Missouri's Pemiscot Bayou*, 115, 139, 349.

67. Stephen Williams, "The Vacant Quarter and Other Late Events in the Lower Valley," in *Towns and Temples Along the Mississippi*, ed., David H. Dye and Cheryl Anne Cox, 170-80; Michael J. O'Brien, *Cat Monsters and Head Pots*, 17–19; O'Brien and Wood, *The Prehistory of Missouri*, 331, 343–44; "The New Madrid Seismic Zone," *United States Geological Survey*, https://www.usgs.gov/natural-hazards/earthquake-hazards/science/new-madrid-seismic-zone?qt-science_center_objects=0#qt-science_center_objects.

68. O'Brien, *Cat Monsters and Head Pots*, 345–47, 349.

69. Theler and Boszhardt, *Twelve Millennia*, 157.

70. Benn quoted in Lance M. Foster, "Sacred Bundles of the Ioway Indians," 15; Alex, *Iowa's Archaeological Past*, 185; O'Brien and Wood, *The Prehistory of Missouri*, 352; Hall, *An Archaeology of the Soul*, 152.

71. James L Theler and Robert F. Boszhardt, "Collapse of Crucial Resources and Culture Change: A Model for the Woodland to Oneota Transformation in the Upper Midwest," 443–45.

72. R. Eric Hollinger, "Conflict and Culture Change on the Plains: The Oneota Example," in *Archaeological Perspectives on Warfare on the Great Plains*, ed. Andrew J. Clark and Douglas B. Bamforth, 270–73.

73. Thomas Edward Berres, *Power and Gender in Oneota Culture: A Study of a Late Prehistoric People*, 16.

74. Berres, *Power and Gender in Oneota Culture*, 8; Foster, *Sacred Bundles of the Ioway Indians*, 12; O'Brien and Wood, *The Prehistory of Missouri*, 350.

75. Hall, *An Archaeology of the Soul*, 52–53, 77–81, 151–53; Richard L. Fishel, et al., "Sourcing Red Pipestone Artifacts from Oneota Villages in the Little Sioux Valley of Northwest Iowa," 170.

76. Berres, *Power and Gender in Oneota Culture*, 27–29.

77. Hollinger, "Conflict and Culture Change on the Plains," 269–72; Berres, *Power and Gender in Oneota Culture*, 46.

78. Berres, *Power and Gender in Oneota Culture*, 29–30.

79. Brewton Berry and Carl Chapman, "An Oneota Site in Missouri," 290–92, 295; O'Brien and Wood, *The Prehistory of Missouri*, 349–54; Chapman and Chapman, *Indians and Archaeology in Missouri*, 90–96.

80. W. Raymond Wood, "Culture Sequence at the Old Fort, Saline County, Missouri," 102, 110–11.

81. Michael E. Ruppert, "Archaeological Excavations at the King Hill Site (23BN1) Buchanan County, Missouri"; O'Brien and Wood, *The Prehistory of Missouri*, 355–356.

82. Waldo R. Wedel, *Prehistoric Man on the Great Plains*, 117–20; Lauren W. Ritterbush, "The Leary Site Revisited: Oneota and Central Plains Tradition Occupation

along the Lower Missouri," 262; Richard L. Fishel, "Dixon to Leary to White Rock: A Hypothesis for Oneota 14th Century Communal Bison Hunts," 1.

83. O'Brien and Wood, *The Prehistory of Missouri*, 356; Hollinger, "Conflict and Culture Change on the Plains," 73.

Voices

1. Paul Radin, ed., "How the Winnebago First Came into Contact with the French and the Origin of the Decora Family," in F. W. Hodge, *Thirty-Seventh Annual Report of the Bureau of American Ethnology, 1915–1916*, 67.

2. Mathews, *The Osages*, 98–99.

3. Louis F. Burns, *A History of the Osage People*, 95.

Chapter Three

1. Steven T. Newcomb, *Pagans in the Promised Land: Decoding the Doctrine of Christian Discovery*, xxv.

2. Dunbar-Ortiz, *An Indigenous Peoples' History of the United States*, 32–34.

3. Robert J. Miller, et al., *Discovering Indigenous Lands: The Doctrine of Discovery in the English Colonies*, 3–4.

4. Francis Paul Prucha, *American Indian Treaties: The History of a Political Anomaly*, 227.

5. Newcomb, *Pagans in the Promised Land*, 38.

6. Dunbar-Ortiz, *An Indigenous Peoples' History of the United States*, 32–33; Patrick Wolfe, "Settler Colonialism and the Elimination of the Native," 390–91.

7. Miller, et al., *Discovering Indigenous Lands*, 9–13.

8. Miller, et al., *Discovering Indigenous Lands*, 12–13.

9. Miller, et al., *Discovering Indigenous Lands*, 18–21.

10. Kathleen DuVal, *The Native Ground: Indians and Colonists in the Heart of the Continent*, 47–54, 55; Louise Barry, *The Beginning of the West: Annals of the Kansas Gateway to the American West, 1540–1854*, 1–2.

11. Mann, *1491: New Revelations of the Americas Before Columbus*, 96.

12. DuVal, *The Native Ground*, 55; Robbie Ethridge, *From Chicaza to Chickasaw: The European Invasion and the Transformation of the Mississippian World, 1540–1715*, 60.

13. DuVal, *The Native Ground*, 35–41; Ethridge, *From Chicaza to Chickasaw*, 119–23; O'Brien and Wood, *The Prehistory of Missouri*, 295, 334, 335.

14. Ethridge, *From Chicaza to Chickasaw*, 60–61; DuVal, *The Native Ground*, 58–59.

15. Lee, *Masters of the Middle Waters*, 15.

16. Carl J. Ekberg, *Stealing Indian Women: Native Slavery in the Illinois Country*, 1; William E. Foley, *A History of Missouri: 1673 to 1820*, 1: 2; A. P. Nasatir, *Before Lewis and Clark: Documents Illustrating the History of the Missouri, 1785–1804*, 1: 1.

17. Lee, *Masters of the Middle Waters*, 257n45; Anton Treuer, *Atlas of Indian Nations*, 161.

18. Lee, *Masters of the Middle Waters*, 34–45; Martha Royce Blaine, *The Ioway Indians*, 26; Burns, *A History of the Osage People*, 9–10.

19. Hall, *An Archaeology of the Soul*, 5, 6–7, 152.

20. Ekberg, *Stealing Indian Women*, 1.

21. Hall, *An Archaeology of the Soul*, 6–7; Lee, *Masters of the Middle Waters*, 17.

22. DuVal, *The Native Ground*, 3, 64; Dates for the Dhegihan migration down the Ohio River vary widely. Anton Treuer places the date at about the year 1200. Treuer, *Atlas of Indian Nations*, 161; Osage historian Andrea Hunter places the date of migration much earlier, between 500 and 900. See Hunter, "Ancestral Osage Geography," in Leach, *The Great Pyramids of St. Louis*, 226.

23. Hall, *An Archaeology of the Soul*, 7.

24. Morris S. Arnold, *The Rumble of a Distant Drum: The Quapaws and Old World Newcomers, 1673–1804*, 1–4; DuVal, *The Native Ground*, 1–2; Ethridge, *From Chicaza to Chickasaw*, 127.

25. Ethridge, *From Chicaza to Chickasaw*, 73–75; Arrell M. Gibson, *The Chickasaws*, 4.

26. Chapman and Chapman, *Indians and Archaeology of Missouri*, 99–102; Stephen Aron, *American Confluence: The Missouri Frontier from Borderland to Border State*, 23; Burns, *A History of the Osage People*, 46–49; Lee, *Masters of the Middle Waters*, 165–66.

27. William E. Foley, *The Genesis of Missouri: From Wilderness Outpost to Statehood*, 4–5; Father Zenobius Membré, "Narrative of the Adventures of La Salle's Party at Fort Crevecoeur, In Illinois," in *Discovery and Exploration of the Mississippi Valley*, ed. John Gilmary Shea, 150–51.

28. Membré, "Narrative of the Adventures of La Salle's Party at Fort Crevecoeur, In Illinois," 150–51; Greg Olson, *The Ioway in Missouri*, 18–20.

29. Willard H. Rollings, *The Osage: An Ethnohistorical Study of Hegemony on the Prairie-Plains*, 82.

30. Lee, *Masters of the Middle Waters*, 55–56; Carl Waldman, *Encyclopedia of Native American Tribes*, 113.

31. Father Zenobius Membré, "Narrative of La Salle's Voyage down the Mississippi," *Discovery and Exploration of the Mississippi Valley*, ed. Shea, 167.

32. Membré, "Narrative of La Salle's Voyage down the Mississippi," 167–68.

33. Membré, "Narrative of La Salle's Voyage down the Mississippi," 169.

34. DuVal, *The Native Ground*, 91; Membré, "Narrative of La Salle's Voyage down the Mississippi," 169–70.

35. Membré, "Narrative of La Salle's Voyage down the Mississippi," 173; Foley, *The Genesis of Missouri*, 5; Miller, et al., *Discovering Indigenous Lands*, 7.

36. DuVal, *The Native Ground*, 5, 101.

37. DuVal, *The Native Ground*, 76–77; Arnold, *The Rumble of a Distant Drum*, xix, 15; Ekberg, *Stealing Indian Women*, 2.

38. M. J. Morgan, *Land of Big Rivers: French and Indian Illinois, 1699–1778*, 52, 55–56; Carl J. Ekberg, *French Roots in the Illinois Country: The Mississippi Frontier in Colonial Times*, 54–55.

39. Ekberg, *Stealing Indian Women*, 31; Eckberg, *French Roots in the Illinois Country*, 153–54.

40. Lee, *Masters of the Middle Waters*, 62–63; Tanis C. Thorne, *The Many Hands of My Relations: French and Indians in the Lower Missouri*, 65–67.

41. Ekberg, *Stealing Indian Women*, 24, 26; Lee, *Masters of the Middle Waters*, 51; Thorne, *The Many Hands of My Relations*, 65; Robert Michael Morrissey, *Empire by Collaboration: Indians, Colonists, and Governments in Colonial Illinois Country*, 97.

42. Morrissey, *Empire by Collaboration*, 9, 156.

43. Lee, *Masters of the Middle Waters*, 73; Bonnie Stepenoff, "Conflict and Conversion: The Jesuit Mission on Missouri's River Des Peres," 242.

44. Stepenoff, "Conflict and Conversion," 237–38; Ekberg, *Stealing Indian Women*, 37–38; Lee, *Masters of the Middle Waters*, 49–50; Willard Hughes Rollings, *Unaffected by the Gospel: Osage Resistance to the Christian Invasion, 1763–1906: A Cultural Victory*, 154–55.

45. Ekberg, *Stealing Indian Women*, 38–39; Lee, *Masters of the Middle Waters*, 81; Stepenoff, "Conflict and Conversion," 244.

46. Morgan, *Land of Big Rivers*, 70–75; Lee, *Masters of the Middle Waters*, 80, 137–141; Ekberg, *French Roots in the Illinois Country*, 34–35, 37.

47. Lee, *Masters of the Middle Waters*, 80–81.

48. Dickey, *The People of the River's Mouth*, 63; John Joseph Mathews, *The Osages: Children of the Middle Waters*, 169.

49. Frank Norall, *Bourgmont: Explorer of the Missouri, 1698–1725*, 7–12; Burns, *A History of the Osage People*, 96; Mathews, *The Osages*, 168.

50. Chapman and Chapman, *Indians and Archaeology of Missouri*, 99–101.

51. Chapman and Chapman, *Indians and Archaeology of Missouri*, 101; Blaine, *The Ioway Indians*, 20; Norall, *Bourgmont*, 17.

52. Norall, *Bourgmont*, 19–21.

53. Norall, *Bourgmont*, 25–47; Foley, *The Genesis of Missouri*, 20–21.

54. Rollings, *The Osage*, 116–17; Carl J. Ekberg and Sharon K Person, *St. Louis Rising: The French Regime of Louis St. Ange De Bellerive*, 20.

55. Norall, *Bourgmont*, 49; Mathews, *The Osages*, 168, 197.

56. Dickey, *The People of the River's Mouth*, 70–71; Rollings, *The Osages*, 117; Ekberg and Person, *St. Louis Rising*, 20.

57. Ekberg, *Stealing Indian Women*, 39–42, 48, Dickey, *The People of the River's Mouth*, 70–72; Norall, *Bourgmont*, 88; Ekberg and Person, *St. Louis Rising*, 147.

58. Dickey, *The People of the River's Mouth*, 73–74; Norall, *Bourgmont*, 53–60; Mathews, *The Osages*, 196–202; O'Brien and Wood, *The Prehistory of Missouri*, 355.

59. Norall, *Bourgmont*, 81.

60. Norall, *Bourgmont*, 83–87; Dickey, *The People of the River's Mouth*, 75–76.

61. Norall, *Bourgmont*, 87–88; Dickey, *The People of the River's Mouth*, 76–78: Mathews, *The Osages*, 210.

62. Ekberg and Person, *St. Louis Rising*, 25.

63. Foley, *The Genesis of Missouri*, 23–24; Dickey, *The People of the River's Mouth*, 62, 78–80.

64. Rollings, *The Osage*, 113–15.

65. Mathews, *The Osages*, 208–9; Burns, *A History of the Osage People*, 97; Dickey, *The People of the River's Mouth*, 61–62; Rollings, *The Osage*, 115–16.

66. Dickey, *The People of the River's Mouth*, 82; Foley, *The Genesis of Missouri*, 23–24; Mathews, *The Osages*, 217–18; Lee, *Masters of the Middle Waters*, 78–79.

67. Mathews, *The Osages*, 218–19; Dickey, *The People of the River's Mouth*, 82.

68. Lee, *Masters of the Middle Waters*, 111.

69. Lee, *Masters of the Middle Waters*, 99–100, 120;. Gibson, *The Chickasaws*, 37–39.

70. Gibson, *The Chickasaws*, 40–41; Ethridge, *From Chicaza to Chickasaw*, 67–68.

71. Nasatir, *Before Lewis and Clark*, 1: 43–45; Lee, *Masters of the Middle Waters*, 109; Morgan, *Land of Big Rivers*, 130–31.

72. Morrissey, *Empire by Collaboration*, 5, 8.

Voices

1. Headmen of the Osages and Missourias speaking to Louis St. Ange de Bellerive and John Ross at Fort Chartres, April 7, 1765, in Clarence Walworth Alvord and Clarence Edwin Carter, eds., *The Critical Period, 1763–1765*, 479–80.

2. Pacanne, a Miami headman, speaking to Louis Lorimier, Aug. 26, 1794, in Louis Houck, ed., *The Spanish Regime in Missouri*, 2: 95–96.

3. Louis F. Burns, *A History of the Osage People*, 88–89.

Chapter Four

1. William E. Foley and C. David Rice, *The First Chouteaus: River Barons of Early St. Louis*, 5–6; Lee, *Masters of the Middle Waters*, 142; Dickey, *The People of the River's Mouth*, 85–88.

2. Patricia Cleary, *The World, the Flesh, and the Devil*, 43–48; Dickey, *The People of the River's Mouth*, 87–88.

3. Lee, *Masters of the Middle Waters*, 118–20; Foley, *The Genesis of Missouri*, 25–26.

4. Foley and Rice, *The First Chouteaus*, 7.

5. Cleary, *The World, the Flesh, and the Devil*, 50; DuVal, *The Native Ground*, 121; Cleary, "Fashioning Identities on the Frontier: Clothing, Culture, and Choice in Early St. Louis," in *French St. Louis: Landscape, Contexts, and Legacy*, ed. Jay Gitlin, Robert Michael Morrissey, and Peter J. Kastor, 114; J. Frederick Fausz, "The Capital of St. Louis: From Indian Trade to American Territory, 1764–1825," in *French St. Louis*, ed. Gitlin, et al., 72; J. Frederick Fausz, *Founding St. Louis: First City of the New West*, 108.

6. Cleary, *The World, the Flesh, and the Devil*, 37; Bonnie Stepenoff, "Conflict and Conversion," 235–48; Ekberg and Person, *St. Louis Rising*, 228, 250; Ekberg, *Stealing Indian Women*, 64–65; Thorne, *The Many Hands of My Relations*, 72.

7. Cleary, *The World, the Flesh, and the Devil*, 59; Lee, *Masters of the Middle Waters*, 132–33.

8. Cleary, *The World, the Flesh, and the Devil*, 60; Burns, *A History of the Osage People*, 101; Gilbert C. Din and Abraham P. Nasatir. *The Imperial Osages: Spanish-Indian Diplomacy in the Mississippi Valley*, 54–55.

9. Cleary, *The World, the Flesh, and the Devil*, 62–63.

10. Cleary, *The World, the Flesh, and the Devil*, 63.

11. DuVal, *The Native Ground*, 95; Cleary, *The World, the Flesh, and the Devil*, 63; Foley, *The Genesis of Missouri*, 29; Lee, *Masters of the Middle Waters*, 161–62; Foley and Rice, *The First Chouteaus*, 7–8.

12. Foley, *The Genesis of Missouri*, 29–33; Cleary, *The World, the Flesh, and the Devil*, 73–75; Lee, *Masters of the Middle Waters*, 162; Dickey, *The People of the River's Mouth*, 90–91; Nasatir, *Before Lewis and Clark*, 1: 65.

13. Burns, *A History of the Osage People*, 102; Foley, *The Genesis of Missouri*, 32–33; Newcomb, *Pagans in the Promised Land*, 35.

14. Mathews, *The Osages*, 237; Burns, *A History of the Osage People*, 103; Blaine, *The Ioway Indians*, 55–56; Aron, *American Confluence*, 59.

15. Cleary, *The World, the Flesh, and the Devil*, 97–99; Foley and Rice, *The First Chouteaus*, 14; Foley, *The Genesis of Missouri*, 33.

16. Blaine, *The Ioway Indians*, 50–52; Foley, *The Genesis of Missouri*, 33.

17. Dickey, *The People of the River's Mouth*, 89–91.

18. Aron, *American Confluence*, 60.

19. Dickey, *The People of the River's Mouth*, 89–91; Aron, *American Confluence*, 61; Cleary, *The World, the Flesh, and the Devil*, 123: Din and Nasatir. *The Imperial Osages*, 79–81.

20. Dickey, *The People of the River's Mouth*, 92–93; Cleary, *The World, the Flesh, and the Devil*, 124; Foley, *The Genesis of Missouri*, 39.

21. Burns, *A History of the Osage People*, 106–7; Tai S. Edwards, *Osage Women and Empire: Gender and Power*, 46; Cleary, *The World, the Flesh, and the Devil*, 125–28; Foley, *The Genesis of Missouri*, 39–40.

22. Foley and Rice, *The First Chouteaus*, 20; Mathews, *The Osages*, 238.

23. Thorne, *The Many Hands of My Relations*, 78.

24. Lee, *Masters of the Middle Waters*, 171; Edwards, *Osage Women and Empire*, 57–58.

25. Thorne, *The Many Hands of My Relations*, 86–87, 94–95; Burns, *A History of the Osage People*, 64, 66; Lee, *Masters of the Middle Waters*, 187; Edwards, *Osage Women and Empire*, 58.

26. Rollings, *The Osage*, 179–80; Edwards, *Osage Women and Empire*, 41.

27. Edwards, *Osage Women and Empire*, 39–42.

28. Mathews, *The Osages*, 238–240.

29. Edwards, *Osage Women and Empire*, 39–41.

30. DuVal, *The Native Ground*, 103; Edwards, *Osage Women and Empire*, 39–41; Rollings, *Unaffected by the Gospel*, 28–31; Burns, *A History of the Osage People*, 112; Rollings, *The Osage*, 180–81.

31. Rollings, *Unaffected by the Gospel*, 31.

32. John Grenier, *The First Way of War: American War Making on the Frontier*, 1, 153–55.

33. Sarah Haskins, "The Shawnee and Delaware Indians in Early Missouri, 1787–1832," 10, 27; Sami Lakomäki, *Gathering Together: The Shawnee People through the Diaspora and Nationhood, 1600–1870*, 165; Foley and Rice, *The First Chouteaus*, 48.

34. Rollings, *The Osage*, 185–186; John P. Bowes, "American Indian Removal Beyond the Removal Act," 68–69.

35. Haskins, "The Shawnee and Delaware Indians in Early Missouri," 56; Edwards, *Osage Women and Empire*, 61–62; Burns, *A History of the Osage People*, 115–18; Rollings, *The Osage*, 180.

36. Burns, *A History of the Osage People*, 118–21; Mathews, *The Osages*, 265: Din and Nasatir, *The Imperial Osages*, 240–42.

37. Burns, *A History of the Osage People*, 120.

38. Burns, *A History of the Osage People*, 121–27; Mathews, *The Osages*, 279–80; Lee, *Masters of the Middle Waters*, 182; Foley, *The Genesis of Missouri*, 69.

39. Dickey, *People of the River's Mouth*, 104–11: Mathews, *The Osages*, 252, 350; Aron, *American Confluence*, 91–92; Jean-Baptiste Truteau, *A Fur Trader on the Upper Missouri; The Journal and Description of Jean-Baptiste Truteau, 1794–1796*, ed. Raymond J. DeMallie, et al., 79.

40. Foley, *The Genesis of Missouri*, 67–68.

41. Mathews, *The Osages*, 283; Lee, *Masters of the Middle Waters*, 184–86; Foley and Rice, *The First Chouteaus*, 52–54; Din and Nasatir, *The Imperial Osages*, 255–61.

42. Burns, *A History of the Osage People*, 128.

43. Lee, *Masters of the Middle Waters*, 185–87; Burns, *A History of the Osage People*, 130; Rollings, *The Osage*, 181, 193, 199–201.

44. Burns, *A History of the Osage People*, 128; Lee, *Masters of the Middle Waters*, 187–89: Foley and Rice, *The First Chouteaus*, 55; Rollings, *The Osage*, 199; Jon D. May, "Claremore," *The Encyclopedia of Oklahoma History and Culture*, Oklahoma Historical Society.

45. Lee, *Masters of the Middle Waters*, 184–85; Stan Hoig, *The Chouteaus: First Family of the Fur Trade*, 21; Foley and Rice, *The First Chouteaus*, 52–54; Lieutenant Governor Zenon Trudeau to Governor Francisco Luis Hector, the Baron de Carondelet, Apr. 18, 1795, in Nasatir, *Before Lewis and Clark*, 1: 320.

46. Burns, *A History of the Osage People*, 129; Lee, *Masters of the Middle Waters*, 185; Carl H. Chapman, "Indomitable Osage In the Spanish Illinois (Upper Louisiana), 1763–1804," in *The Spanish in the Mississippi Valley, 1762–1804*, ed. John Francis McDermott, 301–3.

47. Hoig, *The Chouteaus*, 23.

48. Trudeau to Carondelet, Aug. 30, 1795, in Nasatir, *Before Lewis and Clark*, 1: 346; Mathews, *The Osages*, 286; Foley and Rice, *The First Chouteaus*, 55, 56.

49. Cleary, *The World, the Flesh, and the Devil*, 298.

50. Lieutenant Governor Delassus to Governor Casa Calvo, Sep. 25, 1800, in *The Spanish Regime in Missouri*, ed. Louis Houck, 2: 301–2; Cleary, *The World, the Flesh, and the Devil*, 298–99; Foley and Rice, *The First Chouteaus*, 59–60.

51. Houck, *The Spanish Regime in Missouri*, 2: 304.

52. Houck assumed the Indigenous nation which Delassus listed as the "Avenakis" to be the Abenakis. Houck, *The Spanish Regime in Missouri*, 2: 305–306; Governor Casa Calvo to Don Ramon de Lopez y Angulo, May 8, 1801, in Houck, *The Spanish Regime in Missouri*, 2: 310–11; Din and Nasatir, *The Imperial Osages*, 325.

53. Houck, *The Spanish Regime in Missouri*, 2: 306; Casa Calva to Delassus, Dec. 30, 1800, in Nasatir, *Before Lewis and Clark*, 2: 628.

54. "A Memorial by Lisa and Others to the Governor," Oct. 8, 1801, in Nasatir, *Before Lewis and Clark*, 2: 647; Richard Edward Oglesby, *Manuel Lisa and the Opening of the Missouri Fur Trade*, 18–21.

55. Delassus to Casa Calvo, Oct. 7, 1801, in Nasatir, *Before Lewis and Clark*, 2: 642, 656, 660; Oglesby, *Manuel Lisa*, 21.

56. "Lisa and Others to Salcedo," Jun. 4, 1802, in Nasatir, *Before Lewis and Clark*, 2: 679; Oglesby, *Manuel Lisa*, 22–23; Foley and Rice, *The First Chouteaus*, 61–62; Din and Nasatir, *The Imperial Osages*, 332–36.

57. "Concession by Salcedo to Lisa and Others," Jun. 12, 1802, in Nasatir, *Before Lewis and Clark*, 2: 687–89; Oglesby, *Manuel Lisa*, 24–25; Foley and Rice, *The First Chouteaus*, 62–63.

58. Chapman, "The Indomitable Osage," 307–8; Burns, *A History of the Osage People*, 128.

59. Burns, *A History of the Osage People*, 128; Aron, *American Confluence*, 106–7; Foley and Rice, *The First Chouteaus*, 87–88.

Voices

1. Blackhawk (Fox headman), to Colonel Abraham Eustis, 1833. Alexander Francis Chamberlain, *Wisdom of the North American Indian in Speech and Legend*, 4.

2. Little Turtle (Miami headman), 1793, in Chamberlain, *Wisdom of the North American Indian*, 5.

3. Tecumseh (Shawnee headman), in a message to President James Madison, 1810, in Chamberlain, *Wisdom of the North American Indian*, 5.

4. Mad Bear (Osage) to Missionary William Montgomery when reminded that the Osages had executed a treaty in writing with the US, Aug. 6, 1833, "Extracts from the Journal of Mr. Montgomery," 23.

5. Unidentified Osage, as recorded by William Montgomery, *"Extracts from the Journal of Mr. Montgomery,"* 23.

Chapter Five

1. Burns, *A History of the Osage People*, 133, 139; Mathews, *The Osages*, 354.

2. Blaine, *The Ioway Indians*, 80–81; William T. Hagan, *The Sac and Fox Indians*, 18–19; Cleary, *The World, the Flesh, and the Devil*, 317–18.

3. Blaine, *The Ioway Indians*, 80–81.

4. Stephen Huggins, *America's Use of Terror from Colonial Times to the A-Bomb*, 56–57; Grenier, *The First Way of War*, 198–202.

5. Cleary, *The World, the Flesh, and the Devil*, 319; William E. Foley, *Wilderness Journey: The Life of William Clark*, 64–65.

6. Foley, *The Genesis of Missouri*, 131–33; Peter J. Kastor, *The Great Acquisition: An Introduction to the Louisiana Purchase*, 44–46, 61–65.

7. Foley, *The Genesis of Missouri*, 134–35; Kastor, *The Great Acquisition*, 66–67.

8. Lee, *Masters of the Middle Waters*, 196–97.

9. Colin G. Calloway, *Pen and Ink Witchcraft: Treaties and Treaty Making in American Indian History*, 5; Robert Lee, "Accounting for Conquest: The Price of the Louisiana Purchase of Indian Country," 921.

10. Martin Case, *The Relentless Business of Treaties: How Indigenous Land Became U.S. Property*, 42–44.

11. Even before the Louisiana Purchase, the Louisiana Territory had been divided into two districts for administrative purposes. These were Upper Louisiana (la Haute-Louisiane), which included everything north of the Arkansas River, and Lower Louisiana (la Basse-Louisiane). Foley, *The Genesis of Missouri*, 135–36.

12. Prucha, *American Indian Treaties*, 41.

13. Prucha, *American Indian Treaties*, 1, 41, 230–31; Miller, et al., *Discovering Indigenous Lands*, 44.

14. Julius Wilm, *Settlers and Conquerors: Free Land Policy in Antebellum America*, 19–20; Wolfe, "Settler Colonialism and the Elimination of the Native," 388; Lee, *Masters of the Middle Waters*, 196.

15. Grenier, *The First Way of War*, 1; Dunbar-Ortiz, *An Indigenous Peoples' History of the United States*, 57–58.

16. Dunbar-Ortiz, *An Indigenous Peoples' History of the United States*, 2–7; Grenier, *The First Way of War*, 198–202.

17. Mathews, *The Osages*, 383; Dunbar-Ortiz, *An Indigenous Peoples' History of the United States*, 51–54; Schoolcraft quoted in Foley, *The Genesis of Missouri*, 242–43; James G. Leyburn, *The Scotch-Irish: A Social History*, 213–32.

18. Burns, *A History of the Osage People*, 134.

19. "Annual Report of G. C. Snow, Agent Neosho Agency," *Annual Report of the Commissioner of Indian Affairs, 1868*, 271–72.

20. Jefferson quoted in Burns, *A History of the Osage People*, 140.

21. Burns, *A History of the Osage People*, 141; Rollings, *The Osage*, 203–4.

22. Martin Case, et al., "William Henry Harrison," *Treaty Signers Project*.

23. Timothy James McCollum, "Sac and Fox," *The Encyclopedia of Oklahoma History* Oklahoma; "The Meskwaki Nation's History," *Meskwaki Nation*. https://www.meskwaki.org/history/

24. Robert M. Owens, *Mr. Jefferson's Hammer: William Henry Harrison and the Origins of American Indian Policy*, 87; Hagan, *The Sac and Fox Indians*, 18–21.

25. While Robert Owens claims that by this time "Harrison was making sincere efforts to keep alcohol away from his treaty councils," and that its use "did not fit the general's modus operandi," Colin Calloway and Martin Case, among others, tend to believe alcohol was involved in the negotiations. Owens, *Mr. Jefferson's Hammer*, 90; Case, *The Relentless Business of Treaties*, 42–44; Calloway, *Pen and Ink Witchcraft*, 115–16; Foley, *A History of Missouri, 1673 to 1820*, 1: 87–91.

26. Hagan, *The Sac and Fox Indians*, 21: Rollings, *The Osage*, 180; Burns, *A History of the Osage People*, 48.

27. Black Hawk, *Autobiography of Ma-Ka-Tai-Me-She-Kia-Kiak, or Black Hawk*, 89. According to Hagan, the Sac and Fox prisoner was shot later during an attempt to escape from prison. He had been granted a pardon from President Jefferson in February 1805 but had not yet received it at the time he was killed. Hagan, *The Sac and Fox Indians*, 22; Owens, *Mr. Jefferson's Hammer*, 91.

28. Burns, *A History of the Osage People*, 152.

29. "Treaty with the Sauks and Foxes, 1804," Charles J. Kappler, *Indian Affairs: Laws and Treaties*, 2: 74–76.

30. "Treaty with the Sauks and Foxes, 1822," Kappler, *Indian Affairs*, 2: 202.

31. "Treaty with the Sauks and Foxes, 1804," Kappler, *Indian Affairs*, 2: 75.

32. "Treaty with the Sauks and Foxes, 1804," Kappler, *Indian Affairs*, 2: 77; Case, *The Relentless Business of Treaties*, 43; Foley, *A History of Missouri*, 1: 74.

33. "Treaty with the Sauks and Foxes, 1804," Kappler, *Indian Affairs*, 2: 77; Foley, *A History of Missouri*, 1: 70–73.

34. Case, The Relentless Business of Treaties, 43; "Sauk and Foxes, 1804," *Treaty Signers Project*.

35. "Treaty with the Sauk, 1815," "Treaty with the Foxes, 1815," and "Treaty with the Sauk of the Rock River, 1816," in Kappler, *Indian Affairs*, 2: 121, 122, 126; Foley, *A History of Missouri*, 1: 92–93; Hagan, *The Sac and Fox Indians*, 23.

36. Foley and Rice, *The First Chouteaus*, 116–28; Patricia Cleary, *The World, the Flesh, and the Devil*, 321.

37. Edwards, *Osage Women and Empire*, 66; Burns, *A History of the Osage People*, 31, 47, 57; Lee, *Masters of the Middle Waters*, 185–88.

38. Walter A. Schroeder, "Populating Missouri, 1804–1821," 265.

39. Meriwether Lewis quoted Aron, *American Confluence*, 141.

40. Foley, *A History of Missouri*, 1: 126–27; Lewis quoted in Burns, *A History of the Osage People*, 145.

41. Lewis Quoted in Case, *The Relentless Business of Treaties*, 47.

42. Mathews, *The Osages*, 391.

43. Kathleen DuVal, *The Native Ground*, 201–2.; Aron, *American Confluence*, 142.

44. DuVal, *The Native Ground*, 202; Burns, *A History of the Osage People*, 146.

45. Lee, *Masters of the Middle Waters*, 219–20; DuVal, *The Native Ground*, 203–5.

46. William E. Foley and Charles David Rice, "Pierre Chouteau: Entrepreneur as Indian Agent," 380–82; Mathews, *The Osages*, 389.

47. "Treaty with the Great and Little Osages, 1808," Kappler, *Indian Affairs*, 2: 95–99; Lee, *Masters of the Middle Waters*, 219.

48. "Treaty with the Great and Little Osages, 1808," Kappler, *Indian Affairs*, 2: 95; Robert Lee, "'A Better View of the Country': A Missouri Settlement Map by William Clark," 1, 5, 14.

49. Foley and Rice, *The First Chouteaus*, 148.

50. Burns, *A History of the Osage People*, 157.

51. Burns, *A History of the Osage People*, 154.

52. Edwards, *Osage Women and Empire*, 64–65.

53. Burns, *A History of the Osage People*, 154–55.

54. Lee, *Masters of the Middle Waters*, 209–10; Foley and Rice, *The First Chouteaus*, 145.

55. Jeffrey Ostler, *Surviving Genocide: Native Nations and the United States from the American Revolution to Bleeding Kansas*, 224, 229.

56. Foley and Rice, *The First Chouteaus*, 149–50.

57. Clark quoted in Herman J. Viola, *Diplomats in Buckskins: A History of Indian Delegations in Washington City*, 20.

58. Madison quoted in Viola, *Diplomats in Buckskins*, 21.

59. The Blue and Clermont II quoted in Viola, *Diplomats in Buckskins*, 21.

60. Foley, *The Genesis of Missouri*, 223–27.

61. Clark quoted in Foley, *The Genesis of Missouri*, 227.

62. Michael Dickey, *Arrow Rock: Crossroads of the Missouri Frontier*, 38–41; Mathews, *The Osages*, 393.

63. Clark to the Secretary of War, Sep. 12, 1813, in *The Territorial Papers of the United States*, ed. Clarence Edwin Carter, 14: 697; Dickey, *Arrow Rock*, 41–42; Foley, *The Genesis of Missouri*, 229.

64. Foley, *The Genesis of Missouri*, 231.

65. Oglesby, *Manuel Lisa and the Opening of the Missouri Fur Trade*, 152.

66. Blaine, *The Ioway Indians*, 114; Oglesby, *Manuel Lisa and the Opening of the Missouri Fur Trade*, 153–56; Pekka Hämäläinen, *Lakota America: A New History of Indigenous Power*, 153.

67. Foley, *The Genesis of Missouri*, 233; Prucha, *American Indian Treaties*, 132–33.

68. Foley and Rice, *The First Chouteaus*, 54; Prucha, *American Indian Treaties*, 133.

69. Case, *The Relentless Business of Treaties*, 67–69; Prucha, *American Indian Treaties*, 133; Blaine, *The Ioway Indians*, 115.

70. Burns, *A History of the Osage People*, 156; "Treaty with the Sauk, 1815," and "Treaty with the Fox, 1815," Kappler, *Indian Affairs*, 2: 121 and 122.

71. Arrell M. Gibson, *The Kickapoos: Lords of the Middle Border*, 31–32, 52.

72. Gibson, *The Kickapoos*, 78–80; "Benjamin Stephenson," and "Benjamin Parke," *Treaty Signers Project*.

73. Gibson, *The Kickapoos*, 80–81; "Treaty with the Kickapoo, 1819," in Kappler, *Indian Affairs*, 2: 182–84.

74. Claudio Saunt, *Unworthy Republic: The Dispossession of Native Americans and the Road to Indian Territory*, xiii–xiv; Jeffrey Ostler has estimated the number of Native people deported under the policy of Indian Removal at 123,000. Ostler, *Surviving Genocide*, 247.

75. William Clark and Paschal Cerré quoted in Gibson, *The Kickapoos*, 82, 105; "Paschal Cerré," *Treaty Signers Project*.

76. Gibson, *The Kickapoos*, 100, 106–7; Secretary of War John C. Calhoun to William Clark, Jul. 20, 1820, in Carter, *The Territorial Papers*, 15: 628.

77. "Treaty with the Kickapoo, 1820," in Kappler, *Indian Affairs*, 2: 189; William Clark to Secretary of War, James Barbour, Oct. 12, 1826, "Treaty of Peace and

Friendship Between the Osage Nation and the Delawares, Shawnees, Kickapoos, Weas, Piankeshaws, and Peorias, Entered into at St. Louis, the 7th of October, 1826," *American State Papers: Indian Affairs, 1815–1827*, 2: 673–74.

Voices

1. Big Elk speaking to Major Benjamin O'Fallon at Council Bluff, Oct. 14, 1819, Edwin James, "James's Account of S. H. Long's Expedition, 1819 to 1820," in *Early Western Travels, 1748-1846*, ed. Reuben Gold Thwaites vol. 14.

2. The Ioway headman Maxúthka (White Cloud) speaking to Major Benjamin O'Fallon at Council Bluff, Oct. 4, 1819, in David Meriwether, *My Life in the Mountains and on the Plains: The Newly discovered Autobiography*, ed. Robert A. Griffen, 46–47.

3. Maxúthka speaking to William Clark at a treaty council at Prairie du Chien, Wisconsin, Jul. 8, 1830, "Extracts from Minutes of a Council held at Prairie du Chien," National Archives Records Administration, Record Group 75, Treaty File, Microfilm T494, roll 2, Treaty #159: 17.

4. Waw-ron-esaw speaking to William Clark at a treaty council at Prairie du Chien, Wisconsin, Jul. 9, 1830, "Extracts from Minutes of a Council held at Prairie du Chien."

Chapter 6

1. David Meriwether, *My life in the Mountains and on the Plains*, 43–44.

2. Meriwether, *My life in the Mountains and on the Plains*, 43–44.

3. Foley, *The Genesis of Missouri*, 175–76.

4. John Calhoun to Henry Atkinson, 27 Mar. 1819, in John Gale, *The Missouri Expedition, 1818-1820: The Journal of Surgeon John Gale with Related Documents*, ed. Roger L Nichols, 92; Lance M. Foster, "Native American Perspectives on Forts," in *Frontier Forts of Iowa: Indians, Traders, and Soldiers, 1682-1862*, ed. William E. Whittaker, 48.

5. Gale, *The Missouri Expedition*, x.

6. Hiram Martin Chittenden, *The American Fur Trade of the Far West*, 2: 566; Christina Snyder, *Great Crossings: Indians, Settlers, and Slaves in the Age of Jackson*, 49.

7. Barry, *The Beginning of the West*, 79–80.

8. Gale, *The Missouri Expedition*, 40.

9. Gale, *The Missouri Expedition*, 40.

10. Richard E. Jensen and James S. Hutchins, eds., *Wheel Boats on the Missouri: The Journals and Documents of the Atkinson-O'Fallon Expedition, 1824–26*, 1n1.

11. Gale, *The Missouri Expedition*, 35.

12. Gale, *The Missouri Expedition*, 92.

13. Edwin James, "James's Account of S. H. Long's Expedition, 1819 to 1820," in *Early Western Travels: 1748-1846*, ed. Reuben Gold Thwaites, 14: 187–88; Maxine Benson, *From Pittsburgh to the Rocky Mountains: Major Stephen Long's Expedition, 1819–1820*, 82.

14. Richard H. Dillon, "Stephen Long's Great American Desert," 94.

15. Benson, *From Pittsburgh to the Rocky Mountains*, 81; Big Elk quoted in James, "James's Account of S. H. Long's Expedition, 1819–1820," 260–61.

16. Oglesby, *Manuel Lisa*, 104–9.

17. Schroeder, "Populating Missouri," 267.

18. Henry Rowe Schoolcraft, *Journal of a Tour Into the Interior of Missouri and Arkansaw*, 5.

19. Schoolcraft, *Journal of a Tour Into the Interior of Missouri and Arkansaw*, 46; Aron, *American Confluence*, 161.

20. Schoolcraft, *Journal of a Tour Into the Interior of Missouri and Arkansaw*, 52; Blevins, *A History of the Ozarks*, 1: 131–32.

21. John Mack Faragher, "'More Motley than Mackinaw': From Ethnic Mixing to Ethnic Cleansing on the Frontier of the Lower Missouri, 1783–1833," in *Contact Points; American Frontiers from the Mohawk Valley to the Mississippi, 1750–1830*, eds. Andrew R. L. Cayton and Frederika J. Teute, 305; Thomas Jefferson quoted in Walter Johnson, *The Broken Heart of America: St. Louis and the Violent History of the United States*, 29.

22. Thomas Jefferson quoted in Miller, et al., *Discovering Indigenous Lands*, 82.

23. "Mahaskah," Thomas L. McKenney and James Hall, *History of the Indian Tribes of North America*, 2: 212–13; Viola, *Diplomats in Buckskin*, 113–14; Hagan, *The Sac and Fox Indians*, 95.

24. White Cloud quoted in Blaine, *The Ioway Indians*, 142; Hagan, *The Sac and Fox Indians*, 94–95.

25. "Treaty with The Iowa, 1824" and "Treaty with the Sauk and Foxes, 1824, in Kappler, *Indian Affairs*, 2: 207–9.

26. Gilbert J. Garraghan, *The Jesuits of the Middle United States*, 1: 147, 169; Blaine, *The Ioway Indians*, 143–44.

27. Garraghan, *The Jesuits of the Middle United States*, 1: 151.

28. O'Connor quoted in Gabrielle Hays, "Researchers Unearth the Painful History of a Native Boarding School in Missouri."

29. "Moanahonga," in McKenney and Hall, *History of the Indian Tribes*, 2: 182.

30. Dorothy J. Caldwell, "The Big Neck Affair: Tragedy and Farce on the Missouri Frontier," 396–99.

31. Caldwell, "The Big Neck Affair," 404–8; "Moanahonga," in McKenney and Hall, *History of the Indian Tribes*, 2: 183.

32. "Treaty with the Osage, 1825," in Kappler, *Indian Affairs*, 2: 217; Haskins, "The Shawnee and Delaware Indians in Early Missouri, 1787–1832," 114; Ostler, *Surviving Genocide*, 226.

33. Mathews, *The Osages*, 518; Edwards, *Osage Women and Empire*, 95.

34. "Treaty with the Osage, 1825," in Kappler, *Indian Affairs*, 2: 217.

35. "Treaty with the Osage, 1825," in Kappler, *Indian Affairs*, 2: 218; Prucha, *American Indian Treaties*, 139.

36. Lee, *Masters of the Middle Waters*, 186–87.

37. "Treaty with the Osage, 1825," in Kappler, *Indian Affairs*, 2: 218–20.

38. Mathews, *The Osages*, 529; Burns, *A History of the Osage People*, 168–71; Edwards, *Osage Women and Empire*, 96.

39. Norall, *Bourgmont*, 81–88.

40. Mathews, *The Osages*, 539–41; William Least Heat-Moon and James K. Wallace, eds. and trans., *An Osage Journey to Europe, 1827–1830: Three French Accounts*, 3–10.

41. Mathews, *The Osages*, 540–43.

42. Mathews, *The Osages*, 544–46; Least Heat-Moon and Wallace, *An Osage Journey to Europe*, 20.

43. Mathews, *The Osages*, 546-47.

44. Least Heat-Moon and Wallace, *An Osage Journey to Europe*, 5–10.

45. Gottfried Duden, *Report on a Journey to the Western States of North America*, ed. James W. Goodrich, trans. George H. Kellner, et al., 88.

46. Duden, *Report on a Journey to the Western States of North America*, 88–89.

47. Duden, *Report on a Journey to the Western States of North America*, 91.

48. Perry McCandless, *A History of Missouri: 1820–1860*, 2: 38–39.

49. Lakomäki, *Gathering Together*, 175; Haskins, "The Shawnee and Delaware Indians in Early Missouri," 50–52; Aron, *American Confluence*, 101.

50. Haskins, "The Shawnee and Delaware Indians in Early Missouri, 1787–1832," 98; Stephen Warren, *The Shawnees and Their Neighbors, 1795-1870*, 81.

51. Warren, *The Shawnees and Their Neighbors*, 87–91.

52. Lakomäki, *Gathering Together*, 180–81; "Treaty with the Shawnee, 1825," in Kappler, *Indian Affairs*, 2: 263.

53. "Treaty with the Shawnee, 1825," in Kappler, *Indian Affairs*, 2: 263.

54. Lakomäki, *Gathering Together*, 181–84.

55. "Frank J. Allen" and "Nathan Kouns," *Treaty Signers Project*. http://portal.treaty signers.org/us/Lists/Signers1/Item/displayifs.aspx?List=c07a9a47%2D8a78 %2D4049%2Da09d%2De1e4fe30314a&ID=1212&Source=http%3A%2F%2F- portal%2Etreatysigners%2Eorg%2Fus%2FSitePages%2FSignersPage%2Easpx- %23InplviewHashe21f5ff9%2D3e9f%2D49f1%2Db102%2Df39866f52a69%3D- Paged%253DTRUE%2Dp%5FTitle%253DKinzie%25252c%252520John%2Dp %5FID%253D1195%2DPageFirstRow%253D121%2DFilterFields1%253DA%2 5255Fx002d%25255FZ%2DFilterValues1%253D8%25255FJ%25253B%2525238 %25255FK%2DFilterOp1%253DIn&ContentTypeId=0x0100E1DF37A2DF6F8 8458F62FB152CE3F121.

56. "Treaty with the Shawnee, etc., 1832," in Kappler, *Indian Affairs*, 2: 370–72.

57. Warren, *The Shawnees and Their Neighbors, 1795-1870*, 171–72.

58. Prucha, *American Indian Treaties*, 446; Case, *The Relentless Business of Treaties*, 69; "Treaty with the Delawares, 1818," in Kappler, *Indian Affairs*, 2: 170.

59. C. A. Weslager, *The Delaware Indians: A History*, 361–65.

60. "Treaty with the Delaware, 1829," in Kappler, *Indian Affairs*, 2: 304–5.

61. Weslager, *The Delaware Indians*, 370–71.

62. "Treaty with the Shawnee, etc., 1832," in Kappler, *Indian Affairs*, 2: 370–72.

63. Weslager, *The Delaware Indians*, 373.

64. Treaty Files, "Extracts from Minutes of a Council held at Prairie du Chien, Wednesday, Jul.7, 1830," Treaty 159, RG 75, Microfilm T494, roll 2, National

Archives Records Administration; Clark quoted in Case, *The Relentless Business of Treaties*, 96.

65. Extracts from Minutes of a Council held at Prairie du Chien, Monday, Jul. 12, 1830, NARA, 2–3.

66. Extracts from Minutes of a Council held at Prairie du Chien, Monday, Jul. 12, 1830, NARA, 15.

67. Extracts from Minutes of a Council held at Prairie du Chien, Monday, Jul. 12, 1830, NARA, 16–17.

68. Extracts from Minutes of a Council held at Prairie du Chien, Monday, Jul. 12, 1830, NARA, 19.

69. "Treaty with the Sauk and Fox, etc., 1830," in Kappler, *Indian Affairs*, 2: 305–8.

70. Extracts from Minutes of a Council held at Prairie du Chien, Monday, Jul. 12, 1830, NARA, 22–23.

71. Extracts from Minutes of a Council held at Prairie du Chien, Monday, Jul. 12, 1830, NARA, 22; Blaine, *The Ioway Indians*, 161.

72. Gibson, *The Kickapoos*, 107; Calloway, *Pen and Ink Witchcraft* 132–33.

73. Gibson, *The Kickapoos*, 109–10; Joseph B. Herring, *The Enduring Indians of Kansas: A Century and a Half of Acculturation*, 23.

74. "Treaty with the Kickapoo, 1832," in Kappler, *Indian Affairs*, 2: 365–67.

75. Gibson, *The Kickapoos*, 110–13.

76. Greg Olson, *Ioway Life: Reservation and Reform, 1837–1860*, 14–15.

77. Iowa Agent Andrew Hughes, Jul. 2, 1835, Iowa Agency Records, National Archives Records Administration, RG 75, Microfilm M234, roll 362, frame 462.

78. John Dougherty to William Clark, Aug. 28, 1835, Ioway Agency Records, NARA, M234, roll 362, about frame 490.

79. R. David Edmunds, *The Potawatomis: Keepers of the Fire*, 249–51; R. David Edmunds, "Potawatomis in the Platte Country: An Indian Removal Incomplete," 377–81, 384.

80. McCandless, *A History of Missouri*, 2: 56.

81. Olson, *The Ioway in Missouri*, 114–16; "The Heatherly War," *Livingston County Genealogy Trails*. http://genealogytrails.com/mo/livingston/wars.html

82. Edmunds, *The Potawatomis*, 251–52.

83. Greg Olson, "Slave, Trader, Interpreter, and World Traveler: The Remarkable Story of Jeffrey Deroine," 223–25.

84. Olson, *Ioway Life*, 61.

85. Robert J. Willoughby, *The Brothers Robidoux and the Opening of the American West*, 133; Hugh M. Lewis, *Robidoux Chronicles: French-Indian Ethnoculture of the Trans-Mississippi West*, 137–43.

86. "Treaty with the Ioways, etc., 1836," in Kappler, *Indian Affairs*, 2: 468.

87. "Treaty with the Oto, etc., 1836," in Kappler, *Indian Affairs*, 2: 479.

88. Edmunds, "Potawatomis in the Platte Country," 387–89; Ostler, *Surviving Genocide*, 312.

89. Blaine, *The Ioway Indians*, 168–69.

90. Lee, "Accounting for Conquest: The Price of the Louisiana Purchase of Indian Country," 921–42; The inflation calculation was made using the website https://westegg.com/inflation/infl.cgi.

91. Ioway Agent John Burbank to Superintendent of Indian Affairs W. M. Albin, Sep. 30, 1864, Great Nemaha Agency Records, National Archives Records Administration, RG 75, M234, roll 311, frames 310–14.

92. Johnathan Bean to Joshua Pilcher, Dec. 1, 1839, Great Nemaha Agency Records, NARA, Record group 75, Microfilm publication M234, roll 307.

Voices

1. Siah Hicks (Cherokee) quoted from a 1938 interview in Gregory D. Smithers, *The Cherokee Diaspora: An Indigenous History of Migration, Resettlement, and Identity*, 251.

2. Louis Owens, *Mixedblood Messages: Literature, Film. Family, Place*, 147–48.

3. Beverly Baker Northup, *"We Are Not Yet Conquered": The History of the Northern Cherokee Nation of the Old Louisiana Territory*, 5, 6.

4. Harvey Wyatt quoted in Northup, *"We Are Not Yet Conquered,"* 5.

Chapter 7

1. Ostler, *Surviving Genocide*, 247, 291; Kent Blansett, "Intertribalism in the Ozarks, 1800–1865," 476–78.

2. Ostler, *Surviving Genocide*, 201–3.

3. Saunt, *Unworthy Republic*, 276, 279; Ostler, *Surviving Genocide*, 271–73.

4. Interview with Rachel Dodge, May 14, 1937, interview 5765, Indian-Pioneer Oral History Project, Western History Collections, University of Oklahoma. https://digital.libraries.ou.edu/cdm/ref/collection/indianpp/id/7626; Saunt, *Unworthy Republic*, 278–79.

5. Menominee quoted in Edmunds, *The Potawatomis*, 267.

6. Edmunds, *The Potawatomis*, 267–68; Ostler, *Surviving Genocide*, 312–13; Bowes, "American Indian Removal and Beyond," 72–73.

7. Edmunds, *The Potawatomis*, 272; Jeffrey Ostler, "'To Extirpate the Indians': An Indigenous Consciousness of Genocide in the Ohio Valley and Lower Great Lakes, 1750s–1810," The 589.

8. Quotes from "Removal of Indians," *Democratic Banner* (Bowling Green, MO), Jun. 6, 1846, 2; Ostler, *Surviving Genocide*, 296–310.

9. "The Missouri Delegation to their Constituents," *The Salt River Journal* (Bowling Green, MO), Jul. 25, 1840, 1.

10. Barry, *The Beginning of the West*, 390; "Threaten War on our Frontier," *Boon's Lick Times* (Fayette, MO), Apr. 4, 1840, 3; "Indian Disturbances," *The Salt River Journal*, Apr. 11, 1840, 1.

11. "Frontier Protection," *Boon's Lick Times*, Jan. 16, 1841, 3.

12. "The Frontier," *Boon's Lick Times*, Apr. 17, 1841, 2.

13. "Indian League—Looks Squally," *The Radical* (Bowling Green, MO), Apr. 9, 1842, 2; "Important Military Movements," *The Radical*, Apr. 16, 1842, 1.

14. "An act to suppress Intercourse with Indians," Feb. 9, 1839, *Missouri Session Laws, 1838*, Version 2 (Jefferson City: Calvin Gunn, 1841): 66–67; "An Act to Restrain Intercourse with the Indians," Feb. 27, 1845, *Revised Statutes of the State of Missouri, 1845* (St. Louis: J. W. Dougherty, 1945): 575–76.

15. John W. Kelly to Secretary of War William Marcy, Apr. 29, 1847, and William Rucker to David Rice Atchison, Jan. 22, 1847, Great Nemaha Agency Records, NARA, M234, roll 307.

16. *The State of Missouri vs. John W. Kelly*, Holt County Circuit Court, May Term, 1842.

17. Rudolph Friedrich Kurz, "Journal of Rudolph Friedrich Kurz," ed. J. N. B. Hewitt, trans. Myrtis Jarrell, 30.

18. Lodisa Frizzell quoted in Jacqueline A. Lewin and Marilyn S. Taylor, *The St. Joe Road: Emigration Mid 1800s*, 5.

19. Ethel Grant Inman, "Pioneer Days in Northwest Missouri—Harrison County, 1837–1873," 322–23.

20. L. B. Fleak to Missouri Governor Thomas Reynolds, Aug. 1–3, 1843, Governors Papers, Thomas Reynolds, Box 2, folder 61, Missouri State Archives.

21. McCandless, *A History of Missouri*, 2: 107–11; Fleak to Reynolds, Aug. 1–3, 1843.

22. "Indian Dance," *Boon's Lick Times* (Fayette, MO), Apr. 27, 1844, 2.

23. Olson, *Ioway Life*, 98–104.

24. The historian Joseph Herring defines acculturation as "intercultural borrowing that takes place when two or more diverse people come into close contact." He contrasts this with assimilation, which he defines as a "complete absorption of a minority people . . . into the traditional and cultural mainstream." Herring, *The Enduring Indians of Kansas*, 1–2.

25. Gerald Vizenor, *Fugitive Poses: Native American Indian Scenes of Absence and Presence*, 25.

26. Harry J. Brown, *Injun Joe's Ghost: The Indian Mixed-Blood in American Writing*, 4.

27. Sherilyn Farnes, "'Incongruous Assortment at all Times': Community Relationships in Western Missouri, 1821–1841.'".

28. *State of Missouri v. Henry D. Spear*, Apr. 1840, case no. 1104, Supreme Court of Missouri Files, Missouri State Archives.

29. Lois Ralph and F. Coakley, "William Banks," *Manx Settlement in Holt County, Missouri*, 2019; Barry, *The Beginnings of the West*, 445.

30. Deposition of Frank Dupuis, Abstract, *Oscar Banks et al. v. Catherine Galbraith et al.*, October Term 1898, file ID #8471, Supreme Court of Missouri files, folder 1, Missouri State Archives, 22–28; Deposition of Mahecomi (Mrs. Wilson), Abstract, *Banks v. Galbraith*, 32; Decision, Supreme Court of Missouri, *Banks v. Galbraith*, 1–2.

31. While William Banks Jr. was certain of his birthdate, there is confusion about Joseph Banks's date of birth. William said his brother was born Apr. 7, 1849. However, the timeline laid out in the court proceedings place his birth about 1847.

Deposition of William Banks Jr., Abstract, *Banks v. Galbraith*, 102, 103; Ralph and Coakley, "William Banks"; "Holt County's First Settler," *The Holt County Sentinel*, Mar. 8, 1895, 4; Decision, Supreme Court of Missouri, *Banks v. Galbraith*, 1–2.

32. Deposition of William Banks Jr., Abstract, *Banks v. Galbraith*, 100; Susan K. Suttle White, comp., "1889 Ioway Annuity," and "1891 Iowa Allotment Roll," *Ioway Cultural Institute: Genealogy*. Trans., Juli Kearns, trans. "1891 Census of the Ioway Indians of Pottawatomie and Great Nemaha Agency," *Ioway Cultural Institute*: Census of the Sac and Fox Indians of Pottawatomie and Great Nemaha Agency, 1898, *Ancestry Library*, internet, https://www.ancestrylibrary.com/imageviewer/collections/1059/images/M595_392-0327?pId=3727941.

33. Deposition of William Banks Jr., Abstract, *Banks v. Galbraith*, 101.

34. At the time of the lawsuit, Oscar Banks was the only one of Joseph Banks' children to have reached the age of legal majority. White Cloud, Kansas, lawyer George Nuzum filed on behalf of the minor children as "Next Friend."

35. Decision, Supreme Court of Missouri, *Banks v. Galbraith*, 3–4.

36. Lewis, *Robidoux Chronicles*, 137.

37. Kurz, "The Journal of Rudolph Friedrich Kurz," 67.

38. Willoughby, *The Brothers Robidoux*, 134, 196; Lewis, *Robidoux Chronicles*, 139–42.

39. Mary Alicia Owen, "Among the Voodoos," in *The International Folklore Congress, 1891: Papers and Transaction*, eds. Joseph Jacobs and Alfred Nutt, 241–43; Greg Olson, *Voodoo Priests, Noble Savages, and Ozark Gypsies: The Life of Folklorist Mary Alicia Owen*, 57–58; Jeffrey E. Anderson, *Conjure in African American Society*, 51.

40. Mary Alicia Owen, *Old Rabbit, the Voodoo, and Other Sorcerers*, 2–8, 110–11.

41. Olson, *Voodoo Priests, Noble Savages, and Ozark Gypsies*, 18–19.

42. Roy E. Finkenbine, "The Native Americans Who Assisted the Underground Railroad"; "A talk in Council held by Wm. Harvey Supt of Indian affairs with the Ioway Indians on the 10th of Apr. 1846 in the chapel of the Mission in the Great Nemaha Agency," Apr. 10, 1864, Great Nemaha Agency Records, NARA, M234, roll 307; Robert Collins, *Jim Lane: Scoundrel, Statesman, Kansan*, 106–7.

43. Mary Alicia Owen, *Old Rabbit, the Voodoo, and Other Sorcerers*, 110–11.

44. Owen, *Old Rabbit, the Voodoo, and Other Sorcerers*, 174–78; Andrew Zimmerman, "Guinea Sam Nightingale and Magic Marx in Civil War Missouri: Provincializing Global History and Decolonizing Theory," 150, 171n66.

45. Blansett, "Intertribalism in the Ozarks, 1800–1865," 79.

46. See Richard White, *The Middle Ground: Indians, Empires, and Republics in the Great Lakes Region, 1650–1815*; Blansett, "Intertribalism in the Ozarks, 1800–1865," 494n2.

47. Blansett, "Intertribalism in the Ozarks, 1800–1865," 476; Blevins, *History of the Ozarks*, 1: 77–79.

48. Northup, *"We Are Not Yet Conquered,"* 5, 17.

49. David Edward Walker, "An Open Statement from a Missouri Cherokee Descendent," about page 2, http://davidedwardwalker.com/missouri-cherokee-descendent.html

50. Interview with Lilian Anderson, Aug. 20, 1937, interview 7326, Indian-Pioneer Oral History Project. http://digital.libraries.ou.edu/cdm/ref/collection/in dianpp/id/3059; Interview with Jennie McCoy Chambers, May 3–4, 1937, interview 5625, Indian-Pioneer Oral History Project., https://digital.libraries.ou.edu/cdm/ref /collection/indianpp/id/6948

51. Grant Foreman, *Indian Removal: The Emigration of the Five Civilized Tribes of Indians*, 291–92.

52. Foreman, *Indian Removal*, 310.

53. Ralph Jenkins, "Cherokee Trail of Tears: Other Paths."

54. Angie Debo, "John Rollin Ridge," 59–62. Brown, *Injun Joe's Ghost*, 129–30.

55. Debo, "John Rollin Ridge," 63–65.

Voices

1. Mathews, *The Osages*, 636.

2. Ioway soldier from the Thirteenth Kansas Volunteer Infantry and the Fourteenth Kansas Volunteer Cavalry to President Abraham Lincoln, Jan. 16, 1864, Great Nemaha Agency Records, NARA, M234, roll 311, frames 728–29.

Chapter 8

1. Mary Jane Warde, *When the Wolf Came: The Civil War and the Indian Territory*, 4.

2. Warde, *When the Wolf Came*, 47–52; Annie Heloise Abel, *The American Indian in the Civil War, 1862–1865*, 60; Thomas W. Cutrer, *Theater of a Separate War: The Civil War West of the Mississippi River, 1861–1865*, 72–73.

3. Richard B. McCaslin, "Bitter Legacy: The Battle Front," in *The Civil War and Reconstruction in Indian Territory*, ed. Bradley R. Clampitt, 19–20; Cutrer, *Theater of a Separate War*, 72–74; Warde, *When the Wolf Came*, 52–54, 57–58; Abel, *The American Indian in the Civil War*, 24–25.

4. Warde, *When the Wolf Came*, 25–40; Cutrer, *Theater of a Separate War*, 74–75; McCaslin, "Bitter Legacy: The Battle Front," 20, 22; Stewart Sifakis, *Compendium of the Confederate Armies: Kentucky, Maryland, Missouri, the Confederate Units, and the Indian Units*, 198–99, 202–4; Gary E. Moulton, *John Ross: Cherokee Chief*, 168–73; Angie Debo, *The Road to Disappearance: A History of the Creek Indians*, 142–45.

5. Isaias J. McCaffery, "We-He-Sa-Ki (Hard Rope): Osage Band Chief and Diplomat, 1821–1883," 7–10; Burns, *A History of the Osage People*, 259–64.

6. Warde, *When the Wolf Came*, 97; Abel, *The American Indian in the Civil War*, 25–30; William Shea, "1862: 'A Continual Thunder,'" in *Rugged and Sublime: The Civil War in Arkansas*, ed. Mark K. Christ, 30; Ephraim Anderson quoted in Ingenthron, *Borderland Rebellion*, 152.

7. Cutrer, *Theater of a Separate War*, 88; Alvin M. Josephy Jr., *The Civil War in the American West*, 322.

8. Cutrer, *Theater of a Separate War*, 92; Warde, *When the Wolf Came*, 101; Abel, *The American Indian in the Civil War*, 32–33.

9. Cutrer, *Theater of a Separate War*, 92.

10. Warde, *When the Wolf Came*, 131; Collins, *Jim Lane: Scoundrel, Statesman, Kansan*, 210–11.

11. Albert Castel, *Civil War Kansas: Reaping the Whirlwind*, 78–81; Warde, *When the Wolf Came*, 101–3; Abel, *The American Indian in the Civil War*, 50, 57, 61–77; Laurence M. Hauptman, *Between Two Fires: American Indians in the Civil War*, 31–32.

12. Weslager, *The Delaware Indians*, 416–17; Warde, *When the Wolf Came*, 252–53; Hauptman, *Between Two Fires*, 22–23.

13. E. H. Carruth quoted in Warde, *When the Wolf Came*, 128; Ingenthron, *Borderland Rebellion*, 227, 230: Clint Crowe, *Caught in the Maelstrom: The Indian Nations in the Civil War, 1861–1865*, 86–92.

14. Wiley Britton, *Memoirs of the Rebellion on the Border 1863*, 111–12; W. G. Coffin to William P. Dole, Office of the Superintendent of Indian Affairs, Jan. 5, 1863, "Southern Superintendency," *Report of the Commissioner of Indian Affairs, 1863* (Washington: Government Printing Office, 1864): 192.

15. Wiley Britton, *The Civil War on the Border*, 2: 7–8, 34–35.

16. "Soldiers' Records: War of 1812–World War I," *Missouri Digital Heritage*. https://www.sos.mo.gov/Images/Archives/Military

17. Ingenthron, *Borderland* Rebellion, 102–3, 117–18.

18. My conversations with a much more recent war veteran lead me to question Stith's assertion. Osage Viet Nam War veteran Larry Sellers, who served in the United States Navy, recounted that even in the harsh and unfamiliar conditions of Viet Nam, he was subjected to racism by his peers. Larry Sellers, Osage Nation, Pawhuska, Oklahoma, Oral teaching, personal communication, date not recorded; Matthew M. Stith, *Extreme Civil War: Guerrilla Warfare, Environment, and Race on the Trans-Mississippi Frontier*, 5, 11–12; Earl J. Hess, *The Union Soldier in Battle: Enduring the Ordeal of Combat*, 4–5, 111, 117–22.

19. Quintard Taylor quoted in Johnson, *The Broken Heart of America*, 167.

20. *The WPA Guide to 1930s Missouri*, 54–55; William E. Parrish, *A History of Missouri: 1860-1875*, 3: 199–201.

21. Parrish, *A History of Missouri*, 3: 121; Lawrence O. Christensen and Gary R. Kremer, *A History of Missouri: 1875 to 1919*, 4: 2–3.

22. *John Smith, administrator of the estate of Obadiah Smith, deceased v. Amos Beck, et al.* Cedar County Circuit Court case, April Term, 1865, Missouri State Archives.

23. Patricia Cleary, "The Destruction of the Big Mound: Possessing and Defining Native American Places," 2.

24. Jacob Holland-Lulewicz, "Western Flank Survey Update," 3; Cleary, "The Destruction of Big Mound," 12–14; O'Brien, *Paradigms of the Past*, 45–51.

25. Cleary, "The Destruction of Big Mound," 3–4.

26. Payton quoted in Cleary, "The Destruction of Big Mound," 5; Robert Silverberg, ". . . and The Mound-builders Vanished from the Earth," about page 5 and 6.

27. Quotes from Fagan, *The Great Journey*, 30, 32.

28. Fagan, *The Great Journey*, 32–34.

29. Fagan, *The Great Journey*, 38–39.

30. Wallace D. Farnham, "The Pacific Railroad Act of 1862," 145, 155; Craig Miner, *The Corporation and the Indian: Tribal Sovereignty and Industrial Civilization in the Indian Territory, 1865–1907*, 11–19.

31. "About the Homestead Act," National Homestead Historical Park, National Park Service. https://www.nps.gov/home/learn/historyculture/abouthomesteadact law.htm; "Homesteading by the Numbers," National Homestead Historical Park. https://www.nps.gov/home/learn/historyculture/bynumbers.htm

32. Robert Lee, Tristan Ahtone, et al., "Land Grab University"; Parrish, *A History of Missouri*, 3: 182–87; "University Report," *Journal of the House of the State of Missouri, 1855* (Jefferson City: James Lusk, 1855): 260–61; McCandless, *A History of Missouri*, 2: 201.

33. Jean M. O'Brien, *Firsting and Lasting: Writing Indians out of Existence in New England*, xiii–xv.

34. A. J. Conant, "Archaeology," in *Switzler's Illustrated History of Missouri from 1541 to 1881*, ed. C. R. Barns, 110; O'Brien, *Paradigms of the Past*, 57–60.

35. Conant, "Archaeology," 51–52.

36. William Switzler, ed., *History of Boone County, Missouri*, 21.

37. Joseph Thorp, "The Thorp Letters: 'Early Days in Missouri,'" in *Boone County Chronicles*, eds. David Sapp, et al., 33.

38. Thorp, "The Thorp Letters: 'Early Days in Missouri,'" 35.

39. Thorp, "The Thorp Letters: 'Early Days in Missouri,'" 39.

40. Thorp, "The Thorp Letters: 'Early Days in Missouri,'" 52.

41. O'Brien, *Firsting and Lasting*, xiv.

42. O'Brien, *Firsting and Lasting*, 4–5.

43. Census figures cited here are based on searches made using *AncestryLibrary.com's* US Federal Census database for the decennial census from 1870 to 1940.

44. James P. Collins, "Native Americans in the Census, 1860–1890," 2.

45. *Population Schedules of the Ninth Census of the United States*, 1870, Salt River Township, Shelby County, Missouri; Roll: Microfilm Publication M593, roll 806: 91A.

46. *US Census*, 1870, St. Louis Ward 6, St. Louis, Missouri, M593, roll 816: 387A.

47. *US Census*, 1870, St. Louis Ward 11, St. Louis, Missouri, M593, roll 821: 441B.

48. *US Census*, 1870, Logan, Reynolds County, Missouri, M593, roll 803: 634B.

49. *US Census*, 1870, St. Joseph Ward 5, Buchanan County, Missouri; Roll: M593, roll 762: 633B.

50. *US Census*, 1870, St. Louis Ward 4, St. Louis, Missouri, M593, roll 813: 334A.

51. *US Census*, 1870, St. Louis Ward 3, St. Louis, Missouri, M593, roll 812: 39A.

52. Though Douglass's name is also spelled Douglas in historical records, I use the former spelling because that is how his name appears on both his gravestone and on his death certificate. Gary Scharnhorst, *The Life of Mark Twain: The Early Years, 1835–1871*, 56; "Joe 'Indian Joe' Douglass," *Find A Grave*. https://www.findagrave.com/memorial/22893/joe-douglass; "Joseph Douglas, 1822–1923," *Jim's Journey*. https://jimsjourney.org/hannibals-african-american-notables/; "Joe Douglass," Certificate of Death, September 29, 1923, *Missouri Death Certificates Database*,

1910–1970, Missouri State Archives. https://s1.sos.mo.gov/records/Archives/Arch
ivesMvc/DeathCertificates#searchDB

53. *US Census*, 1900, Boonville, Cooper County, Missouri, Enumeration District
0142; FHL microfilm: 1240850: 2; Leon E. Truesdale, *Fifteenth Census of the United
States, 1930: The Indian Population of the United States and Alaska* (Washington:
United States Printing Office, 1937): 3.

54. Dunbar-Ortiz, *An Indigenous Peoples' History of the United States*, 211–14;
"List of Indian Boarding Schools in the United States," *The National Native American Boarding School Healing Coalition.* https://boardingschoolhealing.org/list/;
Brian Newland, "Federal Indian Boarding School Initiative Investigative Report,"
appendix A and B (working paper, Department of the Interior, 2022).

55. "Guion Miller Roll, 1906–1911," National Archives. https://www.archives.gov
/research/native-americans/rolls/guion-miller-rolls; U.S., Records Related to Enrollment of Eastern Cherokee by Guion Miller, 1908–1910, *Ancestry.com*.https://
www.ancestrylibrary.com/search/collections/60555/

56. "Missouri A. Fleetwood," U.S., Records Related to Enrollment of Eastern
Cherokee by Guion Miller, 1908–1910, *Ancestry.com*. https://www.ancestrylibrary
.com/imageviewer/collections/60555/images/M685_0009_0128?backlabel=Ret
urnSearchResults&queryId=83e5c077f3182d0a855e7ac12d865541&pId=52036;
Missouri Fleetwood, application #36147, U.S., Records Related to Enrollment of
Eastern Cherokee by Guion Miller, 1908–1910, *Ancestry.com*. https://www.ancestry
library.com/imageviewer/collections/60555/images/M685_0005_0348?back
label=ReturnSearchResults&queryId=83e5c077f3182d0a855e7ac12d865541&pId
=36342

57. Grant Gooch, application no. 44054; Adaniza C. Cotter Lisenby, application
no. 19490; James Bruton, application no. 44232; Louisa Ketchum, application no.
37912, all in U.S., Records Related to Enrollment of Eastern Cherokee by Guion
Miller, 1908–1910, vol. 5, *Ancestry.com*. https://www.ancestrylibrary.com/search
/collections/60555/

58. C. Joseph Genetin-Pilawa, *Crooked Paths to Allotment: The Fight over Federal
Indian Policy after the Civil War*, 13–26.

59. Genetin-Pilawa and Rand quoted in Genetin-Pilawa, *Crooked Paths to Allotment*, 26, 27.

Voices

1. Blaine N. Kent quoted in Marth Royce Blaine, *The Ioway Indians*, 305.

2. An unidentified Omaha person testifying to the US Senate quoted in D. S.
Otis, *The Dawes Act and the Allotment of Indian Lands*, 48–49.

Chapter 9

1. Great Nemaha Indian Agent John A. Burbank to Commissioner of Indian
Affairs Dennis N. Cooley, Nov. 24, 1865, Great Nemaha Agency Records, NARA,
M234, roll 312, frame 117; Trouble on the Indian Reserve," *White Cloud Kansas
Chief*, Dec. 21, 1865, 2.

2. "Treaty with the Ioways, etc. 1836," Kappler, *Laws and Treaties*, 2: 468; "Treaty with the Sauk and Foxes, etc., 1861," Kappler, *Laws and Treaties*, 2: 811.

3. Olson, *Ioway Life*, 114; Blaine, *The Ioway Indians*, 272–73.

4. "Man's Best Friend: The Old Drum Story," *Missouri Digital Heritage*, Missouri State Archives. https://www.sos.mo.gov/archives/education/olddrum/Storyof BurdenvHornsby

5. Jeffrey L. Pasley, "The Party of Jefferson in Kansas City," 8.

6. Marian Elaine Dawes, "The Senate Career of George Graham Vest," 36, 49–51; M. Paul Holsinger, "Senator George Graham Vest and the 'Menace' of Mormonism, 1882-1887," 24.

7. *The Lexington Intelligencer*, Oct. 2, 1875, 2; "Concurrent Resolution Instructing Senators and Members of Congress to Prevent Removal of Sioux Indians to the Indian Territory," *Missouri Session Laws*, 1877, Regular Session. https://cdm16795 .contentdm.oclc.org/digital/collection/molaws/id/12738/rec/4: 424

8. Rambler, "Our Indian Neighbors," *The Holt County Sentinel* (Oregon, MO), Jan. 22, 1875, 2.

9. "Our Few Red Neighbors," *The Holt County Sentinel*, Jun. 4, 1875, 2.

10. "Our Few Red Neighbors," 2.

11. Genetin-Pilawa, *Crooked Paths to Allotment*, 95.

12. Prucha, *American Indian Treaties*, 334–36, 346; Wolfe, "Settler Colonialism and the Elimination of the Native," 388.

13. Tom Holm, *The Great Confusion in Indian Affairs: Native Americans and Whites in the Progressive Era*, xii.

14. Dawes, "The Senate Career of George Graham Vest," 50.

15. "Our Few Red Neighbors," 2.

16. Todd Barnett, "Carl Schurz," *Historic Missourians*, State Historical Society of Missouri. https://historicmissourians.shsmo.org/carl-schurz

17. Johnson, *The Broken Heart of America*, 166–68; Schurz was the first of four secretaries of the interior to come from Missouri. Republican John W. Noble served from 1889 to 1893, Democrat David R. Francis served from 1896 to 1897, and Republican Ethan A. Hitchcock served from 1899 to 1907. "Past Secretaries," *U.S. Department of the Interior*. https://www.doi.gov/whoweare/past-secretaries

18. Dawes, "The Senate Career of George Graham Vest," 50.

19. Miner, *The Corporation and the Indian*, 97–98; Dawes, "The Senate Career of George Graham Vest," 49–50.

20. Miner, *The Corporation and the Indian*, 107–8.

21. Miner, *The Corporation and the Indian*, 115.

22. Dawes, "The Senate Career of George Graham Vest," 52; Genetin-Pilawa, *Crooked Paths to Allotment*, 150–53; Holm, *The Great Confusion in Indian Affairs*, 11–12.

23. Herring, *The Enduring Indians of Kansas*, 137–38; Miner, *The Corporation and the Indian*, 116–17.

24. The Ioways split into two groups in the late 1870s and early 1880s. Roughly half of the nation stayed in Kansas and Nebraska, while the other half moved to Oklahoma, where the government established a new reservation for them along

the Cimarron River. Blaine, *The Ioway Indians*, 303–5; Prucha, *American Indian Treaties*, 318–19.

25. Hagan, *The Sac and Fox Indians*, 254–55, 259.

26. Holm, *The Great Confusion in Indian Affairs*, 26–27.

27. K. Tsianina Lomawaima, "The Mutuality of Citizenship and Sovereignty: The Society of American Indians and the Battle to Inherit America," 337.

28. Josiah Hair, "Myths, Misinformation and Motivations Regarding the 1907 Dawes and 1909 Miller Rolls." https://www.powwows.com/myths-misinformation-and-motivations-regarding-the-1907-dawes-roll-and-1909-miller-rolls/, 2; Alysa Landry, "Paying to Play Indian: The Dawes Rolls and the Legacy of $5 Indians," *Indian Country Today*, Sep. 13, 2018. https://indiancountrytoday.com/archive/paying-play-indian-dawes-rolls-legacy-5-indians, 1.

29. Katherine M. B. Osburn, "'Any Sane Person': Race, Rights, and Tribal Sovereignty in the Construction of the Dawes Rolls for the Choctaw Nation," 458, 460; Josiah Hair, "Final Roll of the Cherokee Nation and Freedmen." https://www.powwows.com/final-roll-of-the-cherokee-nation-and-freedman-2/, 2.

30. Landry, "Paying to Play Indian," 1–2; Osburn, "'Any Sane Person,'" 457, 469, 470; Hair, "Final Roll of the Cherokee Nation and Freedmen," 1.

31. Dunbar-Ortiz, *An Indigenous Peoples' History of the United States*, 158–59; Michael Lee Weber, "Redbird Smith Movement," *The Encyclopedia of Oklahoma History*; Kenneth W. McIntosh, "Chitto Harjo," *The Encyclopedia of Oklahoma History*.

32. Katherine Ellinghaus, *Blood Will Tell: Native Americans and Assimilation Policy*, xxv–xxvi; Landry, "Paying to Play Indian."

33. "No More Indian Tribes," *The Laclede Blade*, Oct. 14, 1910, 3; "Indian Forced to Succumb," *Scott County Kicker* (Benton, MO), Jul. 10, 1915: 2.

34. Renato Rosaldo, "Imperialist Nostalgia," 107–22; Holm, *The Great Confusion in Indian Affairs*, 53.

35. Samuel J. Redman, *Prophets and Ghosts: The Story of Salvage Anthropology*, 2.

36. Henry Wadsworth Longfellow, "Hiawatha's Departure," section 22, *The Song of Hiawatha*. http://www.online-literature.com/henry_longfellow/song-of-hiawatha/23/; Olson, *Voodoo Priests, Noble Savages, and Ozark Gypsies*, 119–21.

37. Cecily Hilleary, "Native Americans to Boy Scouts: Stop Plundering our Past."

38. Richard Boehner, "A Short History of the Tribe of Mic-O-Say," Tribe of Mic-O-Say, Ozark Troop 1890, https://sites.google.com/site/ozarktroop1890/tribe-of-mic-o-say; Vincent Schilling, "The Tribe of Mic-O-Say Dance Teams Regularly Perform in 'Native-Style Regalia,'" *Indian Country Today*, Sep. 17, 2019. https://indiancountrytoday.com/news/the-tribe-of-mic-o-say-dance-teams-regularly-perform-in-native-style-regalia

39. Boehner, "A Short History of the Tribe of Mic-O-Say."

40. Schilling, "The Tribe of Mic-O-Say Dance Teams Regularly Perform in 'Native-Style Regalia.'"

41. James W. Loewen, *Lies Across America: What Our Historic Sites Get Wrong*, 145–46; Hazel W. Hertzberg, *The Search for an American Indian Identity: Modern Pan-Indian Movements*, 216–17.

42. "Scalp Dance-Picnic," *The Hayti Herald*, Jul. 1, 1909, 1; Charles H. Litchman, ed., *The Official History of the Improved Order of Red Men*, 11.

43. Loewen, *Lies Across America*, 144–45.

44. Redman, *Prophets and Ghosts*, 2.

45. "The Henry L. George Collection," St. Joseph Museums, Inc. https://www.stjosephmuseum.org/native-american-galleries

46. "Patsy Ryan, 'Short Horse,' Great Indian Curio Collector, Asphyxiated," *Holt County Sentinel* (Oregon, MO), Dec. 16, 1910, 1.

47. Leland quoted in Olson, *Voodoo Priests, Noble Savages, and Ozark Gypsies*, 109.

48. Olson, *Voodoo Priests, Noble Savages, and Ozark Gypsies*, 87–89.

49. Martha Weigle and Barbara A. Babcock, eds., *The Great Southwest and the Fred Harvey Company and the Santa Fe Railway*, xii–xv.

50. David A. Binkley, "Artists Under Glass: The Nelson-Atkins Museum of Art's Native American Dioramas," in *The Great Southwest and the Fred Harvey Company and the Santa Fe Railway*, eds. Weigle and Babcock, 176–81; Kristie C. Wolferman, *The Nelson-Atkins Museum of Art: A History*, 104–5.

51. Steeves, *The Indigenous Paleolithic of the Western Hemisphere*, 30.

52. Johnson, *The Broken Heart of America*, 205.

53. Mark Bennitt quoted in James R. Swensen, "Bound for the Fair: Chief Joseph, Quanah Parker, and Geronimo and the 1904 St. Louis World's Fair," 443.

54. Swensen, "Bound for the Fair," 452.

55. Swensen, "Bound for the Fair," 443–50, 452.

56. Swensen, "Bound for the Fair," 456–61; Johnson, *The Broken Heart of America*, 205; Redman, *Prophets and Ghosts*, 1–7.

57. Geronimo, "At the World's Fair," *Geronimo: His Own Story*. http://www.let.rug.nl/usa/biographies/geronimo/at-the-worlds-fair.php

58. Thomas Hart Benton, *An Artist in America*, 14; Swensen, "Bound for the Fair," 460–61.

59. Nate Dimeo, "Olympic-Sized Racism," *Slate*, Aug. 21, 2008. https://slate.com/culture/2008/08/remembering-the-anthropology-days-at-the-1904-olympics.html; Swensen, "Bound for the Fair," 453; Dave Skretta, "St. Louis Olympics Was Really World's Fair with Some Sports," *The Washington Post*, Jul. 24, 2020. https://www.washingtonpost.com/sports/olympics/st-louis-olympics-was-really-worlds-fair-with-some-sports/2020/07/24/0664ea78-cdc3-11ea-99b0-8426e26d203b_story.html

60. James Ring Adams, "The Sideshow Olympics: Weirdness and Racism at St. Louis, 1904," 2.

61. Holm, *The Great Confusion in Indian Affairs*, xii.

62. Holm, *The Great Confusion in Indian Affairs*, 51–53; Hertzberg, *The Search for an American Indian Identity*, 26–27, 65, 73.

63. Hertzberg, *The Search for an American Indian Identity*, 71–72.

64. Thomas C. Maroukis, "The Peyote Controversy and the Demise of the Society of American Indians," 161; Parker quoted in Holm, *The Great Confusion in Indian Affairs*, 59.

65. Holm, *The Great Confusion in Indian Affairs*, 61–63.

66. Holm, *The Great Confusion in Indian Affairs*, 42–43; Maroukis, "The Peyote Controversy and the Demise of the Society of American Indians," 161–62.

67. Hertzberg, *The Search for an American Indian Identity*, 239, 240.

68. Hertzberg, *The Search for an American Indian Identity*, 246, 272–80.

69. Isaias J. McCaffery, "Before the Powwow: Dance as Spectacle in Early Kansas, 1855–1910," 236; Clyde Ellis, "The Sound of the Drum Will Revive Them and Make Them Happy," in *Powwow*, eds. Clyde Ellis, Luke Eric Lassiter, and Gary H. Dunham, 14.

70. McCaffery, "Before the Powwow: Dance as Spectacle in Early Kansas, 1855–1910," 236, 242; "Powwows," Quapaw Nation., https://www.quapawtribe.com/88/Annual-Quapaw-Powwow; Mathews, *The Osages*, 727–28.

71. Mary Alicia Owen to A. C. Burrill, May 1931, photocopy of handwritten original, Rebecca and Adolf E. Schroeder Papers, Collection CA5648, State Historical Society of Missouri, Columbia.

72. "An Indian Dance," *The Taney County Republican* (Forsyth, MO), reprinted from the *Kansas City Journal*, Apr. 13, 1905, 8.

73. "Big Crowd at the Lake," *The Holt County Sentinel*, Friday, Oct. 8, 1920, 8.

Voices

1. Oren Lyons, "Traditionalism and the Reassertion of Indianness," in *Indian Self-Rule: First-Hand Accounts of White-Indian Relations from Roosevelt to Regan*, ed. Kenneth L. Philip, 244.

2. Philip S. Deloria, "The Era of Indian Self-Determination: An Overview," in *Indian Self-Rule*, ed. Philip, 204–5.

3. "Defend the Graves," *Leavenworth Post*, Jul. 18, 1907, 3.

4. Sandra K. Massey, court deposition, *Sac and Fox Nation v. Missouri Department of Natural Resources*, United States District Court for the Western District of Missouri, Western Division, 2003, quoted in Nicholas Phillips, "Sac and Fox Nation: Missouri Desecrated Our Ancestors. We Want 'Em Back (and Some)!"

Chapter Ten

1. Jessie Kratz, "Terror on the Osage Reservation," *Pieces of History* (blog), *National Archives*, Nov. 24, 2021. https://prologue.blogs.archives.gov/2021/11/24/terror-on-the-osage-reservation/

2. "Citizen Status for Indians Is Favored," *The Springfield News-Leader*, Mar. 30, 1924, 10; Burns, *A History of the Osage People*, 412–13; Kratz, "Terror on the Osage Reservation."

3. "Osage Indian Status Fixed by a New Law," *The Hominy* (Oklahoma) *News*, Mar. 8, 1921: 1, 4.

4. David Treuer, *The Heartbeat of Wounded Knee: Native America from 1890 to the Present*, 200.

5. Dunbar-Ortiz, *An Indigenous Peoples' History of the United States*, 169–70.

6. Elmer R. Rusco, "John Collier: Architect of Sovereignty or Assimilation?," 50; Holm, *The Great Confusion in Indian Affairs*, 182, 191.

7. Holm, *The Great Confusion in Indian Affairs*, 187; Larry W. Burt, *Tribalism in Crisis: Federal Indian Policy, 1953–1961*, 3: Treuer, *The Heartbeat of Wounded Knee*, 201–2.

8. Hertzberg, *The Search for an American Indian Identity*, 288–89; Kenneth R. Philip, "Termination: A Legacy of the Indian New Deal," 169; Floyd A. O'Neil, "Indian New Deal: An Overview," in *Indian Self-Rule*, ed. Kenneth R. Philip, 39–40.

9. Hertzberg, *The Search for an American Indian Identity*, 289; Kenneth R. Philip, "Federal Indian Policy, 1933–1945," in *Indian Self-Rule*, ed. Philip, 59–60; Graham Holmes, "Undoing the IRA," in *Indian Self-Rule*, ed. Philip, 147.

10. Rusco, "John Collier: Architect of Sovereignty or Assimilation?," 50; Wilcomb E. Washburn, "A Fifty-Year Perspective on the Indian Reorganization Act," 280; Rupert Costo, "Federal Indian Policy, 1933–1945 in *Indian Self-Rule*, ed. Philip, 50.

11. Burt, *Tribalism in Crisis*, 4.

12. Tanya Thatcher, James Ring Adams and Anne Bolen, "Patriot Nations: Native Americans in Our Nation's Armed Forces."

13. Donald L. Fixico, *Termination and Relocation: Federal Indian Policy, 1945–1960*, 406; Philip, "Termination: A Legacy of the Indian New Deal," 167; Douglas K. Miller, *Indians on the Move: Native American Mobility and Urbanization in the Twentieth Century*, 44, 53.

14. Colin G. Calloway, *"The Chiefs Now in This City": Indians in the Urban Frontier in Early America,*; Miller, *Indians on the Move*, 45.

15. Truman quoted by Philleo Nash, "Relocation," in *Indian Self-Rule*, ed. Philip, 165; Fixico, *Termination and Relocation*, 11, 42; Philip, "Termination: A Legacy of the Indian New Deal," 180.

16. Larry W. Burt, "Unlikely Activism: O. K. Armstrong and Federal Indian Policy in the Mid-Twentieth Century," 415–24.

17. Quote from House Concurrent Resolution in Fixico, *Termination and Relocation*, 94; Burt, *Tribalism in Crisis*, 4–5: James Officer, "Termination as Federal Policy: An Overview," *Indian Self-Rule*, ed. Philip, 120; Fixico, *Termination and Relocation*, 180–81.

18. Miller, *Indians on the Move*, 71.

19. Burt, *Tribalism in Crisis*, 7.

20. Fixico, *Termination and Relocation*, 63–72.

21. Fixico, *Termination and Relocation*, 136–38; Miller, *Indians on the Move*, 64, 82–89; Joshua Mika, "Indians at the Crossroads: The Native Activism of Bobby and Nancy Blue," 4.

22. "Indian Affairs Bureau Opens First Office Here," *St. Louis Post-Dispatch*, Jul. 31, 1956, 5; "Indians to Be Resettled Here, First to Arrive Next Month," *St. Louis Post-Dispatch*, Aug. 5, 1956, 14.

23. As was the style in the 1950s, the newspaper account of the arrival of first Native relocatees in St. Louis did not name the two married women, referring to them instead only as Mrs. Martime and Mrs. Tongkeamah. "Two Indian Families Arrive, First of About 110 Who Will Live Here," *St. Louis Post-Dispatch*, Oct. 8, 1956, 3; Miller, *Indians on the Move*, 99.

24. Mary Kimbrough, "St. Louis New Home for Indians," *St. Louis Post-Dispatch*, Apr. 14, 1957: 118; Clarissa Start, "Integrating the Indian Into Big City Life," *St. Louis Post-Dispatch*, Feb. 28, 1958: 3F; Miller, *Indians on the Move*, 109.

25. Start, "Integrating the Indian Into Big City Life," 3F.

26. Start, "Integrating the Indian Into Big City Life," 3F.

27. Start, "Integrating the Indian Into Big City Life," 3F.

28. Marguerite Shepard, "Indians Relocated Here Moving Back to Their Reservations," *St. Louis Globe-Democrat*, Jun. 12, 1960: 1F and 5F.

29. Shepard, "Indians Relocated Here Moving Back to Their Reservations," 1F.

30. Samantha Rae Dean, "'As Long as Grass Grows and Water Flows': Lyda Conley and the Huron Indian Cemetery," 23; "Treaty with the Wyandot, 1855," Kappler, *Laws and Treaties*, 2: 677–81; "The Occupation That Saved a Wyandot Cemetery," The first episode of the podcast *A People's History of Kansas City*, February 2020, KCUR Studios. https://www.kcur.org/podcast/a-peoples-history-of-kansas-city/2020-02-06/the -occupation-that-saved-a-wyandot-cemetery

31. Dean, "'As Long as Grass Grows and Water Flows,'" 50; "Defend the Graves," *Leavenworth Post*, Jul. 18, 1907: 3.

32. Dean, "'As Long as Grass Grows and Water Flows,'" 60.

33. Dean, "'As Long as Grass Grows and Water Flows,'" 63.

34. Mika, "Indians at the Crossroads: The Native Activism of Bobby and Nancy Blue," 2–3; Frank E. Melton, "Native Americans in the City" *Kansas City Star*, Aug. 18, 1975: 1, 5.

35. Mika, "Indians at the Crossroads: The Native Activism of Bobby and Nancy Blue," 4; Ellis, "The Sound of the Drum Will Revive Them and Make Them Happy," in *Powwow*, eds. Ellis, Lassiter, and Dunham, 15–18; "The Last Powwow?" *Kansas City Times*, Mar. 31, 1960, 40; "Pow Wow Fires Burn," *Kansas City Star*, Jul. 21, 1963, 8A.

36. Mike North, "Big Pow-Wow is Real Pow-Wow," *Springfield Leader and Press*, Sep. 6, 1964, 1.

37. "It's OK—These Are Our Reds," *Springfield Leader and Press*, Jun. 18, 1967, 38; "Indian Powwow Biggest Since Days of Kickapoo," *Springfield News Leader*, Jun. 17, 1967, 12.

38. Ellis, "The Sound of the Drum Will Revive Them and Make Them Happy," 11.

39. Frank E. Melton, "Native Americans in the City," *Kansas City Star*, Aug. 18, 1975, 1, 5; John T. Dauner, "City Life a Fatal Attraction for Too Many Indians," *Kansas City Star*, May 22, 1973, 12.

40. Melton, "Native Americans in the City," 5

41. Joseph H. McCarty Jr., "Indian Finds City Hostile," *Kansas City Star*, Jan. 18, 1979, 1N and 6N; Martha Shirk, "6,000 Indians Here—The 'Invisible Minority,'" *St. Louis Post-Dispatch*, Nov. 28, 1975, 1C; "Indian Center Opens Here," *Kansas City Star*, Aug. 29, 1971, 23.

42. Kevin Washburn, "Tribal Self-Determination at the Crossroads," 779; "Urban Indians Told to Seek U.S. Funds," *Kansas City Star*, Feb. 11, 1972, 17.

43. Philip S. Deloria, "The Era of Indian Self-Determination: An Overview," In *Indian Self-Rule*, ed. Philip, 196–98; "Indian Center Opens Here," 23.

44. Terrence Thompson, "Indians Losing 'Forgotten' Image," *Kansas City Star*, Dec. 24, 1971, 5.

45. Letter to the Editor by Mary Daniels, "Indians Harassed," *St. Louis Post-Dispatch*, Nov. 13, 1975, 22; Martha Shirk, "6,000 Indians Here—The 'Invisible Minority," *St. Louis Post-Dispatch*, Nov. 28, 1975, 1C.

46. Robert A. Cohn, "ADL Office Assists American Indian Cultural Center in St. Louis," *St. Louis Jewish Light*, Dec. 10, 1975, 32.

47. Edgar A. Albin, "Center Focuses on the Needs of Indians," *Springfield Leader and Press*, Jul. 29, 1979, 4C; Mary Sharp, "Three Groups Help Indians," *Springfield Leader and Press*, Mar. 29, 1987, 23H; Sarah Scarlett, "American Indian Center of Springfield," *Ozark Watch*, Nov. 6, 2020. https://www.ozarksfirst.com /ozarks-tonight/ozarks-tonight-american-indian-center-of-springfield/

48. Joseph H. McCarty Jr., "Indians Decry Cutbacks in Programs," *Kansas City Star*, Jun. 7, 1982, 3A; Christopher Clark, "Funding Fears Shadow Indian Center Festival," *Springfield News-Leader*, Apr. 25, 1993, 11; Tamlya Beasley, "Indian Center Budget Cut in Half," *Springfield News-Leader*, May 24, 1996, 1.

49. Akins and Bauer, *We Are the Land: A History of Native California*, 307–9; Jefferson Strait, "Foes' Vow: No Land, No Gambling," *The Springfield News-Leader*, Jul. 2, 2002, 1A.

50. Strait, "Foes' Vow: No Land, No Gambling," 5A.

51. Strait, "Foes' Vow: No Land, No Gambling," 5A.

52. Strait, "Foes' Vow: No Land, No Gambling," 1A, 5A; "For Justice, Speed Tribal Recognition," *The Springfield News-Leader*, Jul. 2, 2002, 6A.

53. "Getting Started," NAGPRA, National Park Service. https://www.nps.gov/sub jects/nagpra/getting-started.htm; Jim Fisher, "Iowa Tribe Reveres Ancestral Northern Missouri Land," *The Kansas City Star*, May 25, 1997, B-4.

54. Fisher, "Iowa Tribe Reveres Ancestral Northern Missouri Land," B-4, B-5.

55. "Oklahoma Tribe Files Suit Over Treatment of Sacred Sites," *St. Louis Post-Dispatch*, Jul. 7, 2002, 32.

56. "Indian Remains Complicate Efforts to Boost Clarksville," *St. Louis Post-Dispatch*, Aug. 23, 2004, A1, A4; "NAGPRA Policy: Historic Cemeteries and Cultural Resources," Sac and Fox Nation of Oklahoma. https://www.sacandfoxnation-nsn.gov /departments/repatriation-cultural/; Nicholas Phillips, "Sac and Fox Nation: Missouri Desecrated Our Ancestors. We Want 'Em Back (And Some)!."

57. NAGPRA Review Committee Meeting Transcript, vol. 1, Nov. 18, 2015, 12 https://irma.nps.gov/DataStore/DownloadFile/630205; NAGPRA Review Committee Meeting Minutes, Nov. 18–19, 2015. https://irma.nps.gov/DataStore/Down loadFile/630207; *Federal Register*, vol. 78, no. 146 (July 30, 2013): 45960–45961; Meeting Materials for NAGPRA Review Committee Meeting, Nov. 18–19, 2015. https://irma.nps.gov/DataStore/Reference/Profile/2258850

58. William J. Bryan, Deputy Missouri State Historic Preservation Officer, to Melanie O'Brien, Designated Federal Officer, NAGPRA Review Committee, Sep.

29, 2015, Meeting Materials for NAGPRA Review Committee Meeting, Nov. 18–19, 2015; Shannon Shaw Duty, "Missouri State Historic Preservation Office Holding Osage Remains Despite National NAGPRA Committee Finding," *Osage News*, Mar. 20, 2017. https://osagenews.org/missouri-state-historic-preservation-office -holding-osage-remains-despite-natl-nagpra-committee-finding/; Shannon Shaw Duty, "Osage Nation Wins Historic NAGPRA Battle for Missouri Remains," *Osage News*, March 20, 2017. https://osagenews.org/osage-nation-wins-historic-nagpra-battle -for-missouri-remains/

59. O'Brien, *Paradigms of the Past*, 283; Jimmy Meyers, "Artifacts to be Returned," *St. Joseph News-Press*, Nov. 21, 2002, A1, A7.

60. Danielle Zielinski, "Museum Board Returned Artifacts," *St. Joseph News-Press*, Jun. 1, 2006, B1, B3.

61. Danielle Zielinski, "Council Requests Inventory of Artifacts," *St. Joseph News-Press*, Mar. 15, 2006, B1; Steve Booker, "Sorting Out the Museum Squabble," *St. Joseph News-Press*, Jun. 5, 2006, A4.

62. Aaron Bailey, "Museums Inc. Faces Possible Fine," *St. Joseph News-Press*, Apr. 19, 2007, B1, B6; Aaron Bailey, "Museum to Accept Shippee Collection," *St. Joseph News-Press*, May 22, 2007, B1, B2.

63. "Agency: St. Joseph Museums Inc. Did Not Violate the Law," *St. Joseph News-Press*, Jan. 4, 2008, B1, B4.

64. Population figures from *Suburban Stats*. https://suburbanstats.org/race/miss ouri/how-many-american-indian-people-live-in-missouri

Voices

1. Geoffrey Standing Bear, Osage Principal Chief announcing the nation's purchase of land in Missouri. Quoted in Shannon Shaw Duty, "Chief Standing Bear Announces Missouri Land Purchase During Executive Address," Osage News, Sep. 7, 2021.

2. Lance Foster, Vice Chairman of the Iowa Tribe of Kansas and Nebraska discussing the tribe's newly created National Park. Quoted in "Iowa Tribe Creates national Park on Nebraska Kansas Border," Associated Press, Nov. 20, 2020. https://apnews.com/article /iowa-kansas-parks-national-parks-nebraska-e00f719cf2e9f20b5fac09c89073002d

Chapter 11

1. Echo Hawk quoted in Leah Asmelash, "How the Kansas City Chiefs Got Their Name, and Why It's So Controversial," *CNN*, Feb. 1, 2020. https://www.cnn.com/2020 /02/01/us/kansas-city-chiefs-name-race-trnd/index.html

2. Stephanie A. Fryberg, "American Indian Social Representations: Do They Honor or Constrain American Indian Identities?."

3. Asmelash, "How the Kansas City Chiefs Got Their Name, and Why It's So Controversial."

4. Natalie Weiner, "The Kansas City Chiefs Have No Excuse for their Name—Or for the Chop," *Fanbyte*, Feb. 5, 2020. https://www.fanbyte.com/features/kansas-city-chiefs

-chop/?fbclid=IwAR3xYGW-i1hzKrnaqhsQREzsfHhzVuBsTx5gnReKCLMEIJvP
Bitv3aZI6iE

5. "Indian Files Complaint Against K.C. Chiefs," *The Springfield News Leader*,
Dec. 12, 1991, 12.

6. Weiner, "The Kansas City Chiefs Have No Excuse for their Name—Or for the
Chop"; "About," *notinourhonor.com*. https://notinourhonor.com/contact/

7. "A Statement from the Kansas City Chiefs," *Chiefs.com*, Aug. 20, 2020. https://
www.chiefs.com/news/a-statement-from-the-kansas-city-chiefs; Weiner, "The Kansas City Chiefs Have No Excuse for their Name—Or for the Chop."

8. Brian Napier, "As Native American Mascots and Imagery Are Removed, Old
Wounds Stay Intact," *Columbia Missourian*, May 16, 2021. https://www.columbiam
issourian.com/sports/other_sports/as-native-american-mascots-and-imagery-are-
removed-old-wounds-stay-intact/article_bcfde188-a79b-11eb-99cf-b3674df6acb0.
html; "Missouri," *American Indian Sports Team Mascots*. https://www.aistm.org/miss
ouri.htm

9. Napier, "As Native American Mascots and Imagery Are Removed, Old Wounds
Stay Intact."

10. See Philip J. Deloria, *Playing Indian*.

11. Misha Maynerick Blaise, "Creating Boy Scout Ceremonies Without Taking Native American Cultural Property," Mar. 16, 2018. *Medium*. https://medium.com/@
mishablaise/creating-boy-scout-ceremonies-without-taking-native-american-
cultural-property-382ad880cce3

12. "'It's Sickening': How KC-area Boy Scouts' Mic-O-Say Program Demeans Native Americans." Editorial, *The Kansas City Star*, Aug. 10, 2020.

13. Mark L. Willens. "Boy Scouts Mic-O-Say Tribe Honors, Doesn't Demean Native American Culture and Rituals," Guest commentary, *The Kansas City Star*, Aug.
17, 2020.

14. "Our Mission," and "Indian Arts and Crafts Act of 1990," *Indian Arts and
Crafts Board*, US Department of the Interior. https://www.doi.gov/iacb

15. "Odessa Man Sentenced for Selling Fake Indian Art," Western District of Missouri, United States Attorney's Office, US Department of Justice, Sep. 9, 2015. https://
www.justice.gov/usao-wdmo/pr/odessa-man-sentenced-selling-fake-indian
-art; "Missouri Man Convicted Under Indian Arts and Crafts Act, *Cherokee Phoenix*, Sep. 21, 2015; Tony Rizzo, "Missouri Artist Pleads Guilty to Falsely Claiming
to be Cherokee to Sell His Artwork," *The Kansas City Star*, Sep. 9, 2015.; Brenda
Crowley, "What is Authentic Native American Art? Missouri Lawmakers Trying to
Define It," *Columbia Missourian*, Feb. 11, 2018.

16. Chad Garrison, "Going Native," *Riverfront Times*, Nov. 1, 2006. https://www.
riverfronttimes.com/stlouis/going-native/Content?oid=2484117; "Consumers Be-
ware," *Kathy (KiowaKat) Dickerson*. https://www.kiowakat.com/

17. Garrison, "Going Native."

18. Garrison, "Going Native."

19. "Thunderbird Society," *Missouri Online Business Filing*, Missouri Secretary
of State. https://bsd.sos.mo.gov/BusinessEntity/BusinessEntityDetail.aspx?page=be
Search&ID=683032

20. "Federally Recognized Indian Tribes and Resources for Native Americans," *USA.GOV.* https://www.usa.gov/tribes

21. Travis Snell, "Non-Recognized 'Cherokee Tribes' Flourish," *Cherokee Phoenix*, Jan. 19, 2007; Harmeet Kaur, "The Cherokee Nation Acknowledges that Descendants of People Once Enslaved by the Tribe Should Also Qualify as Cherokee," *CNN*, Feb. 25, 2021. https://www.cnn.com/2021/02/25/us/cherokee-nation-ruling-freedmen-citizenship-trnd/index.html

22. Danny Wicentowski, "Inside the Missouri Tribe That Has Made White People Millions," *Riverfront Times*, Sep. 9, 2020. https://www.riverfronttimes.com/stlouis/inside-the-missouri-tribe-that-has-made-white-people-millions/Content?oid=34122145

23. Adam Elmahrek and Paul Pringle, "Claiming to Be Cherokee, Contractors with White Ancestry Get $300 Million," *Los Angeles Times*, Jun. 26, 2019. https://www.latimes.com/local/lanow/la-na-cherokee-minority-contracts-20190626-story.html; Danny Wicentowski, "St. Louis Firms Lose Minority Status Over Claimed 'Cherokee' Ancestry," *Riverfront Times*, Sep. 24, 2121. https://www.riverfronttimes.com/news/st-louis-firms-lose-minority-status-over-claimed-cherokee-ancestry-36289851

24. Twila Barnes, *Thoughts from Polly's Granddaughter* (blog). http://www.pollysgranddaughter.com/

25. Grey Fox, "A Letter to All Cherokee Nation Tribal Citizens," *Northern Cherokee Nation,* accessed Sep. 30, 2021, http://www.northerncherokeenation.com/

26. Kyle Powys Whyte, "Indigeneity and U.S. Settler Colonialism," in *The Oxford Handbook of Philosophy and Race*, ed. Naomi Zack, 93.

27. Whyte and TallBear quoted in Whyte, "Indigeneity and U.S. Settler Colonialism," 99; Dina Gilio-Whitaker, *As Long as Grass Grows: The Indigenous Fight for Environmental Justice, From Colonization to Standing Rock*, 24.

28. While they generally refer to themselves as Ioways, both the tribes in Oklahoma and Kansas and Nebraska are officially recognized by the federal government as "Iowas." "Regenerative Agriculture," *Worage* (Autumn 2021): 12.

29. Untitled Facebook post, *Osage News*, Sep. 15, 2021. https://www.facebook.com/OsageNews/posts/4485055618221897; Isabella Grullón Paz, "Cave Featuring Native American Wall Art is Sold to Anonymous Bidder," *The New York Times*, Sep. 16, 2021.

30. Shannon Shaw Duty, "Chief Standing Bear Announces Missouri Land Purchase During Executive Address," *Osage News*, Sep. 7, 2021, https://osagenews.org/chief-standing-bear-announces-missouri-land-purchase-during-executive-address/; Shannon Shaw Duty, "Osage Nation Announces Plans for a Casino and Hotel Near the Lake of the Ozarks," *Osage News*, Oct. 30, 2021, https://osagenews.org/osage-nation-announces-plans-for-a-casino-and-hotel-near-the-lake-of-the-ozarks/

31. "*McGirt V. Oklahoma*," *Harvard Law Review*, Nov. 10, 2020. https://harvardlawreview.org/2020/11/mcgirt-v-oklahoma/; In June 2022 the Supreme Court issued a decision in the case *Oklahoma v. Castro-Huerta* which narrowed the parameters laid out in the McGirt Case. "Supreme Court Narrows Ruling for Tribes in Oklahoma," *The New York Times*, Jun. 29, 2020.

32. Rudi Keller, "Osage Nation Planning Casino, Hotel of Missouri's Lake of the Ozarks," *Columbia Missourian*, Nov. 3, 2021; "Osage Nation Checks to Governor Have Sticky Implications," *Kansas City Star* Editorial, *Columbia Missourian*, Jun. 7, 2017.

33. "Manifesto," *LANDBACK*. https://landback.org/manifesto/

34. "Federal Land Policy in Missouri," *Ballotpedia*. https://ballotpedia.org/Federal_land_policy_in_Missouri

Voices

1. Lance Foster email post to "Ioways Online," iowaysonline@yahoogroups.com, Oct. 26, 2008.

2. Larry Sellers quoted in Ricki Pryor, "Steady as a Beating Drum: Richmond Powwow Returns for Another Year of Celebration, Education," *Richmond* [Kentucky] *Register*, Sep. 28, 2021. https://www.richmondregister.com/news/steady-as-a-beating-drum/article_bc246967-e399-55b5-ba25-d02e351b4ea5.html

Bibliography

Newspapers

Boon's Lick Times (Fayette, MO)
Cherokee Phoenix (Tahlequah, OK)
Columbia (MO) *Missourian*
Democratic Banner (Bowling Green, MO)
The Guardian (England)
The Hayti (MO) *Herald*
The Holt County Sentinel (Oregon, MO)
The Hominy (OK) *News*
Indian Country Today
Kansas City Star
Kansas City Times
The Laclede (MO) *Blade*
Leavenworth (KS) *Post*
The Lexington (MO) *Intelligencer*
Los Angeles Times
National Post (Canada)
The New York Times
Osage News (Pawhuska, OK)
The Radical (Bowling Green, MO)
Richmond (Kentucky) *Register*
Riverfront Times (St. Louis, MO)
St. Joseph (MO) *News-Press/Gazette*
St. Louis Globe-Democrat
St. Louis Jewish Light
St. Louis Post-Dispatch
The Salt River Journal (Bowling Green, MO)
Scott County Kicker (Benton, MO)
Springfield (MO) *Leader and Press*
Springfield (MO) *News-Leader*

Bibliography

The Taney County Republican (Forsyth, MO)
University Missourian (Columbia, MO)
The Washington Post

Articles

Adams, James Ring. "The Sideshow Olympics: Weirdness and Racism at St. Louis, 1904." *American Indian: National Museum of the American Indian Magazine* 13, no. 2 (Summer 2012).

Anderson, Duane C. "A Long-Nosed God Mask from Northwest Iowa." *American Antiquity* 40, no. 3 (Jul. 1975): 326–29.

Benson, Larry V., Timothy R. Pauketat, Edward R. Cook. "Cahokia's Boom and Bust in the Context of Climate Change." *American Antiquity* 74, no. 3 (Jul. 2009): 467–83.

Berry, Brewton and Carl Chapman. "An Oneota Site in Missouri." *American Antiquity* 7, no. 3 (Jan. 1942): 290–305.

Betts, Colin M. and Dale R. Henning. "Aberrant Earthworks? A Contemporary Overview of Oneota Mound Ceremonialism." *The Wisconsin Archaeologist* 97, no. 2 (Jul.-Dec. 2016): 101–19.

Blakeslee, Donald J. "The Origin and Spread of the Calumet Ceremony." *American Antiquity* 46, no. 4 (Oct. 1981): 759–68.

Blansett, Kent. "Intertribalism in the Ozarks, 1800–1865." *American Indian Quarterly* 34, no. 4 (Fall 2010): 474–97.

Bowes, John P. "American Indian Removal Beyond the Removal Act." *NAIS: Journal of the Native American and Indigenous Studies Association* 1, no. 1 (Spring 2014): 65–87.

Braje, Todd J., et al. "Fladmark + 40: What Have We Learned about a Potential Pacific Coast Peopling of the Americas?" *American Antiquity* 85, no. 1 (Jan. 2020): 1–21.

Burt, Larry W. "Roots of the Native American Urban Experience: Relocation Policy in the 1950s." *American Indian Quarterly* 10, no. 2 (Spring 1986): 85–99.

——— . "Unlikely Activism: O. K. Armstrong and Federal Indian Policy in the Mid-Twentieth Century." *Missouri Historical Review* 94, no. 4 (Jul. 2000): 415–33.

Caldwell, Dorothy J. "The Big Neck Affair: Tragedy and Farce on the Missouri Frontier." *Missouri Historical Review* 64, no.4 (Jul. 1970): 391-412.

Chapman, Carl H. "Indomitable Osage In the Spanish Illinois (Upper Louisiana), 1763–1804." In *The Spanish in the Mississippi Valley, 1762–1804,* ed. John Francis McDermott, 287-313. Urbana: University of Illinois Press, 1973).

Cleary, Patricia. "The Destruction of the Big Mound: Possessing and Defining Native American Places in Early St. Louis." *Missouri Historical Review* 113, no. 1 (Oct. 2018): 1-21.

Clinton, Robert N. "Treaties with Native Nations: Iconic Historical Relics or Modern Necessity." In *Nation to Nation: Treaties Between the United States and American Indian Nations*, ed. Suzan Shown Harjo, 15-33. Washington, DC: Smithsonian Books, 2014.

Bibliography

Collins, James P. "Native Americans in the Census, 1860-1890." *Prologue Magazine* 38, no. 2 (Summer 2006). https://www.archives.gov/publications/prologue /2006/summer/indian-census.html

Danisi, Thomas C. "Reconstructing the Founding of St. Louis." *Missouri Historical Review* 115, no. 2 (Jan. 2021): 134–56.

Debo, Angie. "John Rollin Ridge." *Southwest Review* 17, no. 1 (1932): 59–71.

Dillon, Richard H. "Stephen Long's Great American Desert." *Proceedings of the American Philosophical Society* 111, no. 2 (Apr. 14, 1967): 93–108.

Donahue, Michelle Z. "Lost Native American Ancestor Revealed in Ancient Child's DNA." *National Geographic*. Jan. 3, 2018. https://www.nationalgeographic.com /news/2018/01/alaska-dna-ancient-beringia-genome/

Duncan, James R. and Carol Diaz-Granados. "Of Masks and Myths." *Midcontinental Journal of Archaeology* 25, no. 1 (Spring 2000): 1-26.

Dye, David H. "He-Who-Wears-Human-Heads-As-Earrings: Mississippian Culture Heroes, Reincarnation, and Warfare." In *War and Peace: Conflict and Resolution in Archaeology*, ed. Adam K. Benfer, 86-101. *Proceedings of the 45th Annual Chacmool Archaeology Conference*. Calgary, AB: Chacmool Archaeology Association, 2012.

Edmunds, R. David. "Potawatomis in the Platte Country: An Indian Removal Incomplete." *Missouri Historical Review* 68, no. 4 (Jul. 1974): 375–92.

Ekberg, Carl J. "Antoine Valentin de Gruy: Early Missouri Explorer." *Missouri Historical Review* 76, no. 2 (Jan. 1982): 136–50.

Ekberg, Carl J. and Sharon K Person. "The Making (and Perpetuating) of a Myth: Pierre Laclede and the Founding of St. Louis." *Missouri Historical Review* 111, no. 2 (Jan. 2017): 87–103.

Eren, Metin I., et al. "The *Cinmar* Discovery and the Proposed Pre-late Glacial Maxim Occupation of North America." *Journal of Archaeological Science: Reports* 2 (Jun. 2015): 708–13.

"Extracts from the Journal of Mr. Montgomery." *The Missionary Herald* 30, no. 1 (Jan. 1834): 22-24.

Farnham, Wallace D. "The Pacific Railroad Act of 1862." *Nebraska History* 43 (1962): 141-67.

Fausz, J. Frederick. "Becoming 'A Nation of Quakers': The Removal of the Osage Indians from Missouri." *Gateway Heritage: Quarterly Journal of the Missouri Historical Society* 21, no. 1 (Summer 2000): 28-39.

Finkenbine, Roy E. "The Native Americans Who Assisted the Underground Railroad." *North American News*. Sep. 24, 2019. https://www.globaldiasporanews.com /the-native-americans-who-assisted-the-underground-railroad/

Fishel, Richard L., et al. "Sourcing Red Pipestone Artifacts from Oneota Villages in the Little Sioux Valley of Northwest Iowa." *Midcontinental Journal of Archaeology* 35, no. 2 (Fall 2010): 167–98.

Foley, William E. "Turning the Page: William Clark's Post-Expedition Years." *Missouri Historical Review* 115, no. 3 (Apr. 2021): 227–40.

Bibliography

Foley, William E. and Charles David Rice. "Pierre Chouteau: Entrepreneur as Indian Agent." *Missouri Historical Review* 72, no. 4 (Jul. 1978): 365-87.

Harrington, M. R. "The Ozark Bluff Dwellers." *Indian Notes and Monographs*, vol. 12, Museum of the American Indian, Heye Foundation, New York, 1960.

Haynes, Gary. "How to Kill a Mammoth: The Brutal Act of the Hunt—and an Alternative." *Discovering Archaeology* (Sep./Oct. 1999): 42.

Hays, Gabrielle. "Researchers Unearth the Painful History of a Native Boarding School in Missouri. *PBS News Hour*. Apr. 28, 2002. Pbs.org/newshour/education/uncovering-the-traumatic-history-of-one-native-american-boarding-school-in-the-midwest

Hilleary, Cecily. "Native Americans to Boy Scouts: Stop Plundering Our Past." *Voice of America* Aug. 5, 2019. https://www.voanews.com/usa/native-americans-boy-scouts-stop-plundering-our-past

Hirst, K. Kris. "Is There a Solutrean-Clovis Connection in the American Colonization?" *ThoughtCo.com*. Nov. 16, 2018. https://www.thoughtco.com/solutrean-clovis-connection-american-colonization-172667

Holland-Lulewicz, Jacob. "Western Flank Survey Update." *Cahokian* (Spring 2022): 3.

Holsinger, M. Paul. "Senator George Graham Vest and the 'Menace' of Mormonism, 1882-1887." *Missouri Historical Review* 65, no. 1 (Oct. 1970): 23–36.

Hurt, R. Douglas. "Seeking Fortune in the Promised Land: Settling the Boon's Lick Country, 1808–1825." *Gateway Heritage* 12, no. 1 (Summer 1992): 4–19.

Inman, Ethel Grant, "Pioneer Days in Northwest Missouri—Harrison County, 1837–1873," *Missouri Historical Review* 22, no. 3 (Apr. 1928): 307–30.

Jackson, Edwin H. "Animals as Symbols, Animals as Resources: The Elite Faunal Record in the Mississippian World." In *Animals and Inequality in the Ancient World*, ed. Benjamin S. Arbuckle and Sue Ann McCarty, 107-24. Boulder: University Press of Colorado, 2014.

Jenkins, Ralph. "Cherokee Trail of Tears: Other Paths." *TNGen Web Project*, 1996. https://tngenweb.org/cherokee_by_blood/trail.htm

Kelton, Paul and Tai S. Edwards. "Germs, Genocides, and America's Indigenous Peoples." *The Journal of American History* 107, no. 1 (Jun. 2020): 52–76.

Kennett, Douglas J., et al. "Early Isotopic Evidence of Maize as a Staple Grain in the Americas." *Science Advances* 6, no. 23 (Jun. 3, 2020) https://advances.sciencemag.org/content/6/23/eaba3245

Kraft, Herbert C. "Paleoindians In New Jersey." *Annals of the New York Academy of Sciences* 288, no. 1 (1977): 264–281.

Landry, Alysa. "Paying to Play Indian: The Dawes Rolls and the legacy of $5 Indians." *Indian Country Today*. Sep. 13, 2018. https://indiancountrytoday.com/archive/paying-play-indian-dawes-rolls-legacy-5-indians

Lee, Robert. "'A Better View of the Country': A Missouri Settlement Map by William Clark." *William and Mary Quarterly* 3rd ser. 79, no. 1 (Jan. 2022): 89-120.

———. "Accounting for Conquest: The Price of the Louisiana Purchase of Indian Country." *Journal of American History* 103, no. 4 (Mar. 2017): 921–42.

Bibliography

Lee, Robert and Tristan Ahtone. "Land-Grab Universities." *High Country News*, Mar. 30, 2020. https://www.hcn.org/issues/52.4/indigenous-affairs-education-land-grab-universities

Lomawaima, K. Tsianina. "The Mutuality of Citizenship and Sovereignty: The Society of American Indians and the Battle to Inherit America." *American Indian Quarterly* 37. no. 3 (Summer 2013): 333–51.

McCaffery, Isaias J. "Before the Powwow: Native Dance as Spectacle in Early Kansas, 1855–1910." *Kansas History: A Journal of the Central Plains* 43, no. 4 (Winter 2020–2021): 234–53.

———. "We-He-Sa-Ki (Hard Rope): Osage Band Chief and Diplomat, 1821–1883." *Kansas History: A Journal of the Central Plains* 41, no. 3 (Spring 2018): 2–17.

McMillan, R. Bruce. "Bison in Missouri Archaeology." *The Missouri Archaeologist* 73 (Dec. 2012): 80–136.

———. "Migration Legends and the Origins of Missouri's Siouan-Speaking Tribes." *The Missouri Archaeologist* 75 (Dec. 2014). 5–47.

———. "Objects of Curiosity: Albert Koch's 1840 St. Louis Museum." *The Living Museum* 42, no. 2–3 (1980).

McNutt, Charles H. "The Central Mississippi Valley: A Summary". 1996. *Academia.edu.* https://www.academia.edu/14233814/Central_Mississippi_Valley_Summary_1996

Maroukis, Thomas C. "The Peyote Controversy and the Demise of the Society of American Indians." *American Indian Quarterly* 37, no. 3 (Summer 2013): 161-80.

Marshall, John B. "The St. Louis Mound Group: Historical Accounts and Pictorial Depictions." *The Missouri Archaeologist* 53 (1992): 43–79.

Martin, Terrell. "Late Archaic Evidence in the Moreau River Drainage, Cole County, Missouri." *Missouri Archaeological Society Quarterly* 37, no. 2 (Jul.–Sep. 2020): 12–18.

———. "Middle Woodland Settlement Patterns in Westcentral Missouri." *The Missouri Archaeologist* 77 (2016): 43–80.

———. "Prehistoric Settlement of Western Missouri During the Mississippian Period." *The Missouri Archaeologist* 68 (2007):1–28.

Mika, Joshua. "Indians at the Crossroads: The Native Activism of Bobby and Nancy Blue." *Profiles in Kansas City Activism.* https://info.umkc.edu/kcactivism/?page_id=105

Montagu, M. F. Ashley. "An Indian Tradition Relating to the Mastodon." *American Anthropologist* New Series, 46, no. 4 (Oct.–Dec. 1944): 568–71.

Montaigne, Fen. "The Fertile Shore." *Smithsonian Magazine* (Jan. 2020). https://www.smithsonianmag.com/science-nature/how-humans-came-to-americas-180973739/

Morrow, Lynn. "Trader William Gilliss and Delaware Migration in Southern Missouri." In *The Ozarks in Missouri History,* ed. Lynn Morrow: 19-36. Columbia: University of Missouri Press, 2013.

Munoz, Samuel E. et al. "Cahokia's Emergence and Decline Coincided with Shifts of Flood Frequency on the Mississippi River." *Proceedings of the National*

Bibliography

Academy of Sciences of the United States of America. 112, no. 20 (May 19, 2015): 6319–6324.

Nutter, Charles. "Robert R. Livingston: The Forgotten Architect of the Louisiana Purchase." *Missouri Historical Review* 97, no. 4 (Jul. 2003): 334–50.

O'Brien, Michael J., et al. "On Thin Ice: Problems with Stanford and Bradley's Proposed Solutrean Colonisation of North America." *Antiquity* 88, no. 340 (May 2014): 606–13.

———, et al. "Solutreanism." *Antiquity* 88, no. 340 (May 2014): 622–24.

Olson, Greg. "Slave, Trader, Interpreter, and World Traveler: The Remarkable Story of Jeffrey Deroine." *Missouri Historical Review* 107, no. 4 (Jul. 2013): 222-30.

———. "White Man's Paper Trail: Extinguishing Indigenous Land Claims in Missouri." *Missouri Historical Review* 115, no. 4 (Jul. 2021): 276–95.

Osburn, Katherine M. B. "'Any Sane Person': Race, Rights, and Tribal Sovereignty in the Construction of the Dawes Rolls for the Choctaw Nation." *The Journal of the Gilded Age and Progressive Era* 9, no. 4 (Oct. 2010): 451-71.

Ostler, Jeffrey. "'To Extirpate the Indians': An Indigenous Consciousness of Genocide in the Ohio Valley and Lower Great Lakes, 1750s-1810." *The William and Mary Quarterly* 72, no. 4 (Oct. 2015): 587-622.

Owen, Mary Alicia. "Among the Voodoos." In *The International Folklore Congress, 1891: Papers and Transaction.* ed. Joseph Jacobs and Alfred Nutt, 230-48. London: David Nutt, 1892.

Pauketat, Timothy R. et al., "A Mississippian Conflagration at East St. Louis and Its Political-Historical Implications," *Journal of Field Archaeology* 38 (Jul. 2013): 210–26.

Philip, Kenneth R. "Termination: A Legacy of the Indian New Deal." *Western Historical Quarterly* 14 (Apr. 1983): 165–80.

Phillips, Nicholas. "Sac and Fox Nation: Missouri Desecrated Our Ancestors. We Want 'Em Back (and Some)!" *Riverfront Times*, Jan. 21, 2011. https://www.riverfronttimes.com/news/sac-and-fox-nation-missouri-desecrated-our-ancestors-we-want-em-back-and-some?show--2589722

Radin, Paul, ed. "The Winnebago Tribe." *Thirty-Seventh Annual Report of the Bureau of American Ethnology, 1915–1916.* Washington, DC: Government Printing Office, 1923: 35-550.

Ralph, Lois and F. Oakley. "William Banks. *Manx Settlement in Holt County, Missouri.* 2019. http://www.isle-of-man.com/manxnotebook/famhist/genealgy/holt.htm

Rankin, Caitlin G., et al. "Evaluating Narratives of Ecocide with the Stratigraphic Record at Cahokia Mounds State Historic Site, USA." *Geoarchaeology* 36, no. 3 (2021): 369-87.

Rees, Lydia I. and Jamie C. Brandon. "Beyond the 'Bluff Dweller': Excavating the History of an Ozark Myth." *The Arkansas Historical Quarterly* 76, no. 2 (Summer 2017), 125-43.

Ritterbush, Lauren W. "The Leary Site Revisited: Oneota and Central Plains Tradition Occupation along the Lower Missouri." *Plains Archaeologist* 47, no. 182 (Aug. 2002): 251–64.

Rosaldo, Renato. "Imperialist Nostalgia." *Representations* 26 (Spring 1989): 107-22.

Rusco, Elmer R. "John Collier: Architect of Sovereignty or Assimilation?" *American Indian Quarterly* 15, no. 1 (Winter 1991): 49–54.

Schilling, Timothy. "The Chronology of Monks Mound." *Southeastern Archaeology* 32, no. 1 (Summer 2013): 14–28.

Schroeder, Walter A. "Populating Missouri, 1804–1821." *Missouri Historical Review* 97, no. 4 (Jul. 2003): 263–94.

———. "Spread of Settlement in Howard County, Missouri, 1810-1859." *Missouri Historical Review* 63, no. 1 (Oct. 1968): 1–37.

Silverberg, Robert. ". . . and The Mound-builders Vanished from the Earth." *American Heritage Magazine* 20, no. 4 (Jun. 1969). https://www.americanheritage.com/and-mound-builders-vanished-earth

Skinner, Alanson. "Traditions of the Iowa Indians." *The Journal of American Folklore* 38, no. 150 (Oct.–Dec. 1925): 425–506.

Skousen, B. Jacob. "Posts, Places, Ancestors, and Worlds: Dividual Personhood in the American Bottoms." *Southeastern Archaeology* 31, no. 1 (Summer 2012): 57–69.

Sossamon, Jeff. "Alternate Theory of Inhabitation of North America Disproved." Apr. 27, 2015. *Science X-Phys.Org.* https://phys.org/news/2015-04-alternate-theory-inhabitation-north-america.html

Stanford, Dennis and Bruce Bradley. "Reply to O'Brien et al." *Antiquity* 88, no. 34 (Jun. 2014): 614-21.

Stepenoff, Bonnie. "Conflict and Conversion: The Jesuit Mission on Missouri's River Des Peres." *Missouri Historical Review* 114, no. 4 (Jul. 2020): 235–48.

Swensen, James R. "Bound for the Fair: Chief Joseph, Quanah Parker, and Geronimo and the 1904 St. Louis World's Fair." *American Indian Quarterly* 43, no. 4 (Fall 2019): 439-70.

Thatcher, Tanya, James Ring Adams, and Anne Bolen. "Patriot Nations: Native Americans in Our Nation's Armed Forces." *American Indian* 17, no. 3 (Fall 2016). https://www.americanindianmagazine.org/story/patriot-nations-native-americans-our-nations-armed-forces

Theler, James L. and Robert F. Boszhardt. "Collapse of Crucial Resources and Culture Change: A Model for the Woodland to Oneota Transformation in the Upper Midwest." *American Antiquity* 71, no. 3 (Jul. 2006): 433–72.

Waguespack, Nicole M. "The Organization of Male and Female Labor in Foraging Societies: Implications for Early Paleoindian Archaeology." *American Anthropologist* 107, no. 4 (Dec. 2005): 666–76.

Washburn, Kevin K. "Tribal Self-Determination at the Crossroads." *Connecticut Law Review* 38, no. 4 (May 2006): 777-96.

Washburn, Wilcomb E. "A Fifty-Year Perspective on the Indian Reorganization Act." *American Anthropologist*, New Series, 86, no. 2 (Jun. 1984): 279–89.

"Who Was 'Injun Joe'?." *Journal of the Illinois State Archaeological Society* 5, no. 3 (Jan. 1948): 23.

Bibliography

Wolfe, Patrick. "Settler Colonialism and the Elimination of the Native." *Journal of Genocide Research* 8, no. 4 (Dec. 2006): 387–409.

Wood, W. Raymond. "Culture Sequence at the Old Fort, Saline County, Missouri." *American Antiquity* 38, no. 1 (Jan. 1973): 101–11.

Yerkes, Richard W. "The Woodland and Mississippian Traditions in the Prehistory of Midwestern North America." *Journal of World Prehistory* 2, no. 3 (Sep. 1988): 307–58.

Zimmerman, Andrew. "Guinea Sam Nightingale and Magic Marx in Civil War Missouri: Provincializing Global History and Decolonizing Theory." *History of the Present* 8, no. 2 (Fall 2018): 140–76.

Theses, Papers, Presentations, and Podcasts

Alvey, Jeffrey S. "Paleodemographic Modeling in the Lower Mississippi River Valley." PhD diss., University of Missouri, 2019.

Colvin, Matthew H. "Old-Woman-Who-Never-Dies: A Mississippian Survival in The Hidatsa World." Master's Thesis, Texas State University-San Marcos, 2012.

Dawes, Marian Elaine. "The Senate Career of George Graham Vest." Master's Thesis, University of Missouri, 1932.

Dean, Samantha Rae. "'As Long as Grass Grows and Water Flows ': Lyda Conley and the Huron Indian Cemetery." Bachelor's Thesis, Fort Hays State University, 2016.

Farnes, Sherilyn. "'Incongruous Assortment at all Times': Community Relationships in Western Missouri, 1821–1841." virtual conference presentation. Missouri Conference on History, Mar. 11, 2021.

Fishel, Richard L. "Dixon to Leary to White Rock: A Hypothesis for Oneota 14th Century Communal Bison Hunts." Symposium Paper. 54th Annual Plains Anthropological Conference, 1996. *Academia.edu*, https://www.academia.edu/37436910/Dixon_to_Leary_to_White_Rock_A_Hypothesis_for_Oneota_14th_Century_Communal_Bison_Hunts

Foster, Lance M. "Sacred Bundles of the Ioway Indians." Master's Thesis, Iowa State University, 1994.

Fryberg, Stephanie A. "American Indian Social Representations: Do They Honor or Constrain American Indian Identities?" Symposium paper. *50 Years after Brown vs. Board of Education: Social Psychological Perspectives on the Problems of Racism and Discrimination*. University of Kansas, May 13–14, 2004.

Gilio-Whitaker, Dina and George "Tink" Tinker. "American Indian World View and the Concept of Rights." Virtual lecture. *Beyond the Rhetoric: Civil Rights and Our Shared Responsibility*, Sep. 30, 2021, Rothko Chapel, https://vimeo.com/606777919

Gritts, Galen. "Wait . . . There Are Native People in Missouri?" Missouri Humanities Council Speakers Bureau Presentation. Columbia, Missouri. Aug. 8, 2021. https://missouri2021.org/statehood-day-livestreams/galen-gritts/

Haskins, Sarah. "The Shawnee and Delaware Indians in Early Missouri, 1787–1832." Master's Thesis, University of Missouri-Columbia, 2005.

Bibliography

Lee, Robert. "The Boon's Lick Land Rush and the Coming of the Missouri Crisis." Symposium Paper. *A Fire Bell in the Past: Reassessing the Missouri Crisis at 200.* Kinder Institute of Constitutional Democracy, University of Missouri. Columbia, Missouri, Feb. 15, 2019.

McMahon, Billy J. "'Humane and Considerate Attention': Indian Removal from Missouri, 1803–1838." Master's Thesis, Northwest Missouri State University, 2013.

"The Occupation That Saved a Wyandot Cemetery," The first episode of the podcast *A People's History of Kansas City*, Feb. 2020, KCUR Studios.

Pasley, Jeffrey L. "The Party of Jefferson in Kansas City." Symposium paper. *K.C. in the Golden Age*, University of Missouri-Kansas City, Nov. 5–6, 2015.

Rankin, Caitlin Gail. "Testing Assumptions on the Relationship between Humans and their Environment: Case Studies from Cahokia Mounds, Illinois." PhD diss. Washington University in St. Louis, 2020.

Ruppert, Michael E. "Archaeological Excavations at the King Hill Site (23BN1) Buchanan County, Missouri." Symposium Paper. The 30th Annual Plains Conference, Lincoln, Nebraska, Nov. 2, 1972. http://users.stlcc.edu/mfuller/kinghillwriteup.html

Sall, Candace. "Shoes Older than the Pyramids." PowerPoint presentation, Missouri State Archives, Jefferson City, Missouri. Nov. 12, 2020.

Websites

Case, Martin, et al. *Treaty Signers Project.* Indian Land Tenure Foundation. http://portal.treatysigners.org/us/SitePages/SignersPage.aspx

The Encyclopedia of Oklahoma History and Culture. Oklahoma Historical Society. https://www.okhistory.org/publications/enc/entry.php?entry=CL001

Fuller, Michael. *Michael Fuller Rock Art.* http://www.profmichaelfuller.com/home.html

GoodTracks, Jimm. *Ioway, Otoe, Missouria Language Project.* http://www.iowayotoelang.nativeweb.org/index.htm

Indian-Pioneer Papers Collection. University of Oklahoma. https://digital.libraries.ou.edu/whc/pioneer/

Indian Treaties, 1789–1869. National Archives and Records Administration. https://catalog.archives.gov/id/299798?utm_source=newsletter&utm_medium=email&utm_campaign=treatiesexplorer-oct2020

PowWows.com

"Treaties Explorer." The Indigenous Digital Archive. https://digitreaties.org

"Where the Wilson Meets the James." Center for Archaeological Research, Missouri State University. https://delawaretown.missouristate.edu/index.html

Books

Abel, Annie Heloise. *The American Indian in the Civil War, 1862–1865.* Lincoln: University of Nebraska Press, 1992.

Bibliography

Adovasio, J. M. and David Pedler. *Strangers in a New Land: What Archaeology Reveals About the First Americans.* Buffalo NY: Firefly Books, 2016.

Akins, Damon B. and William J. Bauer Jr. *We Are the Land: A History of Native California.* Oakland: University of California Press, 2021.

Alex, Lynn M. *Iowa's Archaeological Past.* Iowa City: University of Iowa Press, 2000.

Alvord, Clarence Walworth and Clarence Edwin Carter, eds. *The Critical Period, 1763–1765.* Springfield: Illinois State Historical Library, 1915.

Anderson, Gary Clayton. *Ethnic Cleansing and the Indian: The Crime that Should Haunt America.* Norman: University of Oklahoma Press, 2014.

Anderson, Jeffrey E. *Conjure in African American Society.* Baton Rouge: Louisiana State University Press, 2005.

Annual Report of the Commissioner of Indian Affairs, for the Year 1868. Washington, DC: Government Printing Office, 1868.

Arnold, Morris S. *The Rumble of a Distant Drum: The Quapaws and Old World Newcomers, 1673-1904.* Fayetteville: The University of Arkansas Press, 2000.

Aron, Stephen. *American Confluence: The Missouri Frontier from Borderland to Border State.* Bloomington: Indiana University Press, 2006.

Barry, Louise. *The Beginning of the West: Annals of the Kansas Gateway to the American West, 1540–1854.* Topeka: Kansas State Historical Society, 1972.

Barns, C. R., ed. *Switzler's Illustrated History of Missouri from 1541 to 1881.* St Louis: C. R. Barns, 1881.

Bell, John R. *The Journal of Captain John R. Bell, Official Journalist for the Stephen H. Long Expedition to the Rocky Mountains, 1820.* Edited by Harlin M. Fuller and LeRoy R. Hafen. *The Far West and the Rockies, 1820–1875.* vol. 6. Glendale: Arthur H. Clark and Company, 1957.

Benson, Maxine. *From Pittsburgh to the Rocky Mountains: Major Stephen Long's Expedition, 1819–1820.* Golden, CO: Fulcrum, 1988.

Berres, Thomas Edward. *Power and Gender in Oneota Culture: A Study of a Late Prehistoric People.* Dekalb: Northern Illinois University Press, 2001.

Black Hawk. *Autobiography of Ma-Ka-Tai-Me-She-Kia-Kiak, or Black Hawk.* 1833. Oquawka, IL: J. B. Patterson, 1882.

Blaine, Martha Royce. *The Ioway Indians.* Norman: University of Oklahoma Press, 1995.

Blevins, Brooks. *A History of the Ozarks.* 2 vols. Urbana: University of Illinois Press, 2018–2019.

Britton, Wiley. *The Civil War on the Border.* 2 vols. New York: G. P. Putnam's Sons, 1899.

———. *Memoirs of the Rebellion on the Border, 1863.* Chicago: Cushing, Thomas & Co., Publishers, 1882.

Brown, Harry J. *Injun Joe's Ghost: The Indian Mixed-Blood in American Writing.* Columbia: University of Missouri Press, 2004.

Buchanan, Meghan E. and B. Jacob Skousen, eds. *Tracing the Relational: The Archaeology of Worlds, Spirits, and Temporalities.* Salt Lake City: The University of Utah Press, 2015.

Bibliography

Burns, Louis F. *A History of the Osage People.* Tuscaloosa: The University of Alabama Press, 2004.

Burt, Larry W. *Tribalism in Crisis: Federal Indian Policy, 1953–1961.* Albuquerque: University of New Mexico Press, 1982.

Calloway, Colin G. *"The Chiefs Now in This City": Indians and the Urban Frontier in Early America.* New York: Oxford University Press, 2021.

———. *One Vast Winter Count: The Native American West before Lewis and Clark.* Lincoln: University of Nebraska Press, 2003.

———. *Pen and Ink Witchcraft: Treaties and Treaty Making in American Indian History.* New York: Oxford University Press, 2013.

Carter, Clarence Edwin, ed. *The Territorial Papers of the United States,* vol. 14. *The Territory of Louisiana-Missouri, 1803-1814.* Washington, DC: Government Printing Office, 1949.

Case, Martin. *The Relentless Business of Treaties: How Indigenous Land Became U.S. Property.* St. Paul: Minnesota Historical Society Press, 2018.

Castel, Albert. *Civil War Kansas: Reaping the Whirlwind.* Lawrence: University Press of Kansas, 1997.

Cayton, Andrew R. L. and Frederika J. Teute, eds. *Contact Points: American Frontiers from the Mohawk Valley to the Mississippi, 1750-1830.* Chapel Hill: University of North Caroline Press, 1998.

Chamberlain, Alexander Francis. *Wisdom of the North American Indian in Speech and Legend.* Worcester, MA: American Antiquarian Society, 1913.

Chapman, Carl H. *The Archaeology of Missouri.* 2 vols. Columbia: University of Missouri Press, 1988 and 1980.

Chapman, Carl H. and Eleanor F. Chapman. *Indians and Archaeology of Missouri.* Columbia: University of Missouri Press, 1983.

Childs, Craig. *Atlas of a Lost World: Travels in Ice Age America.* New York: Vintage Books, 2018.

Chittenden, Hiram Martin. *The American Fur Trade of the Far West.* 3 vols. 1902, Reprint, Eastford, CT: Martino Fine Books, 2014.

Christ, Mark K. ed. *Rugged and Sublime: The Civil War in Arkansas.* Fayetteville: The University of Arkansas Press, 1994.

Christensen, Lawrence O. and Gary R. Kremer. *A History of Missouri: 1875-1919,* vol. 4. Columbia: University of Missouri Press, 1997.

Clampitt, Bradley R. ed. *The Civil War and Reconstruction in Indian Territory.* Lincoln: University of Nebraska Press, 2015.

Clark, Andrew J. and Douglas B. Bamforth, eds. *Archaeological Perspectives on Warfare on the Great Plains.* Louisville, CO: University Press of Colorado, 2018.

Cleary, Patricia. *The World, the Flesh, and the Devil; A History of Colonial St. Louis.* vol. 1. Columbia: University of Missouri Press, 2011.

Collins, Robert. *Jim Lane: Scoundrel, Statesman, Kansan.* Gretna, LA: Pelican Publishing Company, 2007.

Confer, Clarissa W. *Daily Life in Pre-Columbian Native America.* Westport, CT: Greenwood Press, 2008.

Bibliography

Crowe, Clint. *Caught in the Maelstrom: The Indian Nations in the Civil War, 1861–1865*. El Dorado Hills, CA: Savas Beatie, 2019.

Cutrer, Thomas W. *Theater of a Separate War: The Civil War West of the Mississippi River, 1861–1865*. Chapel Hill: The University of North Carolina Press, 2017.

Debo, Angie. *The Road to Disappearance: A History of the Creek Indians*. Norman: University of Oklahoma Press, 1979.

Deloria, Philip J. *Playing Indian*. New Haven: Yale University Press, 1998.

Deloria, Vine Jr. *Red Earth, White Lies: Native Americans and the Myth of Scientific Fact*. Golden, CO: Fulcrum Publishing, 1997.

Diaz-Granados, Carol and James R. Duncan. *The Petroglyphs and Pictographs of Missouri*. Tuscaloosa: The University of Alabama Press, 2000.

Dickey, Michael. *Arrow Rock: Crossroads of the Missouri Frontier*. Arrow Rock: The Friends of Arrow Rock, Inc, 2004.

———. *The People of the River's Mouth: In Search of the Missouria Indians*. Columbia: University of Missouri Press, 2011.

Dillehay, Thomas D. *The Settlement of the Americas: A New Prehistory*. New York: Basic Books, 2000.

Din, Gilbert C. and Abraham P. Nasatir. *The Imperial Osages: Spanish-Indian Diplomacy in the Mississippi Valley*. Norman: University of Oklahoma Press, 1983.

Dixon, E. James. *Bones, Boats and Bison: Archeology and the First Colonization of Western North America*. Albuquerque: University of New Mexico Press, 1999.

Duden, Gottfried. *Report on a Journey to the Western States of North America*. Edited by James W. Goodrich. Translated by George H. Kellner, et al. Columbia: University of Missouri Press, 1980.

Dunbar-Ortiz, Roxanne. *An Indigenous Peoples' History of the United States*. Boston: Beacon Press, 2014.

DuVal, Kathleen. *The Native Ground: Indians and Colonists in the Heart of the Continent*. Philadelphia: University of Pennsylvania Press, 2006.

Dye, David H. and Cheryl Anne Cox, eds. *Towns and Temples Along the Mississippi*. Tuscaloosa: University of Alabama Press, 1990.

Edmunds, R. David. *The Potawatomis: Keepers of the Fire*. Norman: University of Oklahoma Press, 1978.

Edwards, Tai S. *Osage Women and Empire: Gender and Power*, Lawrence: University Press of Kansas, 2018.

Ekberg, Carl J. *French Roots in the Illinois Country: The Mississippi Frontier in Colonial Times*. Urbana: University of Illinois Press, 1998.

———. *Stealing Indian Women: Native Slavery in the Illinois Country*. Urbana: University of Illinois Press, 2007.

Ekberg, Carl J. and Sharon K. Person. *St. Louis Rising: The French Regime of Louis St. Ange De Bellerive*. Urbana: University of Illinois Press, 2015.

Ellinghaus, Katherine. *Blood Will Tell: Native Americans and Assimilation Policy*. Lincoln: University of Nebraska Press, 2017.

Ellis Clyde, Luke Eric Lassiter, and Gary H. Dunham, eds. *Powwow*. Lincoln: University of Nebraska Press, 2005.

Emerson, Thomas E., et al. *Late Woodland Societies: Tradition and Transformation Across the Midcontinent.* Lincoln: University of Nebraska Press, 2000.

Ethridge, Robbie, *From Chicaza to Chickasaw: The European Invasion and the Transformation of the Mississippian World, 1540-1715.* Chapel Hill: The University of North Carolina Press, 2010.

Fagan, Brian. *The First North Americans: An Archaeological Journey.* New York: Thames and Hudson, 2011.

———. *The Great Journey: The Peopling of Ancient America.* New York: Thames and Hudson, 1989.

Fausz, J. Frederick. *Founding St. Louis: First City of the New West.* Charleston, SC: The History Press, 2011.

Finiels, Nicolas de. *An Account of Upper Louisiana.* Translated by Carl J. Ekberg. Edited by Carl J. Ekberg and William E. Foley. Columbia: University of Missouri Press, 1989.

Fixico, Donald L. *Termination and Relocation: Federal Indian Policy, 1945–1960.* Albuquerque: University of New Mexico Press, 1986.

Flader, Susan, ed. Missouri State Parks and Historic Sites: Exploring Our Legacy. Boonville, MO: Missouri Life Magazine, Inc. and Missouri Parks Association, 2016.

Foley, William E. *The Genesis of Missouri: From Wilderness Outpost to Statehood.* Columbia: University of Missouri Press, 1989.

———. *A History of Missouri, 1673 to 1820*, vol. 1. Columbia: University of Missouri Press, 1971.

———. *Wilderness Journey: The Life of William Clark.* Columbia: University of Missouri Press, 2004.

Foley, William E. and C. David Rice. *The First Chouteaus: River Barons of Early St. Louis.* Urbana: University of Illinois Press, 1983.

Foreman, Grant. *Indians and Pioneers: The Story of the American Southwest Before 1830.* Norman: University of Oklahoma Press, 1975.

———. *Indian Removal: The Emigration of the Five Civilized Tribes of Indians.* Norman: University of Oklahoma Press, 1956.

Fowke, Gerald. "Antiquities of Central and Southeastern Missouri" *Smithsonian Institution Bureau of American Ethnology Bulletin* 37. Washington, DC: Government Printing Office, 1910.

Fritz, Gayle J. *Feeding Cahokia: Early Agriculture in the North American Heartland.* Tuscaloosa: The University of Alabama Press, 2019.

Gale, John. *The Missouri Expedition, 1818–1820: The Journal of Surgeon John Gale with Related Documents.* Edited by Roger L. Nichols. Norman: University of Oklahoma Press, 1969.

Garraghan, Gilbert J. *The Jesuits of the Middle United States.* vol. 1. 1938. Reprint. Chicago: Loyola University Press, 1983.

Genetin-Pilawa, C. Joseph. *Crooked Paths to Allotment: The Fight over Federal Indian Policy after the Civil War.* Chapel Hill: University of North Carolina Press, 2012.

Gibson, Arrell M. *The Chickasaws*. Norman: University of Oklahoma Press, 1971.

———. *The Kickapoos: Lords of the Middle Border*. Norman: University of Oklahoma Press, 1963.

Gilio-Whitaker, Dina. *As Long as the Grass Grows: The Indigenous Fight for Environmental Justice, From Colonization to Standing Rock*. Boston: Beacon Press, 2019.

Gitlin, Jay, Robert Michael Morrissey, and Peter J. Kastor, eds. *French St. Louis: Landscapes, Contexts, and Legacy*. Lincoln: University of Nebraska, 2021.

Graf, Kelly E., Caroline V. Ketron, and Michael R. Waters, eds. *Paleoamerican Odyssey*. College Station: Texas A&M University Press, 2014.

Grenier, John. *The First Way of War: American War Making on the Frontier*. Cambridge: Cambridge University Press, 2005.

Hagan, William T. *The Sac and Fox Indians*. Norman: University of Oklahoma Press, 1988.

Hall, Robert L. *An Archaeology of the Soul: North American Indian Belief and Ritual*. Urbana: University of Illinois Press, 1997.

Hämäläinen Pekka. *Lakota America: A New History of Indigenous Power*. New Haven: Yale University Press, 2019.

Harjo, Suzan Shown, ed. *Nation to Nation: Treaties Between the United States and American Indian Nations*. Washington, DC: Smithsonian Books, 2014.

Hauptman, Laurence M. *Between Two Fires: American Indians in the Civil War*. New York: The Free Press, 1995.

Haynes, Gary. *The Early Settlement of North America: The Clovis Era*. New York: Cambridge University Press, 2002.

Herring, Joseph B. *The Enduring Indians of Kansas: A Century and a Half of Acculturation*. Lawrence: University Press of Kansas, 1990.

Hertzberg, Hazel W. *The Search for an American Indian Identity: Modern Pan-Indian Movements*. Syracuse, NY: Syracuse University Press, 1971.

Hess, Earl J. *The Union Soldier in Battle: Enduring the Ordeal of Combat*. Lawrence: University Press of Kansas, 1997.

Hodge, F. W. *Thirty-Seventh Annual Report of the Bureau of American Ethnology to the Secretary of the Smithsonian Institution 1915-1916*. Washington, DC: Government Printing Office, 1923.

Hoig, Stan. *The Chouteaus: First Family of the Fur Trade*. Albuquerque: University of New Mexico Press, 2008.

Holm, Tom. *The Great Confusion in Indian Affairs Native Americans and Whites in the Progressive Era*. Austin: University of Texas Press, 2005.

Horsman, Reginald. *Expansion and American Indian Policy, 1783–1812*. Norman: University of Oklahoma Press, 1992.

Houck, Louis, ed. *The Spanish Regime in Missouri*. Chicago: R. R. Donnelley and Sons, 1909.

Huggins, Stephen. *America's Use of Terror from Colonial Times to the A-Bomb*. Lawrence: University Press of Kansas, 2019.

Ingenthron, Elmo. *Borderland Rebellion: A History of the Civil War on the Missouri-Arkansas Border*. Branson, MO: Ozarks Mountaineer, 1980.

Bibliography

———. *Indians of the Ozark Plateau*. Point Lookout, MO: The School of the Ozarks Press, 1970.

Iverson, Peter and Wade Davis. *"We Are Still Here:" American Indians since 1890*. Malden, MA: Wiley Blackwell, 2015.

Jacobs, Joseph and Alfred Nutt, eds. *The International Folklore Congress, 1891: Papers and Transactions*. London: David Nutt, 1892.

James, Edwin, et al. *Account of an Expedition from Pittsburgh to the Rocky Mountains Under the Command of Major Stephen H. Long*. 3 vols. Philadelphia: H. C. Carcy and I. Lea, 1822–1823.

Jensen, Richard E. and James S. Hutchins, eds. *Wheel Boats on the Missouri: The Journals and Documents of the Atkinson-O'Fallon Expedition, 1824–26*. Helena: Montana Historical Society Press, 2001.

Johnson, Walter. *The Broken Heart of America: St. Louis and the Violent History of the United States*. New York: Basic Books, 2020.

Joseph, Alvin M. Jr. *The Civil War in the American West*. New York: A. A. Knopf, 1991.

Judson, Katharine Berry. *Myths and Legends of the Great Plains*. Chicago: A. C. McClurg and Company, 1913.

Kappler, Charles J. *Indian Affairs: Laws and Treaties*, vol. 2. Washington DC: Government Printing Office, 1904.

Kastor, Peter J. *The Great Acquisition: An Introduction to the Louisiana Purchase*. Great Falls, MT: Lewis and Clark Interpretive Association, 2003.

———. *William Clark's World: Describing America in an Age of Unknown*. New Haven: Yale University Press, 2011.

Kelley, Dennis. *Tradition, Performance, and Religion in Native America Ancestral Ways, Modern Selves*. New York: Routledge, 2015.

Kelly, Mark William. *Lost Voices on the Missouri: John Dougherty and the Indian Frontier*. Leavenworth, KS: Sam Clark Publishing Company, 2013.

Krech, Shepard III. *The Ecological Indian: Myth and Mystery*. New York: W. W. Norton, 1999.

Kurz, Rudolph Friedrich. "Journal of Rudolph Friedrich Kurz." Edited by J. N. B Hewitt, Translated by Myrtis Jarrell. *Bureau of American Ethnology Bulletin*. vol. 115 (1937).

La Flesche, Francis. *The Osage and the Invisible World: From the Works of Francis La Flesche*. Edited by Garrick A. Bailey. Norman: University of Oklahoma Press, 1995.

Lakomäki, Sami. *Gathering Together: The Shawnee People through Diaspora and Nationhood, 1600–1870*. New Haven: Yale University Press, 2014.

Leach, Mark W. *The Great Pyramids of St. Louis: An Ancient Metropolis*. Self-published, 2017.

Least Heat-Moon, William and James K. Wallace, eds. and trans. *An Osage Journey to Europe, 1827–1830: Three French Accounts*. Norman: University of Oklahoma Press, 2013.

Lee, Jacob F. *Masters of the Middle Waters: Indian Nations and Colonial Ambitions along the Mississippi*. Cambridge, MA: Belknap Press, 2019.

Bibliography

Lewin, Jacqueline A. and Marilyn S. Taylor. *The St. Joe Road: Emigration Mid-1800s.* St. Joseph, MO: The St. Joseph Museums Inc., 1992.

Lewis, Hugh M. *Robidoux Chronicles: French-Indian Ethnoculture of the Trans-Mississippi West.* Victoria, B.C.: Trafford, 2004.

Leyburn, James G. *The Scotch-Irish: A Social History.* Chapel Hill: The University of North Carolina Press, 1962.

Litchman, Charles H., ed. *The Official History of the Improved Order of Red Men.* Boston: The Fraternity Publishing Company, 1893.

Loewen, James W. *Lies Across America: What Our Historic Sites Get Wrong.* New York: The New Press, 1999.

McCandless, Perry. *A History of Missouri: 1820 to 1860.* vol. 2. Columbia: University of Missouri Press, 1972.

McDermott, John Francis, ed. *The Spanish in the Mississippi Valley, 1762–1804.* Urbana: University of Illinois Press, 1974.

McKenney, Thomas L. and James Hall. *History of the Indian Tribes of North America.* vol. 2. Philadelphia: D. Rice and A. N. Hart, 1855.

McNutt, Charles H., ed. *Prehistory of the Central Mississippi Valley.* Tuscaloosa: The University of Alabama Press, 1996.

Mann, Charles C. *1491: New Revelations of the Americas Before Columbus.* New York: Alfred A. Knopf, 2005.

Mathews, John Joseph. *The Osages: Children of the Middle Waters.* Norman: University of Oklahoma Press, 1961.

Meltzer, David J. *First Peoples in a New World: Colonizing Ice Age America.* Berkley: University of California Press, 2009.

Merchant, Carolyn. *Ecological Revolutions: Nature, Gender, and Science in New England.* Chapel Hill: The University of North Carolina Press, 1989.

Meriwether, David. *My Life in the Mountains and on the Plains.* Edited by Robert A. Griffen. Norman: University of Oklahoma Press, 1965.

Miller, Douglas K. *Indians on the Move: Native American Mobility and Urbanization in the Twentieth Century.* Chapel Hill: The University of North Carolina Press, 2019.

Miller, Robert J. et al. *Discovering Indigenous Lands: The Doctrine of Discovery in the English Colonies.* New York: Oxford University Press, 2010.

Miner, Craig H. *The Corporation and the Indian: Tribal Sovereignty and Industrial Civilization in Indian Territory, 1865–1907.* Columbia University of Missouri Press, 1976.

Miner, Craig and William E. Unrau. *The End of Indian Kansas: A Study of Cultural Revolution, 1854–1871.* Lawrence: University Press of Kansas, 1990.

Morgan, M. J. *Land of Big Rivers: French and Indian Illinois, 1699-1778.* Carbondale: Southern Illinois University Press, 2010.

Morrissey, Robert Michael. *Empire by Collaboration: Indians, Colonists, and Governments in Colonial Illinois Country.* Philadelphia: University of Pennsylvania Press, 2015.

Moulton, Gary E. *John Ross: Cherokee Chief.* Athens: University of Georgia Press, 1978.

Murray, David. *Matter, Magic, and Spirit: Representing Indian and African American Belief.* Philadelphia: University of Pennsylvania Press, 2007.

Nasatir, A. P. *Before Lewis and Clark: Documents Illustrating the History of the Missouri,* 2 vols. Lincoln: University of Nebraska Press, 1990.

Newcomb, Steven T. *Pagans in the Promised Land: Decoding the Doctrine of Christian Discovery.* Golden, Colorado: Fulcrum Press, 2008.

Newitz, Annalee. *Four Lost Cities: A Secret History of the Urban Age.* New York: W. W. Norton and Company, 2021.

Nichols, David A. *Lincoln and the Indians: Civil War Policy and Politics.* St. Paul: Minnesota Historical Society Press, 2012.

Norall, Frank. *Bourgmont: Explorer of the Missouri, 1698–1725.* Lincoln: University of Nebraska Press, 1988.

Northup, Beverly Baker. *"We Are Not Yet Conquered": The History of the Northern Cherokee Nation of the Old Louisiana Territory.* Paducah, KT: Turner Publishing Company, 2001.

O'Brien, Jean M. *Firsting and Lasting: Writing Indians out of Existence in New England.* Minneapolis: University of Minnesota Press, 2010.

O'Brien, Michael J. *Cat Monsters and Head Pots: The Archaeology of Missouri's Pemiscot Bayou.* Columbia: University of Missouri Press, 1994.

———. *Paradigms of the Past: The Story of Missouri Archaeology.* Columbia: University of Missouri Press, 1996.

O'Brien, Michael J. and W. Raymond Wood. *The Prehistory of Missouri.* Columbia: University of Missouri Press, 1998.

Oglesby, Richard Edward. *Manuel Lisa and the Opening of the Missouri Fur Trade.* Norman: University of Oklahoma Press, 1963.

Olson, Greg. *Ioway Life: Reservation and Reform, 1837–1860.* Norman: University of Oklahoma Press, 2016.

———. *The Ioway in Missouri.* Columbia: University of Missouri Press, 2008.

———. *Voodoo Priests, Noble Savages, and Ozark Gypsies: The Life of Folklorist Mary Alicia Owen.* Columbia, University of Missouri Press, 2012.

Ostler, Jeffrey. *Surviving Genocide: Native Nations and the United States from the American Revolution to Bleeding Kansas.* New Haven: Yale University Press, 2019.

Otis, D. S. *The Dawes Act and the Allotment of Indian Lands.* 1934, reprint ed. Francis Paul Prucha. Norman: University of Oklahoma Press, 1973.

Owen, Mary Alicia. *Old Rabbit, the Voodoo, and Other Sorcerers.* London: T. Fisher Unwin, 1893.

Owens, Louis. *Mixedblood Messages: Literature, Film, Family, Place.* Norman: Red River Books, 2001.

Owens, Robert M. *Mr. Jefferson's Hammer: William Henry Harrison and the Origins of American Indian Policy.* Norman: University of Oklahoma Press, 2007.

Bibliography

Parrish, William E., *A History of Missouri, 1860 to 1875*. vol. 3. Columbia: University of Missouri Press, 1973.

Pauketat, Timothy R. *An Archaeology of the Cosmos: Rethinking Agency and Religion in Ancient America*. New York: Routledge, 2013.

———. *Cahokia: Ancient America's Great City on the Mississippi*. New York: Penguin Books, 2009.

Pauketat, Timothy R. and Susan Alt, eds. *Medieval Mississippians: The Cahokian World*. Santa Fe: School for Advanced Research Press, 2015.

Philip, Kenneth R., ed. *Indian Self-Rule: First-Hand Accounts of Indian-White Relations from Roosevelt to Reagan*. Salt Lake City: Howe Brothers, 1986.

Prucha, Francis Paul. *American Indian Treaties: The History of a Political Anomaly*. Berkeley: University of California Press, 1994.

Raff, Jennifer. *Origin: A Genetic History of the Americas*. New York. New York: Twelve Books, 2022.

Redman, Samuel J. *Prophets and Ghosts: The Story of Salvage Anthropology*. Cambridge: Harvard University Press, 2021.

Reilly, F. Kent, III and James F. Garber, eds. *Ancient Objects and Sacred Realms: Interpretations of Mississippian Iconography*. Austin: University of Texas Press, 2007.

Rollings, Willard H. *The Osage: An Ethnohistorical Study of Hegemony on the Prairie-Plains*. Columbia: University of Missouri Press, 1995.

———. *Unaffected by the Gospel: Osage Resistance to the Christian Invasion, 1673–1906: A Cultural Victory*. Albuquerque: University of New Mexico Press, 2004.

Rosenthal, Nicolas G. *Reimagining Indian Country: Native American Migration and Identity in Twentieth-Century Los Angeles*. Chapel Hill: University of North Carolina Press, 2012.

Rowe, Mary Ellen. *Bulwark of the Republic: The American Militia in Antebellum West*. Westport, CT: Praeger Publishers, 2003.

Sapp, David, et al. eds. *Boone County Chronicles*. Columbia, MO: Boone County Historical Society, 2000.

Saunt, Claudio. *Unworthy Republic: The Dispossession of Native Americans and the Road to Indian Territory*. New York: W. W. Norton and Company, 2020.

Scharnhorst, Gary. *The Life of Mark Twain: The Early Years, 1835–1871*. Columbia: University of Missouri Press, 2018.

Schoolcraft, Henry Rowe. *Journal of a Tour into the Interior of Missouri and Arkansaw*. 1821. Andesite Press, n.d.

Schwartz, Marion. *A History of Dogs in the Early Americas*. New Haven: Yale University Press, 1997.

Shea, John Gilmary. *Discovery and Exploration of the Mississippi Valley*. New York: Redfield, 1852.

Sifakis, Stewart. *Compendium of the Confederate Armies: Kentucky, Maryland, Missouri, the Confederate Units, and the Indian Units*. New York: Facts on File, Inc., 1995.

Bibliography

Smithers, Gregory D. *The Cherokee Diaspora: An Indigenous History of Migration, Resettlement, and Identity*. New Haven: Yale University Press, 2015.

Snyder, Christina. *Great Crossings: Indians, Settlers, and Slaves in the Age of Jackson*. New York: Oxford University Press, 2017.

Stith, Matthew M. *Extreme Civil War: Guerrilla Warfare Environment, and Race in the Trans-Mississippi Frontier*. Baton Rouge: Louisiana State University Press, 2016.

Steeves, Paulette F. C. *The Indigenous Paleolithic of the Western Hemisphere*. Lincoln: University of Nebraska Press, 2021.

Switzler, William, ed. *History of Boone County, Missouri*. 1882, reprint, Cape Girardeau, MO: Ramfire Press, 1970.

Theler, James L. and Robert F. Boszhardt. *Twelve Millennia: Archaeology of the Upper Mississippi River Valley*. Iowa City: University of Iowa Press, 2003.

Thorne, Tanis C. *The Many Hands of My Relations: French and Indians in the Lower Missouri*. Columbia: University of Missouri Press, 1996.

Thrush, Coll. *Indigenous London: Native Travelers at the Heart of Empire*. New Haven: Yale University Press, 2016.

Thwaites, Reuben Gold. *Early Western Travels: 1748–1846*, 32 vols. Cleveland: The Arthur H. Clark Company, 1904–1907.

Townsend, Richard F., ed. *Hero, Hawk, and Open Hand: American Indian Art of the Ancient Midwest and South*. New Haven: Yale University Press, 2004.

Treuer, Anton. *Atlas of Indian Nations*. Washington DC: National Geographic, 2014.

Treuer, David. *The Heartbeat of Wounded Knee: Native America from 1890 to the Present*. New York: Riverhead Books, 2019.

Truteau, Jean-Baptiste. *A Fur Trader on the Upper Missouri; The Journal and Description of Jean-Baptiste Truteau, 1794–1796*. Edited by Raymond J. DeMallie, et al. Lincoln: University of Nebraska Press, 2017.

Viola, Herman J. *Diplomats in Buckskins: A History of Indian Delegations in Washington City*, Washington, DC: Smithsonian Institution Press, 1981.

Vizenor, Gerald. *Fugitive Poses: Native American Indian Scenes of Absence and Presence*. Lincoln: University of Nebraska Press, 1998.

Waldman, Carl. *Encyclopedia of Native American Tribes*. New York: Checkmark Books, 2006.

Warde, Mary Jane. *When the Wolf Came: The Civil War and the Indian Territory*. Fayetteville: University of Arkansas Press, 2013.

Washburn, Wilcomb E. *The Assault on Indian Tribalism: The General Allotment Law (Dawes Act) of 1887*. Malabar, FL: Robert E. Krieger Publishing Company, 1975.

Wedel, Waldo R. *Prehistoric Man on the Great Plains*. Norman: University of Oklahoma Press, 1961.

Weigle, Martha and Barbara A. Babcock, eds. *The Great Southwest of the Fred Harvey Company and the Santa Fe Railway*. Phoenix, AZ: The Heard Museum and the University of Arizona Press, 1996.

Bibliography

Weslager, C. A. *The Delaware Indians: A History*. New Brunswick, NJ: Rutgers University Press: 1972.

White, Richard. *The Middle Ground: Indians, Empires, and Republics in the Great Lakes Region, 1650-1815*. New York: Cambridge University Press, 1991.

White Hat, Albert, Sr. *Life's Journey-Zuya: Oral Teachings from Rosebud*. Salt Lake City: University of Utah Press, 2012.

Whittaker, William E., ed. *Frontier Forts of Iowa: Indians, Traders, and Soldiers, 1682–1862*. Iowa City: University of Iowa Press, 2009.

Willoughby, Robert J. *The Brothers Robidoux and the Opening of the American West*. Columbia: University of Missouri Press, 2012.

Wilm, Julius. Settlers as Conquerors: Free Land Policy in Antebellum America. Stuttgart: Franz Steiner Verlag, 2018.

Winchester, Simon. *Land: How the Hunger for Ownership Shaped the Modern World*. New York: Harper, 2021.

Wolferman, Kristie C. *The Nelson-Atkins Museum of Art: A History*. Columbia: University of Missouri Press, 2020.

Wood, W. Raymond, et al. *Holocene Human Adaptations in the Missouri Prairie-Timberlands*. Fayetteville: Arkansas Archeological Survey, 1995.

Zack, Naomi, ed. *The Oxford Handbook of Philosophy and Race*. New York: Oxford University Press, 2017.

Index

Page numbers in *italics* refer to illustrations.

Index

Armstrong, John (secretary of war), 159

Armstrong, Orland Kay (Missouri congressman): and termination of tribal governments, 289

Arnold Research Cave, 25

Aron, Stephen: *American Confluence: The Missouri Frontier from Borderland to Border State*, xx, 86

assimilation: of Indigenous Missourians, 255–60: and Pan-Indian Movements, 277; Joseph Herring on, 358n24

Atchison, Kansas, 100

Atkinson, Henry (colonel): with the Sixth US Infantry at Council Bluff, 170

Atlantic and Pacific Railroad, 242

atlatls, 24

Aunt Em'ly (Fox): in *Old Rabbit, the Voodoo, and Other Sorcerers*, 222

Bah-Mary: and the Nelson-Atkins Museum of Art, 269

Bailey, Garrick: on Francis La Flesche, 66

Balio, Paul, 184

Ballinger, Richard A. (secretary of the interior), 263

Baltus, Melissa R.: on Cahokia, 52

Banks, Joseph William (Ioway): children, 219; children and inheritance, 220; date of birth, 358n31; death, 220; marries Elizabeth Ellen Simmons, 220

Banks, William, Sr.: death, 220; marries Giant Woman, 218–19; settles in Holt County, Missouri, 218; and John McIntosh, 218; marries Jane Newasha, 219

Banks, William Jr. (Sac and Fox), 219–21; marries Sarah Helen Wake, 220; in Sac and Fox census, 219

Barbé-Marbois, François: and the Louisiana Purchase, 140

Barlow, Alfred Hinton: and Elisabeth Gibson, 225

Barnes, Twila (Cherokee): on Cherokee tribes without federal recognition, 321

Barron, Joseph, 148

Bartle, H. Roe: nickname, 315; and Tribe of Mic-O-Say, 265, 316–17

Bates, Frederick (acting governor of the Louisiana Territory), 151

Battle of Pea Ridge, Arkansas, 233

Battle of Newtonia, Missouri: Indigenous soldiers in, 234–35

Battle of Thames, 172

Battle of the Sink Hole, 160

Bauer, William J., Jr.: *We Are the Land: A History of Native California*, xx

Beason, Jimmy (Osage), xix

Benn, David: on Oneota culture, 69

Benoît, François Marie, 132

Benson Larry V.: on climate change and Cahokia, 60

Benton, Thomas Hart (artist), xv–xvii, *xvi*; on Geronimo, 272

Benton, Thomas Hart (Missouri senator), 199, 200, 212

Beringia, 12–15, *13*

Berres, Thomas Edward: on contact between Oneotas and Mississippians, 70; on Oneota gender roles, 71

Bible: Genesis 1:28, 78

Big Angy (Ioway): in *Old Rabbit, the Voodoo, and Other Sorcerers*, 222

Big Eddy Site (Missouri), 19

Big Elk (*Ongpatonga*) (Omaha leader): on US military's overhunting, 175; on US military presence, 167; on US military violence, 175; speaking at the Treaty of 1830, 195

Big Mound (St. Louis), 58; destruction of 239–40, *240*

Big Neck (Ioway leader). *See* Great Walker

Big Nemaha River (or Great Nemaha River) (Nebraska): Oneota sites near, 73

Big Soldier (Osage): travels to Europe, 185–88

Big Track (Osage leader), 145; response to Louisiana Purchase, 137; as Osage *Hun Ka*, or Earth People, leader, 127

Black Bird (Osage): dies at sea, 188; travels to Europe, 185–88

396

Index

Index

Dellinger, Samuel: Ozark Bluff Dwellers, 31–32

Deloria, Philip J. (Lakota): on appropriation of Indigenous culture, 316

Deloria, Philip S. (Lakota): on idealizing Indigenous people, 281

Deloria, Vine, Jr., xix; critique of the Land Bridge Migration theory, 12–14; *Red Earth, White Lies: Native Americans and the Myth of Scientific Fact*, 12–14

Deroin, Frank (Ioway): Ioway dances, 279

Deroine, Jeffrey: and Banks and McIntosh, 218; freedom purchased by Ioways, 202; and Joseph Eugene Robidoux, 221; and the Treaty of 1836, 202

diseases: among Quapaws, 84

Deruisseau, Joseph: Fort Cavagnal, 103–4; and trade monopoly, 103

De Soto, Hernando, 76; travels in North America, 79–82, *80*, 244

Descombes, Kenn "Grey Elk": on the Dawes Rolls, 321

Des Peres River (Missouri): site of Kaskaskia mission, 94, 111

Dhegihan (Siouan language and speakers), 63, 65; dates of migration, 344n22; in Oneota culture, 69–74

Diaz-Granados, Carol, xix; on Long-nosed God maskettes, 59

Dickey, Michael, xix; on near annihilation of Missourias, 126

Dickerson, Kathy (Kiowa): and the St. Louis American Indian Consortium, 318; and the Thunderbird Society, 318

Dillehay, Thomas D., 15; on Clovis points, 19–20

Dinhmete, Eliza: in the US Census, 247

Dixon Site (Iowa), 73

Doctrine of Discovery, 78–79; in *Johnson v. M'Intosh*, 177–178; legitimizes La Salle's claim for France, 89–90; Right of Ownership, 78, 148; Right of Occupancy (or Aboriginal Title), 78, 148, 177–78, 198; and the Treaty of 1804, 148–49; in US treaty process, 142

Dodge, Henry (colonel), 159; removes settlers from the Platte Country, 199; and the Treaty of 1815, 161

Dogs: domesticated, 9

Dog Soldier (Little Osage leader): meets with Thomas Jefferson, 144

Doniphan, Kansas: Oneota site near, 72–73

Dougherty, John (Indian agent), 199, 213; and the Treaty of 1836, 203

Douglass, Joseph "Injun Joe": in *The Adventures of Tom Sayer*, 247

Drake, Charles: and the Drake Constitution, 238

Drew, John: and the First Cherokee Mounted Rifles, 233

Ducharme Jean-Marie: defies Spanish Trade restrictions, 119

Duden, Gottfried: encourages German settlement in Missouri, 188–89; observations on Indigenous people, 188

Dugué, Pierre, Sieur de Boisbriant, 95

Dunbar, James: and the Heatherly War, 200–201

Dunbar-Ortiz, Roxanne, xix; colonization of European countries, 77; on Indigenous life in the 1920s, 285; on Scots-Irish, 143

Duncan, James R., xix; on Long-nosed God maskettes, 59

Dunklin, Daniel (Missouri governor): threatens Potawatomis, 201

Dupuis, Frank (Ioway), 219

du Tisné, Charles Claude, 102

DuVal, Kathleen, xix; on Coronado, 81; on Indigenous alliances with European colonizers, 115; on Osage "empire", 122; on Quapaws' attitudes toward French, 90

Dye David H.: on He-Who-Wears-Human-Heads–As-Earrings, 56–57

Earth Mother; 54, 55; cult of, 53; flint clay figurines of, 54–55. *See also* Old-Woman-Who-Never-Dies

East St. Louis, Illinois: fire 62; fortification of, 62; Mississippian mounds, 49–50

402

Index

Easterly, Thomas: photographs Big Mound's destruction, 239, *240*

Eastman, Charles (Dakota): progressive activism, 275–76

Eastman, Elaine Goodale: and the School of the Woods, 275–76

Eaton, John (secretary of war), 199

Echo, Hawk Crystal (Pawnee): on lack of accurate Indigenous representation, 313

Eckberg, Carl J., xix; on enslaved people, 99; on early French explorers, 84; on Kaskaskia, 91;

Eckley, Lillian (Ioway): and traditional clothing, 27

Edwards, Ninian: and the Treaty of 1815, 161

Edwards, Tai S., xix; on William Clark's use of coercion in the Treaty of 1808, 155–56; on Osages' trade strength, 121–22

Elban, Eliza: in the US Census, 247

Elbert, Gustavus M. (captain): and the First Missouri, 233

Elizabeth I (queen), 79

Ellinghaus, Katherine: on unenrolled Natives, 262

Ellsworth, Edward A., 198

Emerson, Thomas: on cult of Earth Mother, 53; on Late Woodland Period, 34

Encircler, The (*Waw-ron-esaw*) (Otoe leader): on assimilation, 168

England, *See* Great Britain

enslaved people: associations with Indigenous people, 222; at Fort Orleans, 99; on the Great Nemaha Agency, 222; at St. Louis, 99; trade in, 99

Europeans; Paleolithic, 15; as conquerors or discoverers, 78; monarchs against peasantry, 77–78

Eustis, William (Secretary of war): authorizes William Clark to bring Indigenous delegation to Washington DC, 157

Exchange (steamboat), 172

Executive Order 44: legalizes the murder of Mormons in Missouri. 214–16

Expedition (steamboat), 172

factories, US trade, 147

Fanning, Kansas, 72

Faragher, John Mack: on forcing Indigenous people to sell land, 178

Fausz, J. Frederick, xix; on Osages importance to St. Louis, 112

Federal Land Office, 148, 191. *See also* General Land Office

Federal Writer's Project: *Arkansas: A Guide to the State*, 32

Fenton, Missouri, 240

Ferdinand (king), 78–79

Fields, Elinor "El," xv–xvii, *xvi*

fire: pyroregeneration (intentional burning), 24–25

Fire Prairie (Missouri): site of Treaty of 1808 negations, 152

firearms, 74, 75; trade at Fort Orleans, 98

First Battalion Creek Cavalry (Confederate), 232

First Battalion Seminole Mounted Rifles (Confederate), 232

First Cherokee Battalion (Confederate): at Battle of Newtonia, 234

First Choctaw and Chickasaw Mounted Rifles (Confederate), 232; at Battle of Newtonia, 234–35

First Choctaw Regiment (Confederate): at Battle of Newtonia, 234

First Creek Mounted Rifles (Confederate), 232

First Missouri: artillery overwhelmed at Pea Ridge, 233

First Regiment US Dragoons: used to end violence between settlers and Indigenous people, 201, 213

Five Civilized Tribes. *See* Cherokees, Chickasaws, Choctaws, Muscogees, *and* Seminoles

Fladmark, Knut: and kelp highway, 15, 16

Fleak, L. B.: warns Governor Reynolds about alleged alliance between Mormons and Potawatomis, 215–16

Index

Index

Index

Index

Index

Index

Mesoamerica, 33, 39

Métis, 93; in Upper Louisiana, 120; in St. Louis, 112

Mexico, 39

Miamis, 87; alliance to Britain, 158; attack on French village, 105; control trade on upper Mississippi River, 104; forced removal to Indian Territory, 211–12; meeting with the Osages and Pierre Chouteau, 131; request permission to move to Spanish territory, 123–24; town raided, 105

Michigameas: wariness of missionaries, 95; town raided, 105; meet with British, 114

micos (leaders of Mississippian chiefdoms), 81

Migration: of ancient Americans, 11; of Chiwere and Dhegihan Siouan speaking people, 64

Miller, Guion: as Special Commissioner to the Eastern Cherokees, 249

Miller, John: as Missouri congressman, 212; and the Treaty of 1815, 161

Miller, Rocky (Cherokee) (Missouri state representative): and law on selling Native art in Missouri, 318

Minor, Eliza: in the US Census, 247

Mississippi River, 24, 40, 44, 64; burial practices, 41–42; dwellings, 41; early Oneota culture near, 69; fortifications on, 116; French presence near, 90–91; La Salle on, 87–90; Marquette and Joliet on, 82–85; Mississippian villages near, 67; pottery, 40; Sioux name for, 82; and the Yellowstone Expedition, 169–75

Mississippian Period, Emergent or Early, 39–44

Mississippian Period, Late: in Missouri, 66–69

Mississippian Period, Middle, 44–69, 55–59; kinship, 58–59; Osage place in, 65–66. See also Cahokia

Missouri, 65; and "An Act to Suppress Intercourse with Indians," 214; annexes Platte Country, 203; Archaic era flora and fauna, 22–24; becomes a state, 178; bicentennial, xvii; border protection, 212–14; constitutional conventions, 238; cost of buying Indigenous land in, 204; extinguishes all Indigenous land title, 203–4, 204; geography and natural resources, 18–19; historical narrative of, 239–40; and the Homestead Act of 1862, 242; Indian boarding schools in, 248; Indigenous inhabitants in 1673, 85–87, 86; Indigenous Inhabitants forcibly removed from, xvii, 169–70, 212; Indigenous presence in, 217–18, 299; legal definition of an Indian in, 218; and legalized gambling, 304; Mississippian culture in, 66–69; petitions Congress for statehood, 177; population growth, 238; and recognition of Indian tribes, 320

Missouri Bootheel, 24, 44, 65; Cairo Lowlands, 61, 64, 66–67; de Soto in or near, 81–82; early corn production, 40; Mississippian culture in, 66–69; New Madrid Seismic Zone, 67

Missouri Department of Natural Resources (DNR): and NAGPRA, 306–8

Missouri Department of Transportation (MoDOT): and NAGPRA, 306–8

Missouri Fur Company: in competition with Pacific Fur Company, 175–76; and the death of Meriwether Lewis, 156

Missouri-Kansas-Texas Railroad (Katy), 258

Missouri Reform School for Boys; Indigenous population, 248

Missouri River, 43, 64; as border between Spanish and British colonies, 110–11; fortifications on, 116; Oneota sites near, 72–73, 73; Osages and Missourias control trade on, 101–3

Missouri State Historic Preservation Office (MoSHPO): and NAGPRA, 306–8

Missouri State Museum: and NAGPRA, 306; and Mary Alicia Owen, 268

Missouri Supreme Court, 218; Banks v. Galbraith, 218–21

Missouri Territory: established, 157; defense of, 158; estimated Indigenous population, 176; white population of, 176

Index

Index

Index

Index

Van Buren, Martin, President, 203

VanDerwarker, Amber: on maize or corn, 40; Cahokia, 53; on Cahokia's decline, 61

Van, Dorn Earl, (major general): as commander of the Confederacy's Trans-Mississippi District, 233

Vanishing Indian, 209; myth of, 216–17, 243–45; Vanishing Policy, 256–57

Van Meter State Park (Missouri). *See* Annie and Abel Van Meter State Park

Vernon County, Missouri: home of Great Osages, 86

Vashon, George (Indian agent): and the Delaware Treaty of 1829, 192–94

Vest, George Graham: on Easterners' views of Indigenous people, 257; "Eulogy for a Dog", 254; and the Missouri-Kansas-Texas Railroad, 258; and Senate Indian Commission, 255; in the US Senate, 254–55

Vetter, Joe (Ioway): and the Jerome Commission, 259–60

Vizenor, Gerald: on Indigenous presence, 217

Voluntary Relocation Program: and Adult Vocational Training, 293; and discrimination, 293; discontinued in St. Louis, 294; established, 290–91; number of participants in St. Louis, 292, 293, 294; number of participants in US, 291; and the rise of Indian centers, 293; and St. Louis, 291–94

Waguespack, Nicole, 21–22

Wah'Kon-Tah, 6, 9, 185

Wake, Sarah Helen: marries William Banks Jr., 220

Wakefield, Elmer, 31

Walker, David Edward: on Cherokee ancestors living in Missouri, 225

Walsh, Robert: and the Treaty of 1815, 161

War of 1812, 157–161

Ward, Mary: in the US Census, 247

Warde, Mary Jane: on Indigenous soldiers in the Civil War, 231

Warrel, S., (lieutenant), 149

Warren, Elizabeth, (Massachusetts senator): and claims of Cherokee heritage, 321

Warrior, Robert (Osage), xix

Washburn, Henry (Ioway): and takeover of Ioway agent's office, 253

Washington Commanders: name change, 314

Washington, DC: Ioways, Sacs and Foxes visit, 178

Washington, George (Ioway): and takeover of Ioway agent's office, 253

Watie, Stand (Cherokee) (general), 226; as commander of the Second Cherokee Mounted Rifles at Pea Ridge, 233; recruits a Confederate regiment, 232

Wayne, Anthony (major general), 145; commits atrocities against Indigenous people, 138, 143

Western Engineer (steamboat), 169–70, *170*; armaments on, 174

Wheeler-Howard Bill. *See* Indian Reorganization Act (IRA)

Whetstone, Terry Lee: and the Indian Arts and Crafts Act of 1990, 318

White Cloud (*Maxúthka* or *Mahaska*) (Ioway leader): on assimilation, 168; defying US, 167; and statue of in Oskaloosa, Iowa, 266; the Treaty of 1824, 179–81

White Cloud, Francis (Ioway leader), 236; and the Treaty of 1836, 202

White, Frank J., (major): commands Indigenous Prairie Scouts, 236

White, Richard: on Middle Ground, 224

White River (Missouri/Arkansas), 42, 123; Quapaws near, 84; Shawnees settle along, 189–90

white settlers: American, 141–44; arriving in Missouri, 138; attack Shawnees, 189; conflict with Ioways near Kirksville, Missouri 181–82; demand removal of Missouri's Indigenous people, 189; overhunting, 177; squat in the Platte Country, 199. *See also* Scots-Irish

423

About the Author

Greg Olson served as the Curator of Exhibits and Special Projects at the Missouri State Archives from 2000–2018 and is the author of six books, including: *The Ioway in Missouri.* He lives in Columbia, Missouri.